Anna of Denmark

Manchester University Press

also available in the series

Windows for the world
Nineteenth-century stained glass and the international exhibitions, 1851–1900
JASMINE ALLEN

The matter of Art
Materials, practices, cultural logics, c.1250–1750
EDITED BY CHRISTY ANDERSON, ANNE DUNLOP AND PAMELA H. SMITH

Critical design in Japan
Material culture, luxury, and the avant-garde
ORY BARTAL

European fashion
The creation of a global industry
EDITED BY REGINA LEE BLASZCZYK AND VÉRONIQUE POUILLARD

The culture of fashion
A new history of fashionable dress
CHRISTOPHER BREWARD

The factory in a garden
A history of corporate landscapes from the industrial to the digital age
HELENA CHANCE

'The autobiography of a nation'
The 1951 Festival of Britain
BECKY E. CONEKIN

The culture of craft
Status and future
EDITED BY PETER DORMER

Material relations
Domestic interiors and the middle-class family, 1850–1910
JANE HAMLETT

Arts and Crafts objects
IMOGEN HART

Comradely objects
Design and material culture in Soviet Russia, 1960s–80s
YULIA KARPOVA

Interior decorating in nineteenth-century France
The visual culture of a new profession
ANCA I. LASC

Building reputations
CONOR LUCEY

The material Renaissance
MICHELLE O'MALLEY AND EVELYN WELCH

Bachelors of a different sort
Queer aesthetics, material culture and the modern interior
JOHN POTVIN

Crafting design in Italy
From post-war to postmodernism
CATHARINE ROSSI

Chinoiserie
Commerce and critical ornament in eighteenth-century Britain
STACEY SLOBODA

Material goods, moving hands
Perceiving production in England, 1700–1830
KATE SMITH

Hot metal
Material culture and tangible labour
JESSE ADAMS STEIN

Ideal homes, 1918–39
Domestic design and suburban Modernism
DEBORAH SUGG RYAN

The study of dress history
LOU TAYLOR

Manliness in Britain, 1760–1900
Bodies, emotion, and material culture
JOANNE BEGIATO

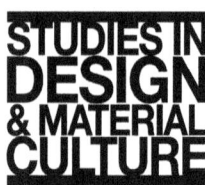

STUDIES IN DESIGN & MATERIAL CULTURE

general editors
Christopher Breward
and
James Ryan

founding editor
Paul Greenhalgh

Anna of Denmark

The material and visual culture of the
Stuart Courts, 1589–1619

Jemma Field

Manchester University Press

Copyright © Jemma Field 2020

The right of Jemma Field to be identified as the author of this work has been asserted by her in accordance with the Copyright, Designs and Patents Act 1988.

Published by Manchester University Press
Oxford Road, Manchester M13 9PL
www.manchesteruniversitypress.co.uk

British Library Cataloguing-in-Publication Data
A catalogue record for this book is available from the British Library

ISBN 978 1 5261 4249 8 hardback
ISBN 978 1 5261 8250 0 paperback

First published 2020
Paperback published 2024

The publisher has no responsibility for the persistence or accuracy of URLs for any external or third-party internet websites referred to in this book, and does not guarantee that any content on such websites is, or will remain, accurate or appropriate.

Typeset in 10/12.5 Compatil Text by
Servis Filmsetting Ltd, Stockport, Cheshire

Contents

List of plates vi
List of figures vii
Stylistic conventions ix
Acknowledgements x
Abbreviations xii

Introduction 1
1 Contexts and networks 18
2 Court places and spaces 43
3 Collecting and display 83
4 Jewellery and apparel 120
5 Representation and self-fashioning 152
6 Ritual and ceremonial 181
Conclusion 219

Select bibliography 223
Index 251

Plates

1. Paul van Somer, *Anna of Denmark*, 1617 (Royal Collection Trust / © Her Majesty Queen Elizabeth II 2019)
2. After Adrian Vanson, *Anna of Denmark*, c.1595 (© Philip Mould & Company)
3. Unknown maker, enamelled gold miniature case set with table diamonds and containing a portrait of Anna of Denmark (© The Fitzwilliam Museum, Cambridge)
4. Adrian Vanson, *King James VI*, c.1595 (© Philip Mould & Company)
5. John de Critz the Elder, *King James VI and I*, c.1606 (© Dulwich Picture Gallery, London)
6. John de Critz the Elder, *Anna of Denmark*, c.1605–1610 (© National Portrait Gallery, London)
7. Isaac Oliver, *Anna of Denmark*, c.1604 (The Rothschild Collection / © The National Trust, Waddesdon Manor)
8. Isaac Oliver, *Anna of Denmark*, c.1605–1610 (© Berkeley Castle, Gloucestershire / Photograph by Peter Yardley)
9. After Marcus Gheeraerts the Younger, *King Christian IV of Denmark*, 1614 (© Princeton University Art Museum, New Jersey)
10. Anonymous, illustrated diagram of the processional order around the royal effigy for the funeral of Queen Anna of Denmark, London, 1619. Royal College of Arms, London, MS I.4, fol. 13r (Reproduced by permission of the Kings, Heralds and Pursuivants of Arms)
11. Attributed to Maximilian Colt, *The Hearse of Anna of Denmark*, 1619. Booke of Monuments, Royal College of Arms, London, MS I.1, p. 1 (Reproduced by permission of the Kings, Heralds and Pursuivants of Arms)

Figures

I.1 Survey Plan of Greenwich Palace, c.1694–1695 from MR1/329 (2) (© The National Archives, London) — 2
2.1 The Queen's House, Greenwich, London, view of the north façade from the river, 2018 — 44
2.2 Robert Smythson, survey plan of additions to the palace and garden, Somerset House, London, c.1609 (RIBA Collections) — 54
2.3 Salomon de Caus, *Dessein d'une volière à oiseaux avec quelques grottes dedans icelle* [design of an aviary with caves] from *Les raisons des forces mouvantes*, Book II, Problesme VII (Paris, 1624) (ETH Library, Zurich) — 62
2.4 Salomon de Caus, *Plan perspectif du précédent dessein* [Perspective of the previous plan] from *Les raisons des forces mouvantes*, Book II, Problesme IX (Paris, 1624) (ETH Library, Zurich) — 62
2.5 Inigo Jones, preliminary elevation for the east or west side of the Queen's House, Greenwich, 1616 (Reproduced with kind permission of the Provost and Fellows of Worcester College, Oxford) — 64
2.6 The Sparepenge of Frederik II at Haderslevhus, detail of an engraving from Georg Braunius and Franz Hogenberg, *Civitates Orbis Terrarum IV*, Cologne, 1588 (Utrecht University Library, MAG: T fol 212 Lk (Rariora)) — 66
2.7 Inigo Jones, design for the read (inner) side of the gateway, Oatlands Palace, Surrey, 1617 (RIBA Collections) — 70
3.1 'FS' cipher in stonework, 1584, inner courtyard of Kronborg Castle, Helsingør (The National Museum of Denmark, Kronborg Castle / photograph by Laura Noelle Kiel) — 86
3.2 'FS' cipher in stonework, 1584, fireplace from the guest room

in the north wing of Kronborg Castle, Helsingør (The National Museum of Denmark, Kronborg Castle / photograph by Laura Noelle Kiel) 87

3.3 Plaster mask from Denmark House, which has traces of gilding and red paint, early seventeenth century (photograph by Jian Wei Lim / © Somerset House and Museum of London) 88

3.4 Plan of the ground floor of Denmark House, *c*.1620. Designed by Simon Thurley and drawn by Melissa Beasley (© Simon Thurley) 94

4.1 After John de Critz the Elder, *Anna of Denmark*, *c*.1603 (© Crown Copyright: UK Government Art Collection) 126

4.2 Unknown, *Anna Regina Scotorum*, *c*. 1603 (© The Trustees of the British Museum) 127

4.3 Unknown, medal commemorating the Coronation of Queen Anna of Denmark, 1603 (© National Maritime Museum, Greenwich, London) 128

4.4 Attributed to Jacob van Doort, *Princess Dorothea of Braunschweig-Wolfenbüttel, later Margravine of Brandenburg*, 1609 (Royal Collection Trust / © Her Majesty Queen Elizabeth II 2019) 130

4.5 Danish made (possibly by Dirich Frying in Odense) gold bracelet with niello, rubies, and diamonds, 1593–1600 (photograph by Kit Weiss / © The Royal Danish Collection, Rosenborg Castle) 144

5.1 Marcus Gheeraerts the Younger, *Anna of Denmark*, *c*.1614 (From the Woburn Abbey Collection / © His Grace the Duke of Bedford and Trustees of the Bedford Estate) 153

5.2 Studio of Nicholas Hilliard, *Anna of Denmark*, *c*.1604–1605 (Yale Center for British Art, Paul Mellon Collection) 163

5.3 Nicholas Hilliard, *King James VI and I*, *c*.1610 (Yale Center for British Art, Paul Mellon Collection) 164

5.4 Paul van Somer, *Anna of Denmark*, *c*.1617–1618 (Royal Collection Trust / © Her Majesty Queen Elizabeth II 2019) 170

Stylistic conventions

This book uses the Gregorian calendar (with the new year starting on 1 January), rather than the Julian, except in a few instances where clarification requires the use of both possible or relevant years (i.e. 1611/12). Printed material has been quoted verbatim, and I have attempted to retain the original capitalisation, spelling, and punctuation of all archival material. Some normalisations have been adopted for readability, such as the silent extension of contractions or the interchangeable use of letters i and j, u and v, and y, c and t. Where interchangeable letters do not seem to obstruct the legibility of the word, they have been left in their original form.

Clarification between the financial currencies of £ Scots and £ Sterling occurs throughout this book, but where not specifically stated it should be assumed that monetary amounts dating to Anna's time in Scotland (1589–1603) refer to £ Scots, whereas those post-1603 are £ Sterling. Discussion of James's decision to rename Anna's principal English residence from Somerset House to Denmark House in 1617 is given in Chapter 2. After this section, to avoid confusion, the palace is referred to as Denmark House irrespective of date except when determined by direct quotes.

Distinction between the kingdoms of England and Scotland are consistently made, although the terms Britain, Great Britain, and British are used on occasion. Such terms are, of course, anachronistic in predating the Acts of Unions of 1707. However, James VI's succession to the English throne engineered a dynastic and personal union of the kingdoms with the formation of a composite Stuart monarchy, and James himself repeatedly used such terms. Furthermore, as Steve Murdoch has demonstrated, Stuart subjects held and asserted a range of local, regional, national, and supra-national identities – including British and Briton – which were not fixed and mutually exclusive but largely dependent on circumstance.[1]

---

[1] For example, *Network North: Scottish Kin, Commercial and Covert Associations in Northern Europe, 1603–1746* (Leiden and Boston, 2006), 49–83; 'James VI and the Formation of a Scottish-British Military Identity', in S. Murdoch and A. MacKillop (eds), in *Fighting for Identity: Scottish Military Experience c.1550–1900* (Leiden, 2002), 3–31.

Acknowledgements

I must begin by acknowledging that this book is part of a project that received funding from the European Union's Horizon 2020 Research and Innovation Programme under the Marie Skłodowska-Curie Actions [706198], for which I am forever thankful. I am particularly grateful to the Principal Investigator of the project, Professor James Knowles, without whom this book would have taken several more years to be published and would likely have taken a very different form. While juggling an eye-watering schedule, James found the time to read and critique numerous drafts, to give sound, considered replies to a myriad of questions and concerns, and, throughout it all, to retain a cheering enthusiasm for the topic – and my approach – that was integral to my perseverance and enjoyment. James's guidance thus helped shape the methodological framework and structure of the book, and to enliven and extend my understanding of early modern female agency and the symbolic and political value of behaviour and ritual. I also give my heartfelt thanks to Associate Professor Erin Griffey, who originally sparked my interest in Anna of Denmark and who has fundamentally shaped me as a scholar. As a supervisor, colleague, and friend she has given me a welcome supply of support, inspiration, and guidance for more than a decade. I am particularly thankful for the countless times she has advocated for me or my work, and for the wonderful conversations shared over cups of coffee and glasses of wine in America, Belgium, England, New Zealand, and the Netherlands.

I have been repeatedly honoured by the vast knowledge, expertise, and unfailing generosity of Dr Michael Pearce, who sent me countless images of documents, copies of his own transcriptions, and relevant references found during his own research. He also assisted me with the transcription of some very challenging hands, and discussed obsolete terminology, matters of finance, and household personnel that were essential to this book. I likewise extend my heartfelt thanks to Professor Steve Murdoch, who has been a wonderful champion of my work and whom I am pleased and proud to call a friend. Steve's boundless generosity – giving time and expertise to critically read draft material, talk through ideas, and share his collection of archival material – was instrumental to the development of several strands of my research, but I am especially thankful for his candour, hospitality, and kindness (at one point, even stepping in for me at a conference and presenting my paper). In addition, Steve's own research has formatively shaped my approach to early modern identity politics and has given light to the imperative of understanding 'Britain' in this time period as a multiple kingdom of the Stuart dynasty.

The geographic scope of this book has incurred the debt of several scholars who have generously given their time and expertise to assist me with the transcription and/or translation of Danish, French, German, Latin, and Swedish material beyond my own proficiency: Dr Alexia Grosjean, Dr Ardis Grosjean, Professor Peter Maxwell-Stuart, Professor Steve Murdoch, Dr Michael Pearce, and Dr Jennifer Rabe – although I take full responsibility for any errors herein. I further extend my thanks to all those who provided helpful comments and feedback on my research, especially Dr Sara Ayres, Associate Professor Timothy McCall, Professor Emeritus R. Malcolm Smuts, and the two anonymous reviewers of the manuscript.

My greatest debt of gratitude remains to my husband, Jamie Nelson, who has given me unconditional love and unfailing emotional, intellectual, and financial support throughout. It is to him that this book is dedicated, with much love and many thanks.

Abbreviations

BL	The British Library (London, England)
CUL	Cambridge University Library (England)
CSPD	Green, Mary Anne Everett, ed. *Calendar of State Papers Domestic: James I, 1603–1625*. 4 vols. London, 1857–1859
CSPD Addenda	Green, Mary Anne Everett, ed. *Calendar of State Papers Domestic: Addenda, James I, 1603–1625*. London, 1872.
CSP Scotland	Bain, Joseph, William K. Boyd, Henry W. Meikle, and Annie Isabella Dunlop, eds. *Calendar of the State Papers Relating to Scotland and Mary, Queen of Scots* ... 13 vols. Edinburgh, 1898–1969
CSPV	Brown, Horatio, and Allen Hinds, eds. *Calendar of State Papers and Manuscripts Relating to English Affairs, Existing in the Archives and Collections of Venice* ... 38 vols. London, 1864–1947
ESRO	East Sussex Record Office (Brighton, England)
ODNB	Matthew, H. C. G., and B. Harrison, eds. *Oxford Dictionary of National Biography*. Online Edition. Oxford, 2004. http://www.oxforddnb.com
NLS	National Library of Scotland (Edinburgh, Scotland)
NRS	National Records of Scotland (Edinburgh, Scotland)
RA	Rigsarkivet (Copenhagen, Denmark)
RCA	Royal College of Arms (London, England)
TNA	The National Archives (London, England)

Introduction

In 1616, Anna of Denmark (1574–1619), queen of Scots and queen consort of England, appointed Inigo Jones (1573–1652), surveyor of the king's works, as the 'accomptaunte' to continue shaping the relationship between the palace and grounds at Greenwich.[1] On the south side of the estate, in place of an old Tudor gateway, a small lodge was to be built as a retreat, where the queen could view both park and river, entertain select guests, and indulge in leisure activities (Figure I.1).[2] The resultant 'module' designed by Jones, envisioned the first truly classical building in England, and once Anna was satisfied with the plan, work began in earnest. Observing the beginnings of this new structure, John Chamberlain (1553–1628) informed Dudley Carleton (1573–1632) that 'the Quene … is building somwhat at Greenwich w[hi]ch must be finished this summer. It is saide to be some curious of devise of Inigo Jones, and will cost above 4000*li*.'[3] The building, however, was not finished by the end of the summer, or even by the close of April 1618 when work was formally stopped. Within a year, Anna was dead, and her 'curious … devise' was not completed until 1638 under the guidance of her daughter-in-law Henrietta Maria (1609–1669).[4] Now known as the Queen's House, it still stands, much altered, in Greenwich and is one of the most celebrated early modern English buildings. Its fame generally rests on it being one of the few remaining examples of Jones's ingenuity, but the building is wholly unusual and extremely significant for having been commissioned, built for, and paid for, by royal women.

A royal female consort in patriarchal early Stuart Scotland and England, Anna's ability to commission and/or fund cultural projects was subject to the largesse of her husband, King James VI and I (1566–1625). In light of her dowry and dynastic prestige, Anna's marriage treaty ensured she was granted a set of jointure possessions (including some royal residences) that yielded her an independent annual income for life.[5] Even so, she did

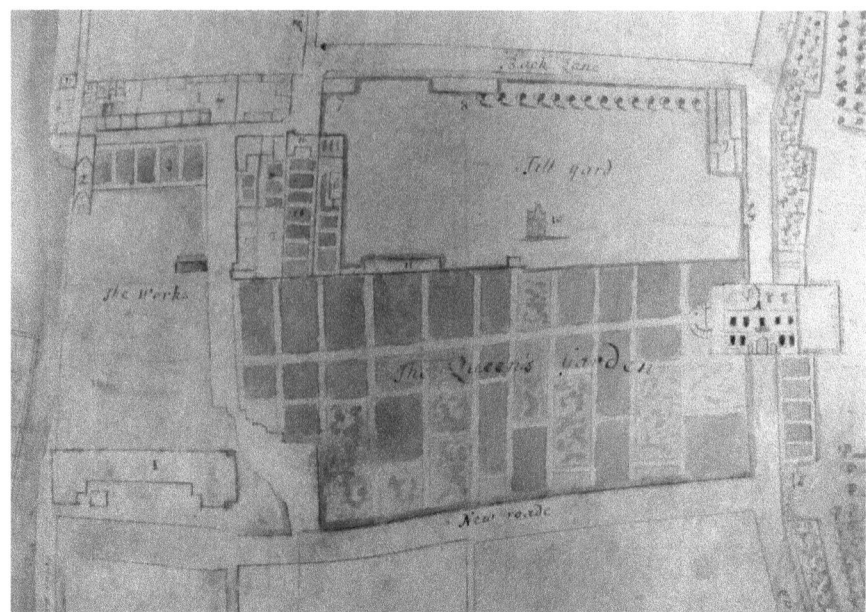

I.1 Survey plan of Greenwich Palace, c. 1694–1695.

not have sole possession and/or occupancy of any of 'her' jointure properties. Although she favoured several residences in her jointure above all others – Dunfermline, Somerset House, Greenwich Palace, and Oatlands Manor – these estates routinely welcomed the king with, or without, the queen.[6] Primarily, the jointure was to protect Anna in case of widowhood, and during her life it was to cover her household costs but, as discussed in Chapter 1, it rarely proved sufficient, and all additional expenditure was sanctioned by James and paid out by the exchequer. Indeed, new or restorative building work at any residence was explicitly excluded from Anna's personal income. First outlined in 1604, when her English jointure was settled, it was reiterated in March 1616 when Sir Edward Coke (1552–1634) drew up twelve 'directions and orders' to reduce the queen's debts and increase her income. Coke's second recommendation called for the queen 'to spend but £1,000 a moneth over and above charges of diet and buildinge', which was clarified by a marginal notation in another hand that 'the king beare all the charges of diet, houskeping and of building'.[7] Yet Anna's actions that year – 1616 – show there was more flexibility and variance than titles, designations, and even rulings sometimes suggest, for she did use her privy purse for building work at Oatlands and Greenwich with payments being made for lengthy brick walls, several monumental gateways, a silkworm house, new lodgings, and the beginnings of the hunting lodge.[8]

The complex relationship between consort and crown finance, and the connective issues of patronage and authority, are a central focus of the following chapters, as this book seeks to arrive at a better understanding of the agency and activities, the cares and concerns, and the motivations of Anna of Denmark. She was, as her name suggests, a Danish princess who, following marriage, became queen of Scotland, and then also queen consort of England. A remarkable woman, her court produced a wide array of important expressive media including art, architecture, garden design, music, and theatre, which influenced the tastes and activities of her connoisseurial son Henry (1594–1612), and her daughter Elizabeth (1596–1662), and helped to reinvigorate and reorientate England's growing dialogue with European forms, styles, and traditions. Throughout it all, Anna helped facilitate James's itinerant mode of kingship, assisted his quest to be seen as both universal and pacific, and championed her natal identity for political leverage. Thus, during the protracted Habsburg-Stuart marriage negotiations, for example, Anna made visual and verbal references to her Oldenburg lineage to remind court attendees that an alliance with Great Britain would facilitate connections with her prestigious kinship network that extended from Denmark-Norway across Brandenburg, Braunschweig-Lüneburg, Electoral Saxony, Mecklenburg, and Schleswig-Holstein.

Mobility and translation

Anna of Denmark's life, as with many of her royal female contemporaries, was one of mobility. This necessitated her negotiation of multiple ethnic, national, social, and religious customs, traditions, and beliefs. In the examination of Anna's agency at the multiple Stuart courts then, this book is broadly concerned with processes and patterns of transcultural exchange, and with the uses and meanings of identifying labels. It confirms that Anna's experiences at the Danish-Norwegian court – tightly connected to much of the German lands – were a key influence on the cultural forms, traditions, and aesthetics that she chose to support in Scotland and England. Yet as the following chapters discuss, Anna did not replicate or transplant the spaces, structures, and fashions of her natal kingdom. Rather, they were adapted and modified as she encountered the practices, expectations, and resources (material and human) of her new marital environs, thereby affirming Peter Burke's theory of cultural translation.[9] Beyond her personal experience, Anna's knowledge of Oldenburg modes and fashions, and her keen sense of natal pride and identity, was reinforced through the high level of contact that she maintained with her siblings and members of her wider familial network through the exchange of letters and gifts, through personal visits and the movement of formal and informal diplomatic envoys.

Contributing to the growing number of studies focused on the role played by northern European, Hanseatic, and Baltic cultural traditions on the development of the early modern British milieu, this book further helps to balance the earlier predominance of attention on Italian modes and precepts.[10] It confirms the existence of a broadly European pre-modern culture largely facilitated by travel and kinship, where artefacts, trends, and traditions spilled across regional divisions, confessional conflicts, and general intolerance. Increasingly gathering acceptance – and fruitfully employed by scholars of architecture, theatre, and festivals – this perspective is yet to become widespread in visual and material histories of the early modern Stuart courts.[11]

The following chapters build on theorisations of the paradigmatic 'queen's court' in early Stuart England, highlighting the fluidity and paradox that was regularly at play in royal women's negotiation of position and influence.[12] Early modern identities are shown to be more multivalent, fluid, and porous than we often give credit, bearing out Ulinka Rublack's observation that 'people across early modern society were not absorbed in large collective cultures dictating uniformity such as "peasants", "artisans", or "Protestants".'[13] Such labels were also inherently subjective, so that notions of what Spanish fashion or Lutheranism looked like varied from court to court and region to region but also from individual to individual. Nevertheless, modern scholars have been quick to assign labels to early modern identities – whether that be religious, national, or dynastic – and they are too often applied in oppositional binaries. Thus, an early modern person was either Catholic or Protestant, Spanish or English, Medici or Habsburg. The tendency to binarise, rather than capture the labile, palimpsestic, and multiple nature of early modern identities has been articulated by Bernard Capp and Barbara Harris, who isolate a similar tendency in scholarship on early modern elite and common English women, who are often characterised as either meekly accepting, or dangerously subverting, the patriarchal status quo.[14]

Anna through history

Anna, like many queens consort before and after her, has suffered a traditionally negative, trivialising historiography that persisted well into the late twentieth century.[15] By this time, however, building on the work of feminist scholars, some historians were also seeking a broader reassessment of early modern women. Central to their efforts has been a redefinition of what constituted the political, moving away from the public/private binary in order to develop an understanding of how women could achieve political value through cultural means and social mores.[16] In the case of Anna of Denmark, literary scholars have been particularly significant to the growing appreciation of the queen as a cultural agent who supported and patronised a range of expressive media that often ran counter to the interests of King James. First articulated by Leeds Barroll and continued in the work of James Knowles, Clare McManus, and Sophie Tomlinson, among others, Anna's masquing activities have been recognised as a central component of early Stuart court culture, and have provided a fertile platform for a reconsideration of her wider political import.[17] As is now well known, the masque was an important occasion in the court calendar, and beyond its cultural significance, it had far-reaching political, diplomatic, and social ramifications.[18] For her part, Anna successfully marshalled the art form to gather together a highly select, influential courtly audience; she strictly guarded invitations, which turned them into a sign of monarchical favour, and carefully selected jewellery and apparel to visualise her support of specific policies and alliances. Moreover, contemporaries acknowledged her determinative guidance of the art form. Ben Jonson (1572–1637) unequivocally credited Anna with the conceit of *The Masque of Blackness*, alleging that it was 'her Majesty's will' to have the masquers presented as 'blackamores at first'.[19] Later, when the paired masque – *The Masque of Beauty* – was danced by the queen and her ladies in 1608, onlookers explicitly ascribed the occasion to Anna and the Venetian ambassador identified her as the 'authoress of the whole'.[20] By controlling or influencing the content and performance site, scholars have shown that Anna challenged concepts of authorship, authority, and female beauty; complicated notions and boundaries of race, gender, and imperialism; staged female marital power; allegorised James, and his monarchy, as a harmonising yet omnipotent force; and even, as McManus states, 'interrogated the very notion of the masque as *court* masque'.[21] Beyond the costly, visionary spectacle of the masque, however, Anna gave ample time, consideration, and money to a host of other art forms including architecture, garden design, painting, music, and jewellery, which have been comparatively overlooked. It is the mode and manner of Anna's engagement with these visual and material goods that forms the heart of this book which, read in conjunction with the extensive socio-political and literary scholarship on early Stuart theatre, provides a more comprehensive understanding of the personal iconography, aims, interests, and alliances of the Stuart consort.

Patronage and agency

A significant difficulty faced by scholars seeking to argue for the cultural agency of early modern women is the lack of documentary evidence surrounding their purchase, commission, and acquisition of visual, textual, and material goods. Among the English formal structures that favoured men and marginalised or excluded women, one of the most detrimental was the common law doctrine of coverture, which ruled that a married woman was an adjunct of her husband, not her own individual person in any economic, social, or legal sense.[22] In practice though, as Harris and Amy Erickson have persuasively demonstrated, this was not a blanket ruling, and it was not enforced on an everyday basis. On the one hand, it was to the benefit of many men to ensure their wives had property rights or wills, and to allow them to manage the household finances and staff. On the other, economic power remained with the husband, who not only fared better in the jointure settlement but was able to sanction (or revoke) his wife's economic independence and control any assets and reserves.[23] It was slightly different for Anna, who, as a royal woman, was not subject to coverture and had her own independent jointure income.[24] But, as mentioned, this income was solely intended for running her establishment and it rarely proved sufficient even for that.[25] Thus, numerous surviving warrants under privy seal clearly show that James routinely ordered large supplementary sums for Anna's use, although it is unclear where this money went. Formally, James was also expected to cover all other costs relating to Anna's household as well as those of her wardrobe, stables, and residences.[26] Furthermore, under this system Anna's wish for new or restorative work to be carried out on her buildings or gardens, or her requests for pieces of furniture, soft furnishings, decorative objects or items of apparel were to be financed by James personally, or sanctioned by him and paid through the exchequer, leaving the queen routinely absent from court records. Thus, if we follow the traditional theory of a patron being 'the person or group who ordered and subsequently paid for the work', then we will naturally preclude Anna of Denmark and most early modern women.[27]

Since the early 2000s, scholars have increasingly recognised that women 'often existed outside the bounds of financial accountability or legal strictures', subsequently advancing patronage studies by questioning the definition, process, and very constituents of patronage. In particular, the pioneering work of Roger Crum on secular female Renaissance patrons persuasively expanded earlier concepts of patronage to include those people 'in charge of its preservation, daily use, and perhaps its display'.[28] For, as Crum maintains, it was the needs, wants, activities, and tastes of these people, who not only frequently occasioned the initial purchase or commission but who had a decisive impact on the materials and aesthetic.[29] Significantly, 'these people' were often women. In turn, Sheryl Reiss and David Wilkins have robustly supported this argument and, coining the term 'conjugal patronage', have asserted that patronage was often a joint endeavour, and that the joining was most commonly between husband and wife.[30] Thus, as Wilkins elaborates, 'a more comprehensive approach to patronage' must be followed – one that allows for the discussion of undocumented works and includes 'those who requested and/or needed the work, as well as those who were intended to use it'.[31] Turning from Italy to England, this patronage model has been fruitfully applied to Anna's daughter-in-law, and successor, Henrietta Maria, who was rarely in the position of directly settling the bills of artisans and tradesmen. Nevertheless, Caroline Hibbard and Erin Griffey have persuasively demonstrated the importance of her 'directorial responsibility', for her approval was required for the building and garden work completed at her palaces, the layout and decoration of her rooms, and the style of her clothing, so that it was her interests, ideas, and tastes that coloured the choice of craftsperson and the choice and look of the finished product.[32] This is similarly true of Anna of Denmark, who was actively involved in shaping her own visual persona; commissioning articles of jewellery and pieces of apparel that she owned and wore; choosing the nature and type of gifts to be given to servants, familial members, and foreign elites; ordering building and refurbishment work for the properties she principally inhabited; and selecting the visual and material goods that furnished those properties. These cultural endeavours, unlike the court masque, rarely solicited contemporary commentary about agency or direction but they did hold intrinsic political value. This was outlined by Harris in a seminal essay of 1990, which she subsequently developed in numerous publications, and which has been employed by cultural and political historians as a framework for the reconceptualisation of female political power in early modern England.[33] Consequently, the concept of conjugal patronage is used throughout this study to provide a richer understanding of the breadth of Anna's interests and some of the meanings generated by her actions, associations, and possessions. This approach moves beyond the socio-cultural restrictions placed on Anna as a woman, and the way in which court finances were structured and controlled in the early Stuart period. In doing so, a more comprehensive evaluation of Anna's role and significance as a cultural patron is provided, which is not hampered by narrow models, or obscured by the bureaucratic mechanics of courtly financial control and distribution.

Visual display

A paucity of evidence likewise affects our knowledge of the audience and reception of Anna's visual display. The role of inference is often therefore inevitable, but surviving inventories and accounts, coupled with contemporaneous opinions do offer valuable insights into the virtues, aims, and allegiances that Anna endeavoured or managed to project. As queen consort, she was a visual symbol of the Stuart monarchy and her appearance and comportment were repeatedly held to political account.[34] Having been privy to the 1608 performance of the *Masque of Beauty*, for example, the Venetian ambassador stated that 'what beggared all else, and possibly exceeded the public expectation was the wealth of pearls and jewels that adorned the Queen and her ladies, so abundant and splendid that in everybody's opinion *no other court* could have displayed such riches.'[35] If Anna's physical presence was scrutinised at the Stuart court, it was similarly analysed throughout the European courtly community through epistolary networks and the ritual exchange of portraits. Beyond monarchical power and prestige, however, recent scholarship has shown how early modern royal women could – and did – make conscious sartorial decisions to legitimise their position, demonstrate national and dynastic belonging, and illustrate political intentions and alliances.[36] This has been observed of Élisabeth of Valois (1545–1568), Élisabeth of Bourbon (1602–1644), and Maria de Médici (1575–1642), for instance, and the same is true of Anna of Denmark who used bodily display in the form of familial badges, miniatures, and specific colours and styles of clothing, to visualise her verbal concerns, ensuring that her onlookers were made well aware of her dignified lineage, influential kinship networks, Spanish favour, and of her wish for Prince Henry to marry the Infanta Ana María (1601–1666).

Beyond her physical body, Anna's visual display extended to her properties of primary occupancy in England: Greenwich Palace, Oatlands Manor, and Somerset House. These residences regularly hosted local and international elites, both singularly by the queen and jointly by the monarchical couple, although James's frequent absences from London coupled with their separate calendars meant that Anna probably presided over more state audiences than most consorts. Yet visitors to Anna's court rarely, if ever, record their impressions of the interiors. Rather, the increasing importance of precedence and courtesy fostered an almost obsessive focus on these matters to the neglect of just about everything else. Rather than relaying details of fashion or setting at any one reception or event, ambassadorial dispatches are generally filled with information concerning whether it was 'for publicke, or for private', the route that was taken, the type of seating provided, their position in the room relative to others, and their proximity to the royal person.[37] The squabbles over precedence between the Spanish and French ambassadors in this period are legendary, and it is no coincidence that James was the first English monarch to create a formal post for strictly regulating issues of status and access – a master of ceremonies – held by Sir Lewis Lewknor (c.1560–1627) from 1605 and assisted by Sir John Finet (1570/71–1641) who took over from Lewknor on his death in the Caroline period.[38] These concerns are palpably apparent in the lengthy description by Horatio Busino of the 'audience of the queen' enjoyed by his master – the Venetian ambassador extraordinary, Pietro Contarini – at Oatlands in September 1618. Contarini must have been provided with an account of the expected proceedings, for Busino notes that 'it would have been exceedingly grand and pompous by the instructions given, but on the appointed day a provoking rain fell incessantly.' Nevertheless, the occasion was still considered 'most stately and grave' due to the identity, order, and seating arrangements of the guests. Modes of entry and the royal touch also drew Busino's attention, who was pleased to report that Contarini 'was led by the Lord Chamberlain into the presence chamber and was graciously received by her Majesty, who gave him her hand.' After the audience, 'they led his Excellency [Contarini] to dinner', and of the dinner itself, Busino happily recalls that 'the table was distributed beautifully and profusely.'[39] However, on the specifics of the foodstuffs, of Anna's formal attire, or the decoration of the room, he is regrettably quiet, and the same is true of earlier ambassadors. Giovanni Carlo Scaramelli, who, having 'passed into the Queen's [Anna] apartments', merely sighed that 'it would be tedious to describe her splendour', while the chief concern of Francesco Contarini and Marcantonio Correr was that they be 'most courteously received' – as an indication of the queen's favour for Venice – and are pleased to report that Anna 'caused us to be seated, and engaged us in conversation for some time'.[40]

Despite the dearth of eyewitness descriptions, an analysis of the extant inventories, accounts, and objects make it clear that the placement of functional and decorative goods at Anna's palaces – as with other Tudor and Stuart residences – was determined by the guiding principles of suitability, audience, and precedence.[41] These documents further demonstrate that, in the same manner as her bodily attire, the queen's household goods operated as 'complex visual codes' signifying her social standing and financial position – and therefore that of the Stuart kingdom – together with her interests and aesthetics, piety, factional leanings, and dynastic pedigree.[42] The hierarchy of the queen's rooms was made manifest in a sliding scale of the fabric types and dyestuffs used for textiles and upholstery, and in the manner and quantity of furniture and decorative objects.[43] Thus, the state apartments and other important reception rooms such as the Great Gallery at Somerset House were equipped with suites of furniture in crimson velvet, complete with a canopy of state and a large quantity of portraits of local and foreign elites that showcased the power and breadth of the Stuart network. Comparatively lesser rooms, such as the library at Oatlands, sported furniture upholstered in silver camlet with green flowers and special tables made to hold and display books. Rooms with restricted access, such as the cabinet or closet, contained more personalised, intimate objects such as pieces of porcelain, agate, and coral, as well as curios and a select number of books. The cabinet at Oatlands even touchingly contained a portrait of Anna's deceased brother Hans, Prince of Schleswig-Holstein (1583–1602). In the relatively private rooms of her residences, Anna placed goods that invited close inspection, while in the chambers and galleries that accommodated formal audiences, and at court more generally, she took care to visualise her factional and familial connections, her political loyalties and opinions, and her tastes and connections. This was communicated through the iconography of the jewels and the colour of the clothes that she chose to wear; in the portraits that she hung; in the unusual and imported objects and pieces of furniture that she displayed; in the heraldry that branded her palaces (her cipher, motto, and the Danish-Norwegian arms); and in the visual persona she crafted.[44]

Terminology and sources

A central intention of this study has been to move beyond the Anglocentric approach traditionally applied to studies of Anna of Denmark. Remarkably, despite Anna's geographical and cultural mobility, she is consistently referred to as queen consort of England, and her time at the Stuart court in England is almost the sole focus of research.[45] This approach has obfuscated our understanding of how Anna's Oldenburg birthright and European connections shaped her role and value at court and impacted Stuart foreign policy, and how her transnational experiences underpinned her aims, activities, networks, and behaviour. Concerted effort has therefore been made to include Anna's time as queen consort in both Scotland and England, and to consider the influential role that her childhood experiences in Denmark-Norway had on her cultural endeavours and conception of status. This book draws on a wealth of untapped archival material primarily held in the collections of the National Archives (London) and the National Records of Scotland (Edinburgh) but including those from other repositories in Austria, Denmark, the United Kingdom, and Sweden. These manuscripts – household lists, accounts, warrants, bills, inventories, and letters – have been supplemented by a range of printed primary materials that have not heretofore featured in studies of Anna of Denmark and are contextualised within the secondary source literature relating to the two Stuart courts. However, it does not claim to be an exhaustive study of Anna of Denmark, and it is hoped that the new material uncovered here will encourage future cross-cultural research that looks to encompass additional sources still waiting to be found in other European repositories.

Chapter structure

This book is a sustained examination of the role, activities, and significance of Anna of Denmark, as Stuart queen consort in Scotland and England. Anna is, therefore, the primary focus while other important historical figures including King James, the royal children, and powerful male courtiers – such as Thomas Howard, Earl of Arundel (1585–1646), George Villiers, Duke of Buckingham (1592–1628), Henry Howard, Earl of Northampton (1540–1614), Robert Cecil, Earl of Salisbury (1563–1612), and Robert Carr, Earl of Somerset (c.1587–1645) – are not subject to detailed analysis but feature only when they serve to elucidate the actions or agency of the queen.[46] On the one hand, such parameters are dictated by the practical matter of space but, on the other, they intentionally recognise that these figures have all received individual, focused studies that can, and should, be read in conjunction with this book if the aim is for a comprehensive understanding of the Stuart courts.

In approaching the Stuart courts through the lens of the queen consort, this study is underpinned by three key themes: translating cultures; female agency and clientage; and the role of kinship networks and genealogical identity for early modern royal women. Taking a thematic approach, it follows a spatial trajectory beginning with Anna's exterior spaces, before moving to the interior furnishings of her palaces, the material adornment of the royal body, an examination of Anna's visual persona, and finishing with a discussion of Anna's performance of extraordinary rituals that follow her life cycle. While this introduction has presented the key methodological pathways used throughout this book, the following chapter builds on this foundation by examining the role of the queen consort, contextualising Anna's place and value within the wider socio-political environment of the Stuart courts in Scotland and England, and introducing the reader to Anna's consanguineous and affinal kingship networks that were valued by both Stuart king and queen consort, and serviced through letters, gifts, and travelling personnel.

Chapter 2 examines the ways in which Anna conceived of, and transformed, her court spaces in Scotland and England. It uncovers the significance of setting – both immediate and further afield – to Anna's conception of a palace, discusses her strong sense of possession, and traces notable consistencies in taste and style across her projects. The importance of Anna's Danish upbringing is approached as a source for her knowledge of, and interest in, innovative gardens and buildings while a detailed examination of Anna's jointure, income, and modes of mobility furthers our understanding of the financial, geographic, and hierarchic structures that made up the Stuart court.

In Chapter 3, the male-dominated tradition of collecting and display at the Stuart court, and the use of the Italianate as the standard for cultural sophistication, is complicated through the examination of Anna's preference for Dutch and Flemish artworks that were concurrently favoured at the Oldenburg court. Our knowledge of cultural transfer operating between the courts of the Oldenburg siblings is extended through a consideration of their parallel tastes, interests, and patronage, which is particularly noticeable in the realms of painting and music. Importantly, the discussion of Anna as a figure of exchange is approached through Burke's framework of 'cultural translation', acknowledging that modes, traditions, and fashions were not transferred wholesale between kingdoms but were dynamically reshaped in line with the trends, materials, and resources already in practice at the destination.[47] The chapter further uncovers Anna's role as a representative of the monarchy and her use of space, access, and visual and material goods to strategically showcase amity and consanguinity.

Situated across the sartorial landscape of Denmark-Norway, Scotland, and England, Chapter 4 draws on textual and pictorial evidence to critically evaluate the ability of garments and jewellery to make statements of identity, allegiance, and belonging. The discussion extends beyond the body of the queen to consider the apparel of her householders – many of whom were issued with garments in distinct, denotative colours, fabrics, and styles – and the place that clothing and jewels held for Anna in the highly politicised world of gift-exchange. This chapter presents new evidence concerning the Stuart consort's relationship to the almost mythic sartorial legacy of her predecessor, Queen Elizabeth I (1533–1603), and charts the political significance of Anna's apparel at key junctures including her international journeys from Denmark-Norway to Scotland in 1590 and from Scotland to England in 1603. It specifically extends our understanding of the type and frequency of Anna's jewellery purchase and argues that she continued Danish traditions in the strategic use of bodily display to visualise her dynastic identity and support her political aspirations.

Chapter 5 examines easel and miniature portraits of Anna produced in Scotland and England, to track the queen's increasing control over her own image in the development of a highly individualised iconography that formed around familial pride, court networks, and personal interests. It uncovers Anna's patronage of European artists – notably Isaac Oliver (1565–1617), Marcus Gheeraerts (1561–1636), and Paul van Somer (1577–1621) – to secure a cosmopolitan mode of representation that radically contrasted with the artists and styles supported by James and his court, and those favoured by Queen Elizabeth. The chapter argues that in portraiture, as in architecture and garden projects, Anna's outward-facing stance helped to establish a new direction for royal patronage, aligning England with its European counterparts and setting an important precedent for Prince Henry, who was quick to patronise the same artists as his mother and to adopt a comparative manner of presentation. Anchored within the domestic and international socio-political context, this chapter unpacks the intention and significance of format, iconography, and display in Anna's portraits, and it increases our general understanding of the ability of portraiture to connect with wider cultural, dynastic, and diplomatic issues.

The final chapter focuses on the extraordinary rituals that Anna of Denmark underwent in Scotland and England: birth, baptism, churching, and the marriage of her only daughter who survived to adulthood, Elizabeth. It concludes with her final performance for the Stuart monarchy with the magnificent state funeral that was mounted in honour of her death in March 1619. Throughout, the high diplomatic, dynastic, and sociocultural importance of the figure of the queen consort to the Stuart monarchy is uncovered. While there is a substantive body of literature on death, mourning, and burial rites and practices in early modern England, those staged for Anna of Denmark have not been subject to sustained discussion. Much of the material on the queen's funeral is therefore presented here for the first time, with close attention to the material goods provided for Anna's mourning, the form and nature of the procession, and the sociopolitical hierarchy and cultural identity of her household as seen through the funerary accounts. The event is importantly contextualised within the international political climate of 1619 – when Europe teetered on the brink of the Thirty Years' War – and argues that King James marshalled the occasion as a diplomatic strategy intended to secure a Stuart–Habsburg marriage that would, in turn, secure European peace. This chapter highlights Anna's role as a figure of negotiation and mediation which is, perhaps, most significantly demonstrated by the fact that Kings James VI and I and Christian IV of Denmark-Norway (1577–1648) acknowledged her death as having removed the familial element between their dynasties and the resultant need for a formal agreement. This was the first alliance signed between the Houses of Oldenburg and Stuart since James had become the head of a composite monarchy in 1603.

By exploring the impact that Anna's Danish experiences and connections had on her later patronage and collecting, this book challenges us to rethink the influence that the Stuart queen consort had – and the Baltic had – on the formation of early modern culture in Scotland and England. While Anna is the prime focus, the analyses help more generally to extend our knowledge of the myriad ways in which early modern royal women used visual and material culture to communicate political aims, support, and allegiances together with their sense of factional, dynastic, or religious belonging. This book does not intend to have the final word on Anna of Denmark but to analyse her prevailing historiography and ensure that far from being 'one of the least attractive courts in history', the early Stuart courts are seen as characterised by a unique and compelling diversity of styles, policies, values, and factions.[48]

Notes

1. TNA, E351/3389; TNA, AO1/2487/356.
2. TNA, E351/3250; TNA, E351/3251; TNA, SC6/JASI/1653; H. Colvin, *History of the King's Works*, 6 vols (1485–1660) (London, 1982), vol. 4, 113–114.
3. N. E. McClure (ed.), *The Letters of John Chamberlain*, 2 vols (Philadelphia, 1939), 1: 83, no. 268 (21 June 1617). Anna spent £2,400 on the building before her death, at which point only the foundations and a couple of layers of brick had been completed. Henrietta Maria was to spend a further £7,600 on the building and an additional £500 on the gardens. Overall, this was not a significant amount, and comparisons can be drawn with Jones's Banqueting House at Whitehall, which cost the Crown £15,000. See Colvin, *King's Works*, 114–115; S. Thurley, *Somerset House: The Palace of England's Queens, 1551–1692* (London, 2009), 31.
4. Colvin, *King's Works*, 119–122. The very last account for the Queen's House is 1639/40, but the majority of the building work was completed by 1638, and interior decoration began as early as 1633.

5 A major difference was the common law principle of coverture, which did not apply to royal women. Receiving an income was not restricted to royal women, and many elite and middling women were allocated annual 'pin money' to manage the household: B. Capp, *When Gossips Meet: Women, Family, and Neighbourhood in Early Modern England* (Oxford, 2003), ch. 2, esp. 29–30; A. Erickson, *Women and Property in Early Modern England* (London, 1993), 24–26; B. Harris, *English Aristocratic Women, 1450–1550: Marriage and Family, Property and Careers* (Oxford, 2002), 17–26.

6 Somerset House was the major exception to this pattern, as discussed in Chapter 2.

7 TNA, SP14/86 fols 173r–v (24 March 1616); TNA, SP14/86, fols 175r–v (March 1616), here fol. 175r. See also J. Cramsie, *Kingship and Crown Finance under James VI and I, 1603–1625* (London, 2002), 143.

8 TNA, SC6/JASI/1653; TNA, AO1/2485/344, fol. 1r.

9 P. Burke, 'Translating Knowledge, Translating Cultures', in M. North (ed.), *Kultureller Austausch in der Frühen Neuzeit* (Cologne, 2009), 69–77, esp. 69–71. See also B. Roeck, 'Introduction' in H. Roodenburg (ed.), *Cultural Exchange in Early Modern Europe: Forging European Identities, 1400–1700* (Cambridge, 2007), vol. 4, 1–29: 2–5.

10 See, in particular, the essays of R. Malcolm Smuts ('Cultural Diversity and Cultural Change at the Court of James I') and Pauline Croft ('Robert Cecil and the Early Jacobean Court') in L. L. Peck (ed.), *The Mental World of the Jacobean Court* (Cambridge, 1991); L. L. Peck, *Court Patronage and Corruption* (London, 1993); R. M. Smuts, *Court Culture and the Origins of a Royalist Tradition* (Philadelphia, 1987).

11 T. D. Kaufmann has been particularly influential in calling attention to the multidirectional cultural exchange constantly at work across the interconnected European courts. Other scholars who have been instrumental to my thinking about cross-cultural paradigms include Mara Wade, Krista De Jonge, Konrad Ottenheym, and Helen Watanabe-O'Kelly. Specific mention must also be made of two collections of essays: *Reframing the Danish Renaissance: Problems and Prospects in a European Perspective* (Copenhagen, 2011) and *Queens Consort: Cultural Transfer and European Politics, c.1500–1800* (London, 2017), which focus on exchange processes underpinning case studies of sculpture, theatre, architecture, interior furnishings, and the pictorial arts in Europe, while the latter uncovers the central role played by female consorts as agents and facilitators of transfer. Publication details are provided in the following chapters and bibliography.

12 For Jacobean and Caroline England, this has been explored most extensively by scholars of literature and theatre and considered discussions are found in, for example, L. Barroll, *Anna of Denmark, Queen of England: A Cultural Biography* (Philadelphia, 2001), esp. chs 1 and 3; C. McManus, *Women on the Renaissance Stage: Anna of Denmark and Female Masquing in the Stuart Court (1590–1619)* (Manchester, 2002); C. McManus, 'Introduction: The Queen's Court', 1–17: 1–12 and J. Knowles, '"To Enlight the Darksome Night, Pale Cinthia Doth Arise": Anna of Denmark, Elizabeth I and the Images of Royalty', 21–48: 21–24, 30–42, both in C. McManus (ed.), *Women and Culture at the Courts of the Stuart Queens* (Basingstoke, 2003); S. Tomlinson, *Women on Stage in Stuart Drama* (Cambridge, 2005); K. Britland, *Drama at the Courts of Queen Henrietta Maria* (Cambridge, 2006); E. Griffey (ed.), *Henrietta Maria: Piety, Politics and Patronage* (Aldershot, 2008); E. Griffey, *On Display: Henrietta Maria and the Materials of Magnificence* (New Haven, 2015). For later Stuart and Hanoverian England, see C. Campbell-Orr (ed.), *Queenship in Britain, 1660–1837: Royal Patronage, Court Culture and Dynastic Politics* (Manchester, 2002).

13 U. Rublack, *Dressing Up: Cultural Identity in Renaissance Europe* (Oxford, 2010), 11.

14 B. Capp, 'Separate Domains? Women and Authority in Early Modern England', in P. Griffiths et al. (eds), *The Experience of Authority in Early Modern England*

(Basingstoke and London, 1996), 117–145, esp. 125; Capp, *When Gossips Meet*, 31–36; Harris, *English Aristocratic Women*, 14–15.

15 For Maurice Ashley, she was 'a dumb blonde', *House of Stuart: Its Rise and Fall* (London, 1980), 116; Michael Lynch labels her 'a largely anonymous figure' in *Scotland: A New History* (London, 1991), 233; and, as late as 1997, Timothy Wilks characterised her patronage as being influenced by the fact that she was 'subject to extreme mood swings, and though given to gaiety and frivolity, could lapse into a depressed state in which brooding and rage alternated' in his 'Art Collecting at the English Court from the Death of Henry, Prince of Wales to the Death of Anne of Denmark (November 1612–March 1619)', *Journal of the History of Collections* 9 (1997), 31–48: 42.

16 For England, the work of Barbara Harris is foundational. See her 'Women and Politics in Early Tudor England', *The Historical Journal* 33 (1990), 259–281. Later scholarship that has driven forward Harris's findings include O. Hufton, 'Reflections of the Role of Women', *The Court Historian* 5 (2000), 1–13; C. Hibbard, 'The Role of a Queen Consort: The Household and Court of Henrietta Maria, 1625–1642', in R. Asch and A. Birke (eds), *Princes, Patronage, and the Nobility* (Oxford, 1991), 393–414; E. Griffey, 'Introduction', in Erin Griffey (ed.), *Henrietta Maria* (Aldershot, 2008), 1–11; R. M. Smuts and M. J. Gough, 'Queens and the International Transmission of Political Culture', *The Court Historian* 10 (2005), 1–13.

17 See those publications listed in n. 12.

18 Beyond those texts already cited by Barroll, Knowles, McManus, and Tomlinson, others that specifically focus on Anna's theatrical activities include (alphabetically): H. Aasand, '"To Blanch an Ethiop and Revive a Corse": Queen Anne and *The Masque of Blackness*', *Studies in English Literature* 32 (1992), 271–285; B. Andrea, 'Black Skin, The Queen's Masques: Africanist Ambivalence and Feminine Author(ity) in the *Masques of Blackness and Beauty*', *English Literary Renaissance* 29 (1999), 246–281; L. Barroll, 'Inventing the Stuart Masque', in D. Bevington and P. Holbrook (eds), *The Politics of the Stuart Court Masque* (Cambridge, 1998), 121–143; M. Butler, *The Stuart Court Masque and Political Culture* (Cambridge and New York, 2008); B. K. Lewalski, *Writing Women in Jacobean England* (Cambridge, MA, 1993); C. McManus, 'When is a Woman Not a Woman? Or, Jacobean Fantasies of Female Performance (1606–1611)', *Modern Philology* 105 (2008), 437–474; K. L. Middaugh, '"The Golden Tree": The Court Masques of Queen Anna', Unpub. PhD diss. (Case Western Reserve University, 1994); B. Ravelhofer, *The Early Stuart Masque: Dance, Costume and Music* (New York, 2006); K. Schwarz, 'Amazon Reflections in the Jacobean Queen's Masque', *Studies in English Literature* 35 (1995), 293–319.

19 M. Wynne-Davies, 'The Queen's Masque: Renaissance Women and the Seventeenth-Century Court Masque', in S. P. Cerasano and M. Wynne-Davies (eds), *Gloriana's Face: Women, Public and Private in the English Renaissance* (Hemel Hempstead, 1992), 79–104; McManus, *Renaissance Stage*, 4.

20 *CSPV*, vol. 11, no. 154: 24 January 1608.

21 C. McManus, 'Memorialising Anna of Denmark's Court: *Cupid's Banishment* at Greenwich Palace', in C. McManus (ed.), *Women and Culture at the Courts of the Stuart Queens* (Basingstoke, 2003), 81–99: 82–87; quote from 83.

22 Harris, *English Aristocratic Women*, 18, 61–62; Erickson, *Women and Property*, 99–101, 104–106, 146–151.

23 Harris, *English Aristocratic Women*, 17–19; Erickson, *Women and Property*, 24–28, 119–122, 224–229. See also Capp, *When Gossips Meet*, 71–72, 78–80; H. Wunder, *He Is the Sun, She Is the Moon*, trans. T. Dunlop (Cambridge, MA and London, 1998), ch. 4.

24 It is beyond the scope of this study, but it should be pointed out that while ordinary women were always subject to coverture, many were able to broker marriage settlements that shielded them from 'the more incapacitating aspects', see Erickson, *Women and Property*, 102–113, 224–227, quote from 225.

25 T. Riis, *Should Auld Acquaintance Be Forgot … Scottish–Danish Relations c.1450–1707*, 2 vols (Odense, 1988), 1: 272, 274–278; A. Juhala, 'The Household and Court of King James VI', Unpub. PhD diss. (The University of Edinburgh, 2000), 63–64, 172.
26 TNA, SP14/86, fol. 175r; E. Lodge, *Illustrations of British History, Biography and Manners in the reigns of Henry VIII, Edward VI, Mary, Elizabeth, and James I … etc.*, 3 vols (London, 1791), 3: 207.
27 D. G. Wilkins, 'Introduction', in S. E. Reiss and D. G. Wilkins (eds), *Beyond Isabella: Secular Women Patrons of Art in Renaissance Italy* (Kirksville, 2001), 1–17: 1.
28 R. J. Crum, 'Controlling Women or Women Controlled? Suggestions for Gender Roles and Visual Culture in the Italian Renaissance Palace', in S. E. Reiss and D. G. Wilkins (eds), *Beyond Isabella: Secular Women Patrons of Art in Renaissance Italy* (Kirksville, 2001), 37–51: 38.
29 Crum, 'Controlling Women', 37–38, 41–43; Wilkins, 'Introduction', 1, 6, 12–13.
30 This observation is directed at secular Italian Renaissance women generally, using the model of 'conjugal patronage' to 'encourage scholars to move yet further 'beyond Isabella' in their assessment of women's patronage of art and architecture'. See 'Prologue', in their edited collection *Beyond Isabella*, xv–xvii.
31 Wilkins, 'Introduction', 12.
32 C. Hibbard, '"By Our Direction and For Our Use": The Queen's Patronage of Artists and Artisans seen through her Household Accounts', in E. Griffey (ed.), *Henrietta Maria: Piety, Politics and Patronage* (Aldershot, 2008), 115–139; Griffey, *On Display*, 14–21, 118–132; quote from 18.
33 Harris, 'Women and Politics'; 'The View from my Lady's Chamber', *Huntington Library Quarterly* 60 (1999), 215–247; 'Aristocratic Women and the State', in C. Carlton, R. L. Woods, M. L. Robertson, and J. S. Block (eds), *State, Sovereigns, and Society in Early Modern England: Essays in Honour of A. J. Slavin* (Stroud, 1998), 3–24; *English Aristocratic Women*. See also those essays in J. Daybell (ed.), *Women and Politics* (Aldershot, 2004) and particularly Daybell's 'Introduction', 1–21; those publications cited in n. 16, and A. Morton and H. Watanabe-O'Kelly (eds), *Queens Consort: Cultural Transfer and European Politics, c.1500–1800* (London and New York, 2017).
34 R. M. Smuts, 'Art and the Material Culture of Majesty', in R. M. Smuts (ed.), *The Stuart Court and Europe* (Cambridge, 1996), 86–112: 90–94, 107.
35 *CSPV*, vol. 11, 86, no. 154 (emphasis mine).
36 E. Andersson, 'Foreign Seductions', in T. E. Mathiassen et al. (eds), *Fashionable Encounters: Perspectives and Trends in Textile and Dress in the Early Modern Nordic World* (Oxford, 2014), 15–31; L. O. Santaliestra, 'Isabel of Borbón's Sartorial Politics', in A. J. Cruz and M. G. Stampino (eds), *Early Modern Habsburg Women: Transnational Contexts, Cultural Conflicts, Dynastic Continuities* (Farnham and Burlington, VT, 2013), 225–243; S. Édouard, 'The Hispanicization of Elisabeth de Valois', in J. L. Colomer and A. Descalzo (eds), *Spanish Fashion at the Courts of Early Modern Europe*, vol. 2 (Madrid, 2014), 237–266: 239–241; I. Paresys, 'The Dressed Body: The Moulding of Identities in Sixteenth-Century France', in H. Roodenburg (ed.), *Cultural Exchange in Early Modern Europe: Forging European Identities, 1400–1700* (Cambridge, 2007), vol. 4, 227–258.
37 J. Finet, *Finetti Philoxenis: som choice observations of Sr. John Finett knight, and master of the ceremonies to the two last Kings … etc.* (London, 1656), 12, 13, 19–20, 200; here 12. The terms 'public' and 'private' referred to whether the event was to be seen by others at court. See also, Griffey, *On Display*, 21–23.
38 J. Dillon, *The Language of Space in Court Performance, 1400–1625* (Cambridge, 2010), 80–81. This was a first for England, but it was a well-established tradition in Europe.
39 *CSPV*, vol. 15, no. 535: 14 September 1618 (to the Signori Giorgio, Francesco and Zaccharia Contarini).

40 *CSPV*, vol. 10, no. 102: 30 July 1603; *CSPV*, vol. 11, no. 801: 25 February 1610.
41 Griffey, *On Display*, 13–26, 63–79, 97–109. Tara Hamling's work shows that these values likewise governed the layout and furnishing of rooms in Protestant gentry houses, see her *Decorating the 'Godly' Household: Religious Art in Post-Reformation Britain* (New Haven and London, 2010), 67–85, and Chapter 4. On the signification of household objects see Smuts, 'Art and the Material Culture of Majesty', esp. 86–87, 90–96, 107; and for portraiture see J. Peacock, 'The Politics of Portraiture', in K. Sharpe and P. Lake (eds), *Culture and Politics in Early Stuart England* (Basingstoke, 1994), 199–228: 215–226, esp. 213, 215–216.
42 Smuts, 'Art and the Material Culture of Majesty', 112.
43 The physical and hierarchical structure and function of the early Stuart court has been well mapped by Neil Cuddy, who demonstrates sensitivity to the bonded politics of access and patronage. His analyses do not extend to material furnishings or decoration, but he provides a sound spatial framework on which the politics of these choices and goods can be determined. See his 'The Revival of the Entourage', in D. Starkey (ed.), *The English Court: from the Wars of the Roses to the Civil War* (London, 1987), 173–225; 'Reinventing a Monarchy', in E. Cruickshanks (ed.), *The Stuart Courts* (Stroud, 2000), 59–86. For further information on the topography of early modern palaces in England, see D. Starkey, 'Introduction', 1–25 and 'Intimacy and Innovation', 71–119, both in D. Starkey (ed.), *The English Court* (London, 1987). The classic piece on the layout and function of royal apartments remains H. M. Baillie's 'Etiquette and the Planning of the State Apartments in Baroque Palaces', *Archaeologia* 101 (1967): 169–199. See also E. Cole, 'The State Apartment in the Jacobean Country House, 1603–1625', unpub. DPhil Thesis (University of Sussex, 2010), esp. 55–120.
44 See various entries in the palace inventories: ESRO, Glynde MS 314; ESRO, Glynde MS 317; ESRO, Glynde MS 320; M. T. W. Payne, 'An Inventory of Queen Anne of Denmark's "Ornaments, Furniture, Householde Stuffe, and Other Parcells" at Denmark House, 1619', *Journal of the History of Collecting* 13 (2001), 23–44; O. Millar (ed.), 'Abraham van der Doort's Catalogue', *The Thirty-seventh Volume of the Walpole Society* (1958–1960), 196–198. This was a relatively common practice, and can be observed of both Prince Henry and Henrietta Maria, for example, but the quantity of Anna's badges in her palaces, and those worn about her person, were pronounced. For Henry, see T. Wilks, 'Introduction', in T. Wilks (ed.), *Prince Henry Revived: Image and Exemplarity in Early Modern England* (London, 2007), 10–22: 12; for Henrietta Maria, see Griffey, *On Display*, 69, 79, and S. A. Sykes, 'Henrietta Maria's "house of delight"', *Apollo* 133 (1991), 312–336: 332–334.
45 Exception is found in McManus's study of Anna's masquing activities, which includes Scotland, and in the few chapters by M. R. Wade and M. Meikle. See, for example, McManus, *Renaissance Stage*; M. Meikle, 'Anna of Denmark's Coronation and Entry into Edinburgh, 1590: Cultural, Religious and Diplomatic Perspectives', in J. Goodare and A. MacDonald (eds), *Sixteenth-Century Scotland: Essays in Honour of Michael Lynch* (Leiden, 2008), 277–294; 'A Meddlesome Princess: Anna of Denmark and Scottish Court Politics, 1589–1603', in J. Goodare and M. Lynch (eds), *The Reign of James VI* (East Linton, 2000), 126–140; Wade, 'The Queen's Courts: Anna of Denmark and Her Royal Sisters – Cultural Agency at Four Northern European Courts in the Sixteenth and Seventeenth Centuries', in C. McManus (ed.), *Women and Culture at the Courts of the Stuart Queens* (Basingstoke, 2003), 49–81. However, even Wade opens the latter chapter by stating that it was at the 'London' court that Anna 'made an indelible mark on arts and learning', 49.
46 These publications are included in the bibliography.
47 Burke, 'Translating Knowledge', 69–71.
48 Starkey, 'Introduction', 2.

1

Contexts and networks

On 21 October 1611, Antonio Foscarini, the Venetian ambassador in England, updated the Doge and Senate on matters unfolding at the Stuart court for 'the Danish Ambassador [Dr Jonas Charisius (1571–1619)], by means of the Queen [Anna], has seen the King [James] in private at Hampton Court several times. He has been successful and conciliated his Majesty. The Queen worked to this end.'[1] Sent from Christian IV, Charisius had arrived in England on 31 August 1611, with the task of securing assistance from James for the Danish attack on Sweden.[2] While King James disapproved of the war and looked to secure peace, Anna was interested in her brother's success and safety and she interceded with James on Charisius's behalf to ensure the needs of the Danes were met.[3] This is just one of many examples of Anna acting as an intercessory figure between her husband and brother – a mantle she repeatedly held throughout her life as she brokered some of the needs and demands that flowed between her natal and marital dynasties. Anna likewise interceded with her husband on a local level, petitioning him on behalf of her clients and favourites and vocalising her wants and opinions but, as this chapter makes clear, she always played a careful balancing act.

This chapter sets the stage for the thematic chapters that follow, outlining the importance of Anna's natal identity and remapping her political and marital dynamic with James. It discusses the related issues of maternal agency, confessional identity, and power-brokering, together with the pronounced influence of the ongoing ties within her family network. New archival evidence – principally drawn from the declared accounts of the treasurers of the chamber to the pipe office, the receivers' accounts to the office of the auditors of land revenue (both England), the exchequer records (Scotland), and numerous letters (Scotland and England) – combined with secondary source literature that has not hitherto informed research into the Stuart courts, provides a richer understanding of the parameters of Anna's consortship by exploring the international relations between the Oldenburgs and Stuarts, and the domestic relations between Anna and powerful male courtiers. The chapter builds on earlier studies of the political structures and spaces of the Stuart court, but it offers a new focus on the material manifestations of Anna's political agency which are strongly evinced by her involvement in gift-exchange.

Negotiating dependence and autonomy

On the one hand, Anna was a prestigious asset to the Stuarts, providing access to an important pan-European kinship network and valuably fulfilling her expected duties in the provision of heirs and the visible practice of Protestant piety. She actively supported James's manoeuvrings for the English throne and the quest for a Catholic bride for the Stuart heir, and her household was connected to James's (and Henry's) through shared administrative and financial departments, and the movement of courtiers, players, and artisans.[4] On the other hand, however, Anna often backed different factions and clients to those favoured by James, and she engaged artisans and supported styles that were not seen at James's court. As consort, Anna received an independent income, maintained a distinct establishment, followed her own, separate, court calendar, and had a personal judiciary court to deal with the legalities of her jointure estates. Unprecedented for a royal female consort in Scotland or England, Anna's ability to exercise such autonomy was predicated on her individual relationship with the king and the ideological plurality of the Stuart court.[5] In 1991, Malcolm Smuts posited a new conceptualisation of the Jacobean court in England as a 'polycentric world' where aristocratic and princely households could operate as 'focal points of opposition to royal favourites and policies'. Crucially, as he continued, 'such opposition did not entail rejecting the court as an institution' but 'often represented an alternative model of the court, both in political terms and with respect to matters of taste, style and ambience'.[6] At the time of writing, Smuts only looked to male centres of power (the king, the heir, and the powerful aristocrats of Salisbury, Buckingham, and Arundel), but literary critics have since recognised the queen consort's court as a central player in this multiplicity of power bases, and have extended the consideration to Anna's time in Scotland, pointing to her theatrical and factional independence, and her performative appropriation of male modes of patronage and authority.[7] Operating in a patriarchal patronage society, any position and influence that Anna enjoyed ultimately stemmed from favour with the king; as a woman and a consort she remained firmly under his authority in the wider court hierarchy.[8]

For Anna, as for all courtiers, the personal preservation of harmonious inter-court relations was vital to survival and preferment. Helen

Watanabe-O'Kelly's overview of some axioms of the role of the queen consort is useful to understanding the limits, expectations, and concessions that Anna faced. In addition to providing the marital dynasty with at least two male children who survived infancy, and personifying its 'religion and charitable deeds', Watanabe-O'Kelly identifies the crux of a consort's success as her ability to negotiate key relationships with the king, his mistress/es, and his mother.[9] Likewise, Clarissa Campbell-Orr earlier observed that 'the one person they [queens consort] needed most as an ally, [was] their husband',[10] and that their prime responsibility was 'to suggest in idealised form the symbolic harmony of male and female, the potency and fertility of the ruling male, and the continuity of the dynasty'.[11] For Anna, managing relationships with the mistress and/or mother-in-law was not applicable, but she did have to contend with a string of powerful male favourites and councillors. As far as James was concerned, these men were not a threat to his wife's position, favour, or authority. In 1603, following Anna's fallout with John Erskine, Earl of Mar (1558–1634) over the custody of Prince Henry and her indignation that Mar had told James she was on a 'papiste or Spanish course', the king counselled his wife that should she heed 'everie flattering sicphante that will persuade you that when I account well of an honest servant for his tru service to me that it is to compare or preferre him to you then will neither ye or I be ever at reste.'[12] Nevertheless, on more than one occasion Anna deemed it necessary to actively oppose them. In Scotland, for instance, she was unrelenting in her quest to establish her authority and position over John Maitland of Thirlestane (1537–1595), and then over Mar. Later, while in England, she worked with Prince Henry – and then with the faction centred around Henry Wriothesley, Earl of Southampton (1573–1624), and William Herbert, Earl of Pembroke (1580–1630) – to counter the rising dominance of Somerset and she took bold steps against Northampton.[13] In many of these instances though, and in Anna's sphere of activity more generally, she was careful not to isolate herself at court, working in concert with men who enjoyed proximity and influence with the king. Beyond those already mentioned, this is most notable in Scotland in her periodic alignment with Francis Stewart, Earl of Bothwell (c.1562–1612) and Ludovic Stewart, Duke of Lennox (1574–1624), and in England with her close ties to Salisbury.

Anna was not an antagonistic force at court, although the recognition of her frequently oppositional stance and the distance between the royal courts has occasionally run counter to determining the extent and consequences of her agency.[14] Rather, Anna did work separately from – and sometimes against – James's policies, interests, and/or clients, but her actions, like those of her non-elite female contemporaries, should be approached through a conceptual lens of 'accommodation or negotiation'. Moreover, we cannot forget that she concurrently fulfilled her expected duties in the support and continuation of the Stuart dynasty. Bernard Capp's model of non-elite women's engagement with the structures of male power examines how they were 'able to soften and sometimes bypass male authority without challenging it outright'.[15] At the Stuart court, the king permitted space for the expression of royal female word and action as Anna, who may not always have been able to realise her intentions – the initial custody battle over Henry being a prime example – was able to pursue her own agendas without being ostracised from court or punished by James. This was a space occasioned by the confluence of Stuart polycentrism and the personal, marital relationship.

Despite physical distance between the Stuart courts, the level of personal affection between James and Anna remained a frequent topic of comment. In 1612, the Venetian ambassador stated that James 'tells her [Anna] any thing she chooses to ask, and loves and esteems her', while Chamberlain observed, in August 1613, that 'love and kindness increases daily between them, and it is thought they were never on better terms.'[16] Later, in March 1615, Thomas Erskine, Viscount Fenton (1566–1639) noted that 'his Majestie and the Quein, I thank God, was never in better tearmes and lyking then at this tyme.'[17] However, the need to stress cordial relations hints at a latent anxiety that the royal relationship was susceptible to breach, and several fractious periods in Scotland must have remained at the forefront of the collective memory. Chief among these were Anna's sustained antagonism towards Maitland over some of his lands south of the Forth that she considered part of her jointure; her custody battle with James and Mar over Prince Henry; and her unwavering support of the Ruthven sisters, despite their familial connection to the Gowrie Plot and consequent banishment from court.[18] Indeed, just prior to the English succession, George Nicholson wrote to Salisbury that 'the King and Queen do agree very well and lovingly, God be thanked, and all well.'[19] Prior to this – and on more than one occasion – reports had issued from Scotland that 'the King and the Queen are in very evil ménage', which gave rise to beliefs in England that 'there is no good agreement but rather open diffidence between the King of Scots and his wife.'[20] In this case, as in previous episodes, reconciliation was quickly achieved, and letters written a couple of months later confirmed that 'the King is still better and better pleased with the Queen who obeys and pleases him very respectively and greatly to his joy and contentment.'[21]

This was the general pattern as upheavals were shortly followed by reunion. Children continued to arrive until 1607 and the pair remained fond of each other until Anna's death in 1619. In the aftermath of Anna's conflict with Mar over her wish to take Prince Henry to England, for example, James was concerned for Anna's health and angered by her disobedience, but he wrote to her in kind and loving terms that simultaneously evidenced his high regard for the sanctity of marriage: 'I thanke

God I carrie that love and respecte unto you quhiche be the law of God and nature I ought to do to my wyfe and nother of my children, but not for that ye are a kings dauchter; for quhither ye waire a king's or a cook's dauchter, ye must be all alyke to me, being once my wife.'[22] As we shall see, while away on the hunt, James often sent gifts of his success back to his wife, the royal couple continued to spend the summer months and the major annual festivals together, and care and concern was observed between them.[23] In March 1618, when 'divers' of James's bedchamber including Buckingham could not 'perswade and entreat' Anna to leave Denmark House, James personally went 'to visit her', and even when Anna was deathly ill and lying 'still at Denmarke House', she prioritised the effort of 'two or three journies to White-hall to visit the King whiles he kept within doore' suffering through an illness.[24] James also made repeated decisions to place his wife in positions of political delicacy, ordering the privy council to meet at Anna's court during his absences from London and entrusting her to carry out separate state audiences. He valued her judgement above all others in the appointment of posts to his bedchamber, allowed her to complete her own, independent progresses, and he continued to have her accompany him on the main summer progress until at least 1616.[25]

Some critics have interpreted James's establishment of a ruling council in England during his journey to Scotland in 1617 as a failure on Anna's behalf to gain regency (and within that of James's distrust). But such matters are not clear cut. In the first instance, it is debatable whether Anna ever requested to be regent, for the only evidence is Chamberlain's suspicion 'that she dreames and aimes at a Regencie'.[26] Secondly, Anna did achieve a position of authority and power: the prince and the council clustered around her at Greenwich; she firmly established the socio-cultural heart of the court at her residence; and the council paid particular deference to her by retitling Greenwich Palace in her honour and deliberating over her income in case of widowhood. All of this is discussed in more detail in the succeeding chapters and, when contextualised within the patriarchal, hierarchical, yet polymorphic structure of the Jacobean court, allows for a more comprehensive mapping of the political space that Anna secured. Rather than marital strife, the Stuarts' geographical separatism should be interpreted in line with Heide Wunder's theorisation of early modern matrimony as a 'partnership'. Reiterating that women – across all classes – were subordinate to men in terms of legal, civic, and economic power, Wunder argues for marriage according women power as it facilitated their exercise of authority over the household and the children and often put them in the important position of representing, and upholding, the honour of their husband. This was, of course, determined on an individual basis, but Wunder stresses the frequency with which husbands and wives joined together 'in defending the material and nonmaterial position of the household', which often entailed separate, yet complementary, roles.[27] In the case of the elite 'ruling couple', or 'father and mother' of the kingdom, Wunder adds that the woman was not only tasked with the governance of her household, and the management of her dowry, but with the preservation and furtherance of her marital house through the production of heirs, the brokerage of dynastic alliances, and, often, as governor or regent.[28] James himself acknowledged as much in 1603 when, having acquiesced to Anna's wish to personally bring Henry with her to England, he wrote to her that 'for the respect of youre honorable birthe and discente I married you, but the love and respect I now beare you is that *ye are my married wife and so pairtaker of my honore as of all my other fortunes.*'[29] Thus, while the Stuarts' personal relationship was periodically tumultuous, it was buttressed by a successful working partnership and their frequent physical distance should be read as yet another example of the pair adopting divergent positions, opinions, and approaches as a 'ruling couple' to facilitate James's style, concept, and performance of monarchy. If the Stuarts' factional, aesthetic, and religious differences assisted James to fulfil his self-styled persona of 'universal king' and 'peacemaker', then their geographical distance allowed James to indulge his need for 'open air and exercise' while maintaining a royal presence in London.[30]

Apart from the custody battle over Henry – which has specific roots in Anna's firm sense of her own royal entitlement and her awareness of the power to be gained from a close relationship with the heir – James did not view Anna's independent activities or position as a challenge, and he very rarely reprimanded her.[31] A wider view of their relationship over the course of the Scottish and English courts reveals a couple who often worked separately of one another for a united goal. In fact, even when Anna *appeared* to be labouring in opposition to James, her actions often worked to his advantage, which raises questions around the extent of James's complicity. On the surface, Anna's support of the Catholic circle in Scotland, for instance, could be construed as an antagonising thorn in James's side, but a closer look at the factional situation suggests that it held benefits for the king, for he was able to profess a staunchly Protestant position (most importantly to Queen Elizabeth I and the kirk) while remaining abreast of the intrigues of the Catholic earls and ensuring a climate of relative stability and balance. A relationship of cooperation and accommodation underpins the Stuarts' factional and aesthetic difference, geographical distance, and the question of Anna's confessional identity.[32] On the other hand, it rationalises their ability to be concurrently united in the quest for Spanish peace and a Habsburg bride, to share a passion for hunting, and an appreciation of architecture and theatre. For example, reports of the pair hunting together are found as early as May 1590 and, as discussed in greater detail in Chapter 2, they were active architectural patrons individually commissioning highly classicising structures that set a new direction for building in England.[33]

The first Stuart heir, Henry Prince of Wales

During his own lifetime and posthumously, Henry, Prince of Wales and first heir to the multiple Stuart monarchy, was lauded as a Renaissance prince who embodied the hopes and dreams of a new, chivalrous, militantly Protestant Stuart kingdom.[34] The tragedy of his early death at eighteen years of age has suffused his historiography with lamentation, and has bequeathed a mythic quality to his character, talents, and achievements. Thus, for the most part, his two modern biographers, Roy Strong and Timothy Wilks, assert that he was confident, athletic, measured, fervently Protestant, an ambitious architectural patron, a talented collector, and was possessed of a 'general irresistibility'.[35] However, as Smuts rightly reminds us, this merely repeats much seventeenth-century rhetoric that was designed to embellish 'the virtues of young princes'.[36] But while Smuts, together with Kevin Sharpe and Aysha Pollnitz, among others, have tempered this approach, the Henrician ideal continues to be used as a benchmark to highlight the failings of his parents.[37] It is still common to read, for example, that 'there were very obvious differences in the characters of the two courts – indecorum and intemperateness prevailing at James's, order and sobriety insisted upon at Henry's', or that great efforts were made 'to save Henry from Anna's potentially ruinous influence'.[38] Furthermore, while previous generations have argued that from 1604 'until Henry neared his sixteenth birthday, he and Anne of Denmark saw each other infrequently', a different interpretation of the evidence is equally, if not more persuasively, tenable.[39] Anna finally gained control of Henry prior to her leaving Edinburgh in 1603 and the two of them – together with Princess Elizabeth and a large entourage – jointly made their way to London. Once there, Henry was established with his own court at Oatlands, but this lasted little more than a year, and by at least 1607 he was back in regular contact with his mother. On 4 July 1607, the Venetian ambassador, Zorzi Giustinian, was able to plan to give Henry the Doge's gratitude when he next went 'to visit the Queen', as she 'is devoted to him and never lets him away from her side'.[40]

Anna's attempts to gain custody of Henry and manage his household have been mostly interpreted in maternal terms, but her political motivations also need to be recognised.[41] Anna's parental intimacy with her children was slight, since they were raised by appointed guardians from a young age. But she was well aware of the position and leverage to be gained from a close relationship with the heir apparent and aligned with Henry on political opinion, favourites, and aesthetics. Indeed, observation of her affections, such as that by the Venetian ambassador, who noted in 1609 that 'the Queen especially caresses [Henry] and tries by every means in her power to secure his good-will', was tellingly undercut by the belief that 'her object is to secure her fortune and increase her income in case of accidents.'[42] Such 'accidents' referred to the possibility of King James's death, and Anna's concomitant widowhood in which situation she would need to rely on the good graces of the new king – her eldest son. Certainly, from the outset of 1610, Anna and Henry joined forces against the rising influence and power of James's first English favourite, Robert Carr (Kerr), made Viscount Rochester in 1611 and Earl of Somerset in 1613, and her cultural activities proved influence for Henry's patronage.

Male favourites and faction

Carr had been in ascendance since breaking his leg at the Accession Day tilt of 1607,[43] but it took a unique confluence of events – the power vacuum occasioned by the successive deaths of George Home, Earl of Dunbar (c.1566–1611) in January 1611, the Earl of Salisbury in May 1612, and Prince Henry in November 1612, the growing influence of Sir Thomas Overbury (1581–1613), and James's decision to increase his personal involvement in policy with Carr as broker – for the favourite to cease being satisfied with personal reward and control of clientage and to begin meddling in court politics and growing factionalism.[44] With Carr's move from 'bedchamber to the bureaucracy', writes James Knowles, he achieved 'unrivalled control over patronage and access to the King', and by August 1612, George Calvert, Baron Baltimore (1579–1632), was compelled to characterise Carr as 'the *primum mobile* of our court, by whose motion all the other spheres must move, or stand still; the bright sun of our firmament, at whose splendour or glooming all our marigolds of the court open and shut'.[45]

By 1612, Carr's favour with James was almost complete, but he was not universally popular. Just weeks before Calvert called Carr 'the *primum mobile*' of the court, Viscount Fenton observed that while 'Rotchester is exceeding great vith his Majestie ... yet can he not find the rycht waye to pleis ather the Quein or the Prince, but thaye are bothe in the conceat of this Court not weill satisfied vith him.'[46] This extended to prominent courtiers including Pembroke who, in August 1612, was reportedly 'so far out' with Carr 'as it is almost come to a quarrel'.[47] Furthermore, as Leeds Barroll determines, Anna and Henry spent the best part of 1612 working together against the young Scotsman. Confirmation of their politicking is clear in January 1612, when Carr was created chief clerk of the court of common pleas and then, notably, was required to share the office with John Harington (1592–1614), one of Henry's most intimate companions and the younger brother of Anna's principal lady-in-waiting Lucy Russell, Countess of Bedford (née Harington) (1580–1627).[48] That same year, Anna and Henry joined forces in their support for the secretaryship, it being known that they were 'earnest in Sir Henry Wotton's behalf', it was perceptively reported that 'the Lord Rochester [Carr] is not willing, after his late reconciliation, to oppose himself, or stand in the breach against such assailants.'[49] Sir Ralph Winwood (1562/63–1617) also perceived the unity of consort and heir, and when having returned from The Hague in July 1612, and desiring the secretariat for himself, he chose to spend a day 'with the Queen who used him extraordinarily well', and then 'took his leave of the Prince and had the same usage'.[50] Barroll's supposition that Anna and Henry 'were a faction at this time' might be taking their unity a step too far, but it is clear that they were very far from having the 'little significant contact' that an earlier generation of scholars assumed.[51]

The factional connection between Anna and Henry during the period of Carr's rise extended beyond the political into the visual arts as the prince followed his mother's lead in patronising Isaac Oliver (c.1565–1617) and Robert Peake the Elder (c.1551–1619). By this time, as discussed in Chapter 5, Oliver had been in the queen's services since 1604, and it was that same year that Anna became Peake's first royal Stuart patron with orders for portraits of herself and Henry.[52] By comparison, it was only in 1608 that Henry began patronising Oliver, and Peake does not enter the prince's privy purse accounts until 1611. Henry was, however, familiar with Peake before this point, for in addition to his mother having commissioned his portrait from the painter, several English elites (as is now well known) ordered his portrait from Peake and even if Henry did not personally sit for them, they must have been completed with his knowledge.[53] Such patterns of patronage clearly establish Anna's cultural influence on Henry and call for a reconsideration of scholarship that has traditionally maintained Henry as the aficionado who led Anna in her cultural endeavours.[54]

The deaths of Cecil and Henry weakened Anna's position against Carr and assisted his rise. On 3 November 1613, he was created Earl of Somerset, and on 26 December 1613, he formalised his relationship to the Howards with his marriage to the Earl of Northampton's newly divorced niece, Frances Howard (1590–1632).[55] Anna remained steadfast in her aversion to the Howard-Carr faction, turning her support to the opposing network headed by the earls of Pembroke and Southampton, which, like Anna, nurtured relations with the Cecils until Salisbury's death in 1612. Through her household personnel, Anna already enjoyed multifaceted and longstanding connections to this faction – not least of all by the fact that Pembroke was Lucy Harington's second cousin and the pair collaborated on cultural projects and marriage matches – but Anna's alliance to the group was cemented by the events of 1612 and their joint opposition was evident throughout 1613 and 1614.[56] As discussed in Chapter 2, Anna entered into a rivalry with Northampton over the keepership of Greenwich Park, and she ensured that Carr was not the only courtier to be married with royal support in the Christmas season of 1613/14. The Carr-Howard marriage at Whitehall Palace on 26 December 1613 was competitively followed by the marriage of Jane Drummond (c.1585–1643) to Robert Ker, Earl of Roxburghe (1569/70–1650) at Somerset House on 3 February 1614.[57] As the queen's principal lady-in-waiting and chief confidant, Drummond's wedding was sponsored by Anna and 'the entertainment' was considered to be 'great and cost the Quene ... over £3,000'.[58] Beyond the bridal couple and royal residence, the attendant festivities have been interpreted as examples of the cultural divergence between James and Anna's courts through the choices of playwright and the resultant tone, content, and poetic style.[59] This was certainly perceived by contemporaries, who discussed the marriages in relation to the royal patron and host – James or Anna – with Chamberlain reporting to Carleton that 'all the talk now is of masking and feasting at these towardly marriages ... the King bears the charge of the first, all saving the apparel, and no doubt the Queen will do as much of her side.'[60] Anna's display of difference from the palaces, favourites, and playwrights associated with James and the Carr-Howard faction served to solidify the notion of her having a distinct physical court, with the wedding masque for Drummond and Roxburghe having been staged 'at Somersethouse or Quenes court (as it must now be called)'.[61]

Significantly, it was also 1614 that Anna worked with the Southampton-Pembroke network to advance Villiers as a replacement for Carr.[62] In July 1614, Sir William Sanderson (1586–1676), secretary to Henry Rich, Earl of Holland (1590–1640), recounted that members of 'the family of Herberts, Hertford, and Bedford' met at Baynard's Castle to discuss 'the design to bring in Villiers'.[63] Subsequently, on 3 August 1614, Villiers was introduced to James at Althorp and by the following month he was already being described as 'in favore with his Majestie'.[64] Anna's role in promoting Villiers was pivotal and George Abbot, Archbishop of Canterbury (1562–1633), recalled:

> The King began to cast his eye upon George Villiers, who was then Cupbearer, and seemed a modest and courteous youth. But King James had a fashion, that he would never admit any to nearness about himself, but such a one as the Queen should commend unto him, and make some suit on his behalf ... In the end, upon importunity, Queen Anne condescended and so pressed it with the King, that he assented ... And when the King gave order to swear him [Villiers] of the Bed-chamber, Somerset [Carr], who was near, importuned the King with a message, that he might be only sworn a Groom: But my self and others that were at the door, sent to her Majesty, that she would perfect her work, and cause him to be sworn a Gentleman of the Chamber.[65]

The Venetian agent Foscarini also credited Anna with Villiers's triumph, writing that 'since the fall of her [Anna's] enemy, the Earl of Somerset, Mr Villiers has risen, supported by her and dependent on her.'[66] As is now well known, the placement of Villiers was enormously successful, and an affable relationship continued between consort and advancing favourite.

When Villiers accompanied James to Scotland in 1617, Sir Francis Bacon (1561–1626) wrote to him of Anna's activities for he knew 'your Lordship hath a special care of anything that concerneth the Queen.'[67] For her part, Anna's few surviving letters to Villiers show her having used him as a conduit to the king. Villiers was to inform James that she had received twelve mares from her brother Christian IV and was going to put them into Byfield Park, and she thanked him for 'remembering the King for the pailing one of me parke'. As a result of these services, she signed off with the promise to 'doe you [Villiers] anie service I can'.[68] Managing a working relationship with Villiers was to Anna's distinct advantage in increasing her leverage with the king, but she also took care to remind Villiers of her superiority. Her letters are indicative of congeniality rather than formality and her use of the appellation 'my kind dog' points to both intimacy and condescension, where the latter is reinforced by her opening statement that she found Villiers's letter 'acceptable'. This combination of care and jest extended directly to the king, building a picture of a harmonious triumvirate of royal couple and chief favourite: Anna thanked Villiers for doing so 'verie well in lugging the Sowes [James's] eare' and added that she wished him to 'continue a watchfull dog to him [James] and be alwaies true to him'.[69] Such jovial terms of address were likewise used by James – and Queen Elizabeth before him – where a repertoire of personalised names in 'rough humour' were allocated to close ministers and favourites.[70]

There were both physical affection and emotional bonds between king and favourite, but whether any of the bodily contact that passed between them could be identified as sex or sexual (in James's relationship with Carr or in his later relationship with Villiers) remains conjectural. A number of historians – including Alastair Bellany, Robert Shephard, and Curtis Perry – have convincingly argued that contemporary allegations of sexual impropriety (and related accusations of effeminacy) should be understood as grievances around corruption and nepotism.[71] Furthermore, as William Stockton and James Bromley remind us, 'there is no single, transhistorical definition of sex', which complicates the ability to categorise forms of physical contact as sexual, social, affective, or other.[72] Important for this study is the further recognition that James's male favourites had little bearing on Anna's position, for they were no rival to the queen in her ability to bear legitimate children, they were not divinely ordained with royal blood, and they could not provide James with access to a powerful Protestant network on the Continent. These were the reasons for which Anna had been chosen as James's wife in 1588. Indeed, they were the reasons that protected her place and power at the Stuart courts throughout her life and were dramatically fêted in her state funeral as seen in Chapter 6.

Carr's advancement throws the unique space that Anna occupied at court into sharp relief, for of all James's favourites it was Carr that she uniquely opposed. As scholars have recognised, Carr was a novel type of favourite in England for his combination of political and cultural influence – a mantle inherited and extended by Villiers.[73] The reason for Anna's antipathy towards Carr and the Howard faction has never been satisfactorily explained. It is not clearly elucidated in the contemporary correspondence, but evidence suggests that Anna's dislike of Carr stemmed from their time in Scotland when Carr served as a page to George Home, Earl of Dunbar – one of James's principal favourites and chief advisors, and a target of Anna's displeasure. The first hint of such conflict comes in August 1592 when it was noted that 'the Queen is greatly offended against … Sir George Hume' and such discord was still apparent nearly three years later when, on 18 January 1601, Thomas Douglas informed Cecil that 'the Queen and her faction' were working against the Earls of Dunbar and Mar, and Sir Thomas Erskine.[74] The rivalry was still news at court in April when George Nicholson wrote that 'the Queen' remained 'constant in her dislike of her conceived enemies', and by the close of May rumours were circulating that Anna would topple Dunbar since he was 'of her Majesty's enemies' but 'the love twixt his Majesty and his Queen … was never so hot and earnest', which suggests that the court expected James to heed his wife's wishes.[75] A formal reconciliation between Anna and Dunbar is not recorded, but if the queen's antipathy continued it did not affect the position of either the earl or his page.

The exact date of Carr's admittance to the Stuart household is unknown, but it may have been as early as 1598 and he was definitely serving as a page of honour by April 1602.[76] The following year (as page to Dunbar), Carr travelled to London with his master and the king where Dunbar was promptly made chancellor of the exchequer and a member of the English privy council and, in summer 1604, Carr was promoted to groom of the bedchamber.[77] Yet Anna's actions following Dunbar's death in January 1611 suggest that her animosity had not abated. In March 1611, the queen's lodgings at Whitehall were readied in anticipation of her arrival, but she significantly gave additional orders for 'hanginge the lodginges that were the Erle of Downbarres for her Ma[jes]ty', thereby physically recasting and claiming Dunbar's court spaces as her own.[78]

In addition to fears that Carr would draw power away from Henry, Anna also resented Carr for disrespecting rank and after being subject to his disdain, she caustically recalled that he was 'beholden to none but himself'.[79] For his part, James certainly treated Carr like a loving father as he nursed him through broken bones, taught him Latin, encouraged him in politics, and gave him expensive gifts and prestigious titles so that, as Bellany contends, James 'made him anew' and 'acted out one of the fantasies of Renaissance royal power, the king's ability to shape the characters and hearts of his subjects'.[80] In England, despite James's close ties to Carr, he tolerated and probably endorsed Anna's support of the group that countered his own because it aided his quest for factional balance.

This broadened the king's self-promoted image of peace and concord, and James himself deliberately kept the oppositional Earls of Southampton and Pembroke in royal favour by treating them to offices and perquisites. James's concern for factional balance was perceived by contemporaries with Chamberlain noting in 1617 that Bacon, had 'oppose[d] himself so violently against' Winwood, 'but the King according to his pacificall disposition hath made all frends'.[81] It is also worth repeating at this point that, despite this factional divergence, there is no evidence of growing geographical separatism between the royal couple. Warrants issued for readying the royal lodgings show that James and Anna continued to stay together for parts of the court calendar and to host ambassadors together. Whitehall remained the key site for celebrating the major court festivals, and the palace annually welcomed the couple for such occasions as the Accession Day, Easter, Maundy Thursday, the Feast of St George, All Saints Day, Christmas, and New Year, although the summer festival of Whitsun was customarily observed at Greenwich. In those years that Anna did not accompany James for part of the summer progress – between June and September – the royal couple still converged at a number of the royal residences including Greenwich, Hampton Court, Nonsuch, Oatlands, Theobalds, Whitehall, Windsor Castle, and Woodstock.[82] Even after the competitive Christmas season of 1613, James and Anna celebrated the following Easter and St George's Day together, as usual, at Whitehall and that summer saw the royal couple jointly lodge at Greenwich, Hampton Court, and Whitehall.[83] It is undeniable that James had extremely close relationships with particular men throughout his life but these did not disrupt the working royal relationship or reduce Anna's position or status.

Confessional identities

In addition to Anna's involvement with the masque, one other area of her life has received sustained scholarly focus: her confessional identity.[84] Raised a strict Lutheran and accompanied to Scotland – and then England – by her German Lutheran chaplain, Johan Sering (1589–1619), two reports claim that Anna converted to Catholicism around 1592 or, perhaps, around 1600. This was not publicised and knowledge was restricted to James, a handful of Catholic dignitaries, and a select number of elite Scottish and English Catholics. While the queen is thought to have performed Catholic observances in the relative privacy of her palaces, in the comparatively public courtly arena she upheld an appearance of conformity. To this end, she accompanied James to quasi-public reformed services, made sure as the king's proxy that she 'never missed one Lent sermon' during James's 1617 Scottish progress, supported Protestant preaching in her palaces, maintained Protestant chaplains in her household, and did not display any paintings or devotional items or indeed wear any pieces of jewellery that could be interpreted as popish.[85] Perhaps unsurprisingly, this confessional performance posed problems for the queen, giving rise to multiple misgivings and doubt among both Catholics and Protestants. It has also resulted in conflicting, oblique, and questionable evidence with the majority of subsequent scholarship seeking to *prove* the genuine nature of Anna's conversion or to map the difficulties that her Catholicism brought to James.

Revisionist scholarship by Peter McCullough, Alexandra Walsham, and others has stressed the existence of multiple confessional positions – including the 'church papist' – in early modern England, moving religious studies beyond the basic Protestant/Catholic divide.[86] What commonly remains a blanket assumption, however, is that early modern women – irrespective of which religion they conformed to – were deeply, studiously, pious. This, of course, was true of many in the period, as private writings attest, but as Bernard Capp has demonstrated of ordinary women, it was not true of them all.[87] Yet a different caution needs to be exercised when considering royal women, for we need to acknowledge that their religious observances – just like their sartorial choices, cultural projects, or social activities – were often heavily inflected with political meaning. This is not to belittle or discredit the authenticity of their faith, but to recognise that their confessional identities contained an inherently political and performative quality. Indeed, 'the symbolic significance of women's religious beliefs in early modern England', writes Patricia Crawford, 'awaits attention'.[88] Furthermore, we must recognise that royal women constantly negotiated a shifting scale of priorities where politics could, at times, even trump religious practice. As a representative of the Stuart monarchy, Anna of Denmark's religious observances not only provided a model of emulation for English women but signified the state of national practice and devotion to foreign elites. Perhaps expectedly then, her Catholic beliefs were not visualised in any conclusive, public manner, and the vast majority of courtly onlookers were only ever privy to a display of certain Protestantism, which was made patently manifest, for example, in the churching ceremonies that she underwent after the births of princesses Mary (d.1607) and Sophia (d.1606) in 1605 and 1606 respectively.[89] On the other hand, Anna was quick to profess her Catholic faith to co-religionists, especially when political benefits were within reach: Spanish envoys charged with negotiating peace in 1604; Pope Paul V (1550–1621) when dispensation was required for a cross-confessional match with Tuscany; Spanish officials when religious freedom was a condition for the Infanta María Ana's (1606–1646) marriage into the Stuart kingdom. Thus, as I have argued elsewhere, Anna was fully aware of the benefits to be gained from upholding a position of confessional duality.[90] Moreover, James's complicity, coupled with his own infamous posturing to numerous Catholic officials in the lead up to the English succession shows that he could likewise use religion in support of politics.

Gift-exchange across networks

It has long been recognised that the giving and receiving of gifts was a key component in the creation and augmentation of the patron–client relationships and kinship bonds that underwrote many early modern court systems – Denmark, England, and Scotland included. Gifts were routinely presented to foreign rulers and their representatives, household and family members, local elites and favourites; they were given away at weddings and christenings; offered as rewards for devoted service; and exchanged on Valentine's Day, New Year's Day, and while on progress. At the Stuart courts, they commonly took the form of jewels and plate but also included money, animals, plants, garments, soft furnishings, and foodstuffs, and extended beyond physical goods to perquisites, titles, and hospitality.[91] Exchanged liberally within Stuart Scotland and England, the practice extended to visiting diplomats, foreign rulers, and faraway relatives. In each case, the gift was transacted within established repertoires of socio-cultural significance as honour, political intimacy, or favour was performed, and complexities of connection, gratitude, obligation, and reciprocity were created.[92]

In the Stuart world of international diplomacy, two examples of Anna giving and receiving gifts highlight Stuart England as a gift economy, demonstrate the queen's political role and value to the monarchy, and showcase her involvement in highly ceremonial exchanges. In the first instance, in April 1606, having determined that Anna had influence with King James, Spain sought her support of the Stuart-Habsburg marriage alliance, ordering their ambassador-extraordinary, the Marquis de San Germano, to give Anna 'large presents … [to] win her to their side'.[93] On the other hand, when, in April 1611, the Venetian ambassador, Marcantonio Correr, witnessed Anna giving 'presents of some value' to the daughter-in-law of the French ambassador, he concluded that such 'special signs of graciousness' proved that France was in high favour and Prince Henry would therefore marry a French princess.[94] Gifts were also a central rubric in Anna's preservation of bonds with her wider kinship network, especially with her brother Christian and her mother Sofie. Beyond the jewels and miniatures that Anna and Christian exchanged, which are discussed in Chapter 4, Anna commissioned her principal jeweller, George Heriot (1563–1624) to make a diamond-encrusted tablet 'to be sent to her mats mother ye Queene of Denmark', which must have contained a miniature of Anna herself.[95] When Christian's 1606 visit to England came to an end, Anna presented him with 'some fine horses handsomely caparisoned' to give to their mother, who ran a highly successful stud farm on Falster.[96] A decade later, Anna received twelve horses from Christian, together with a solid gold sideboard, to which she reciprocated by sending him a bed and a suite of 'brocaded hangings of great richness'.[97] These were individualised gifts, carefully attuned to the tastes of the recipient and they showcased the craftsmanship and fashion of the respective court, which would have then been appropriately displayed and discussed in rooms of ceremonial and diplomatic importance.

A principal argument made in the following chapters is that Anna's natal network was of considerable value and prestige to James. Writing to her brother Christian, on 13 May 1609, James admitted that

> it does not escape us how great (both for your dignity and also for the communion of religion) is the authority of Your Serene Highness among all of the princes in Germany ... among them there is almost no one of great name and reputation who does not come in contact with you through kinship or marriage.[98]

As for Anna, one of the main ways in which James serviced this relationship (and Christian reciprocated) was by gifting commodities and personnel. Given the kings' mutual love of hunting, it is perhaps expected that the corresponding animals – namely dogs, deer, hawks, and horses – were the frequent choice of gift between the two kingdoms, although in August 1596 Christian deemed it appropriate to send a more exotic hunting beast, gifting James a lion complete with a German keeper, Wilhelm Froelich.[99] For his part, James repeatedly framed the gifts as a sign of the personal affection according to 'the law of friendship and fraternal intimacy'. Yet the personal was always political, and James also voiced the need to preserve the balance of power by playing both donor and receiver, taking care to remind Christian that 'nothing will be more pleasing to us than to have the ability to present very often to you proofs and tokens of our good will.'[100]

Other members of the Oldenburg network were likewise fêted with gifts from the Stuarts, and personnel moved between the courts. In 1601, having received a representative from Anna's grandfather, Duke Ulric of Mecklenburg-Güstrow (1527–1603), James sent him back with 'ane greit cheinyie of gold wt his hienes portrait hingand [hanging]' for the duke that cost a considerable £611.18s.4d. Scots.[101] In 1609, 1612, and again in 1613, horses were sent to Anna's brother Duke Ulrik of Holstein (1578–1624), and dogs were sent to her brother-in-law Heinrich Julius of Braunschweig-Lüneburg (1564–1613).[102] This extended to broader instances of cross-cultural exchange as people moved between the centres gaining knowledge of other customs, languages, traditions, and fashions as they went. Beyond the elite circles of royalty, nobility, and sovereign representatives, this was seen among more common folk such as Mr Rider, one of James's gentlemen 'harbengers', who attended Duke Ulrik on his entry into the Stuart kingdom in 1607, and then returned with him to the Continent where he remained for a full year.[103] The preservation of the wider consanguineal and affinal Oldenburg bonds through gift-giving was also beginning to be in evidence among the next generation of Stuarts in

England with Prince Henry, just prior to his death, sending Heinrich Julius a suit of armour 'and other things'.[104]

This small but instructive number of newly documented examples extends Mara Wade's important research into the networks of exchange operating between the Oldenburg siblings' courts, where she has drawn particular attention to the regular gifts, letters, and personnel that moved between Saxony and Denmark. As Wade elaborates, Hedevig, Electress of Saxony (1581–1641) sent her brother Christian IV a dog and a master of the hounds; he sent her animals – a lion, a lioness, and a tiger – for her menagerie; and the pair discussed sending servants to the courts in England and Wolfenbüttel.[105] Hedevig's husband, Elector Christian II of Saxony (1583–1611), was well aware of the strong bonds of personal affection between the familial members writing, in August 1603, that 'deliebten geschwister in gutter Leibesgesundheit zusammen kommen, sich fruendltich miteinander ... ergotzen, auch durch göttliche beschirmung in dergleichen wolfärigen zustandt zu mehrmaln einander besuchen mögen' [We furthermore wish that your royal highness might come together with your beloved siblings in good health to enjoy each other's company, and through god's patronage in good health may visit each other again and again].[106] There is less evidence of the sisters sending gifts and letters between themselves, which points to the politics that underwrote these exchanges whereby Christian IV, as the most powerful of the siblings, was the focal point.

Further down the social scale in England, the strict system of clientage and reciprocity is thrown into sharp relief through the records of 'guifts & rewards paid by warrant' preserved in the accounts of Anna's receiver-general, George Carew, Earl of Totnes (1555–1629). These documents have not been analysed in this manner before, and the general pattern saw Carew record the amount of money dispensed from the queen's privy purse as a gift. Occasions that warranted such gift-giving included times when Anna served as godmother, when she offered thanks for items (most commonly foodstuffs but also literary dedications, letters, and performances) that she was given, and when gifting rewards for specific acts of service.[107] The servants of aristocrats, courtiers, and ambassadors who delivered Anna gifts from their superiors were generally given ten shillings for their efforts; performers and musicians were more generously rewarded but in any single case the sum rarely exceeded 100 shillings. These records clearly show Anna regularly giving money to petitioners from Denmark-Norway and the German lands. As well as donating funds (usually between ten and sixty shillings) to poor Danes and Germans, on at least three occasions she gave monetary aid to Danish and Norwegian sailors who had suffered at sea. Such records are suggestive of Anna having some sense of duty – personal and/or political – to her compatriots, and it is plausible that they provided her with welcome reminders of language, custom, or appearance.[108] On at least one instance the reminder was edible, with

Anna rewarding 'Dutch [German] men' for gifting her 'wildbore westfalia bacon', and it is possible that the 'distilled watters' she received from a German woman had been similarly brought in from the Continent.[109] More commonly, the victuals she received were locally sourced with commoners, elites, and the king himself gifting the queen quantities of fresh fish, shellfish, fruit, fowl, nuts, and deer. The majority of these goods – from the mullet, sturgeon and 'ffish from the Thames' that were delivered by fisherman, to the 'green pease [peas]' gifted by John King, Bishop of London (d.1621), or the boxes of dried cherries and grapes from Frances Howard, Countess of Kildare (c.1572–1628) – would have been grown in their own holdings or personally sourced through their trades. As Natalie Zemon Davis points out, such food-gifts were accorded a much higher value than had they been bought at market and therefore, irrespective of the terms and expectations of the individual relationship, were more successful in realising the giver's aim of honour, gratitude, supplication, or favour.[110] As such objects and goods literally changed hands, the ritualised process of exchange extended ties between the court to the country, and the Stuart kingdom and the Continent.

As the subsequent discussions make clear, the wealthy Denmark-Norway of Anna's youth housed an active and diverse court culture marked by drama, tournaments, festivals, and dance, as the crown established itself as a leader in the patronage of architecture, painting, music, and learning.[111] In turn, these were inflected by the trends and traditions of its southern neighbours (Italy included), for Denmark-Norway was intricately tied to most of the German lands by kinship, politics, and/or religion. These connections, combined with its geographic position more generally, saw the kingdom shaped by the results of increasing travel and a burgeoning print culture; it was the centre of constant exchange as people, goods, and graphic material filtered across its borders. Thus, as the following analyses emphasise, Anna came to Scotland and England with personal knowledge and experience of cosmopolitan cultural forms and a firm understanding of their ability to visualise aims and allegiances: this is repeatedly evident in her engagement with theatre, building, landscaping, painting, and her own bodily attire.[112] Indeed, an important finding of this study is that irrespective of her marital country of residence – Scotland or England – Anna identified first and foremost as a member of the House of Oldenburg with proud, pan-European alliances of blood, marriage, and politics, and that it was these connections and experiences which shaped her cultural activities and her conception of etiquette, and underwrote her value to the Stuart dynasty.

Notes

1 *CSPV*, vol. 12, no. 355: 21 October 1611.
2 *CSPV*, vol. 12, nos. 316, 342: 2, 30 September 1611.
3 James's multifaceted diplomatic approach to the Kalmar War between Denmark-

Norway and Sweden is discussed in Chapter 5. For Anna's involvement see *CSPV*, vol. 12, nos. 250, 277, 316, 325, 355.

4 Smuts, 'Cultural Diversity and Cultural Change', 99–113: 104–105; Knowles, 'Images of Royalty', 23. The movement of personnel is particularly marked in the case of musicians, as discussed in Chapter 3.

5 This is aptly summarised by Clarissa Campbell-Orr, who, writing on early modern royal women, states that 'even if they accepted that their chief role was to produce legitimate offspring and be as supportive of their husbands as possible ... individual women managed [this] similar role very differently, *depending on their education, personality, circumstance, and evolving relationship with the men in question*'. See her 'Introduction: Court Studies, Gender and Women's History, 1660–1837', in C. Campbell-Orr (ed.), *Queenship in Britain, 1660–1837: Royal Patronage, Court Culture and Dynastic Politics* (Manchester, 2002), 1–53: 1 (emphasis mine).

6 Smuts, 'Cultural Diversity and Cultural Change', 104–105. A male model of Jacobean polycentrism is also discussed in P. Croft, 'Robert Cecil and the Early Jacobean Court', 134–148: 135–138, 142–143, and L. L. Peck, 'An Introduction', in Peck (ed.), *The Mental World of the Jacobean Court*, 1–17: 3–4; Peck, *Court Patronage and Corruption*, 68–74; Smuts, *Court Culture*, 59–60, 65.

7 Barroll, *Anna of Denmark*, esp. chs 1 to 3; L. Barroll, 'The Court of the First Stuart Queen', in L. L. Peck (ed.), *The Mental World of the Jacobean Court* (Cambridge, 1991), 191–208; 'Theatre as Text: The Case of Queen Anna and the Jacobean Court Masque', *Elizabethan Theatre* 14 (1996), 175–193; McManus, *Renaissance Stage*; Knowles, 'Images of Royalty', esp. 23, 30–33; McManus, 'Introduction', 1–17; esp. 1–8; McManus, 'Memorialising Anna of Denmark's Court', 81–99: esp. 86–90. See also Tomlinson, *Women on Stage*.

8 Cuddy, 'Reinventing a Monarchy', 63; McManus, 'Introduction', 1–8; A. Morton, 'Introduction', 1–14: 3–4, and H. Watanabe-O'Kelly 'Afterword', 231–250: 238–240, both in A. Morton and H. Watanabe-O'Kelly (eds), *Queens Consort: Cultural Transfer and European Politics, c.1500–1800* (London and New York, 2017).

9 Watanabe-O'Kelly 'Afterword', 234, 238–242; quote from 238. For the difficulties that Anna faced in performing a public, outward display of Protestant piety – given that she is thought to have converted to Catholicism while in Scotland – see J. Field, 'Anna of Denmark and the Politics of Religious Identity in Jacobean Scotland and England, c.1592–1619', *Northern Studies* 50 (2019), 87–113, and Chapter 6 below.

10 Campbell-Orr, 'Introduction: Court Studies', 17. Campbell-Orr also highlights the need for historians to reconceptualise the Renaissance court through an awareness of their base polycentrism.

11 C. Campbell-Orr, 'Introduction', in C. Campbell-Orr (ed.), *Queenship in Europe 1660–1815: The Role of the Consort* (Cambridge, 2004), 1–15: 5.

12 NRS, GD124/10/82.

13 Anna's relationships to James's male favourites are discussed below.

14 For instance, see the work of B. K. Lewalski who, writing in the early 1990s, stated: 'The Queen's oppositional activities and subversions could not substantially alter her actual position in James's patriarchal regime, nor had she the intellectual power or political consciousness to mount a consistent oppositional policy': *Writing Women*, 43. Knowles is similarly critical of the argument that Anna used Elizabethan imagery for an 'oppositional' position, asserting that it 'understates the varied uses of such ideologies and how they played within the complex, polycentric structure of the Jacobean court': 'Images of Royalty', 23.

15 Capp, 'Separate Domains?' 125–126. Heide Wunder argues for a similar interpretation of early modern gender relations, writing that the political and social hierarchy, which privileged men, comprised 'comparative differences' but rather than being innately binarised, it 'depended on the delicate balance of mutual obliga-

16 *CSPV*, vol. 12, no. 462: 16 March 1612; T. Birch, *The Court and Times of James I*, 2 vols (London, 1849, reprint 1973), vol. 1, 261: 1 August 1613 (to Dudley Carleton).
17 H. Paton (ed.), *Supplementary Report on the Manuscripts of Mar and Kellie preserved at Alloa house, Clackmannanshire* (London, 1930), 59.
18 See Chapters 2, 5, and 6, and see also Barroll, *Anna of Denmark*, 17–35.
19 *CSP Scotland*, vol. 13, part 2, no. 900: 9 February 1603.
20 *CSP Scotland*, vol. 13, part 2, no. 572: 31 October 1600 (The Master of Gray to Sir Robert Cecil); E. Sawyer, *Memorials of Affairs of State in the Reigns of Q. Elizabeth and K. James I Collected (chiefly) from the Original Papers of the Right Honourable Sir Ralph Winwood, Kt. Sometime one of the Principal Secretaries of States*, 3 vols (London, 1725), vol. 1, 274: 15 November 1600 (Sir Henry Neville to Sir Ralph Winwood).
21 *CSP Scotland*, vol. 13, part 2, no. 613: 28 January 1601 (George Nicholson to Sir Robert Cecil).
22 NRS, GD124/10/82.
23 TNA, LR7/137, fols 23r, 24r; TNA, E351/543, fols 247r, 247v, 260r, 260v, 261v, 262r, 262v, 263r; TNA, E351/544, fols 8v, 10r, 10v, 11r, 11v, 26r, 26v, 27r, 27v, 43v, 44r, 58r, 58v, 59r, 59v, 78v, 79r, 91r, 91v, 92r, 99v, 100v.
24 McClure (ed.), *Chamberlain*, vol. 2, 149, 152, nos. 290, 291: 16 and 27 March 1618 (Chamberlain to Carleton).
25 Cuddy, 'Revival of the Entourage', 194–195; Cole, 'State Apartment', 25. Examples of Anna giving independent audiences include: TNA, SP14/12, fols 19r–v (9 January 1605); TNA, E351/543, fol. 247v; TNA, E351/544, fols 8v, 10v, 26r, 43v, 60r, 78v, 79r, 91r, 91v; *CSPV*, vol. 10, no. 102: 30 July 1603; *CSPV*, vol. 11, nos. 477, 801: 15 April 1609; 25 February 1610; *CSPV*, vol. 12, nos. 389, 400: 9, 23 December 1611; *CSPV*, vol. 14, nos. 139, 340: 1 January 1616; 1 July 1616; *CSPV*, vol. 15, nos. 183, 525, 535: 28 March 1618; 7, 14 September 1618). Paton (ed.), *Supplementary Report*, 53: 15 August 1613 (Thomas, Viscount Fenton to John, Earl of Mar); J. Rushworth, *Historical Collections of Private Passages of State, Weighty Matters in Law, Remarkable Proceedings in Five Parliaments Beginning the Sixteenth Year of King James, Anno 1618 and Ending the Fifth Year of King Charles, Anno 1629* (London, 1659), 456–457.
26 McClure (ed.), *Chamberlain*, vol. 2, 47, no. 256: 4 January 1617 (to Dudley Carleton).
27 H. Wunder, *He Is the Sun*, chs 9 and 10: quotation from 174. Wunder levels this at women burghers and peasants, but it finds resonance with royal relationships in their joint defence of the dynasty/kingdom within the wider courtly community.
28 Wunder, *He Is the Sun*, 162, 202–203, 205; Campbell-Orr, 'Introduction', 5–14.
29 NRS, GD124/10/82; italics mine.
30 TNA, SP14/12, fols 19r–v (9 January 1605). On the nature of James's kingship, with specific reference to his self-fashioning as a peacemaker and universal king, see J. Goodare and M. Lynch, 'James VI: Universal King?' in J. Goodare and M. Lynch (eds), *The Reign of James VI* (East Linton, 2000), 1–31: 4–5, 19–22, 31. Although beyond the scope of this book, it is worth noting that James's projected image did not align with his actions, for he also led a remarkable military career. The persona was hugely successful, however, for James is still most commonly remembered (and critiqued) as a pacifist king. On James's military escapades see, most concisely, Murdoch, 'James VI', 5–11.
31 Barroll, *Anna of Denmark*, 20–24, 28–35. Far from being unique to Anna, this was

an awareness among early modern consorts generally, and is perceptively detailed in Watanabe-O'Kelly, 'Afterword', 232–233.
32 For a detailed treatment of Anna's performance of confessional identity see Field, 'Anna of Denmark and the Politics of Religious Identity'; also Chapter 6, this volume.
33 *CSP Scotland*, vol. 10, no. 409: 31 May 1590 (Bowes to Burghley). Unlike Anna, James did not perform in any masques, but he was a regular attendee and frequently sanctioned Anna's expenditure through centralised court office. James's interest in masquing is neatly encapsulated by McManus's observation that 'between 1609 and 1611 … the king's, queen's, and prince's courts vied for ownership of the masquing stage', in her 'When Is a Woman Not a Woman', 439.
34 T. Wilks, 'Introduction' 11–17 and Smuts, 'Prince Henry and his World', 19–31, both in C. MacLeod, Timothy Wilks, R. M. Smuts, and Rab MacGibbon, *The Lost Prince: The Life and Death of Henry Stuart* (London, 2012).
35 R. Strong, *Henry Prince of Wales and England's Lost Renaissance* (London, 1986); T. Wilks, 'The Court Culture of Prince Henry', Unpub. PhD diss. (The University of Oxford, 1987); T. Wilks, 'Art Collecting at the English Court'; T. Wilks, '"Forbear the Heat and Haste of Building": Rivalries among the Designers at Prince Henry's Court, 1610–12', *The Court Historian* 6 (2001), 49–65; T. Wilks 'Introduction: Image and Exemplarity'; Wilks, 'Introduction', in *Lost Prince*, quotation from 17.
36 Smuts, 'Prince Henry and his World', 19–20.
37 K. Sharpe, *Politics and Ideas in Early Stuart England: Essays and Studies* (London, 1989), 288–291; Smuts, 'Prince Henry and his World', 19–31; A. Pollnitz, 'Humanism and the Education of Henry, Prince of Wales', in T. Wilks (ed.), *Prince Henry Revived* (London, 2007), 22–65: 22–25.
38 Wilks, 'Introduction', in *Lost Prince*, 14; Wilks, 'Art Collecting at the English Court', 42.
39 Wilks, 'Court Culture of Prince Henry and his Circle', 290.
40 *CSPV*, vol. 11, no. 18: 4 July 1607.
41 D. Stevenson, *Scotland's Last Royal Wedding: The Marriage of James VI and Anne of Denmark* (Edinburgh, 1997), 74–75; E. C. Williams, *Anne of Denmark: Wife of King James VI of Scotland, James I of England* (London, 1970): 53–57. McManus recognises the political dimension of Anna's actions, writing that 'while the influence of maternal concerns cannot be denied, Anne's conception of queenship and James VI's own response to her opposition formulate her actions as political', *Renaissance Stage*, 81. The following reading draws on Barroll, *Anna of Denmark*, 119–134.
42 *CSPV*, vol. 11, no. 511: 20 May 1609.
43 Orders were given In April 1607, for 'certan lodgings' to be readied at Whitehall 'for his Ma[jes]tie to see master Carre who lay sicke there': TNA, E351/543, fol. 174r.
44 M. Lee, *Great Britain's Solomon: James VI and I in His Three Kingdoms* (Urbana and Chicago, 1990), 240, 241–244; A. Bellany, *The Politics of Court Scandal in Early Modern England: News Culture and the Overbury Affair, 1603–1660* (Cambridge, 2002), 29; P. Croft, 'Can a Bureaucrat Be a Favourite? Robert Cecil and the Strategies of Power', in J. H. Elliott and L. W. B. Brockliss (eds), *The World of the Favourite* (New Haven and London, 1999), 81–95: 91; J. Knowles, *Politics and Political Culture in the Court Masque* (London, 2015), 58.
45 Knowles, *Politics and Political Culture*, 58; Birch, *Court and Times*, vol. 1, 191: 1 August 1612 (to Sir Thomas Edmondes).
46 Paton (ed.), *Supplementary Report*, 41: 22 June 1612 (to Mar).
47 Birch, *Court and Times*, vol. 1, 191: 1 August 1612 (George Calvert to Sir Thomas Edmondes).
48 Barroll, *Anna of Denmark*, 133.

49 Birch, *Court and Times*, vol. 1, 177: 17 June 1612 (Chamberlain to Carleton); Barroll, *Anna of Denmark*, 134.
50 McClure (ed.), *Chamberlain*, vol. 1, 368: 9 July 1612 (to Carleton); Barroll, *Anna of Denmark*, 133, 207–208. For a different interpretation see Cuddy who argues that following Cecil's death, Carr worked with both the Howards and the Southampton group; first supporting Sir Henry Neville (1561/62–1615) for Secretary, but by the close of 1612 backing Winwood. Cuddy makes no mention of Anna and Henry, but Henry's sudden death in November 1612 was a likely factor in Winwood changing patron. He was eventually confirmed on 29 March 1614 and credited the favourite with his success. This was not the first time that Anna and Carr had been in separate favour of the same candidate; in June 1612, they both backed Sir George Carew (1556–1612) for master of the wards. See Cuddy, 'Revival of the Entourage', 210–211; McClure (ed.), *Chamberlain*, vol. 1, 357–358.
51 Barroll, *Anna of Denmark*, 207–208, notes 34, 35. See letters in McClure (ed.), *Chamberlain*, vol. 1, 368, 359–360, 521. Winwood did eventually succeed to the secretaryship on 29 March 1614, although Chamberlain thought it was at Carr's behest: McClure (ed.), *Chamberlain*, vol. 1, 521. See also L. L. Peck, *Northampton: Patronage and Policy at the Court of James I* (London, 1982), 31–32.
52 R. Strong, *Tudor & Jacobean Portraits*, 2 vols (London, 1969), vol. 1, 9 citing Folger Shakespeare Library MS V.a.334. In 1607 Anna made a second commission to Peake for 'sundry pictures': TNA, SC6/JASI/1648. Princess Elizabeth later followed with commissions to Oliver, paying him £10 from her privy purse between Michaelmas 1612 and Lady Day 1613 'for a picture of her graces, w[hi]ch was appointed by her grace to be made': TNA, E407/57/2, p. 6.
53 E. Town, 'A Biographical Dictionary of London Painters, 1547–1625', *The Seventy-Sixth Volume of the Walpole Society* (London, 2014), 149, 153; MacLeod et al., *Lost Prince*, 35–38, 56, 70, 94, 142.
54 See statements to this effect by, for example, Strong, *Henry, Prince of Wales*, 11, 186; Wilks 'Art Collecting at the English Court', 31.
55 Peck, *Northampton*, 31–37; Barroll, *Anna of Denmark*, 135–136; Lee, *Great Britain's Solomon*, 241–242, 244–245.
56 On the intricacies of this network, the identities of influential members, and their connections to Anna, see Barroll, 'Court of the First Stuart Queen', 200–205; Barroll, *Anna of Denmark*, 40–44, 51–53, 135–136; Lewalski, *Writing Women*, 23–25; H. Payne, 'Aristocratic Women and the Jacobean Court, 1603–1625' (PhD diss., University of London, 2001): 35, 38–44; M. O'Connor, 'Godly Patronage', in J. Harris and E. Scott-Baumann (eds), *The Intellectual Culture of Puritan Women, 1558–1680* (New York, 2011), 71–83: 72.
57 The sense of competition between the two events was well known among contemporaries: McClure (ed.), *Chamberlain*, vol. 1, 487, no. 185: 25 November 1613.
58 McClure (ed.), *Chamberlain*, vol. 1, 507, no. 192: 10 February 1614 (Chamberlain to Carleton).
59 Barroll, *Anna of Denmark*, 138–142; Knowles, *Politics and Political Culture*, 55–57, 68–92, esp. 56, 76, 81, 84, 86–87; Knowles, 'Images of Royalty', 33; McManus, *Renaissance Stage*, 166–171. See also J. Field, 'Anna of Denmark and the Arts in Jacobean England' (unpub. PhD diss., University of Auckland, 2015), 221–225, and on the masques more generally see D. Lindley, 'Embarrassing Ben: The Masques for Frances Howard', *English Literary Renaissance* 16 (1986), 343–359; A. Scott, *Selfish Gifts: The Politics of Exchange and English Courtly Literature, 1580–1628* (Madison, NJ, 2006), 175–187.
60 McClure (ed.), *Chamberlain*, vol. 1, 487, no. 185: 25 November 1613.
61 McClure (ed.), *Chamberlain*, vol. 1, 507, no. 192: 10 February 1614 (Chamberlain to Carleton). On Denmark House as 'the queen's court' see Chapter 2. The change in name is reflected in the works accounts: TNA, E351/544, fol. 26r.

62 Barroll, *Anna of Denmark*, 144–145; L. H. Roper, 'Unmasquing the Connections between Jacobean Politics and Policy: The Circle of Anna of Denmark and the Beginning of the English Empire, 1614–18', in C. Levin, J. Eldridge Carney, and D. Barrett-Graves (eds), *'High and Mighty Queens' of Early Modern England: Realities and Representations* (New York, 2003), 45–59: 45–46.
63 Quoted in Barroll, *Anna of Denmark*, 145.
64 Paton (ed.), *Supplementary Report*, 56: 2 September 1614 (Viscount Fenton to the Earl of Mar).
65 Rushworth, *Historical Collections*, 456–457. Abbot's account is often cited by scholars, see for example Barroll, *Anna of Denmark*, 146; Lewalski, *Writing Women*, 24–25.
66 *CSPV*, vol. 15, no. 658: 19 December 1618 (Relation of England of Foscarini).
67 J. Spedding, R. Leslie Ellis, and D. Denon Heath (eds), *The Life and Letters of Francis Bacon*, 6 vols (London, 1861–1874; electronic edition, Virginia, 1998), here vol. 6, 208: 25 May 1617.
68 H. Ellis (ed.), *Original Letters Illustrative of English History*, 3 vols (London, 1969), vol. 3, 100, no. CCLXII [undated]. See too, Anna and Bacon using Buckingham as a conduit to James for extending the queen's income in case of widowhood: Spedding et al. (eds), *Life and Letters*, 170, 195.
69 Ellis (ed.), *Original Letters*, vol. 3, 100–101, nos. CCLXII, CCLXIII [undated].
70 Croft, 'Can a Bureaucrat Be a Favourite?', 88.
71 For a balanced overview of the evidence couched within contemporary notions of homosexuality, and the political value and moral implications of such sexual misconduct, see Bellany, *Politics of Court Scandal*, 28–32, 254–261; R. Shephard, 'Sexual Rumours in English Politics: The Cases of Elizabeth I and James I', in J. Murray and K. Eisenbichler (eds), *Desire and Discipline: Sex and Sexuality in the Premodern West* (Toronto, 1996), 101–122; C. Perry, '1603 and the Discourse of Favouritism', in G. Burgess et al. (eds), *The Accession of James I: Historical and Cultural Consequences* (Basingstoke, 2006), 155–176. See also Lee, *Great Britain's Solomon*, 233–260, although statements such as 'James had very little use for women ... his relations with his wife were never very close. Anne was no intellectual' (247–248), is reflective of the time of writing and should be treated with caution.
72 W. Stockton and J. M. Bromley, 'Introduction: Figuring Early Modern Sex', in W. Stockton and J. M. Bromley (eds), *Sex before Sex: Figuring the Act in Early Modern England* (Minneapolis, 2013), 1–23: 3. For recent scholarship on sex and sexuality in the early modern period, see also V. Traub, *Thinking Sex with the Early Moderns* (Philadelphia, 2016); L. Gowing, *Gender Relations in Early Modern England* (Harlow and New York, 2013); K. Crawford, *European Sexualities, 1400–1800* (Cambridge, 2007); *The Sexual Culture of the French Renaissance* (Cambridge, 2010); J. Bromley, *Intimacy and Sexuality in the Age of Shakespeare* (Cambridge, 2012).
73 Knowles, *Politics and Political Culture*, 58–60; Bellany, *Politics of Court Scandal*, 29. On Carr as a collector see, for example, A. R. Braunmuller, 'Robert Carr, Earl of Somerset, as Collector and Patron', in L. L. Peck (ed.), *The Mental World of the Jacobean Court* (Cambridge, 1991), 230–250; T. Wilks, 'Robert Carr, Earl of Somerset (1587–1645), Reconsidered', *Journal of the History of Collections* 1 (1989), 167–177. On Buckingham as collector see, for example, P. McEvansoneya, 'Italian Paintings in the Buckingham Collection', in E. Chaney (ed.), *The Evolution of English Collecting: Receptions of Italian Art in the Tudor and Stuart Periods* (New Haven and London, 2003), 315–336; S. Bracken and R. Hill, 'Sir Isaac Wake, Venice and Art Collecting in Early Stuart England: A New Document', *Journal of the History of Collections* (2012), 183–198.
74 TNA, SP52/67, fol. 7; *CSP Scotland*, vol. 10, no. 736 (News from Scotland); Barroll, *Anna of Denmark*, 26, 179, n. 34.

75 *CSP Scotland*, vol. 13, nos. 641, 665 (to Robert Cecil).
76 NRS, E21/76, fol. 241. Juhala, 'Household and Court', 314. On Carr's background and early years at the Scottish court see Bellany, *Politics of Court Scandal*, 26–28.
77 Bellany, *Politics of Court Scandal*, 28.
78 TNA, E351/543, fol. 247r.
79 Quoted in Lee, *Great Britain's Solomon*, 247.
80 Bellany, *Politics of Court Scandal*, 31–32: quote from 32.
81 McClure (ed.), *Chamberlain*, vol. 2, 102, no. 273: 11 October 1617 (to Carleton).
82 TNA, E351/543, fols 246v, 247r–v, 260r–263r; TNA, E351/544, fols 8r, 10r–11v, 26r–27v, 43v–44r, 58r–59v, 78v–79r, 91r–92r, 99v, 100r–v. The only deviation from the rule of spending Christmas at Whitehall, as discussed in Chapter 6 below, was made in 1618 when, in deference to Anna, James ordered the court to observe the period at Hampton Court where the queen was incapacitated due to ill health.
83 TNA, E351/544, fol. 26r–27v.
84 For a sustained engagement with the extensive scholarship on Anna's religious position see Field, 'Politics of Religious Identity'; Chapter 6.
85 TNA, SP14/92, fol. 83: 9 May 1617 (George Gerrard to Dudley Carleton).
86 P. McCullough, *Sermons at Court: Politics and Religion in Elizabethan and Jacobean Preaching* (Cambridge and New York, 1998), 169–209; A. Walsham, *Church Papists: Catholicism, Conformity, and Confessional Polemic in Early Modern England* (Woodbridge, 1993), 50–72, 77. See also M. M. Meikle and H. Payne, 'From Lutheranism to Catholicism', *The Journal of Ecclesiastical History* 64 (2013), 45–69: 46, 62; Payne, 'Aristocratic Women', 241–255.
87 Capp, *When Gossips Meet*, 353–363, providing evidence of women absconding from sermons, sleeping through catechisms, and enjoying the social dimension of religious practice. See also P. Crawford, *Women and Religion in England 1500–1720* (London and New York, 1993), 1–17, 53–55.
88 Crawford, *Women and Religion*, 3. Crawford was writing in 1993, but this is an area still awaiting sustained scholarly attention.
89 J. Stow, G. Buck, and E. Howes, *Annales, or Generall Chronicle of England, begun first by maister Iohn Stow, and after him continued and augmented with matters forreyne, and domestique, anncient and moderne, vnto the ende of this present yeere 1614* (London, 1615), 863–864. Notably, Anna's Catholic successor, Henrietta Maria, pointedly refused to observe these rituals: Griffey, *On Display*, 111. On these rites see W. Coster, 'The Churching of Women, 1500–1700', in W. J. Sheils and D. Wood (eds), *Women in the Church* (Oxford, 1990), 377–387; Barroll, *Anna of Denmark*, 104–107. This is discussed in Chapter 6.
90 Field, 'Politics of Religious Identity'.
91 M. Mauss, *The Gift*, expanded edition selected, annotated, and translated by J. I. Guyer (Chicago, 2016), 61.
92 This is a vast and rapidly expanding field of study by anthropologists and historians that was pioneered by M. Mauss with 'Essai sur le Don. Forme et Raison de l'Échange dans les Sociétés archaïques', *L'Année sociologique*, n.s., 1 (1923–1924), 30–186 (I have consulted the 2016 English translation by Guyer (Chicago, 2016)). For studies of gift-exchange and court patronage in Tudor and Stuart England see J. Lawson (ed.), *The Elizabethan New Year's Gift Exchanges, 1559–1603* (Oxford, 2013), esp. 3–26; Harris, 'Women and Politics', esp. 266–268; L. L. Peck, 'Court Patronage and Government Policy: The Jacobean Dilemma', in G. F. Lytle and S. Orgel (eds), *Patronage in the Renaissance* (Princeton, 1981), 27–46; Peck, *Court Patronage and Corruption*, 30–46; F. Heal, *Hospitality in Early Modern England* (Oxford, 1990); F. Heal, 'Royal Gifts and Gift-Exchange', in S. Boardman and J. Goodare (eds), *Kings, Lords and Men in Scotland and Britain, 1300–1625: Essays in Honour of Jenny Wormald* (Edinburgh, 2014), 283–300; F. Heal, *The Power of*

Gifts: Gift-Exchange in Early Modern England (Oxford, 2014); Scott, *Selfish Gifts*; G. Ungerer, 'Juan Pantoja De La Cruz and the Circulation of Gifts between the English and Spanish Courts, 1604–5', *Shakespearean Studies* 26 (1998), 145–186: 149–157; M. Jansson, 'Measured Reciprocity: English Ambassadorial Gift Exchange in the 17th and 18th Centuries', *Journal of Early Modern History* 9 (2005), 348–370. For the European context see, for example, N. Z. Davis, *The Gift in Sixteenth-Century France* (Oxford, 2000); S. Kettering, *Patronage in Sixteenth and Seventeenth Century France* (Aldershot, 2002); S. Kettering, *Patrons, Brokers and Clients and Clients in Seventeenth-Century France* (New York and Oxford, 1986); G. Algazi, V. Groebner, and B. Jussen (eds), *Negotiating the Gift: Pre-Modern Figurations of Exchange* (Göttingen, 2003); V. Groebner, *Liquid Assets, Dangerous Gifts: Presents and Politics at the End of the Middle Ages*, trans. P. E. Selwyn (Philadelphia, 2002); L. R. Clark, *Collecting Art in the Italian Renaissance Court: Objects and Exchanges* (Cambridge, 2018).

93 *CSPV*, vol. 10, no. 515: 27 April 1606.
94 *CSPV*, vol. 12, no. 202: 14 April 1611.
95 TNA, LR2/122, fol. 24r: June to September 1607.
96 *CSPV*, vol. 10, no. 566: 24 August 1606; Wade, 'The Queen's Courts', 49–80: 53.
97 *CSPV* vol. 14, no. 410: 26 August 1616; *CSPV* vol. 14, no. 577: 29 December 1616.
98 R. M. Meldrum (ed.), *The Royal Correspondence of King James I of England (and VI of Scotland) to his Royal Brother-in-Law, King Christian IV of Denmark, 1603–1625* (Hassocks, 1977), 98.
99 Meldrum (ed.), *Royal Correspondence*, 17–18, 24, 26–27, 78, 83, 85; NRS, E21/68, fol. 178; NRS, E23/11/16. See also TNA, E403/2732, fol. 13r, for James ordering the 'redd deare that came out of Denmark' to be distributed among 'divers' of his parks.
100 Meldrum (ed.), *Royal Correspondence*, 27. On the ability of gift-gifting to balance power or incur indebtedness see Clark, *Collecting Art*, 5; Heal, *Power of Gifts*, 18–19, 22–23.
101 NRS, E21/76, fol. 165.
102 TNA, E403/2728, fol. 131r; BL Lansdowne MS 164, fols 76v, 144r.
103 TNA, E403/2727, fol. 222r. Another Englishman – 'John Douglas' – with no given profession or rank was sent to Heinrich Julius in February 1613: BL Lansdowne MS 164, fol. 154r. On Ulrik's possible whereabouts at this time see M. R. Wade, 'Duke Ulrik as Agent, Patron, Artist: Reframing Danish Court Culture in an International Perspective c.1600', in M. Andersen, B. Bøggild Johannsen, and H. Johannsen (eds), *Reframing the Danish Renaissance: Problems and Prospects in a European Perspective* (Copenhagen, 2011), 243–263: 244–245.
104 TNA, E403/2732, fol. 103r.
105 Wade, 'Duke Ulrik', 255; Wade, 'Widowhood', 11.
106 Quoted in Wade, 'Duke Ulrik', 255. See also M. R. Wade, 'Dynasty at Work: Danish Cultural Exchange with England and Germany at the Time of the Palatine Wedding', in S. Smart and M. R. Wade (eds), *The Palatine Wedding of 1613: Protestant Alliance and Court Festival* (Wiesbaden, 2013), 479–514.
107 TNA, SC6/JASI/1648; TNA, LR7/137.
108 TNA, SC6/JASI/1648; TNA, SC6/JASI/1650; TNA, SC6/JASI/1655.
109 TNA, SC6/JASI/1655.
110 Davis, *The Gift*, 58.
111 Wade, 'The Queen's Courts', 52–53, 55; Barroll, *Anna of Denmark*, 15–17; S. Heiberg (ed.), *Christian IV and Europe: The 19th Art Exhibition of the Council of Europe: Denmark* (Herning, 1988), 73–151, 301–351, 446–464.
112 Like Anna, the later Stuart consorts were foreign-born women who thus endowed the English court with a notable cosmopolitanism as French, Italian, Spanish, Dutch, and German influences made their mark on court culture, see Campbell-Orr, 'Introduction: Court Studies', 8–12.

2

Court places and spaces

In November 1611, Anna's principal lady-in-waiting and favourite, Jane Drummond, returned a bill, signed by the queen, to Robert Cecil, together with a letter in which she quipped 'I acquented her ma[jes]tie with what your lor[dship] wrote of her loving no body, bot dead pictorris in a peltry gallery: her Ma[jes]tie comanded me to returne this answer, that she is more contented amongst those hamles [harmless] picturs, in the paltry gallery, then your lo[rdship] is with your greate imployments, in fair roumes all thing's considdered.'[1] Evocatively conjuring an image of state business being executed in large and ornate court rooms, and the queen happily choosing to forgo these areas in favour of small galleries lined with inert portraits, Drummond's letter raises significant questions around Anna's use of space and the extent of her autonomy. It suggests that the queen crafted intimate spaces in her palaces, and that she was granted the freedom to choose whether she withdrew to her private quarters or resided in the more open, public spaces of the Stuart court, thereby signalling a consciousness of spatial meanings. Whether Drummond (and, through her, Anna) was faithfully recounting the queen's preferential habits, or merely replying in jest, remains unknown. However, we do know Anna was afforded an unprecedented degree of legal, financial, and geographic independence. Not only did she maintain an entirely separate household to the king, but she also received an independent income, followed her own, separate, court calendar, and had her own judiciary court to deal with the legalities of her jointure estates. This chapter examines the nature and extent of that independence – financially, culturally, and spatially – and argues for a new reading of the royal Stuart relationship as one defined by cooperation and accommodation where the queen's individual actions and policies benefitted James in the realisation of his image as a king who brought peace and transcended faction.[2]

Anna placed considerable importance on the design and setting of her residences in Scotland and England, initiating large-scale, and often highly innovative, building programmes that James was willing to fund despite his comparative disinterest. James did not build, or renovate, on the same scale as his wife, although he appreciated the importance of magnificent court settings. He was quick to adopt new styles – commissioning the classical Banqueting House at Whitehall in 1619 – and his itinerant approach to kingship necessitated the purchase and renovation of several properties including Royston, Newmarket, Theobalds, Holdenby, and Thetford.[3] Anna though, demonstrated a pronounced interest in the form, style, and layout of her residences, with architectural historians concluding that her work on Somerset House, in particular, was 'unparalleled in the palace-building sphere since Henry VIII's time', and recognising her important commission of Inigo Jones to design the first classical building in England with the Queen's House at Greenwich (Figure 2.1).[4] In this chapter, these two projects are woven into a larger narrative of Anna's architectural agency that extends to her other activities at Somerset House and Greenwich Palace, as well as her work at Dunfermline and Oatlands Manor. This broader history extends our understanding of how Anna conceived of her residences and of the sources that provided her with inspiration, which allow us to determine patterns in her patronage.[5]

In Stuart England, the concept of a house was one that encompassed the main building together with its immediate gardens, orchards, and courts, as well as any subsidiary structures and adjoining lands. This integrated approach was first articulated by Pliny, and later emphasised and extended by Leon Battista Alberti (1404–1472) in *De re aedificatoria*

2.1 The Queen's House, Greenwich, London, 2018.

(1452), wherein the garden – as well as the built structure/s – was the domain of the architect.[6] It emphatically shaped the aesthetic and practical experience of household members and visitors alike, and it was impossible for contemporaries to separate a dwelling from its grounds.[7] Importantly though, Anna was already familiar with this attitude from her time in Denmark-Norway, where it similarly dominated her father's and brother's approach to building, and informed one of the most famous – and unique – properties of the time, Tycho Brahe's (1546–1601) Uraniborg on the island of Hven. It is unclear whether Anna ever personally visited Uraniborg, but it is highly possible since her father, mother, husband, members of James's Scottish entourage, and her brother-in-law Heinrich Julius, all made trips there at various times between 1588 and 1590.[8] Furthermore, considering the fame and eccentricity of the property, Anna must have at least gained knowledge of it at court for it would have been an interesting and appropriate topic for discussion. It is perhaps unsurprising then, that Anna's vision for her principal English residences included strong ideas about the layout and design of their physical surrounds. In each case, the grounds were one of the first areas to receive her attention, and she transformed them into dramatic expressions of her European outlook, importing Italianate and French aesthetic traditions – as specifically interpreted and experienced at the Oldenburg court, and therefore inflected with both Netherlandish and Nordic traditions – which aligned her with a select number of the English elite who, in the newfound Stuart peace, were rapidly transforming the aristocratic identity.[9]

Financial independence

Anna's ability to govern a household that inhabited different royal residences and followed a different court calendar to that of the king was the result of several key factors: her upbringing, her sense of her own royal status, her jointure, and James's style of kingship. Of significant importance to royal women in early modern England and Scotland, jointure possessions provided an income during the term of marriage, and were to provide for them in the case of their widowhood.[10] The majority of a royal jointure comprised forests, lands, and dwellings that generated revenue in the form of fees, leases, rents, and/or fines. In the case of a royal residence being assigned to the jointure, the issue of ownership became complicated. Granted for life, or a fixed number of years, the residence yielded income from its associated lands, lodgings, and/or industry, which was allocated to the consort's privy purse. However, the palace itself still accommodated the king whenever he saw fit, and the centralised office of works (in both Scotland and England) covered all maintenance and building, which was then financed through the exchequer. While several of Anna's jointure palaces were described as being 'reserved for her majesties access and pleasure', these properties were not her exclusive domain. Indeed, several of them – Oatlands, Greenwich, Havering, Nonsuch, and Theobalds – were commonly frequented by James (with or without Anna), while the latter three received the king more often than the queen.[11] Moreover, while palace lodgings were also designated as belonging to the king or queen, there was fluidity in habitation and on occasion Anna occupied James's suite of rooms, or ordered that both sides be readied for her use.[12] The contents of Anna's jointure is important, least of all for funding her privy purse, but it is the residences that James and Anna chose to occupy, and the frequency of those occupations, that provide telling information about their individual preferences, sense of ownership, and the nature of their relationship.

Included in the Scottish-Danish marriage contract, and scrupulously checked over by the Danish delegation prior to the coronation, Anna's Scottish jointure consisted of the palaces of Falkland (Fife), Linlithgow (West Lothian), and Dunfermline (Fife) together with a third of their associated lands. This generated £4,541.13s.11d. Scots, which was supplemented by a substantial amount of foodstuffs including wheat, oats, oatmeal, barley, capons, geese, and hens.[13] When later residing in England, Anna continued to receive her Scottish jointure and she was also frequently allocated cash payments from the Scottish treasury for her ordinary and household uses. In February 1605, for example, she signed a receipt at Whitehall for £14,000 Scots.[14] Anna's English jointure was considerably larger and more lucrative – and somewhat more complicated – than her estates in Scotland. In the absence of a pre-existing set of possessions, it took nearly three years to finalise, with letters patent issued on 29 September 1603, 13 May 1604, and 25 February 1606, by which time it consisted of 139 possessions in twenty-nine counties, and brought in a total annual revenue of £9,918.2s.1d.qua.di. sterling.[15] Following precedent set by Henry VIII (1491–1547), James assigned Anna her own council to administer her estates, and gave her the authority to grant leases, but he extended her autonomy beyond that of her Tudor predecessors by establishing an official court of law for Anna – the 'Queen's Court of Chancery' – which was to resolve all matters pertaining to the legalities of her jointure.[16]

Intended to generate income to cover Anna's household expenditure – both ordinary and extraordinary – the queen's jointure was never fixed but increased significantly over the course of James's reign. Thus, when Carew, Anna's receiver general, came to declare his annual account in September 1617, the queen's jointure now covered an extensive 523 entries in forty-two counties with revenue totalling £21,498.19s.4d. sterling.[17] While this growth was partly due to Anna's spending patterns, it was also the result of wider economic trends, for, as economic historian Amy Erickson has shown, throughout the sixteenth and seventeenth centuries, 'freehold prices rose consistently faster than other commodities, as agricultural prices and rents fell, producing a lower relative income from land.'[18] In addition to the revenue generated from the rents, leases, and fines associated with Anna's jointure lands and estates, from late 1608 or early 1609 the queen's personal income was supplemented by her lease of import duties on sugar.[19] Yet despite these efforts in Scotland and England, Anna's income rarely covered her outgoings and her expenditure was consistently supplemented by James through promissory notes and warrants.[20]

Aside from the estates mentioned, Anna's English jointure encompassed a number of royal residences. Hatfield (Hertford), Havering at Bower (Essex), Nonsuch (Surrey), and Somerset House (Middlesex), were included from the outset of the Stuart reign, with the latter two being expressly noted as 'reserved for her majestie accesse and pleasure without value', or, to put it another way, they were not intended to yield revenue.[21] Later additions to the jointure included Oatlands Manor (Surrey) on 30 August 1611 and Greenwich Palace (Kent) on 18 February 1614.[22] The other substantial change to royal properties in Anna's jointure concerned Hatfield House. Having been 'surrendred ... to the king's majesty', James exchanged the property on 22 May 1607 (along with additional manors, tenements, and mills in some thirteen counties) with Robert Cecil for his principal property of Theobalds in Hertfordshire.[23] Officially passing into royal ownership as a replacement for Hatfield, Theobalds was allocated to the queen's jointure where it remained for the rest of her life.[24] Even so, Theobalds became one of James's favoured houses while Anna was infrequently in residence, spending most of her time between the centralised, accessible properties of Greenwich, Hampton Court, Whitehall, and Somerset House, the latter of which became her main residence from 1614 and which rarely welcomed James.[25]

Royal mobility and the implications of independence

Geographic distance was a defining feature of the royal Stuart relationship, as the practical result of James's itinerant style of kingship. Evident during the Stuarts' time in Scotland, it became more pronounced in England due to the greater number of royal residences coupled with Cecil's administrative dominance and Anna's ability to represent the crown. The king's largely peripatetic lifestyle was fuelled by his passion for the hunt, but it was importantly buttressed by his keen understanding of the political benefits of mobility. In Scotland, James rarely stayed in one place for more than three weeks at a time, constantly moving between the royal palaces of Stirling, Linlithgow, Falkland, Holyroodhouse, and Dunfermline.[26] He also frequented a large number of noble residences (the most common being Dalkeith), and in the summer months covered large parts of the country while hunting or on progress, with his usual route encompassing

Inverness, Fortrose, and Cromarty in the north, Carlisle and Dumfries in the south, and as far west as Dumbarton.[27] Anna, on occasion, joined James on progress and reports issued from Robert Bowes, in March 1591, that 'the King and Queen have gone to Dalkeith, the house of the Earl of Morton, for six or seven weeks: after which they repair to Linlithgow, Stirling, and Falkland for the most part of the summer.'[28] Later, in October 1595, it was noted that Anna followed James to St Johnstone from whence the royal pair jointly moved to Falkland, Dunfermline, Linlithgow, and then onto Stirling.[29] More frequently, however, the couple kept divergent calendars which meant that even though they frequented the same palaces, they were often at different residences at different times.[30]

In England, James and Anna's courts continued to be clearly, physically, distinguished from one another, although ceremonial points of the year – particularly Easter and Christmas – saw the royal family gather together at Whitehall, and from early to late summer (May to September) Anna frequently travelled to stay with James at royal residences further afield from London: Greenwich, Hampton Court, Nonsuch, Oatlands, Theobalds, Windsor Castle, and Woodstock.[31] Their continued good graces were also seen in the frequent exchange of letters and gifts, a warrant being issued on 1 August 1606, for example, to pay for 'ryding post from the courte at Newmarkett in the night wth l[ett]res and prsentes from his Ma[jes]tie to the Queene at whitehall and back againe wth annswere and likewise with like ymplymt [employment] from the courte at Royston to the Queene at Whitehall'.[32] James was also partial to sending Anna the spoils of the hunt and between March and November 1611, she received five stags and a hind, as well as poultry and dotterels from the king.[33] In any given year though, James was absent from London for between six and nine months, choosing to spend most of his time at his favoured residences of Royston, Newmarket, Thetford, and Theobalds.[34] Located in Cheshunt, Theobalds was only nineteen kilometres from London, but Newmarket in Cambridgeshire and Royston in Hertfordshire, were significantly further afield being more than 70 kilometres north of London, while Thetford in Suffolk was some 120 kilometres north-east. In striking comparison, the majority of Anna's time was spent close to the administrative and ceremonial heart of Jacobean London at her palaces of Somerset House and Greenwich, although she also resided for periods at Oatlands and Hampton Court, and completed her own progresses.

The marked itinerancy of the king was facilitated by Cecil and Anna, while a network of royal and standing posts kept James abreast of state matters and he maintained a definite interest in religious policy and international politics.[35] A councillor who bridged the reigns of Queen Elizabeth and King James, and was a major figure in ensuring the latter's peaceful succession, Cecil was an indispensable feature of Stuart governance. By 1608, he had gained unprecedented control over central bureaucracy and a near monopoly on crown patronage through an extraordinary trifecta of office as secretary of state, master of the court of wards, and lord treasurer, in addition to which he was also a privy councillor. While James travelled large parts of the country, Cecil stayed in London keeping a protective hand over matters of state.[36] In like manner to Cecil, the majority of Anna's time was spent in London between the main palaces of Somerset House, Whitehall, Greenwich, and Hampton Court. Anna's central location positioned her as James's royal substitute, being readily accessible for ambassadors and visiting dignitaries who valued her as a monarchical representative and an important conduit to the king. On 16 March 1612, Foscarini, the Venetian ambassador in England, declared that James 'tells her [Anna] anything', and the ambassadorial dispatches and records of the pipe office of the period are filled with orders for rooms to be readied for Anna to give independent audiences.[37] In January 1605, James granted Anna a formal role during his absences from London for 'open air and exercise'. Not only were the privy council instructed to assemble 'once every weeke … in such places as our dearest wife [Anna] shall keepe her courte', but she was also a trusted recipient of the king's correspondence, for it was at Anna's court that the councillors were to 'receive dispatch … w[hi]ch doe depend upon our owne [James's] directions to you [Anna]'.[38] In a letter to Cecil a couple of months earlier, James referenced his increasing absence from London and the political role that Anna was to shoulder, proclaiming that 'ye and your fellows there are so proud now that ye have gotten the guiding again of a feminine court in the old fashion as I know not how to deal with you.'[39] On the other hand, the king may well have been making a satirical barb at Elizabeth's (and therefore Anna's) inability to rule, casting both royal women as mere figureheads, and acknowledging that the true mechanics of rule were implemented by the male council led by Cecil. As these divergent interpretations suggest, personal correspondence can be a questionable and ambiguous form of evidence for, as Steve Murdoch succinctly acknowledges, aside from misleading survival rates, 'letters are sent for a variety of reasons even, at times, to deceive the recipient.'[40] Indeed, it is impossible from our vantage point to determine the meaning or authenticity of James's statement. However, if, at the very least, Anna was only to play a token part in the theatre of power, it was still an important and necessary part: visibly stationed in London, she was a reassuring, legitimate, and accessible representative of monarchy, who guarded against the mistaken impression that councillors and courtiers had taken full and unfettered run of the Stuart court and kingdoms in the absence of the king. Even when journeying away from London – the queen's own court calendar extending to four progresses to Bath – Anna directly promoted the image of Stuart authority, generosity, and loyalty.[41] Ostensibly undertaken for reasons of 'health and recreacon',[42] these journeys were matters of state and took the queen to parts of England that

James had never visited (notably Bristol, Bath, Newbury, Warminster, and Wells). The Venetian ambassador's report of Anna's visit to Wells, in September 1613, pointedly notes the political value of the consort as a monarchical representative:

> Her Majesty was surrounded by a somewhat greater number of ladies and gentlemen than ordinary, and all the nobility of the province gathered together. Because the king has never been here, all sorts of people hasten to see the queen, and show their pleasure at seeing her, by offering the greatest honours and service ... In passing from place to place, all the streets were full of people and blessings and good wishes were showered upon the queen, who thanked everyone and gave her hand to many to kiss, which they did kneeling. The queen showed her delight at these honours and the affection bestowed upon her by everyone, which is truly great.[43]

Indeed, surviving accounts of civic expenditure for the entertainment and reception of the queen are clear evidence of the strong political import that these progresses held, with Anna spending eight days at Wells 'for beholding of pageants shows and sportes'.[44] Preparations were also made for reuniting the Stuarts on Anna's 'retourne from the Bathe' with Windsor Castle readied for James 'meetinge her'.[45] Such periodic separation expressly helped, rather than hindered or antagonised, the king and it was not indicative of marital disharmony. Working independently of one another for mutual benefit, it often fell to Anna to maintain a Stuart presence in the capital where she could spend ample amounts of time in 'paltry' galleries if she wished, while James satisfied his need for 'open air and exercise', but was kept informed of state business and remained secure in the knowledge that there was a royal body in the capital.[46]

The interior and exterior spaces of Anna's courts

It is often asserted that Anna of Denmark was a prodigious architectural patron, for her programme at Somerset House in London was, in the words of Simon Thurley, the 'single most important and expensive royal domestic architectural work of the early Stuart period'.[47] Yet, in the shadows cast by this mammoth undertaking, Anna crafted a sequence of innovative and influential court spaces – interior and exterior – that remain comparatively unexplored. To be sure, Anna did not personally pay for the majority of these endeavours, for it was the traditional responsibility of the crown to cover all building costs associated with royal residences, whether they were part of the queen's jointure or not.[48] Her direction is nevertheless clear, for not only did the projects take place at her favoured residences – Dunfermline, Greenwich Palace, Oatlands Manor, and Somerset House – but they were united by a classical aesthetic that Anna had first experienced in Denmark-Norway. It is further significant that many of the artisans brought in to work on Anna's properties were otherwise not in crown employment, but had either lived or trained on the Continent, and were therefore conversant with the styles and trends that the queen wished to import to Scotland and England. Unfortunately, due to the poor nature of the surviving evidence of Anna's buildings in Scotland, combined with the comparative wealth of the English treasury which afforded her far more scope, the following discussion mainly centres on the queen's activities in England.[49]

Dunfermline: Danish and Italo-Netherlandish trends

A large proportion of the Dunfermline Abbey estates were included in Anna's jointure, although the palace was in a state of disrepair at the time of her arrival in Scotland in 1590.[50] Almost nothing survives of the gardens and setting of Dunfermline, and very little physical or archival material remains of the building programme, but it seems to have adhered to the tradition of Danish palace design in the conscious melding of renaissance and gothic elements. Appropriately, the architect chosen to oversee construction was William Schaw (c.1550–1602), a man who had personal knowledge of the urban landscape in Denmark-Norway, having been part of the 1589/90 retinue that accompanied James to retrieve Anna after inclement weather had forced her wedding party to seek refuge in Norway.[51]

In the last ten years, a significant body of research has determined a better understanding of the impact that high levels of migration from the Low Countries, coupled with the dissemination of Netherlandish architectural models, sources, and ideas had on the built environments of central and northern Europe.[52] In so doing, valuable light has been shed on the influences and traditions that physically shaped the Oldenburg court during Anna's childhood and teenage years, and these can be seen affecting her many years later when, as queen, she undertook her own building projects. An avid builder, it was Anna's father, King Frederik II of Denmark-Norway (1534–1588), who began the radical step to transition the Danish court from one of medieval informality to one of baroque ceremony and splendour – a move that was fully realised during the reign of his son Christian IV. Some of Frederik's endeavours are further discussed below, but it is significant for a consideration of Anna's later building activities that as the Danish king sought to make over the landscape of his kingdom, it was predominantly Netherlandish artisans who were called upon to realise his wants, who worked in an architectural language combining the imported and innovative with the local and traditional.[53] It is no coincidence that many of Anna's new and restorative building projects in Scotland and England were a stylistic fusing of the classical and the decorative. In the first case of Dunfermline, Anna inherited a palace where the southern range was anchored by heavy buttresses to the top of the precipitous incline of Pittencrieff Glen, which afforded spectacular views over the countryside.[54] When modernising the building, efforts were made to capitalise on this dramatic outlook and to increase the connection between house and land: a number of large cross-windows were installed and three bays – symmetrical in design – were added at the west end.[55] However, as we find with Frederik's building programmes in Denmark-Norway, Anna's palace block was not made over in a completely classicising language of architecture, for the gothic-arched pend was preserved, as were the crenellated rooflines and turrets, and this mixture of the symmetrical and the decorative was also in evidence in the range to the west of the Abbey.[56] Thus, the tentative inclusion of classical elements links the palace to other, slightly later, examples in Scotland and foreshadows the pronounced classicism that Anna was to commission in England. Yet the retention of local, decorative elements firmly connects Dunfermline to the Danish building tradition of Anna's father and brother. The queen's impact on Dunfermline – physically shaped through her building activities and conceptually shaped by her frequent presence – led to an identification between person and place. By 1601, Dunfermline was commonly referred to as 'residence of the Queen', an act of renaming that was to be repeated, even more strongly, at Anna's primary residence in England: Somerset House.[57]

Somerset House: relocating the queen's court in London

The discussion of Anna's residences in England follows the hierarchical order of importance established by the declared accounts of the office of works: Somerset House, Greenwich Palace, and Oatlands Manor. Anna's favour of these three palaces over the multitude of other properties in her jointure was predicated on issues of location, royal precedent, scale of the property, state of repair, current furnishings, and the seasonal calendar. Both Somerset House and Greenwich Palace enjoyed strategic positions close to the centre of London and were easily accessed from the Thames. Somerset House was within a kilometre of Whitehall, Westminster, and St James, while Greenwich, although more distant, had the added allure of a strong and symbolic history of royal use. Oatlands, on the other hand, was much further away, lying some 48 kilometres south-west of Whitehall and central London, although it too could be easily accessed via the Thames. Anna favoured Oatlands more in her later years, and the majority of her building work at the palace was completed between 1616 and 1618. During this time, Anna often spent the summer months at Oatlands (with short stays at other palaces) and the colder period at Greenwich, Somerset House, or Whitehall in a pattern of occupancy known at court where it was observed that 'the queen returned from Oatlands on Monday, where she has spent this summer, to her usual residence at Greenwich.'[58]

Several parallels link Anna's main palaces in Scotland and England: Dunfermline and Somerset House were granted to her at the beginning of her time in each country; they enjoyed strategic locations and a rich history of royal ownership; they were ripe for transformation by the time of Anna's arrival, and, crucially, they were chosen by the queen as appropriate sites for the transmission of European fashions. The major difference, however, was in financial scope. Covered by the comparatively wealthy English crown, Anna's project of remodelling Somerset House was infinitely more ambitious, and as indicated above, it constituted the biggest building project of the entire Stuart period. Between 1609 and 1613, the exchequer disbursed more than £34,500 as Somerset House received a new suite of royal apartments, two new galleries, new lodgings on the east and west, a rebuilt upper court, and a restored Strand frontage.[59] Anna's integrated approach to the relationship between house and grounds is evident in Robert Smythson's (1535–1614) 1609 plan (Figure 2.2) where the new palace block, to the east of the original building, comprises a symmetrical three-sided courtyard that extends into the new privy garden and down to the Thames.[60]

The ranges of lodgings that ran along the east and west sides of the internal courtyard were rebuilt in stone, and they must have included adequate rooms for James and Prince Henry who both stayed at the palace on occasion. During the festivities for the wedding of Princess Elizabeth and Friedrich, Elector Palatine (1596–1632) in 1613, for example, orders were given 'for making ready the queenes ma[jes]t[ie]s lodgings and the Princes at Somersetthouse against the wedding and for making ready the king's ma[jes]t[ie]s lodgings there allsoe'. The following year, in March 1614, the king and queen's lodgings at Whitehall were prepared for 'there comeing from Somersetthouse', which was followed in May 1614 with warrants for 'wayting, attending and making ready divers lodgings for the king's ma[jes]tie and for the prince and allsoe for divers other rooms for the feast and play at the Queenes Courte [Somerset House]'.[61] Such preparations prove that Somerset House contained suites of rooms for accommodating the king (and the prince) in addition to the queen, but it is highly possible that the palace only housed one set of state apartments.[62] These were reserved for Anna as the primary resident while James was very rarely present, but the flexibility of use witnessed at other Stuart palaces indicates that James would have used her rooms if required. He certainly did so at Greenwich where, in May 1606, the queen's side was readied 'with rich stuffe Sparvers and seeling the roofe with Arras for his Ma[jes]t[i]e lying'. Similarly, as mentioned, at Greenwich, Hampton Court, and Windsor Anna did, on occasion, occupy James's suite of rooms or ordered that both sides be made up for her use, and when Anna and Elizabeth journeyed to Greenwich in November 1611, it was James's apartments that were prepared for the Princess.[63] Furthermore, given the proximity of

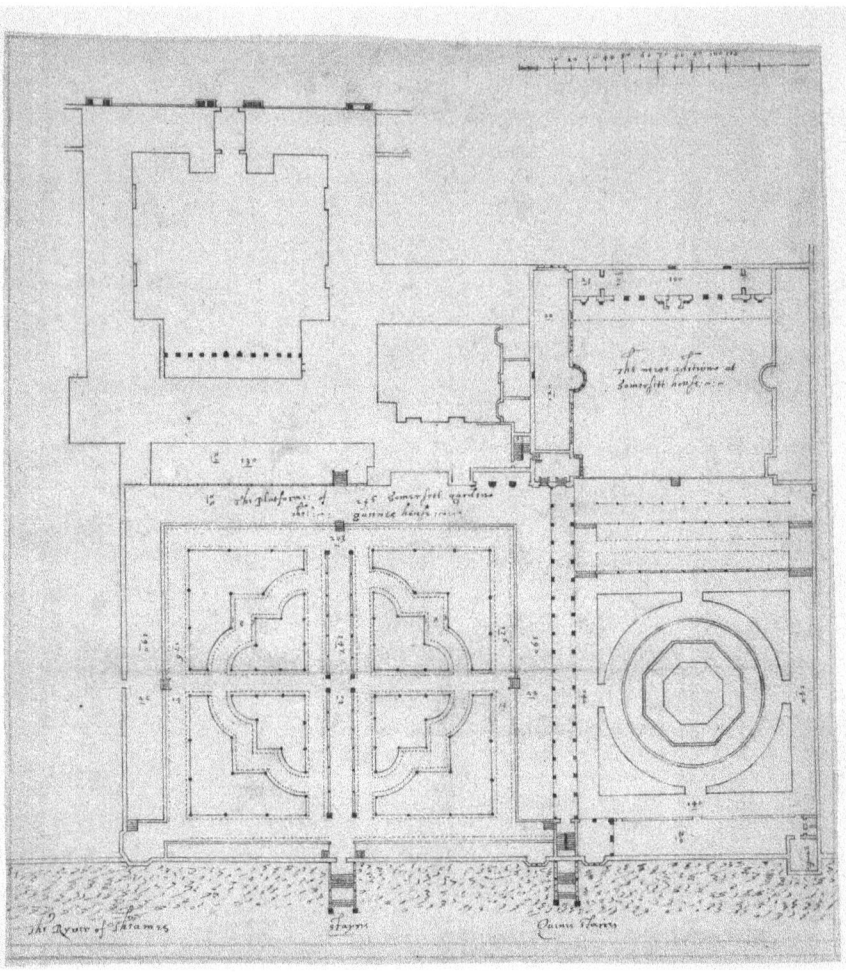

2.2 Survey plan of additions to the palace and garden, Somerset House, London, by Robert Smythson, c.1609.

Somerset House to Whitehall Palace, the decision to have one set of state apartments holds a practical, economic element. Whitehall remained the ceremonial heart of the Stuart court: it was here that James chose to stay when in London; where he opted to entertain dignitaries and guests; and where the royal couple spent the majority of the celebratory points of the year including the Coronation Day, Easter, St George's Feast, Christmas, and New Year.[64] By comparison, the lengthy periods that Anna spent at Somerset House coupled with her extensive remodelling programme, led the palace, like Dunfermline before it, to be firmly conceived as her domain and by May 1614, as the warrant quoted above evidences, it was formally called 'the queen's court'.[65]

Somerset House to Denmark House

James formally acknowledged the presence of Anna's autonomous court in London, when he officially changed the title of the palace to Denmark House. On 8 March 1617, Chamberlain reported that 'the king dined that day [Shrove Tuesday] with the Quene at Somerset House, which was then new christened, and must henceforward be called Denmarke House.'[66] Chamberlain's assertion is corroborated by the works accounts, which register the new title in the accounts for 1617/18.[67] This was a unique and momentous decision and while it is frequently mentioned by historians, the king's impetus has never been satisfactorily explained.[68] It is generally accepted that it was made in celebration of Anna's ambitious building programme or to mark her decision to finally take up residence, but both proposals are unlikely since renovations had largely finished by the close of 1613, and Anna had been staying there since at least July 1614.[69] A more feasible explanation for the change in name is found in the context of Anna's close relationship with her brother, Christian IV, and the international political climate of 1617.

Playing a major role in the peace negotiations between Sweden and Russia to end the Ingrian War, Britain finally concluded a treaty in February 1617 that gave highly favourable terms to Denmark's traditional enemy – Sweden.[70] The war had been raging since 1610 as Karl IX of Sweden (1550–1611), and then Gustav II Adolph (1594–1632), sought to place a Swedish duke on the Russian throne. The latter was further driven by his wish to prevent the unification of Poland-Lithuania-Russia under Sigismund III (1566–1632), which would undoubtedly look to absorb Sweden.[71] Christian IV of Denmark was doubtless relieved that Sweden's imperial aims had failed, but was severely chagrined by the terms that were laid out in the Treaty of Stolbovo, and by the fact that Britain had worked with the Dutch on its negotiation. Christian's antipathy to the Dutch was well known, having been compounded by the anti-Danish alliance that they signed with Sweden in 1614, which had severely curtailed his own plans for expansion.[72] Anna's fierce Danish pride and her support of Christian, to whom she was 'passionately attached', were equally well known in England and contemporaries observed that the queen was 'not very fond of the Dutch, owing to their differences with the King of Denmark, her brother'.[73] In March 1617 – the month after the conclusion of the peace treaty – the Venetian Secretary, Giovanni Battista Lionello, vehemently reiterated this sentiment when he observed Anna giving her nephew, Frederik III, Duke of Holstein-Gottorp (1597–1659), a frosty welcome to London and opined that it was due to 'his alliance with the Dutch; whom she hates so much on account of the king of Denmark, so that she has never allowed their ambassador to visit her'.[74]

It was the terms granted to Sweden by the treaty, more than the Stuart decision to work with the Dutch, that riled Christian. The large and strategic territorial gains (Ingria and Kexholm), coupled with Russian peace, laid the groundwork for Sweden's rise to dominance in the Baltic – superseding that of Denmark-Norway.[75] James's decision to rename Somerset House in the months immediately following the treaty was a logical attempt to curry favour with Christian – and Anna – after England had assisted Sweden's triumph, and the choice of palace was pointed. For Christian, Somerset House was indelibly linked to his sister Anna, with whom he shared a particularly close bond. It was also here that Christian stayed when he visited England in 1606, and again in 1614 at which time he experienced, first hand, Anna's architectural projects that shared marked parallels with, and served as inspiration for, his own building work at Frederiksborg Castle in Hillerød. Whether communication was shared via letters or plans remains unknown, but both palaces featured the unusual decision to have a gallery extend from the inner lodgings and culminate in a free-standing chamber.[76] In addition, as Patrick Kraglund has recently pointed out, Anna's noteworthy garden structure of Mount Parnassus (discussed below) found later echo at Frederiksborg as Christian chose to have his Audience House fronted by a ceremonial gateway topped with a life-size statuary group of Minerva and the Muses.[77] In turning Somerset House into Denmark House, James's choice of name and choice of palace was highly calculated: it endorsed Anna's autonomous court, celebrated her lineage, and recognised the bond between Anna and Christian as one that extended beyond bloodlines and natal pride, to shared cultural interests (including architecture). More pointedly though, it established an English royal palace, strategically located in the centre of London, that paid homage to the Oldenburg kingdom and announced James's continued goodwill, respect, and support of the Danes.

The setting of Denmark House

Denmark House, more than any other property, was well and truly conceptualised as the physical manifestation of Anna's independent position and court. It was the location of her most impressive building programme, but it was also the important site of major earthworks, and the importation of French and Italian gardening traditions that were still rare in England, and entirely absent from royal patronage.[78] Even before work commenced on the palace, a terraced privy garden was laid in the east, with William Goodrowse being paid £400, in 1609, for 'raising and levelling' the new garden.[79] Later payments in 1613/14 for 'rayling about the walke and knottes' confirm that this was an early example of the raised, symmetrically patterned garden based on French designs that originated in Italy, and were present in Denmark during Anna's youth.[80] The geometric forms at Denmark House were carefully highlighted by laying the paths with black and white stone, in a notable departure from the commonly used materials of sand or crushed brick.[81] Anna also drew inspiration from French fashions in her decision to build one of the first orangeries in England, which was erected at Denmark House between 1610 and 1611.[82] The precise location of the orangery is unknown, but it was evidently large with a roof requiring almost 22 metres of slate. Once the 'framing and setting up a house for orrenge trees in the garden' was complete, Francis Renche, a slater, was brought in to lay 4 and 1/3 rods (approximately 21.8 metres) of slate 'over the oreng trees'.[83] The cultivation of fruit trees, especially those bearing exotic specimens such as oranges, was a noted indicator of the resources and rank of the owner.[84] Such signs were also transmitted through unusual, foreign plants and Anna engaged in transnational courtly exchange with Louis XIII of France (1601–1643) to this end, sending the king 'six horses and thirty couple of hounds' in return 'for plants and bulbs received from him'.[85] In addition to France, English gardeners repeatedly looked to Holland and Flanders for rare, costly botanical specimens that visualised their cultural capital, and it is important to note that many of these would not have been native examples but were imported from other parts of Europe and the Americas.[86] Thus, in 1611, Cecil's gardener, John Tradescant (1570–1638), was tasked with importing 'strang and rare' botanical species from Holland (Haarlem and Leiden) and France (Paris) for the garden at Hatfield.[87] The Stuarts' desire for the prestige associated with garden stock and designs procured in France extended beyond Anna's interaction with Louis XIII to a notable transfer of people and horticultural goods in 1611 and 1612. Unnoticed by historians, by December 1611, the royal Bourbon gardener Jean Le Nôtre (1575–1655) 'and other ffrenche gardiners' had arrived in England and were paid £100 for their work. The following March saw a further £108 issued to the 'ffrenche gardiner' (presumably Le Nôtre) for 'repaire of gardens'.[88] The order books of the exchequer of receipt clarifies that the December payment was made to 'John de Nostre gardener to the quene regent of ffrance [Anne of Austria]' for safeguarding a horticultural gift from the Bourbons, and he was reimbursed for 'his charges & hire of a barque for transportacon of certen fruit trees sent from the said Queene [of France]'.[89] It unfortunately remains unclear as to which English palace/s Le Nôtre was tasked to 'repaire' and for which Stuart (Anna's interest in gardens certainly makes her a logical candidate), and what he was able to achieve, but the presence of a French royal gardener working in England for at least a couple of months, and bringing a substantial amount of fruit trees from central Europe, speaks volumes about the desirability of European specimens and styles and confirms the Stuarts leading a reorientation of the English garden through cosmopolitan influences and mediation. Anna's cut-turf parterre and orangery were innovative developments for English gardens, but her most impressive and influential patronage came with her engagement of the French hydraulic engineer Salomon de Caus (1576–1626).

Salomon de Caus at Denmark House and Greenwich Palace

One of the most talented and extraordinary polymaths to work at the Stuart court, De Caus arrived in London towards the end of 1610, or in the early months of 1611. The dating of De Caus's early work in England is imprecise and has led to conflicting interpretations as to whether Anna or Prince Henry was the French gardener's first patron.[90] Anna, as Roy Strong contends, may very well have been responsible for securing De Caus's passage to England and providing him with initial employment, for the exchequer accounts from the ninth year of James's reign (1611/12) describe De Caus as 'Gardener to the Queen' and record him 'beautifying the gardens' at Greenwich and Denmark House.[91] Without a more specific date, however, it is impossible to determine whether this was prior to Lady Day, and therefore referred to 1611 (n.s.). The same problem hampers our reading of the works accounts wherein explicit mention is made of 'sundry woorkes about the fountaine in the Garden and buildinge a house towards the Thames for Monnzer de Cois to make the Rocke in for the ffountaine' at Denmark House but, running from 1 October 1611 through to 30 September 1612, the accounts leave it unclear as to which year the expenditure occurred.[92] Yet, in light of the projected scale and cost of the work that Anna sought from De Caus, the engineer must have been in concert with the queen prior to his commencement of work, and Denmark House must have required some degree of preparation. Indeed, the works accounts from the previous year (October 1610 to September 1611) strongly suggest that this was the case, with charges lodged 'for framing and fittinge a new crane for the works', and for two carpenters 'saweinge workeinge framing and settinge up a newe house in the base courte of two stories and a garrett for the gardner', and for a plasterer to finish the 'gardners new house' with lime and hair.[93] Most logically, the 'gardner' was De Caus, and the crane was moved in readiness for the intended earthworks. The crane was certainly in use during De Caus's paid time at Denmark House, with the 1612 expenditure including payments for 'soape and oyle for the engine and crane' and for 'ropes for the crane and slynge', while Richard Barnwell was further paid for 'makeinge and settinge upp of an engine to force upp water from a well at the end of the terrasse in the garden to the great cesterne over the Strand Lane which serveth the new ffountaine with water'.[94] Roy Strong and Luke Morgan have pointed to the paucity of descriptive documentary information for De Caus's work at Denmark House and Greenwich Palace, but the exorbitant costs – indicative of substantial scale – have been underplayed. By 7 October 1612, Anna's projects were already considerable with an account drawn up of the 'money received out of the receipt by Salomon de Caus for the workes att Greenewich and Som[er]set gardens since his first entry to that service', totalling £998.11s.[95] Subsequently, between November 1612 and April 1613, De Caus received a further four payments amounting to £275.10s.8d.,[96] and in 1615, he was still in receipt of extraordinary money with £565.11s. issued to him at Easter term and a further £205 disbursed at Michaelmas.[97]

Anna's unifying concept for Denmark House gave rise to her largest refurbishment and building project, and one of the key steps that she took was to reorient the state lodgings in order that they overlook her new gardens and earthworks.[98] Originally, the presence, privy, and withdrawing chamber – the most important rooms of the house – had windows overlooking the interior courtyard. These were filled in and replaced with windows along the southern walls to face over the gardens and towards the river. Anna's most distinguished visitors were now invited into the state apartments and given a carefully orchestrated view to acquaint them with their host's international outlook. Beyond these windows lay Anna's most remarkable commission: a dominating water feature of Mount Parnassus. Featuring a basin with a diameter of 100 feet, Anna's fountain of Parnassus demanded De Caus's expertise to construct an intricate network of pipes, taps, cisterns, and valves that would supply it with an adequate and constant water supply from the Thames.[99] Beyond his hydro-engineering skills, De Caus's knowledge of sixteenth-century Tuscan garden design must have endeared him to the queen, and it was this style that he brought to Denmark House.[100] The most evocative description of De Caus's complex and innovative garden mount comes from Johann Wilhelm Neumayr (1572–1641), who visited the palace in 1613 and reported to Duke Johann Ernst of Saxe-Weimar (1594–1626) that in the garden there was

> a Mount Parnassus: the mountain or rock is made of sea-stones, all sorts of mussels, snails, and other curious plants put together ... On the side facing the palace it is made like a cavern. Inside it sit the Muses, and have all sorts of instruments in [their] hands. Uppermost at the top stands Pegasus ... water flows into the basin about four good paces wide ... Among others there stands above such a female figure in black marble in gold letters *Tamesis*. It is the river on which London lies, and [which] flows next to this garden ... It is thus a beautiful work and far surpasses the Mount Parnassus in the Pratolino near Florence.[101]

Iconographically and hydraulically complex, the mount, as Morgan asserts, cast Anna as 'a "tenth muse" if not a new Apollo'.[102] In Greek mythology, Mount Parnassus was home to the nine Muses and, therefore, to knowledge and the arts. During the Renaissance, it became closely connected to Mount Helicon where the winged horse Pegasus stamped his hoof and released the Hippocrene, a sacred spring of inspiration. Consequently, in fifteenth- and sixteenth-century poetry, Parnassus, the Muses, Apollo, or the Hippocrene Spring, were invoked to praise a ruler as a patron and guardian of the arts and literature.[103] At this time too, fountains of Parnassus or Pegasus were becoming common features in Italian gardens and could be seen, for example, at the Villa Lante at Bagnaia, at the 'Park of Monsters' in Bomarzo, the Villa Medici at Pratolino, and the Villa d'Este at Tivoli. There, as at Denmark House, they cast the residence as the home of the Muses; as a place of reflection and thought under the inspiration of nature, which in turn inspired the arts.[104] Rising in European popularity, Anna gained personal knowledge of this *topos* at her natal court where Brahe built his famous complex on Hven complete with the mythic figures of Apollo and the Muses and with several automatons powered by wind and/or water.[105] Likewise, Anna's father Frederik II was interested in the magical, mysterious, and amusing effects of hydraulic engineering, which in addition to moving automata could also produce sound – notably of rain, thunder, and birdsong – that delighted and surprised guests. At Kronborg, Frederik's monumental fountain rose some 6 metres in height and the water supply caused the crowning statue of Neptune to rotate.[106] Anna's Parnassus at Denmark House made a similarly dramatic statement. The towering form was readily visible to people travelling on the river and, more importantly, it was easily seen by distinguished visitors from the state apartments. It connected Anna to a wider European dialogue centred on the revocation of mythological tropes to flatter the patron, and on hydraulic innovation that mastered natural resources. Placed within the context of Anna's broader patronage, the Parnassus was a logical manifestation of her interests, which centred on the history, trends, and fashions, of Italian design – which she had been exposed to in Denmark-Norway – and they similarly coloured her projects at Greenwich.

Innovation in the gardens at Greenwich

For Anna, Greenwich was, as it had been for Elizabeth I and Henry VIII before her, a 'place of pleasure and decorative exuberance', and she appropriately sought to heighten the restorative and enchanted nature of the grounds.[107] Aside from maintaining the Tudor banqueting house, garden seats, orchards, arbours, and fountains, Anna embarked on several major projects – a set of new lodgings, a garden, a grotto aviary, and a garden lodge (the Queen's house) – that transformed the palace and its setting into an integrated whole and reflected her internationalist outlook.[108]

Anna's aviary at Greenwich was under construction for several years, and by the close of the 1611/12 works accounts it had an interior finished with lime and hair, a slate roof, 90 yards of wire netting, five archways that extended more than 50 feet with sixteen entry points for birds in the manner of a dovecote, and its own water supply.[109] At this time, there were only two complex grottoes in England, but large and decorative aviaries had a distinguished Italian tradition, with Marcus Lænius Strabo's aviary in Brindisi being extolled by Pliny, and celebrated Renaissance examples encompassing those of the Villa Lante at Bagnaia and the Villa Medici at Pratolino. They also enjoyed a rich history in medieval English, Scottish, and Danish gardens, where they added a magical, exotic element.[110] The most suggestive description of Anna's Greenwich aviary is again provided by Neumayr's 1613 account that in the gardens

> one comes to a grotto. [It] is a small house from the front and on both sides mostly open, with great iron railings there. On the wall are three different arches ... In the middle arch stands a figure, half a woman and half a horse in the right size ... it gave water from itself unto the ground. In the other two arches were other figures, from which water also sprang ... This house was also in the roof open in several places, although protected by wire grating, so that the birds, of which a great number were flying around inside could not get out.[111]

This must have been the same grotto/aviary recorded in the works accounts, and while the two do not entirely match, there are notable similarities. Both structures had arcaded frontages, both were finished with wire grating, both were designed to contain a multitude of birds, and both were furnished with their own water supply. Logically too, it would be extremely unusual to find two ornate garden structures at Greenwich that housed birds and water features, with one missing from the works accounts and the other being kept from Neumayr during his tour of the palace.[112] It was De Caus who was engaged to design and/or oversee the installation of the aviary's water system, which involved an intricate system of pipes, cisterns, stopcocks, and vaults, very much like that of the Parnassus.[113] De Caus was paid, by writ dated 22 March 1612/13, for 'works done in the garden att Som[er]st. House, as in the garden founteins & birdhouses att Greenwch', costing £70.13s.6d.[114] He was later to publish designs for structures that combined aviaries with grottoes, which may have drawn on that at Greenwich (Figures 2.3 and 2.4).[115] Inspired by his mother's admiration for Italian (specifically, Florentine) gardens, and her patronage of European artisans, Prince Henry followed Anna's lead, employing De Caus to transform his gardens at Richmond, and singling out Pratolino as the model of emulation – as it had been for the Denmark House Parnassus.[116] The same was true for Princess Elizabeth, who not only took De Caus with her to Heidelberg in 1613, but the surviving designs of the *Hortus Palatinus* show that her garden was also to boast a Parnassus with a 'parterre of the muses' and a fountain of Neptune (father of Pegasus), while extraordinary mechanised water features, grottoes, and an orange grove were also notable components.[117] Again, as with those gardens De Caus designed for Anna, and then Henry, the *Hortus Palatinus* drew heavily on Pratolino.[118] Beyond her immediate family, Anna's influence extended to her court circle and into the next generation of Stuarts. Sometime between 1617 and

1630, at Moor Park in Hertfordshire, the Countess of Bedford (or, possibly, the Earl of Pembroke) had the garden made over in the Italianate manner with a grotto and water works, and at Wimbledon in 1642, Henrietta Maria had André Mollet (1600–1665) design her an aviary with a fountain.[119]

2.3 Design for an aviary with caves by Salomon de Caus from *Les raisons des forces mouvantes* (Paris, 1624).

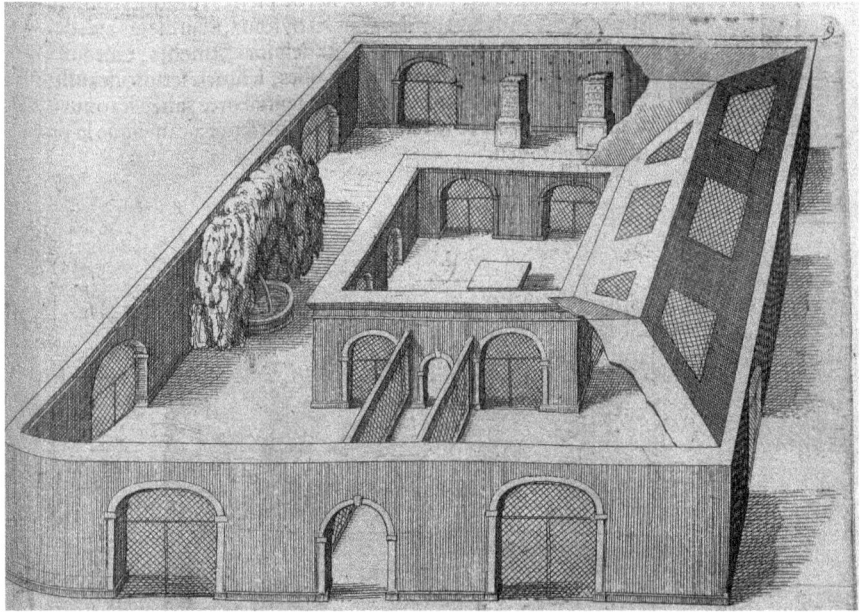

2.4 Perspective of a design for an aviary with caves by Salomon de Caus from *Les raisons des forces mouvantes* (Paris, 1624).

Reconfiguring gardens and buildings at Greenwich

Between 1609 and 1611, a new two-storey brick section was built on the southwest side of the palace block at Greenwich and adjoined the presence and privy chambers. Containing the queen's lodgings, a gallery, and a study, it overlooked the new gardens that Anna had had De Caus concurrently lay to the west. Then, in 1614, Anna improved the dialogue between palace and grounds by ordering a brick-and-stone building to extend straight out from her lodgings towards De Caus's garden beyond. When finished, it comprised 'a three-arch loggia' and 'a return front facing the garden' which 'had a two-storey rectangular bay with a parapet and above this a curved gable containing a three-light window' (Figure I.1).[120] The result was a building that was not only physically connected to Anna's new garden, but whose views generally encouraged the contemplation and admiration of the grounds and parkland beyond. Interestingly, the building was begun under the surveyorship of Simon Basil (*fl*.1590–1615), at which time costs were declared before the exchequer as expected.[121] But when the final payments were being made – between September 1616 and September 1617 – Jones was now head of the works, and payments were made to him directly from the queen's privy purse. Carew, the receiver-general, recorded having seen seven 'severall bookes under the handes of Indigo Jones Esquier the kings majesties surveyor of his works and Henrie Herne clearke of the kings workes', and payments had been made for labour and materials (limestone and brick specifically noted, along with £158.7s. for marble 'and other materialls' in August 1617), which gave a total of £1,627.2s.10d. 'for the queenes majesties buildings at her highnes house at Greenwich'. This was in addition to £500 that Carew had earlier sanctioned for 'the payment of her majesties buildings at Greenewich'.[122] It is possible that some of this money was allocated to Anna's latest project for a hunting lodge to link the palace with the park (Figure I.1), as that building (now known as the Queen's House) was entirely paid for by the privy purse and was under construction at this time (Figure 2.1). Desiring a retreat where Anna could escape the stresses of public court life, entertain select guests, and indulge in leisure activities such as hunting, the designs for the lodge were realised by Jones and show a building akin to a sixteenth-century Italian villa (Figure 2.5). While the impact of Italian renaissance traditions on this ancillary building (and on Jones) have been carefully mapped, little consideration has been given to the range of influences at play on the patron, Anna of Denmark, which spurred her to insist on, or at least accept, a type of building, and an architectural style that was still unusual in the Stuart kingdom. The answer can be found in a number of court spaces and buildings from the late sixteenth-century Danish court of Anna's youth.

In the first instance, Uraniborg and Kronborg were particularly renowned for their introduction of Italian Renaissance styles. Built between

2.5 Preliminary elevation for the east or west side of the Queen's House, Greenwich, by Inigo Jones, 1616.

1576 and 1581, Brahe's castle of Uraniborg was a ground-breaking combination of Italian classicism with Netherlandish and Nordic traditions. Personally familiar with Andrea Palladio's (1508–1580) work in Venice and Vicenza, the plan of Brahe's castle was based on the Villa Rotunda with two symmetrical axes and Venetian arched gables, while the gardens followed the layout of the Villa d'Este outside Rome.[123] A plurality of medieval and Renaissance forms were likewise found at Kronborg, which was concurrently under construction for Anna's father Frederik. Here, over a period of eleven years, the medieval fortified castle was transformed in a piecemeal fashion into a Renaissance palace that paid homage to Italian and Netherlandish traditions: towers, gables, and spires dominated in some sections, while others offered symmetry, restraint, and the correct use of the classical orders.[124] Having been originally conceived in brick, throughout the 1580s it was clad in pale sandstone, offering an intentionally antique Italianate appearance.[125] Yet, importantly, both buildings were realised by a taskforce dominated by artisans from the Low Countries, so that the 'Renaissance' or 'antique' motifs realised in Denmark were based on a form of Italian classicism that had been introduced, interpreted, and adapted in the Netherlands some forty years earlier.[126]

Arguably though, other precedents weighed still more heavily on Anna's commission of Jones at Greenwich: Frederik's use of garden lodges (*Sparepenge*) at his major residences, and the royal hunt with its associated buildings, spaces, and rituals. The latter was, of course, not a tradition unique to the Danish crown but, as John Robert Christianson has determined, it held a particularly strong importance for Frederik. Not only did the Danish King spend large amounts of time, money, and manpower on transforming vast tracts of his kingdom into exclusive royal hunting reserves, but he also repaired and extended existing properties and built a number of new structures.[127] Ostensibly used to accommodate small hunting parties, or the entire court for extended periods, Frederik also considered them appropriate for private acts of diplomacy. In 1586, Frederik met with Fabian von Dohna (1550–1621), an envoy from Johann Casimir, Count of Pfalz (1543–1592), at one such lodge before deciding to grant him financial aid for the French Huguenots.[128] Unsurprisingly, as Christianson elaborates, these buildings were a mixture of age and style. The inherited three-storey lodge at Grøngaard in Schleswig bore the influence of Vitruvius and was of the French Renaissance style with a loggia at the entrance and a tower in each of the four corners while, by comparison, the two-storey lodge at Hørsholm, newly built between 1567 and 1571, was Netherlandish in style with five towers and a large grange as well as stables and kennels.[129] Having spent time in the royal hunting reserves, Anna was personally familiar with many of these properties. In 1587, for instance, she spent at least three weeks at the Great Hunt (*storjagt*), during which time she stayed at the castles of Hald and Silkeborg as well as the hunting lodges at Vinderslev (now Vinderslevholm) and Løgager.[130]

When conceiving of her new lodge in the gardens of Greenwich, Anna must have thought back on the royal hunting properties that formed her experience of the Danish kingdom beyond the urban centres, but along with these large houses she must also have recalled the suite of small yet sumptuous garden buildings (*Sparepenge*) that her father delighted in at Frederiksborg, Antvorskov, and Haderslev. In the same manner that Anna's hunting lodge at Greenwich was wont to do, these buildings operated as intimate and informal spaces for Frederik to escape the hustle and expense of a large court, but where he could still readily entertain a select number of guests. The Sparepenge at Haderslev was a three-storey turreted building complete with flying pennants (Figure 2.6), while the interior of that at Antvorskov was decorated with tapestries, tablecloths, cushions, and a canopy – all green – together with a brass chandelier, and pewter tableware.[131] Returning to Kronborg, and bridging the gap between the hunting lodges and the Sparepenge, is one further building that sets a clear precedent for Anna's lodge at Greenwich in terms of position, function, and style: Lundehave. Envisioned as a pavilion or garden house for leisure and hunting, Lundehave was built at Kronborg in 1587 and, crucially, was the first Italianate villa built in Denmark-Norway. In his work on Frederik II's use of informal court spaces, Poul Grinder-Hansen notes that Lundehave 'had an open loggia, a balcony, and a flat roof behind a balustrade' and it is not mere coincidence that these were to be characterising features of Jones's designs for Anna at Greenwich some thirty years later.[132] But, importantly, while Renaissance Italy may have been the original source of such classicism, this *all'antica* language of architecture had long been present in the Low Countries and parts of Germany

2.6 The Sparepenge at Haderslevhus from Georg Braunius and Franz Hogenberg, *Civitates Orbis Terrarum IV* (Cologne, 1588).

where it had not been transferred wholesale but adapted and transformed and from these centres it filtered further north into Denmark-Norway.[133] Additionally, the brick façade of Lundehave was painted to imitate brown ashlar interspersed with joints and strips of sandstone – perhaps linked to the gradual introduction of stone cladding at Kronborg throughout the 1580s – which served to place the building within the broader Danish fashion for, what Grinder-Hansen has termed, 'Flemish-inspired architecture'.[134] Thus, what emerges from the sources is a recreational building conceived on a relatively small scale, which drew stylistic influence from the classicism present in the southern Netherlands at the Habsburg court of Charles V (1500–1558) and his sister, the regent Mary of Hungary (1505–1558).[135] The most probable model for Lundehave is the cube-shaped hunting lodge built at Mariemont, for Mary of Hungary, between 1547 and 1549 and designed by Jacques Du Broeucq (c.1505–c.1584). Set in a royal hunting reserve and annexed to the palace at Binche (also by Du Broeucq) some miles distant, it featured a flat roof complete with balustrade, two rusticated portals and further rustication around the windows and at the corners – many elements of which later reached a wide audience through the prints of Hans Vredeman de Vries (1527–1607).[136] Thus, Lundehave was, like many royal Danish buildings, both Netherlandish and Italian in stylistic origin, and Danish and Netherlandish in execution – and serves as yet another example of the complexities of architectural influence and transfer, and the difficulties of drawing strict trends in style along national lines.

There are two important considerations in bringing these precedents to bear on Anna's work at Greenwich: the first is to realise the central role that informality and retreat played in late sixteenth-century Danish court culture and diplomacy, which was often realised by the careful consideration of a building's location, form, and demesne. Secondly, royal Danish architecture offered a complex, conscious assimilation of elements from Netherlandish (and within that Habsburg) and Italianate traditions that were frequently executed by Netherlandish artisans – much of which really started to come to fruition during Anna's teenage years at court. Some decades later when, in 1616, Anna came to commission her own garden lodge at Greenwich, she had first-hand knowledge of a classicism informed by several European architectural languages, as well as her father's use of informal spaces and their role in court leisure and ceremonial. There is clear evidence that Anna had a preconceived concept of the lodge, for when Jones delivered the 'first module [design] of the newe building at Grenewich', it failed to satisfy the queen and changes were ordered. Jones was paid £10 for his first design and then received an additional £16 for 'making and pfecting the second module of the same buildinges at Grenewich in the form the same was to be builded and finished by the Quene Majesties commaundement'.[137] It should also be remembered that Jones, too, had personal knowledge of the fabric of the Danish court having been included in the embassy, headed by Roger Manners, Earl of Rutland (1576–1612), to mark the baptism of Prince-Elect Christian (1603–1647) in Copenhagen in the summer of 1603.[138] While Jones was drawing on the work of Palladio, Giuliano da Sangallo, and Vincenzo Scamozzi, Anna was drawing on her personal experiences of classicism – Netherlandish classicism – in Denmark-Norway. This is not to discredit or challenge the Italianate origins of Jones's influences and interests, but to consider that Anna's suggestion for, or consent of, the style was rooted in her exposure to a stylistic pluralism of models and fashions.

Exercising a strong directorial role in the commission, Anna secured herself further control by paying for the workmanship and materials from her privy purse, and the expenses were recorded in her household accounts. These documents show that beyond the intangible Danish influence of personal remembrance, a physical Danish connection had made an impact at Greenwich for the better part of a year: in 1618, a payment of £50 was disbursed for the transport costs of 'Baron Benson [and] Nicholas Stocker, the two stonemen sent from the Kinge of Denmarke unto her Majesty for ix monethes', to return to Denmark.[139] That the queen was paying for her own building programme is unusual and it is without precedent in her patronage, but it was not the only example seen that year. As earlier stated, it was customary in England, as it was in Scotland, for the king to cover all royal building work, and James had done so up until this point. It is possible that Anna was making up for a shortfall in crown finance, although this seems doubtful since the crown had been plagued by financial difficulties throughout the decade, and this had had no prior impact on the office of the works, where financial outlay continued at a steady rate.[140] Moreover, the expectation continued that James would pay for Anna's building programmes. In March 1616, Sir Edward Coke submitted his 'directions and orders' for reducing Anna's debts, curtailing her expenditure, and increasing her income, from which he explicitly excluded building since the king was to 'beare all the charges of diet, houskeping and of building'.[141] In light of these circumstances, it is reasonable to conclude that Jones received payment from Anna as part of his role as her 'accomptaunte' – appointed from 8 October 1616 until 30 April November 1618 – which also required him to report directly to the queen.[142] This was certainly the case with the building that Jones was tasked to finish as a joining piece between the queen's lodgings and De Caus's garden at Greenwich, and it was also true of the two classicising gateways Jones designed and built for Anna at Oatlands Manor.

Anna's last building at Greenwich, like Frederik's *Sparepenge* and his hunting residences, combined the recreational with the ceremonial in the realisation of two principal functions: a hunting lodge on the south and a viewing platform on the north.[143] As Gordon Higgott has demonstrated, the south (park) side, with its large loggia, was the original entrance. From here, Anna and her guests would be able to comfortably watch a royal hunt, and conveniently retire to the great hall or to the state apartments beyond.[144] By comparison, the north (river) side celebrated the traditional role of Greenwich Palace as a site of international diplomacy and ritual (Figure 2.1). Under the Stuarts, the palace hosted welcome receptions for visiting dignitaries and ambassadors, and the lodge afforded views eastward along the Thames to Gravesend where guests would arrive by boat.[145] As is well known, however, Anna's lodge was not completed during her lifetime, and by the close of Jones's account on 30 April 1618, labour and materials had only resulted in demolishing the old Tudor gateway, digging the foundations and cellars, and laying several levels of brickwork.[146] Instead, Jones's first truly classical building came to fruition under James's aegis with the 1619 commission of the Banqueting House at Whitehall, which was completed in 1622.[147] A key site of court ceremonial, the Banqueting House – articulated in white stone – was a monument to Stuart internationalism and innovation, and a radical departure from its red-brick Tudor surrounds.[148] This was a defining commission in English architecture, but it must be remembered that Jones's first designs for a planned, coherently classicising building, were completed for Anna and predated the Banqueting House by almost three years. For Anna, her favourite properties provided the ideal canvas for the transmission of

Oatlands Manor: vineyards and gates

Between 10 August 1616 and 30 September 1618, Anna, using her privy purse, engaged Sir John Trevor, the keeper of Oatlands, to build a new silkworm house and to surround the vineyard, the long privy walk, and the 'newe garden' with brick walls, which were to be punctuated by gateways designed by Jones.[149] The existence of a vineyard, while not common in England, was not wholly unusual either, and contemporary examples included those of both Cecils – Thomas Cecil, Earl of Exeter at Wimbledon (1542–1623), and Robert Cecil, Earl of Salisbury at Hatfield House.[150] Alongside the provision of fruit – and rarely of wine – they were generally valued as sites for relaxation, reflection, and exercise.[151] Ensuring that Anna's vineyard at Oatlands was enclosed and exclusive, Trevor's wall rose just over 3 metres in height, stretched for more than 213 metres, and was only entered by way of Jones's gates.[152] Generally, as Paula Henderson outlines, Stuart gateways were informed by highly personal and/or symbolic choices of decoration, were diverse in design, and their simple form made them ideal sites for experiments in classicism.[153] Jones's gateways at Oatlands, much like the proposed hunting lodge at Greenwich, harked back to classical principles and, built over the course of June and July 1617, may have enabled him to test some of his ideas for Greenwich. At 3.65 metres high, the 'greate gate' topped Trevor's wall with 'doricke columnes cutt rusticke with a frontispice [pediment] and a square table of marble sett over the same'.[154] Inspired by Palladio and Sebastiano Serlio (1475–c.1554), the reverse side of the Great Gate – which faced into the vineyard and was therefore visible from the palace – featured the same rough-cut treatment of stone intended for the walls of the lodge (Figure 2.7).[155]

Clearly visible in the background of Anna's stately 1617 hunting portrait by Paul van Somer, Trevor's wall and Jones's gate marked a clear boundary between Anna's private domain and the wider, open, and more public space beyond (Plate 1). Interestingly though, in the portrait Anna has placed herself – in an extremely confident posture – some distance from the manor, suggesting that her conception of ownership extended well beyond the confines of her palace walls. This was likewise true of the queen's approach to Dunfermline and Greenwich. Between 1591 and 1593, the queen (and several Danish ambassadors) were involved in a dispute with the Scots over her Dunfermline jointure estates (north of the Forth), which had not been wholly ceded to her and were therefore adversely

2.7 Design for the inner side of the gateway at Oatlands Palace, Surrey, by Inigo Jones, 1617.

affecting her income.[156] In the subsequent negotiations, Anna demanded restitution of all Dunfermline lands – north and south of the Forth – despite the fact that James had not originally assigned her the southern portion, for it comprised the hereditary estates of elite Scots including Chancellor Maitland, who owned Musselburgh.[157] Attempts were made to reach a compromise, but Anna refused to accept anything less than complete ownership and her animosity towards Maitland steadily increased.[158] On 28 January 1592, the English ambassador in Scotland, Sir Robert Bowes (c.1535–1597), reported to William Cecil, Baron Burghley (1520–1598), that 'to the great danger of the Chancelor' he was now in 'thevil conceitt of the Q[ueen]', and by August 1592 Maitland had withdrawn from both court and council.[159] Anna united a disparate faction against Maitland and divided the court, and numerous attempts were subsequently made 'with the Q[ueen] to pacyfie her wrathe against the Channcellor that he mighte be restored to her good countenance, and retourne to the courte to serve the K[ing]', which were to no avail.[160] Anna's resolve eventually paid off, and by the close of July 1593 all occupants of Dunfermline lands had resigned their estates to the king, who, in turn, granted them to his consort. This included Musselburgh and having succeeded in her quest, Anna allowed for reconciliation with Maitland.[161]

The queen's pronounced sense of ownership caused further problems in England. Having received her initial jointure settlement, Anna was displeased that Nonsuch Palace did not include the Great Park with Sir Thomas Chaloner (1559–1615) observing that 'the queen cannot conveniently keep house at Nonsuch without she could procure the Great Park, of which Lord Lumley has a lease, and some of his lordship's adjoining lands; without these parcels the fair house of Nonsuch will be nothing pleasing to the queen.'[162] Despite rarely visiting the palace, Anna demanded the Great Park from the current leaseholder, Baron John Lumley (c.1533–1609), but the matter was not resolved until 1605 when Lumley acquiesced to the queen's wishes and received annual compensation in return.[163] More heated was Anna's bitter rivalry with Northampton over land and control in Greenwich. By 1613, the earl had sizeable possessions in the borough including a lodge, the keepership of Greenwich Park, the lease of the meadow and parsonage, and custody of the orchard, garden, pond, and game birds.[164] Towards the close of 1613, however, it was known that Anna was to gain title to the royal residence, and with it came an unbridled sense of her rights over its surroundings. In November, Anna openly pitted herself against Northampton for the stewardship of the park.[165] The enmity between them is conspicuous in Northampton's surviving letters, which also reveal his fear of Anna's power and swift action (to be contained only by James), and his personal and political investment in retaining his post. Seeking aid from Lake and Somerset to entreat with James on 'the fickele state of my poor tenure', Northampton complained that his 'wrathfull mistresse [Anna]' had driven him to suffer 'dayly alarmes' that she will 'thrust me out of both the lodge and of the keepinge of game' as soon as she has the grant of Greenwich, and even before the letters patent have passed. According to Northampton, not only were his 'spirites' therefore threatened, but his reputation and status were in jeopardy for 'to enjoy the lodge without the care of the parke wold make me ridiculouse'.[166] Anna, on the other hand, was driven by a strong sense of possession, although this was probably encouraged by her contempt of Northampton and the associated Howard faction. If she gained keepership of the park, Anna could then disburse it to one of her own clients and increase her standing in the area while simultaneously reducing Northampton's position. Unlike the situations over Dunfermline and Nonsuch, on this occasion – likely thanks to Somerset's intervention – Northampton prevailed and James confirmed the earl in his keepership with rights to 'herbage and pannage' at the close of 1613.[167]

Conclusion

Anna's extensive, and hugely expensive, refurbishment of Denmark House is the most conclusive example of her architectural patronage, but it was only one of several important projects that she undertook. Arguably for Anna, the most significant of these may well have been the planned hunting lodge at Greenwich, for this was the only building that she ordered completely anew and it bore direct connections to the spaces of her natal court. In the palace hierarchy of the Stuarts, Greenwich was not as prestigious or central as Denmark House, but it was a celebrated and frequent site for court ceremony and diplomacy, and it held a richer history of royal use.[168] Both palaces were, in conjunction with Anna's other principal residences of Dunfermline and Oatlands Manor, the location for landscaping, planting, and ancillary buildings that drew on the European traditions, design principles, and styles that had surrounded the queen in Denmark-Norway. The considerable time and money that Anna poured into the natural surroundings of her properties evidences her approach to the palace complex as one that extended beyond the main building into the gardens, orchards, subsidiary structures, and wider landscape. It is also evident in her fierce sense of proprietorship over the lands annexed to her residences, which led her to contest the ownership rights of Maitland in Fife, Lumley in Surrey, and Northampton in Greenwich. This was demonstrative of early Stuart attitudes wherein house and setting were conceived as a single integrated unit and were intimately connected to issues of status and pride.

The queen's outward-facing, European, interests resulted in the patronage of De Caus and Jones to realise the design and construction of innovative earthworks, formal gardens, and classicising forms. Again, as with her conception of the interconnection of property and setting, this was not wholly unique but representative of a growing movement among Stuart elites to overcome Elizabethan isolationism and develop a dialogue with the courts, traditions, and trends of European collecting, connoisseurship, architecture, and gardening. Yet, within the realm of royal – and especially of *royal female* – patronage, she was little short of revolutionary

– re-establishing the crown as the arbiter of fashion and influencing the cultural pursuits of her children. Anna's ability to realise her avant-garde ventures resulted from her accommodating marital relationship, James's itinerant kingship, and the polycentric structure of the Stuart court. A key figure in facilitating James's wish to be a universal king and peacemaker who spent the majority of his time in rural spaces, Anna was granted a significant level of independence. She presided over her own household, followed her own court calendar, and supported factions, styles, opinions, and cultural avenues that were not favoured by James or his court. However, Anna was a strong supporter of James and the monarchy, and, as befit her position of queen consort, she remained firmly under him in the hierarchy of the court. Rather than being indicative of opposition or antagonism, these differences were, in fact, central to maintaining the factional balance that James desired, and for retaining a royal representative in the capital while the king was travelling and hunting. Thus, while James did not share Anna's fervour for transforming court spaces, he supported her endeavours and frequently financed them through crown resources. As we shall see in the next four chapters, this delicate balancing act was central to all of Anna's cultural undertakings and it fundamentally underpinned her position and value at court.

Notes

1. TNA, SP14/67, fol. 104.
2. Goodare and Lynch, 'James VI: Universal King?' 4–5, 22–25, 31. For an overview of the factionalism that divided Scotland during James's rule and likely gave rise to his want for domestic peace, see J. Goodare, 'Scottish Politics in the Reign of James VI', in J. Goodare and M. Lynch (eds), *The Reign of James VI* (East Linton, 2000), 32–54: 32–55. For these principles continuing to govern James's reign in England see, for example, W. B. Patterson, *King James VI and I and the Reunion of Christendom* (Cambridge, 1997), 293–299, 334–340; R. Lockyer, *James VI and I* (London and New York, 1998), 138–157; Lee, *Great Britain's Solomon*, 263–293.
3. Cole, 'State Apartment', 98; Colvin, *King's Works*, 31, 153, 175, 237–240, 273–279.
4. Quoted in Colvin, *King's Works*, 255. As a result of the existing literature on Somerset House and the Queen's House at Greenwich, neither building is treated in great detail here. For Somerset House, see, for example, Colvin, *King's Works*, 254–260; M. Girouard, *Elizabethan Architecture: Its Rise and Fall, 1540–1640* (New Haven and London, 2009), 122, 142–145; Thurley, *Somerset House*, 31–44; Griffey, *On Display*, 25–27, 63–69, 73–80, 201–221. For Greenwich, see, for example, S. Thurley, 'Architecture and Diplomacy: Greenwich Palace under the Stuarts', *The Court Historian* 11 (2006), 125–135; G. Higgott, 'The Design and Setting of Inigo Jones's Queen's House 1616–40', *The Court Historian* 11 (2006), 135–149; J. Harris, 'Disneyland in Greenwich: The Restoration of the Queen's House', *Apollo* 122 (1990), 56–60; J. Harris, S. Orgel, and R. Strong, *The King's Arcadia: Inigo Jones and the Stuart Court* (London, 1973); J. Harris, 'Inigo Jones and the Courtier Style', *Architectural Review* 154 (1973), 17–24; J. Bold, *Greenwich: An Architectural History of the Royal Hospital for Seamen and the Queen's House* (London, 2000); J. Harris and G. Higgott, *Inigo Jones: Complete Architectural Drawings* (London and New York, 1989).

5 This methodology is used to great effect by Paula Henderson, although Anna's projects are not subject to sustained analysis: *The Tudor House and Garden: Architecture and Landscape in the Sixteenth and Early Seventeenth Centuries* (New Haven and London, 2005), 46–47, 99–104.

6 R. Strong, *The Renaissance Garden in England* (London, 1979), 15.

7 Henderson, *Tudor House and Garden*, 1–5, 11–12, 31; P. Henderson, 'The Architecture of the Tudor Garden', *Garden History* 27 (1999), 54–72: 54.

8 J. R. Christianson, 'Terrestrial and Celestial Spaces of the Danish Court, 1550–1650', *The Court Historian* 12 (2007), 129–153: 146–148; V. Parrott, 'Celestial Expression or Worldly Magic? The Invisibly Integrated Design of Uraniborg: A Look at some Philosophical Aspects of the Ground Plan of Tycho Brahe's House and Garden', *The Garden History Society* 38 (2010), 66–80: 73; A. Ørum-Larsen, 'Uraniborg – The Most Extraordinary Castle and Garden Design in Scandinavia', *Journal of Garden History* 10 (1990), 97–105: 100–101. Like Anna, Christian's building programmes often started with the gardens, which is particularly notable at Rosenborg.

9 Smuts, *Court Culture*, 82–84, 98–108, 117–120; Smuts, 'Cultural Diversity and Cultural Change', 104–105, 110–112; E. Chaney, 'The Italianate Evolution of English Collecting', in E. Chaney (ed.), *The Evolution of English Collecting* (New Haven and London, 2003), 1–124: 2, 8–9, 40–57.

10 For elite women, see Erickson, *Women and Property*, 25–28, 102–105; Harris, *English Aristocratic Women*, 22–24.

11 Cole, 'State Apartment', 8–9, 12, 98, appendix 2: 365–405; Colvin, *King's Works*, 153.

12 TNA, E351/543, fols 155r, 247r, 260v, 262v; TNA, E351/544, fol. 26r.

13 P. Graves, 'The Danish Account', in D. Stevenson, *Scotland's Last Royal Wedding* (Edinburgh, 1997), 79–122: 79–84, 102–103; Riis, *Auld Acquaintance*, vol. 1, 270–274, 277–278. For the separate financial system of apparel see J. Field, 'Dressing a Queen: The Wardrobe of Anna of Denmark at the Scottish Court of King James VI, 1590–1603,' *The Court Historian* 24 (2019), 152–167: 154–155.

14 NRS, E23/12/8, no. 9. My thanks to Michael Pearce for this reference.

15 TNA, LR7/137, this included £2,210.18*s.ob.qua.* in arrears. The patent rolls are TNA, C66/1610 (part 4); C66/1626 (part 20); TNA, C66/1631 (part 1), confirmed by private statute, Parliamentary Archives, London, HL/PO/PB/1/1603/1J1n35. See also TNA, SC6/JASI/1648.

16 N. R. R. Fisher, 'The Queenes Courte in her Councell Chamber at Westminster', *English Historical Review* 108 (1993), 314–337: 314–320. Anna's Council included a High Steward of Revenue (Robert Cecil, Earl of Salisbury), a Chancellor (Sir Roger Wilbraham), a Master of Game (Henry Wriothesley, Earl of Southampton), a Surveyor General (Robert Sidney, Viscount Lisle), a Receiver General (George Carew), an Attorney General (Sir Robert Hicham), an Auditor General (Ralph Ewens), and a Solicitor (Lancelot Lowther). It was further serviced by three Sergeants at Law (Sir Thomas Forster, James Altham, and Sir Edward Cooke), two Counsellors at Law (John Dodridge, and John Walter), a Clerk of the Council, a Keeper of the Register of the Chancery (both held by Daniel Powell), two Deputies to the Attorney General (Thomas Waller, and William Ackwell), a Clerk to the Receiver-General (George Hooker), and an Underkeeper of the Court at Westminster (Owen Garvey); TNA, SC6/JASI/1646.

17 TNA, SC6/JASI/1653.

18 Erickson, *Women and Property*, 121.

19 TNA, SP14/86, fol. 175r. Coke puts Anna's annual income from sugar impositions at £5,000 per annum. Anna was presumably granted the licence in 1608, or early 1609, for a warrant issued on 3 March 1609 states that Anna is to receive 12*d.* per hundredweight of Muscovado sugar, and 10*d.* per hundredweight of sugar

imported from St Thomas in the Caribbean: *CSPD* (1603–1610), 623: 10 July 1610; TNA, SP14/40, fol. 12: undated, 1608?. On the common law and the provision of a bride's dowry and jointure in Tudor England see, Harris, *English Aristocratic Women*, 22–24, 44–58.

20 Riis, *Auld Acquaintance*, vol. 1, 274–275, 277; Juhala, 'Household and Court', 63–64, 172.
21 TNA, LR6/154/9. Hatfield House and Havering at Bower generated £71.10s.4d. *ob.qua* and £18.18s.1d.*ob.* respectively per annum. Colvin, in *King's Works*, does not mention Havering or Nonsuch being in Anna's jointure, although Havering was evidently a traditional jointure property as it had been granted by Henry VII (1457–1509) to Elizabeth of York (1466–1503) in 1487, and then successively given by Henry VIII to Catherine of Aragón (1485–1536), Anne Boleyn (c.1501–1536), and Jane Seymour (c.1508–1537). Nonsuch was later included in Henrietta Maria's jointure in 1628, see Colvin, *King's Works*, 150–151, 204.
22 For the letters patent for Oatlands manor see TNA, C66/1924, for Greenwich Palace see TNA, C66/1990 (nos. 4, 7, 8). For income generated by Oatlands and Greenwich see, for example, TNA, SC6/JASI/1653 (1616–1617).
23 TNA, SC6/JASI/1653 (1616–1617); TNA, SP14/27/31 (Act for the Assurance of Theobalds). On the problematics of the exchange and the commemorative celebrations that Cecil commissioned from Ben Jonson see G. Heaton, *Writing and Reading Royal Entertainments: From George Gascoigne to Ben Jonson* (Oxford, 2010), 169–172.
24 TNA, LR7/137; TNA, SC6/JASI/1653 (1616–1617); Cole, 'State Apartment', 10, 12, 98, and esp. 360–416.
25 Cole, 'State Apartment', 360–416.
26 Cole, 'State Apartment', 6, 360–416; Juhala, 'Household and Court', 121.
27 Juhala, 'Household and Court', 61, 121, 127–128, 130, 132–135; Cole, 'State Apartment', 21. The ownership of Dalkeith Palace changed hands several times following the execution of James Douglas, earl of Morton (b.1525) for treason in 1581. It was under the control of Esmé Stewart, Duke of Lennox (1542–1583) between 1581 and 1584, but by 1589 it was back in the possession of the Douglas family.
28 *CSP Scotland*, vol. 10, no. 537: 9 March 1591 (to Burghley).
29 *CSP Scotland*, vol. 10, no. 30: 3 October 1595 (George Nicholson to Bowes).
30 Cole, 'State Apartment', 19–21; Juhala, 'Household and Court', 61, 127–128, 132–136, 139, 142, 144–146.
31 TNA, E351/543, fols 246v, 247r–v, 260r–263r; TNA, E351/544, fols 8r, 10r–11v, 26r–27v, 43v–44r, 58r–59v, 78v–79r, 91r–92r, 99v, 100r–v. As discussed in Chapter 6, the only deviation to the rule of spending Christmas at Whitehall was made in 1618 when, in deference to Anna, James ordered the court to observe the period at Hampton Court where the queen was incapacitated.
32 TNA, E351/543, fols 163r–v.
33 TNA, LR7/137.
34 Cole, 'State Apartment', 8–10; Barroll, *Anna of Denmark*, 38–39; Croft, 'Robert Cecil and the Early Jacobean Court', 136–137. See also Colvin, *King's Works*, 175, 144, 237–239, 278, 321–322.
35 M. Brayshay, 'Royal Post-Horse Routes', *Journal of Historical Geography* 17 (1991): 373–389. These were still James's prime concerns in 1615: Cramsie, *Kingship and Crown Finance*, 144.
36 Croft, 'Robert Cecil and the Early Jacobean Court', 134–135, 138–140; Croft, 'Can a Bureaucrat Be a Favourite?' 83, 85–87. This was a continuation of James's peripatetic style of government in Scotland: Goodare and Lynch, 'James VI: Universal King?' 21–22.
37 *CSPV*, vol. 12, no. 462. For Anna giving audiences see TNA, E351/543, fols 132v,

134r, 134v, 135r, 155r, 175r, 188r, 190v, 191r, 211v, 212r, 212v, 246v, 247r, 247v, 248r, 260r, 260v, 261r, 261v, 262v, 263r; TNA, E351/544, fols 8v, 9r, 9v, 25v, 26r, 28r, 43r, 43v, 57r, 59v, 60r, 91v, 92r; *CSPV*, vol. 10, no. 102: 30 July 1603; *CSPV*, vol. 11, nos. 477, 801: 15 April 1609; 25 February 1610; *CSPV*, vol. 12, nos. 389, 400: 9, 23 December 1611; *CSPV*, vol. 14, nos. 139, 340: 1 January 1616; 1 July 1616; *CSPV*, vol. 15, nos. 183, 525, 535: 28 March 1618; 7, 14 September 1618. See also M. Brayshay, *Land Travel and Communications in Tudor and Stuart England* (Liverpool, 2014), 239–240, 247–249; Cramsie, *Kingship and Crown Finance*, 56; Cole, 'State Apartment', 9–10.
38 TNA, SP14/12, fols 19r–v (9 January 1605); Cramsie, *Kingship and Crown Finance*, 56–57.
39 G. P. V. Akrigg (ed.), *Letters of King James VI and I* (Berkeley, 1984), 234, no. 109: 5 August 1604.
40 Murdoch, *Network North*, 7–8.
41 Cole, 'State Apartment', 25. Knowles further interprets the first 1613 progress as a political move by Anna to showcase her independence in the aftermath of the deaths of Cecil and Prince Henry, see his 'Images of Royalty', 33–42. Anna accompanied James on six of his summer progresses and joined him for parts of a further four. For the route taken on the 1613 progress see TNA, E351/544, fols 8v, 9r.
42 M. Pilkinton (ed.), *Records of Early English Drama: Bristol* (Toronto, 1997), 177.
43 *CSPV*, vol. 13, no. 70: 2 September 1613; Cole, 'State Apartment', 26.
44 Quote from TNA, E351/544, fol. 9r; J. Stokes (ed.), *Records of Early English Drama: Somerset*, 2 vols (Toronto, 1996), 1: 21–24, 371–377; Pilkinton (ed.), *Records*, xliii–xliv, 173–194, 200, 202–204; Cole, 'State Apartment', 25–26.
45 TNA, E351/544, fol. 11r.
46 TNA, SP14/12, fols 19r–v: 9 January 1605.
47 Thurley, *Somerset House*, 31.
48 Fisher, 'Queenes Courte', 316–317. For a discussion of the patronage model used here see Chapter 1.
49 On the economic difficulties of late sixteenth-century Scotland see, for example, J. Goodare, 'James VI's English Subsidy', in J. Goodare and M. Lynch (eds), *The Reign of James VI* (East Linton, 2000), 110–126; Goodare and Lynch, 'James VI: Universal King?' 10, 15–16, 22–23; Riis, *Auld Acquaintance*, 1: 265–266; Juhala, 'Household and Court', 63.
50 J. Dunbar, *Scottish Royal Palaces: The Architecture of the Royal Residences during the Late Medieval and Early Renaissance Periods* (East Linton, 1999), 93; D. Howard, *Scottish Architecture: Reformation to Restoration, 1560–1660* (Edinburgh, 1995), 26.
51 *CSP Scotland*, vol. 10, 174–186. For a considered discussion of the some of the motivating reasons for, and the results of, James's journey set within a wider consideration of the king as politician and diplomat, see C. Fry, 'Diplomacy & Deception: King James VI of Scotland's Foreign Relations with Europe (c.1584–1603)' (Unpub. PhD diss., University of St Andrews, 2014), ch. 2: 56–79.
52 See, in particular, K. Ottenheym and K. De Jonge (eds), *The Low Countries at the Crossroads: Netherlandish Architecture as an Export Product in Early Modern Europe (1480–1680)* (Turnhout, 2013); K. De Jonge and K. Ottenheym (eds), *Unity and Discontinuity: Architectural Relations between the Southern and Northern Low Countries 1530–1700* (Turnhout, 2007); B. Noldus, *Trade in Good Taste: Relations in Architecture and Culture Between the Dutch Republic and the Baltic World in the Seventeenth Century* (Turnhout, 2004); Andersen et al. (eds), *Reframing the Danish Renaissance: Problems and Prospects in a European Perspective* (Copenhagen, 2011). See also those articles in the special 2003 edition of *Scandinavian Journal of History* (vol. 28).
53 K. De Jonge, 'A Netherlandish Model?' in M. Andersen et al. (eds), *Reframing the Danish Renaissance* (Copenhagen, 2011), 219–233: 219, 222–224.

54 Howard, *Scottish Architecture*, 26–27; Juhala, 'Household and Court', 137.
55 A. MacKechnie, 'James VI's Architects and Their Architecture', in J. Goodare and M. Lynch (eds), *The Reign of James VI* (East Linton, 2000), 154–169: 162; Howard, *Scottish Architecture*, 26.
56 Heiberg, *Christian IV and Europe*, 463–468; Christianson, 'Terrestrial and Celestial Spaces', 142; Ørum-Larsen, 'Uraniborg', 99; Howard, *Scottish Architecture*, 26–28.
57 Howard, *Scottish Architecture*, 28–29; Juhala, 'Household and Court', 88, 92.
58 *CSPV*, vol. 14, no. 484: October 1616. Barroll even refers to Denmark House as Anna's 'own winter palace': *Anna of Denmark*, 39.
59 Colvin, *King's Works*, 255–259; Thurley, *Somerset House*, 33–36.
60 Colvin, *King's Works*, 255.
61 TNA, E351/544, fols 25v, 26v.
62 Only one set is mentioned in the works accounts for the Jacobean period, and a new (probably second) set of state rooms were built between 1636 and 1639: Thurley, *Somerset House*, 55–56.
63 TNA, E351/543, fols 154v, 155r, 247r, 260v, 262v; TNA, E351/544, fol. 26r.
64 TNA, E351/543, fols 110v; 111r, 111v, 132r, 132v, 133r, 133v, 134r, 135r, 153v, 154r, 155r, 155v, 173v, 175r, 188r, 189r, 190r, 192r, 210v, 211r, 211v, 246v, 247r, 247v, 260r, 260v, 261r, 262v; TNA, E351/544, fols 8r, 9r, 10r, 10v, 25v, 26r, 26v, 27v, 28r, 43v, 44r, 57r, 59r, 59v, 60r, 78v, 79r, 91r, 91v, 99v.
65 McClure, *Chamberlain*, vol. 1, 507, no. 192; Birch, *Court and Times*, vol. 1, 340. That James would change the title of the palace was subject to rumour some months prior, with Fenton writing to Mar 'that on the 12 daye [of Christmas] the King shalbe at the Queins houss and geve it sume uther name, and at that tyme Rosborow [Roxburghe] and Jeane Drummond shall be maried': Paton (ed.), *Supplementary Report*, 56: 19 November 1613.
66 McClure, *Chamberlain*, vol. 2, 60, no. 260 (to Carleton); Colvin, *King's Works*, 260.
67 TNA, E351/3252.
68 Barroll, *Anna of Denmark*, 39; Knowles, 'Images of Royalty', 23; Thurley, *Somerset House*, 36.
69 Birch, *Court and Times*, vol. 1, 340: 29 July 1614 (Thomas Lorkin to Thomas Puckering).
70 M. Roberts, *Gustavus Adolphus: A History of Sweden, 1611–1632*, 2 vols (London, 1958), vol. 1, 87–88. On the competitive nature of Swedish–Danish relations in the period, see 38–47, 60–72; P. D. Lockhart, *Denmark, 1513–1660: The Rise and Decline of a Renaissance Monarchy* (Oxford, 2000), 149–158.
71 P. D. Lockhart, *Sweden in the Seventeenth Century* (New York, 2004), 41–44; A. Grosjean, *An Unofficial Alliance: Scotland and Sweden, 1569–1654* (Leiden and Boston, 2003), 42–43. On the intricacies of Russo-Swedish relations during the Ingrian war, see Roberts, *Gustavus Adolphus*, 72–91; S. Lundkvist, 'The Experience of Empire', in M. Roberts (ed.), *Sweden's Age of Greatness, 1632–1718* (London, 1973), 20–57: esp. 21, 30–31.
72 Heiberg, *Christian IV and Europe*, 59.
73 *CSPV*, vol. 15, no. 658: 19 December 1618 (relation of England of Foscarini); *CSPV*, vol. 14, no. 170: 5 February 1616.
74 *CSPV*, vol. 14, no. 665: 2 March 1617.
75 Lockhart, *Sweden*, 38, 41–43; Roberts, *Gustavus Adolphus*, 82–83, 88–91.
76 J. Skovgaard, *A King's Architecture: Christian IV and his Buildings* (London, 1973), 128–129. It has long been thought that Christian took inspiration from Anna's layout at Somerset House during his 1614 stay, but the configuration had already been determined at Frederiksborg by this point. See, most recently, P. Kragelund, *A Stage for the King: The Travels of Christian IV and the Building of Frederiksborg Castle* (Copenhagen, 2019), 118–120.
77 Kragelund, *Stage for the King*, 153–157, fig. 7.28.

78 There was no English royal precedent for symmetrical compartmentalised gardens, although Robert Cecil had one laid out at Hatfield with crushed-brick paths, see P. Henderson, 'A Shared Passion: The Cecils and their Gardens', in P. Croft (ed.), *Patronage, Culture and Power: The Early Cecils* (New Haven and London, 2002), 99–120: 111, 113–114. It is also possible that the 'impressive formal gardens' planted by Thomas Cecil at Wimbledon – perhaps inspired by his travels through France – were also of this style: C. Knight, 'The Cecils at Wimbledon', in P. Croft (ed.), *Patronage, Culture and Power* (New Haven and London, 2002), 47–66: 54, 56.
79 TNA, E351/3243; Colvin, *King's Works*, 255.
80 TNA, E351/3248; R. Strong, *The Artist and the Garden* (New Haven, 2000), 14, 35–36; Ørum-Larsen, 'Uraniborg', 99–100, 104.
81 Henderson, *Tudor House and Garden*, 100; Henderson, 'A Shared Passion', 111.
82 TNA, E351/3245; Henderson, *Tudor House and Garden*, 146, although Henderson misquotes Strong in her assertion that it was 'designed by Salomon de Caus'. Henderson attributes the first orangery in England to William Cecil, see her 'A Shared Passion', 99. Conversely, Strong accords the honour to Sir Francis Carew: 'Sir Francis Carew's Garden', in E. Chaney and P. Mack (eds), *England and the Continental Renaissance* (Woodbridge, 1990), 229–238: 234–235. See also, V. Black, 'Beddington – "the best Orangery in England"', *Journal of Garden History* 3 (1983), 113–120.
83 TNA, E351/3245. Renche was paid 34*s*.8*d*. for his labour.
84 J. Francis, '"A ffitt place for any Gentleman"? Gardens, Gardeners and Gardening in England and Wales, *c*.1560–1660' (unpub. PhD diss., University of Birmingham, 2011), 142–143, 145–147; L. L. Peck, *Consuming Splendor: Society and Culture in Seventeenth-Century England* (Cambridge, 2005), 225–228.
85 *CSPV*, vol. 15, no. 287: 21 March 1618.
86 Francis, 'Gardens', 98–99, 174–176. Notably, in 1611 Cecil had John Tradescant the Elder, his gardener, import fruit trees and flowers from France and Holland for his garden at Hatfield.
87 R. T. Gunther, *Early British Botanists and their Gardens* (Oxford, 1922), 328–329; Peck, *Consuming Splendor*, 225–226.
88 BL Lansdowne MS 164, fols 10r, 48r.
89 TNA, E403/2731, fol. 58v.
90 For a reading that favours Anna as De Caus's first patron see Strong, *Renaissance Garden*, 87–110; and for Henry, see L. Morgan, *Nature as Model: Salomon De Caus and Early Seventeenth-Century Landscape Design* (Philadelphia, 2007), 99–123. They agree that by November 1611 De Caus was also working for Cecil at Hatfield House. Neither scholar recognises that Henry granted De Caus an annual pension of £50 that the exchequer continued to pay after his death: BL Lansdowne MS 164, fols 188r, 190r, 224v, 237v.
91 Strong, *Renaissance Garden*, 87; BL Add MS 24705, fol. 24v.
92 TNA, E351/3246. This is also the problem with De Caus's work at Richmond for Prince Henry.
93 TNA, E351/3245.
94 TNA, E351/3246; Strong, *Renaissance Garden*, 90; Morgan, *Nature as Model*, 112.
95 BL Lansdowne MS 164, fols 447r–v, see also fols 48r, 50r, 110r, for payments to De Caus.
96 BL Lansdowne MS 164, fols 126r, 144r, 146r.
97 BL Lansdowne MS 164, fol. 451v, dated 'Termino Pasche A° xiii°' and 'Tertio Michas Anno xiii°'. These payments were in addition to his pension cited above.
98 Thurley, *Somerset House*, 36, 41. On the layout and function of the rooms in the state apartments during James's reign see Cole, 'State Apartment', 103–114;

S. Thurley, *Royal Palaces of Tudor England: Architecture and Court Life* (New Haven, 1993), 113–143; H. M. Baillie, 'Etiquette and the Planning of the State Apartments in Baroque Palaces', *Archaeologia* 101 (1967): 169–199: 172–181; R. O. Bucholz, 'Going to Court in 1700: A Visitor's Guide', *The Court Historian* 5 (2000): 198–211.
99 M. Girouard, 'The Smythson Collection of the Royal Institute of British Architects', *Architectural History* 5 (1962), 21–184: 33, 75, no. 1/13.
100 Strong, *Renaissance Garden*, 97; Henderson, *Tudor House and Garden*, 101, 103; Morgan, *Nature as Model*, 115–119.
101 Quoted in Strong, *Renaissance Garden*, 90–91. De Caus later published a design – in *Les Raisons des forces Mouvantes* (Frankfurt, 1615) – for a Parnassus that is almost identical to that described by Neumayr.
102 Morgan, *Nature as Model*, 120–121. For an examination of the role and place that mechanical and magical effects held in the contemporary literary world see the essays in W. B. Hyman (ed.), *The Automaton in English Renaissance Literature* (Farnham, 2011).
103 Morgan, *Nature as Model*, 120.
104 C. Lazzaro, 'The Villa Lante at Bagnaia: An Allegory of Art and Nature', *Art Bulletin* 59 (1977): 555; C. Lazzaro, *The Italian Renaissance Garden* (New Haven and London, 1990), 132–134, 266–269.
105 Parrott, 'Celestial Expression', 71, 74; Christianson, 'Terrestrial and Celestial Spaces', 139, 142. Anna visited Hven at least once with James in 1590: Ørum-Larsen 'Uraniborg', 104.
106 P. Grinder-Hansen, *Frederik 2: Danmarks Renæssancekonge* (Copenhagen, 2013), 247–250; Christianson, 'Terrestrial and Celestial Spaces', 139, fig. 5.
107 Colvin, *King's Works*, 107.
108 BL, RP 9392 (November 1609); TNA, E351/3248; TNA, E351/3249; TNA, E351/3250; TNA, E351/3253; Colvin, *King's Works*, 107, 110.
109 TNA, E351/3242; TNA, E351/3243; TNA, E351/3244; TNA, E351/3246; Colvin, *King's Works*, 113, 115–116. Work commenced in 1606/7 and the specific wording of the taskwork underscores Anna's directorial role with bills for material itemised as 'for the quenes birdcage'.
110 Henderson, *Tudor House and Garden*, 149; Henderson, 'Architecture of the Tudor Garden', 57, 68, 70; Parrott, 'Celestial Expression', 74; Lazzaro, *Italian Renaissance Garden*, 13, 251–252; J. Dent, *The Quest for Nonsuch*, 2nd edn. (Sutton, 1981), 60; Strong 'Sir Francis Carew's Garden', 237–238.
111 As quoted in Strong, *Renaissance Garden*, 96.
112 De Caus is absent from the works accounts since he, like Jones, kept his own books of expenses, which have unfortunately not survived: TNA, E403/2732, fol. 181v.
113 TNA, E351/3243.
114 TNA, E403/2732, fol. 126r.
115 Morgan and Strong state that the structure Neumayr describes was the work of De Caus, but they fail to link it to the aviary in the works accounts. Morgan acknowledges that 'a "Birdhouse and fountain" are singled out' in the 1611/12 accounts but adds that 'exactly what these consisted of is not indicated', thereby brushing over the extensive information preserved in the individual taskwork in TNA, E351/3246, see Morgan, *Nature as Model*, 99, 113, 115; Strong, *Renaissance Garden*, 95–97, fig. 50.
116 Strong, *Renaissance Garden*, 97–102; Henderson, *Tudor House and Garden*, 103–107.
117 B. Franke, 'Salomon de Caus', in W. Thomas and L. Duerloo (eds), *Albert and Isabella: Essays* (Turnhout, 1998), 202–204; W. Metzer 'The Perspective of the Prince', in S. Smart and M. R. Wade (eds), *The Palatine Wedding of 1613* (Wiesbaden, 2013), 567–596: 572–573, 585, 587–590. Interestingly, as part of the

1613 welcome celebrations for Friedrich and Elizabeth into Heidelberg, a Mount Parnassus complete with Apollo and the muses, was built.
118 Metzer, 'Perspective of the Prince', 579–580.
119 K. Hearn, 'A Question of Judgement: Lucy Harington, Countess of Bedford, as Art Patron and Collector', in E. Chaney (ed.), *The Evolution of English Collecting* (New Haven and London, 2003), 221–239: 223, 224; Henderson, *Tudor House and Garden*, 149.
120 Colvin, *King's Works*, 113–114.
121 TNA, E351/3249 (1614–1615); TNA, E351/3250 (1615–1616); Colvin, *King's Works*, 113.
122 TNA, SC6/JASI/1653. A further £600 was disbursed for reparations at Byfleet (Surrey), which Anna must have been granted sometime before September 1615, as it first appears in her Receiver General's accounts for that year: TNA, SC6/JASI/1651.
123 Skovgaard, *A King's Architecture*, 15; Ørum-Larsen, 'Uraniborg', 97, 99; Christianson, 'Terrestrial and Celestial Spaces', 141–145.
124 Skovgaard, *A King's Architecture*, 17–20; Heiberg, *Christian IV and Europe*, 465–466; Grinder-Hansen, *Frederik 2*, 251–257.
125 De Jonge, 'A Netherlandish Model?' 222.
126 K. Ottenheym, 'Introduction', in K. De Jonge and K. Ottenheym (eds), *Unity and Discontinuity* (Turnhout, 2007), 1–15: 1–2; K. Ottenheym and K. De Jonge, 'The Architecture of the Low Countries', in K. Ottenheym and K. De Jonge (eds), *The Low Countries at the Crossroads* (Turnhout, 2013), 15–30: 20–27. This finds interesting parallel with the arguments put forward by Bjarke Moe for the diffusion, reception, and adaptation of 'Italian' music and musicians in northern Europe – particularly Denmark – which is discussed in the next chapter of this book. See his 'Italian Music at the Danish Court during the Reign of Christian IV: Presenting a Picture of Cultural Transformation', *Danish Yearbook of Musicology* 38 (2010/11), 15–32: 22–32.
127 J. R. Christianson, 'The Spaces and Rituals of the Royal Hunt', in B. B. Johannsen and K. Ottenheym (eds), *Beyond Scylla and Charybdis: European Courts and Court Residences outside Habsburg and Valois/Bourbon Territories 1500–1700* (Odense, 2015), 159–171: 160–165.
128 P. Grinder-Hansen, '"Im Grünen": The Types of Informal Space and their use in Private, Political and Diplomatic Activities of Frederik II, King of Denmark', in B. B. Johannsen and K. Ottenheym (eds), *Beyond Scylla and Charybdis* (Odense, 2015), 171–183: 179–180.
129 Christianson, 'Spaces and Rituals', 162–163; J. R. Christianson, 'The Hunt of King Frederik II', *The Court Historian* 18 (2013), 165–187: 168, 174.
130 Christianson, 'Spaces and Rituals', 166.
131 Grinder-Hansen, 'Types of Informal Space', 174–175.
132 Grinder-Hansen, 'Types of Informal Space', 177; Grinder-Hansen, *Frederik 2*, 259–260.
133 The term 'all'antica' is taken from Ottenheym and De Jonge, *Low Countries at the Crossroads*.
134 Grinder-Hansen, 'Types of Informal Space', 177–178. On the origins of this 'generically "Netherlandish"' style, see De Jonge, 'A Netherlandish Model?' 219–233, esp. 219–222, 224.
135 Ottenheym, 'Introduction' in *Unity and Discontinuity*, 2. See also T. DaCosta Kaufmann's assertion that 'when we find works that seem to resemble the classicism of Versailles, we may actually be encountering the traces of Netherlanders and their pupils', and while he highlights France in this instance, the same point can be made for Italy: quotation from *Court, Cloister, and City: The Art and Culture of Central Europe 1450–1800* (Chicago, 1995), 280.

136 K. De Jonge, 'Antiquity Assimilated', in K. De Jonge and K. Ottenheym (eds), *Unity and Discontinuity* (Turnhout, 2007), 55–78: 69–70; Grinder-Hansen, 'Types of Informal Space', 178; De Jonge, 'A Netherlandish Model?' 224. Not incidentally, De Caus had first-hand knowledge of Mariemont, having worked there during his decade at the Brussels court (1600–1610): Morgan, *Nature as Model*, ch. 3.
137 TNA, AO1/2487/356. A transcription of the account is in G. H. Chettle, *The Queen's House, Greenwich* (London, 1937), 97–103.
138 Wade, 'Duke Ulrik', 249–250.
139 As quoted in S. Carney, 'The Queen's House at Greenwich: The Material Cultures of the Courts of Queen Anna of Denmark and Queen Henrietta Maria, 1603–69' (unpub. PhD thesis, University of Roehampton, 2013), 99, citing TNA, SC6/JASI/1655. Unfortunately, the manuscript is now missing, and I have been unable to check this reference.
140 Cramsie, *Kingship and Crown Finance*, 145–150. Expenditure in the 1615/16 accounts remained consistently high at £11,619.14s.2d., and a significant proportion of that was spent on Anna's properties. Greenwich was second only to Newmarket, and the principal cost was a new building extending from Anna's lodgings into the garden: TNA, E351/3250; Colvin, *King's Works*, 113–114.
141 TNA, SP14/86, fols 173r–v (24 March 1616); TNA, SP14/86, fols 175r–v (March 1616); Cramsie, *Kingship and Crown Finance*, 143.
142 TNA, E351/3389 (1616–1618).
143 Colvin, *King's Works*, 114–115; Harris and Higgott, *Inigo Jones*, 64–71; Higgott, 'Design and Setting', 141–143, 145–146.
144 Higgott, 'Design and Setting', 136–138, 143–145. See also Henderson, *Tudor House and Garden*, 174–177.
145 Thurley, 'Architecture and Diplomacy', 125–128; Higgott, 'Design and Setting', 137–138.
146 TNA, E351/3389; Colvin, *King's Works*, 114–115.
147 Colvin, *King's Works*, 330.
148 The facing stone used on the Banqueting House included Oxfordshire, Purbeck, Portland, and Northamptonshire, see TNA, E351/3391; Colvin, *King's Works*, 329, 330. Elements of classicism in England date back to the 1540s, but the Banqueting House was set apart by the clarity of the classical language, and the function and location of the building. The classical Strand facade of Somerset House evidently preceded this, although Girouard points out that it barely covered the traditional frontage, see Girouard, *Elizabethan Architecture*, 142–160.
149 TNA, AO1/2485/344, fol. 1r.
150 Henderson, *Tudor House and Garden*, 108; Henderson, 'A Shared Passion', 107, 111. Cecil's vineyard at Hatfield comprised more than 30,500 vines imported from France: Gunther, *Early British Botanists*, 328.
151 Henderson, *Tudor House and Garden*, 73. The poor state of English wine was bemoaned by William Harrison in 1587: G. Edelen (ed.), *Description of England: The Classic Contemporary Account of Tudor Social Life* (Washington and New York, 1994), 435. Frederick, Duke of Württemberg, was to later observe the absence of English wine production in 1592, see W. B. Rye, *England as Seen by Foreigners in the Days of Elizabeth and James the First* (London, 1865), 52.
152 Colvin, *King's Works*, 213.
153 Henderson, *Tudor House and Garden*, 65; Henderson, 'Architecture of the Tudor Garden', 57.
154 TNA, E351/3389.
155 Harris and Higgott, *Inigo Jones*, 76, 78, cat. no. 17.
156 Riis, *Auld Acquaintance*, vol. 1, 271; G. P. McNeill (ed.), *The Exchequer Rolls of Scotland: Rotuli Scaccarii Regum Scotorum* (Edinburgh, 1908), vol. 23, nos. 12, 16, 21, 60.

157 Maitland had bought Musselburgh from Dunfermline in July 1587: Riis, *Auld Acquaintance*, vol. 1, 273, n.44.
158 Riis, *Auld Acquaintance*, vol. 1, 273–274.
159 TNA, SP 52/48, fol. 8r. (28 January 1592).
160 TNA, SP 52/50, fol. 51v. (7 April 1593). Anna's rift with Maitland is well described by Barroll, although he attributes it to the Chancellor having held her 'queenship in light regard': *Anna of Denmark*, 17–20.
161 Maitland's legal rights were evident in the charter, however, for it specified that Musselburgh was to return to a hereditary fief of Maitland and his wife on the death of the queen: Riis, *Auld Acquaintance*, vol. 1, 274.
162 Dent, *Quest for Nonsuch*, 185.
163 Dent, *Quest for Nonsuch*, 184–185; M. S. Giuseppi (ed.), *Calendar of the Manuscripts of the Most Hon. the Marquis of Salisbury* (London, 1938), vol. 17, 433, nos. 830, 831.
164 TNA, SP14/75, fol. 80 (December 1613); *CSPD* (1611–1618), 216; Peck, *Northampton*, 73–74.
165 Chamberlain wrote to Carleton, on 25 November 1613, that Anna had received Greenwich into her jointure, and Foscarini reported to the Doge and Senate, on 4 January 1614, that 'the king has given to the queen the palace of Greenwich.' The palace and lands were confirmed by letters patent dated 18 February 1614, but the change in ownership was knowledge at court well in advance: McClure (ed.), *Chamberlain*, vol. 1, 487, no. 185; *CSPV*, vol. 13, no. 166; for the letters patent see TNA, C66/1990 (nos. 4, 7, 8).
166 TNA, SP14/75, fols 70, 78; Peck, *Northampton*, 74.
167 TNA, SP14/141, fol. 161; Peck, *Northampton*, 74.
168 This is discussed in greater detail in Chapter 5, but for a substantial period Greenwich was the favoured palace of both Henry VII and Henry VIII, and it was also notable as the birthing location of Henry VIII, Elizabeth I, and Mary I.

3

Collecting and display

In April 1619, Lady Anne Clifford (1590–1676) travelled to Denmark House to pay her respects to the recently deceased Stuart queen. Later recalling in her diary that she had dutifully 'sat a good while there by the Queen's corpse', she added that she 'then went into the privy galleries and showed my cousin Mary those fine delicate things there'.[1] Although Clifford is regrettably circumspect in her description, her actions and comments are importantly suggestive of Anna of Denmark's reputation as a collector who piqued the interest of her contemporaries.[2] The statement is not indicative of the insignificant nature of Anna's acquisitions, for even Clifford's account of visiting Arundel House in 1616 is taciturn as she merely notes having seen 'all the pictures in the gallery & the statues in the lower rooms'.[3] Other pieces of contemporary evidence – letters, reports, and accounts – likewise yield little specific information in regard to the contents and reception of Anna's palace interiors, which, as discussed in detail below, is characteristic of Jacobean collecting more generally. Yet the means and manner of Anna's collecting are particularly poorly evidenced and have contributed to her omission from the literature.

What does survive are inventories of two of Anna's main properties in England – Denmark House and Oatlands Manor – dating to the time of her occupancy. From these documents, coupled with entries found among the accounts of the pipe office, the queen's receiver-general, and the exchequer, and commentary contained within ambassadorial dispatches, a firm image emerges of a consort who took a directorial role in the layout and furnishings of her main residences; who was central to Stuart diplomatic relations and ceremonial; and who was cognisant of the power and meaning that could be attached to palace rooms through the use of spatial protocols and material culture.[4] It is this image of the queen that takes centre stage in this chapter, nuancing the male-dominated history of collecting and display at the early Stuart court and the traditional scholarly use of the Italianate as the benchmark of cultural erudition.[5] This body of scholarship, including the work of Edward Chaney, David Howarth, and Timothy Wilks, has focused on the activities and interests of the Stuart princes – Henry, and then Charles (1600–1649) – together with a select group of elites, who are celebrated for bringing England into dialogue with the Continent as they amassed collections to rival those of the European courts and changed the fabric of aristocratic identity in the process.[6] While there is much value in this argument, it often takes the further, exclusive view that the acquisition of classicising Italian artworks and artefacts equated to the exceptional and connoisseurial, while other European markets, skills, and traditions have been disregarded as being of considerably lesser value and significance. This narrowly subjective view is complicated in what follows, for Anna's palaces were largely filled with Flemish and Dutch artworks which, far from being a sign of her disinterest or naïveté, were a tool for building affinity with her Danish ancestors and siblings while highlighting the continued currency of artistic centres outside of Italy.

Paintings are treated here as an important means of visualising networks, tastes, and alliances, but they are integrated within a broader, and more expensive, programme of visual and material display that encompassed objects, musical instruments, furniture, and textiles. In turn, these goods are approached as a constituent factor – in combination with palace layout, access protocol, and the physical presence and movement of the royal body – in visualising a range of specific meanings including power, status, honour, and affection. The following discussions of Anna's use and decoration of her palace rooms therefore locate the queen within wider scholarship on the structural, material, and spatial topographies of the early modern court.[7] In the same manner as preceding and subsequent chapters, contextualisation for Anna's undertakings and interests is sought in the Danish court of her father and comparative material is drawn from the activities of her siblings. New evidence is thereby added to our understanding of the precedents that influenced Anna, of the use of cultural activities to celebrate family and lineage, and of the complex processes and patterns of exchange that connected the Oldenburg natal network. Due to the nature of the extant documentary evidence, this chapter is heavily focused on Anna's English residences. To my knowledge, no inventory of any of the royal Scottish palaces pertaining to Anna's period of residence (or even her lifetime) survives, and orders or purchases of interior goods rarely, if ever, feature in the extant records of the exchequer, office of works, or the treasury.[8] It is probable that merchants kept their own order books that have not survived, for this was certainly the case with fabric suppliers as discussed in Chapter 4. While efforts have been made to include information on Scotland where possible in this chapter, it is regrettably slight, and it is hoped that more textual evidence will be uncovered in the future to remedy this imbalance.

The refurbishment of Denmark House

In the early years of the Stuarts in England, Denmark House continued to function – as it had done under Queen Elizabeth – as accommodation for state visitors.[9] But in 1609, as evidenced in Chapter 2, an extensive programme of reconstruction began as the privy apartments and the Privy Gallery were remodelled, a new arched three-storey gallery was built to connect them and to open onto the garden, the upper court was rebuilt, the Cross Gallery was added, and the classicising Strand frontage was restored.[10] The building work followed Elizabethan modes of palace planning but, as Howard Colvin first observed, innovation was a hallmark of the interior, where a greater level of decoration, and a more liberal use of ornate materials was deployed than in any previous Stuart building project.[11] As the works accounts demonstrate, over the course of the renovations, Denmark House received large quantities of ornamental panelling, eleven fretwork ceilings, decorative chimney-pieces, and elaborate plaster- and wood-work, much of which was painted and gilded. Expensive stonework was carried out using liberal amounts of black 'dornix' (small stone) and red Rance (variegated 'marble') imported from the Wallonia region, white and black marble, alabaster from Derbyshire, and black or dark grey 'touch-stone' (hard stone) that was quarried in Sussex, which provided an elaborate, avant-garde confluence of colours, materials, and textures.[12]

There may have been no Stuart precedent for such opulent refurbishing in England, but some of the palaces that the Stuarts inherited – particularly Nonsuch and Greenwich – were highly ornate. The Henrician palace of Nonsuch, as is now well known, was finished with an incomparably high level of decoration and a complex iconographical programme.[13] Drawing on François I's (1494–1547) gallery at Fontainebleau, the external walls of Nonsuch were covered in sculptured plaster-stucco panels, carved and gilded pieces of slate, and possibly painted work as well to create 'statues pictures and other Antik formes of excellent art and workmanshipp and of noe small cost'.[14] Ornate stucco panels were also seen at Greenwich where, in 1583, Queen Elizabeth paid more than £2,800 to remodel the exterior in one of the few renovations she undertook.[15] The appearance of these two residences may well have encouraged Anna's later approach at Denmark House, but she certainly left Denmark-Norway with a personal knowledge and experience of the material and ceremonial splendour appropriate for European royalty. A central part of her father's programme of conspicuous consumption had centred on building with attention given to the architectural edifice, the interior layout, and the furnishings. Frederik's extension and refurbishment of Kronborg Castle, undertaken throughout Anna's teenage years, insisted on an elaborately decorative scheme. Ornamentation in wood, stone, and stucco was widely disbursed throughout the castle, ranging from simple star-studded ceilings to complex arrangements featuring foliage, fruits, animals, birds, and angels, while the carved initials of Frederik II's motto adorned the staircase portal into the eastern octagonal corner tower, or *Kackelborg*.[16] Many of the window sills, jambs, and mullions featured the carved heads of lions and women, fantastical beasts, and shaped designs of volutes, squares, and curvilinear forms.[17] The coffered ceiling of the new great hall in the south wing was entirely painted and gilded, and its ornately carved sections were punctuated with 900 turned roses.[18] Scanian sandstone tablets were chosen to complete the watching gallery in the south wing, featuring carved profile heads, serpents, anchors, acanthus leaves, and the conjoined cipher of the royal Oldenburg couple, 'FS', clasped in a hand and extending from a cloud; several of which are extant. The crowned cipher, set on a shield or a heart, was also chosen for decorating stone fireplaces and featured above doorways and windows throughout the inner courtyard (Figures 3.1 and 3.2).[19]

A comparable decorative programme governed Anna's refurbishment of Denmark House, where elaborate ceilings of fretwork or plasterwork were installed in the attiring, presence, withdrawing, privy, and cabinet chambers, and the bedchamber, library, and privy gallery, where the

3.1 'FS' stonework cipher in the inner courtyard of Kronborg Castle, Helsingør, 1584.

3.2 'FS' stonework cipher on a fireplace in the north wing of Kronborg Castle, Helsingør, 1584.

latter featured painted roses, marigolds, mask-heads, and both round and square pendants (Figure 3.3).[20] A telling indication of the widespread use of such ornamentation throughout the palace is found in the accounts for 1611/12, when the plasterer James Leigh was paid for stopping and white-washing 1,312 yards of fretwork.[21] In addition, costly chimneypieces – in combinations of alabaster, white marble, black touch, and red variegated limestone from Rance – were installed in the Great Gallery, Cross Gallery, and the privy chamber. Those in the bedchamber, library, and the cabinet, attiring, and closet chambers were further enriched with 'fine gold' and 'fine bice lacke & other riche cullours' at the hands of the serjeant-painter, John de Critz the Elder (d.1642).[22] In general, the works accounts for Denmark House are redolent with entries for wainscoting, fretwork, tafferels, friezes, painting and gilding, and for vaguer payments to masons for 'other enrichements of carveinge woorke' and to the carver Maximillian Colt (d. after 1641) for 'overseeinge and directing the carvers' of wood and stonework that was carried 'about chaires doors and chymneys'.[23] The palace was also richly furnished, with a combination of pieces being requisitioned from the standing wardrobes and newly ordered to suit the transformation of the palace into the main London residence of the queen consort.

The remodelling of Denmark House, as already mentioned, cost just over £34,500, and Simon Thurley estimates the furnishings to have cost

3.3 Plaster mask from Denmark House, which has traces of gilding and red paint from the early seventeenth century.

an additional £10,000.[24] It may have been considerably more, for there is little known documentary evidence of the acquisition of interior goods and by the time Denmark House was inventoried in 1619, many of the rooms had been cleared for the queen's corpse to be laid out in state.[25] That it was one of the queen's jointure properties did not have any bearing on the centralised system of Stuart finance, for the majority of expenditure on royal properties (exterior and interior) went through the exchequer. While not involved in purchasing goods for her palaces, references to Anna's directorial role do survive, such as the warrant issued in September 1612 'for altertons of divers of her Ma[jes]t[ie]s lodgeings at Oatelandes which by her Ma[jes]t[ie]s Comaunde were altered and furnished againe'.[26] Although the records of Anna's palace interiors are incomplete, the textual information that survives of Denmark House and Oatlands Manor is enough to build an understanding of the layout and function of key rooms under the Stuart queen; to evidence her ritualised use of space; and her intentional use of textiles, paintings, and objects to make her dynastic and factional identity visually and materially manifest.

The politics of space, furnishings, and behaviour

Research into the political significance of the use of space at the early modern court has shown how the location and decoration of individual rooms were determined by ceremonial function, and that access was governed by strict rules of rank and honour so that movement between rooms visualised and reinforced social relationships and hierarchies – domestic and international.[27] Leading on from this, and highlighting the importance of furniture and decoration to the performance of diplomacy, Tracey Sowerby argues that rulers varied the rooms they used or modified 'the visual and material culture they contained', to communicate their position vis-à-vis a representative's ruler.[28] This was clearly observed at Denmark House in 1604 when, after the Spanish ambassadorial contingent had been granted their wish to stay at the palace, it was freshly 'decorated with the most gorgeous hangings that belong to the crown' in a move that was expressly 'taken as an indication of good-will towards Spain'.[29] The interrelationship between material furnishings, behavioural protocols, function, and movement of any given environment is also picked up by Lena Cowen Orlin in her research into domestic Tudor spaces, where she argues – to take one example discussed further below – that not only was the long gallery significant in its length and sparsely furnished to allow for walking, but that walking enabled occupants to exchange confidences away from prying eyes and keen ears; in turn, a prime use of the long gallery was privacy.[30] Beyond visual and material culture, the work of Janette Dillon, Malcolm Smuts, and George Gorse has underscored the politicisation of space as a fluid and dynamic construct determined by the occupier's cultural, social, and political needs, as well as by their negotiation of inherited spatial protocol and tradition.[31] The subsequent analyses of Anna's performance of rank and authority, consumption and display, and dynasty and network within her built environments follows an interdisciplinary approach sensitive to this confluence of factors.

Changes in modes of access and etiquette were apparent once the Stuarts relocated to England and spatial, ceremonial, and social Tudor precedents were confronted. As early as 15 May 1603, the Venetian secretary in England, Giovanni Carlo Scaramelli, reported that 'three days ago his Majesty began to live with English attendants in the English style at Theobalds up to that time he had followed his Scottish custom.'[32] He later clarified that this entailed stricter rules of access, although these only applied to the king's English servitors, none of whom, 'be his rank what it may, can enter the Presence Chamber without being summoned, whereas the Scottish Lords have free entree of the privy chamber, and more especially at the toilette, at which time they discuss those proposals which, after dinner are submitted to the Council'.[33] These changes were still topical a month later, at which time Scaramelli opined that James 'of his own accord, would probably hardly have changed his modest habit of life which he pursued in Scotland, where he lived hardly like a private gentleman, let alone a sovereign, making many people sit down with him at table, waited on by rough servants, who did not even remove their hats', but that the English council, cognisant of the need to visualise the rank and 'dignity' of the multiple Stuart monarchy, were 're-introducing the ancient splendours of the English Court' and the king was seen 'day by day' adopting 'the practices suitable to his greatness'. Interestingly, Scaramelli's understanding of Scottish court protocol was that the king and queen followed different principles; while James favoured informality, 'all expenditure and pomp' had to be observed 'for the service of the queen'.[34] William Dundas observed a further connection between Anna's mode of etiquette and Danish culture, reporting shortly after her arrival in Scotland that 'things are beginnand to be greatly altered here; the court wondrus solitary, & ye patron [pattern] of the court of Denmark is greatly before ye king's eye.'[35] This concept of Danish formality is complicated by a puzzling interaction between Anna and her brother, Duke Ulrik of Holstein in England in 1605. Anna, maintaining a high level of reserve, was reportedly outraged by Ulrik's presumption to enter her 'rooms whenever he chose' and ordered that he was 'not to be admitted without being announced' and 'for two months … refused to speak to him'.[36] It is plausible that in the intervening years since their time in Denmark together, Ulrik's travels and experiences in Croatia, France, Hungary, the Low Countries, and Germany had softened his expectations of decorum at the familial level or, more feasibly, that he thought it prudent to extend James's penchant for informality to Anna.[37] Rules and expectations of access at the king and queen's courts were notably distinct, adding another layer to the individualised modes and styles that distinguished these two centres. Looking forward to the subsequent reign of Charles I, it was his mother's preference for reserve and regulation that was followed, and it became a hallmark of both king and court.[38] Charles's insistence on gravitas was immediately apparent. In a matter of days following the succession, Zuane Pesaro, the Venetian ambassador, reported that 'the king observes a rule of great decorum. The nobles do not enter his apartments in confusion as heretofore, but each rank has its appointed place.'[39] Even on the 'great and extraordinary occasion' of the birth of his own son and heir, Prince Charles (1630–1685), the king was noted to be 'as reserved as usual'.[40]

At the Stuart courts, Anna, as queen consort, occupied a central position in ceremonial and diplomacy, and while she often joined James for the first welcoming reception of international guests, the greater part of her role was in giving independent audiences. These were regularly granted to ambassadors at any one of her main palaces – Denmark House, Greenwich Palace, or Oatlands Manor – where the favour and honour of each represented state was exchanged, a suite was put forward and the queen's support requested, or her opinion was sought – especially apropos James's sentiments and actions, and the marriage matches of the Stuart children.[41] In June 1603, a Danish embassy was sent to England to congratulate James on the accession and after 'a private audience of the king', even took the subsequent trouble to travel all the way to Edinburgh for an audience with the queen.[42] In England, Anna regularly entertained ambassadors with James and she hosted receptions alone.[43] Such occasions were carried out in respect of formal diplomatic protocol, and numerous accounts make mention of the queen's material and social gravitas, with Anna 'covered with jewels and strings of pearls' and seated 'under the baldacchino ... attended by a great company of ladies and gentlemen'.[44] More than a figurehead of monarchy, Anna's diplomatic weight and respect was due in large part to the belief among the ambassadorial community that she had the ear of the king. Most emphatically, George Nicholson wrote to Cecil from the Scottish court that 'always the Queen knows all', while later, in April 1606, the Venetian ambassador reported that Spain had begun courting Anna having learnt of her 'great weight with the king'.[45] In 1612, Antonio Foscarini reiterated that 'the king tells her any thing that she chooses to ask, and loves and esteems her.'[46] There was some truth to these suppositions, for although not always successful Anna frequently chose – since her early days in Scotland – to actively petition James on behalf of her clients.[47]

The regulated politics of space, access, and décor, and the importance of visualising rank and precedence at the Stuart court in England are evocatively preserved in Finet's detailed notebooks although, as noted, he only served as assistant to Lewknor throughout the Jacobean period. Finet's entries reveal that favour was demonstrated well before the prime event, with much significance – and anxiety – placed on the route that was chosen, and then being signified in the form of seating provided, the position allocated in the room relative to others, and proximity to the royal person – where touching or kissing was a particular show of favour for the diplomat's represented ruler. Importance was also given to the level of privacy, where ambassadors were regularly concerned to know whether the event was 'for publicke' and therefore seen by other courtiers, or 'for private' and therefore removed from the wider eyes of the court and, hence, more intimate and confidential.[48]

A detailed account of Anna's engagement with the politics of space and display in her preservation of Stuart majesty and honour is evident in her reception of the Venetian ambassador extraordinary, Pietro Contarini, at Oatlands, in September 1618. As mentioned in the introduction, an outline of proceedings was issued to the Italian contingent, one of whom later commented that 'it would have been exceedingly grand and pompous by the instructions given, but on the appointed day a provoking rain fell incessantly.' Nevertheless, due to the great 'display' of 'the chief ladies of title ... and some of the principal noblemen', and with rank and precedence carefully preserved in spatial hierarchies and types of seating, the occasion was still considered by the Venetians to be 'most stately and grave'. The esteem the Stuart monarchy showed for the Republic was consolidated through the use of space and touch when Contarini 'was led by the Lord Chamberlain into the [queen's] presence chamber and was graciously received by her Majesty, who gave him her hand. After he had kissed it respectfully her Majesty gave him her arm, a singular favour.' Having communicated concord and affection between their nations, Anna completed the ceremony with a showcase of Stuart wealth and generosity in a dinner for Contarini's honour. Anna's knowledge of European – specifically Italian – modes of stately hospitality, and her role in bringing European fashions to England was underscored by Contarini's compatriot, who opined that the feast 'was distributed beautifully and profusely ... indeed it would compare as a whole with the most famous banquets of Italy or elsewhere.'[49] Although not commonly described in detail, requisite components for affecting displays of stately grandeur included costly furnishings, objects, and plate as well as the apparel of the royal host. One example of such judgement comes from the earlier Venetian ambassadors, Marc' Antonio Correr and Francesco Contarini, during a dinner hosted by James in 1610. At this time, the king's sartorial display gave cause for delighted comment, for it consisted of 'a [hat] jewel made of five diamonds of extraordinary size, and also a chain of diamonds from which hung the George, that is the Order of the Garter'. But, rather than James's costly and chivalric jewellery, it was 'on account of the great number of silver-gilt vases upon the side-board, piled up to the ceiling, and for a service of flagons holding goblets of precious stone studded with gems', that the ambassadors were able to define the evening as having been noticeably 'royal'.[50] Likewise, the layout and furnishings of the rooms at Oatlands, through which the later Venetian ambassador, Pietro Contarini, and his train were ushered in 1618, showcased the wealth, tastes, and ceremonial custom of the Stuarts. The presence chamber, where the ambassador had been privileged with the queen's arm, was equipped with a suite of state furniture that was likely moved there for the occasion. Consisting of a curtained canopy, a high chair, a footstool, eight high stools, two long cushions, and one square cushion, the set was upholstered in green velvet, trimmed with lace and silk fringes in green and gold, and notably embroidered with the queen's crowned letters AR in gold.[51]

Anna's primary English residences reflected her diplomatic responsibilities, being laid out and furnished as ceremonial reception sites for ambassadors, courtiers, and both domestic and international figures of rank and title. A chamber in the state apartments – generally the withdrawing, privy, or presence chamber – served for matters ceremonial, but the centralised location of the galleries in the queen's palaces, and their proximity to the apartments, meant that they frequently featured in the ceremonial route through the palace.[52] On the other hand, the length of the gallery afforded privacy, as distance could be maintained from other occupants and this made them suitable spaces for the exchange of confidences; both James and Anna are known to have separately used the gallery at Greenwich in this capacity.[53] As a result, their decoration was politically significant; all furnishings and objects were appraised as signs of Stuart wealth, merit, and honour. When Denmark House was inventoried on 19 April 1619, sets of state furniture remained in the two galleries, but the other furnishings had been relegated to the wardrobe.[54] During Anna's lifetime they had been in periodic service in the privy and presence chambers, but when the palace was dressed for the mourning period of the queen, these rooms were appropriately rehung with 'Cloathes of Estates' in black velvet with the impaled arms of multiple Stuart and Oldenburg kingdoms under an imperial crown.[55] Sets of 'sutable' state furniture consisting of two chairs of estate, four high stools, and two footstools – all upholstered in black velvet, and finished with black silk cushions, lace, fringes and tassels – had also been installed.[56]

The inventory of Denmark House provides more information as to the location and the furnishings of the two galleries, indicating that the Cross Gallery was the more intimately social and spatially restricted of the two. It was situated in the eastern reaches of the palace and flanked by ante-rooms on each end, allowing Anna to easily guard access as a sign of favour, and it was filled with goods that would have delighted guests: mirrors, elaborate clocks, Persian carpets, and tables, stools, and cabinets in ebony, marble, crystal, and walnut (Figure 3.4). The ebony tables, cabinets, and mirrors were extremely elaborate, being inlaid with mother-of-pearl and/or garnished with silver, such as a 'rich cabonett of ebony inlaid wth silver white and guilt wth flowers and beasts'.[57] Such items suggest an interesting concurrency of fashion at the Stuart and Oldenburg courts, for Christian IV famously equipped all of his main rooms at Frederiksborg with ebony furniture inlaid with a combination of silver, ivory, and mother-of-pearl.[58]

The Cross Gallery at Denmark House was also primed for receptions

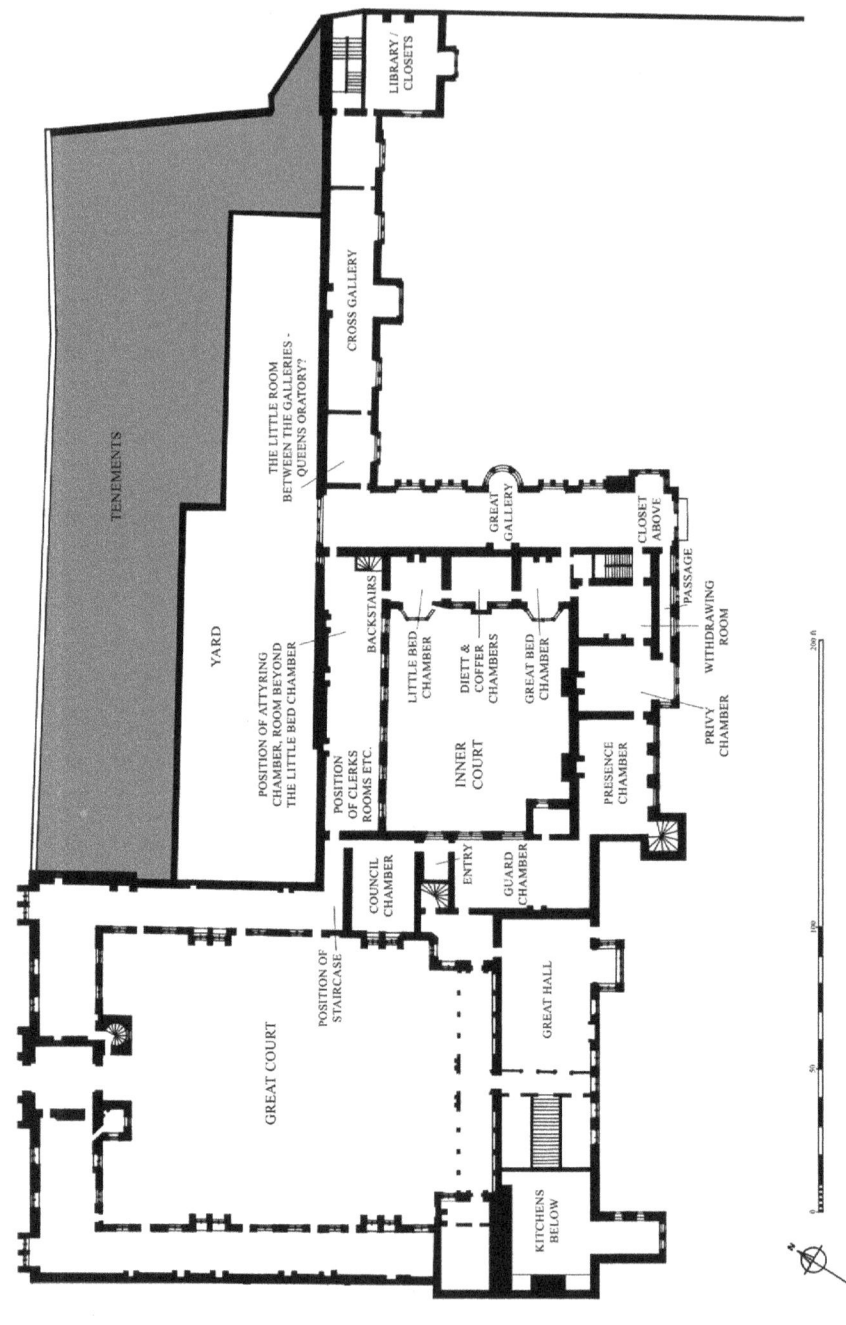

3.4 Plan of the ground floor of Denmark House, c.1620.

with a suite of state furniture – two high chairs (one of which was canopied and curtained), two square stools, two footstools, two square cushions, twelve stools, and twelve long cushions – upholstered in cloth of silver, wrought with green and hair-coloured silk flowers, and trimmed with gold and silver lace.[59] Yet the much richer textiles, of crimson velvet embroidered with gold heraldry, and the much larger set of state furniture in the Great Gallery marked it as an important site of court ceremonial. When the inventory was taken, the only other objects in the Great Gallery were two mirrors, a small painted panel of walnut wood, a billiard board covered with a green cloth, two brass candlesticks, and a pair of andirons – a paucity that has led Thurley and Griffey to conclude it had been emptied for the queen's mourning period.[60] Yet it is likely to have been just as sparsely furnished during Anna's occupancy, for it was not a central space for the mourning and, as Orlin's research shows, the gallery was a 'walking space' defined by its long length, its proximity to the garden, and its 'paucity of goods and furnishings'.[61] The intention of the space, as Orlin elaborates, was to provide intimacy, or 'private exchange', where the householder could walk, sit, and talk beyond the hearing range of others.[62] At Denmark House, the Cross Gallery was a space of contemplation and conversation, while the Great Gallery served a greater ceremonial purpose. Spanning the length of the privy apartments and connected to the state apartments – specifically the privy chamber – by way of a corridor, the Great Gallery occupied a central position in the ceremonial topography of palace and would have been readily traversed by diplomats, envoys, and distinguished guests (Figure 3.4).[63]

Visualising genealogy and faction

Despite the absence of information concerning the acquisition methods of the goods in Anna's residences, enough evidence survives in the inventories to show that she took a central, directorial role in their decorative programmes. With large quantities of visual and material goods bearing the identifying badges of the queen and her natal court, together with a carefully selected suite of portraits, Anna transformed her rooms into highly personalised statements about her genealogical networks and domestic alliances. At Oatlands, care was taken to upholster the rooms used for state occasions – the south gallery, bedchamber, the outer withdrawing (presence) chamber and even the privy chamber and bedchamber on the king's side – with references to the main occupant, Anna of Denmark. Hangings, curtains, carpets, cloths of state, and upholstered pieces of furniture were embroidered with Anna's coat-of-arms, her cipher AR, or her personal Italian motto *La mia grandezza dal eccelso* ('My power is from the most high').[64] This was similarly true of Denmark House, where the queen's coat-of-arms were painted above the fireplace in the bedchamber and where one of the queen's beds even featured a headcloth embroidered with all three identifying badges. As it had been at Kronborg under Frederik II, Anna's most common choice of identifying sign at Denmark House were her letters AR, which appeared on pillows, cushions, mattresses, quilts, pieces of tapestry, blankets, the backs of chairs, and even the frames of mirrors, while the Danish coat-of-arms adorned silver andirons, fire shovels, velvet canopies, comb cases, and cloths of state.[65] The wainscot chimneypiece in the presence chamber was 'fairely carved with the Queenes armes in it and two wilde men on each side', while the Cross Gallery was even furnished with a wooden screen bearing the 'wilde man' of Denmark 'on the topp'.[66]

It is highly likely that some of these goods, branded with Anna's familial origins, were made in Denmark for her bridal trousseau. Entries in the 1619 inventory of Denmark House detailing 'twoe yron chestes called Denmarke Chestes' in the coffer chamber, and 'two Denmark Chestes of Iron' in the pages gallery, further hint at such a possibility.[67] Ancestral pedigree and material cost – perhaps coupled with a small degree of sentimentality – saw Charles retain many of these pieces after Anna's death and they are identifiable in the 1627 inventory of Denmark House and, later, in the 1649 Commonwealth Sale.[68] For Charles, invested as they were with hereditary pedigree and heraldic significance, such goods aptly demonstrated his genealogical links. Throughout the 1630s and early 1640s they may well have been strategically used to stress amity with his maternal uncle Christian IV, visually reminding onlookers of the Stuart king's powerful blood relation who could provide diplomatic and military support – a need that intensified as internal dissent in all three Stuart kingdoms rapidly escalated.[69]

Portraiture in the palaces

Throughout each of the queen's three principal residences in England – Denmark House, Greenwich Palace, and Oatlands Manor – portraits were displayed, but beyond the traditional grouping of European rulers to broadly state the monarchy's connections and allies, Anna's personal connections and political agendas were readily identifiable. The queen fashioned the display to signify her natal network in Denmark-Norway and the German courts; her local English court faction; and close members of her household, while, unusually, portraits of members of the Houses of Tudor and Stuart – even Anna's own husband and children – were conspicuously rare. This considered display, or what John Peacock has termed the 'calculated and tendentious arrangement' of portraits to make 'statements of relationship and alliance', was not unusual for the time, but it is significant in raising awareness of Anna's use of visual culture to showcase specific aspects of her political and dynastic position.[70]

Looking to Oatlands under Anna, the rooms were hung with twenty-two portraits which, aside from two portraits of Anna herself, included four portraits of her nephews – the sons of Christian IV – and, as mentioned, a portrait of her deceased brother John. The queen's local affiliations were visualised through portraits of her maids of honour, Jane Drummond and Mary Middlemore (d.1618), her jester Tom Derry, and her close affiliates Pembroke and Carew.[71] There was also, rather remarkably, a portrait of the Spanish ambassador, Diego Sarmiento de Acuña, Count Gondomar (1567–1626), which was perhaps intended to remind onlookers of Anna's connections to, and esteem for, the Habsburgs and her desire for a marriage match between their kingdoms. On the other hand, the only paintings that bore reference to Anna's Tudor and Stuart connections were a portrait of Queen Elizabeth I, and one of King James's grandfather, Matthew Stewart, Earl of Lennox (1516–1571).[72]

There were considerably more portraits on display at Denmark House than at Oatlands, and there were more ancestral – marital – portraits with images of Henry VIII, Edward VI when Prince of Wales (1537–1553), Queen Elizabeth I, Mary Queen of Scots (1542–1587), and one of King James but, again, there were none of the Stuart children. As Griffey points out, this stands in stark contrast to the patterns of display in operation under Anna's successor, Henrietta Maria, who repeatedly fashioned herself as wife and mother.[73] For Anna, by contrast, her Oldenburg connections were the main source of her pride and position and, as at Oatlands, the queen used portraiture at Denmark House to physically showcase the reach of her amity and affinity. The Great Gallery held images of Christian IV, and his eldest son and heir (Anna's nephew) Christian Prince-Elect of Denmark (1603–1647), while visitors to the Cross Gallery were greeted by a display of Anna's genealogical connections to the Habsburgs and to the German-speaking courts in the Holy Roman Empire. There hung portraits of Joachim Frederick, Elector Brandenburg (1546–1608) (father-in-law to Anna's brother, Christian IV); pendants of the Lutheran Duke Frederick of Württemberg (1557–1608) and his wife Sibylla of Anhalt (1564–1614); independent portraits of their five daughters; pendants of King Philip III of Spain (1578–1621) and his wife Margaret of Austria (1584–1611); and pair portraits of Albert VII, Archduke of Austria (1559–1621) and Archduchess Isabel Clara Eugenia (1566–1633), the latter of which is still in the Royal Collection in London.[74] This was the more intimate and reserved of the two galleries at Denmark House, but Anna would still have used the space for audiences where she wished to impart a particular element of familiarity or affection, and it would therefore have been appropriate to have a visual record of her international, familial alliances.[75]

Building on these personal and dynastic elements, Denmark House also boasted a noticeable concentration of portraits of members of Anna's English court circle, a circle that she supported in contrast (and often outright opposition) to the Howard-Carr faction favoured by James, which is detailed in Chapter 1.[76] Portraits of Southampton, Arundel, Winwood, Edward Somerset, Earl of Worcester (1553–1628), and Robert Sidney, Earl of Leicester (1563–1626) were displayed, along with, as at Oatlands, portraits of both Carew and Derry.[77] This pattern continued at Greenwich where three of the eight portraits in that palace were of members of Anna's natal family: her maternal grandfather Ulric, her brother-in-law Christian II, and her niece Sophia Hedevig of Braunschweig-Wolfenbüttel, Countess of Nassau-Dietz (1592–1642).[78] Although contemporary impressions of Anna's portrait display, and the means of acquisition, have not survived, the prominence given to genealogy and faction is clear evidence of the queen's direction: international and domestic visitors to one of Anna's palaces cannot have failed to comprehend the nature and extent of her pride and connections.

Amassing an art collection

There have been few sustained considerations of Anna's collection of artworks and interior goods. As suggested above, this is probably due to the patchy nature of the evidence and the predilection of the queen for paintings that devolved from Holland and the Low Countries. Griffey's recent study of Henrietta Maria's material agency and display includes a comparative view of Anna's collections at Oatlands Manor and Denmark House, where she draws useful conclusions around her engagement with governing modes of precedence and suitability, her 'affinity with Passion imagery', and observes that 'diversity' was a defining feature of 'the display of pictures' at Oatlands.[79] The most focused consideration, however, remains that of Timothy Wilks, but, published in 1997, it is in need of updating and is filled with frustratingly derisive statements. In general, Wilks refuses to accord any agency to the queen, and he dismisses the political value of portraiture by conceiving of Anna's interest in purely personal, emotional terms: the queen 'was less interested in having a strident collection than in having one that could absorb her and comfort her'.[80] Concluding that 'Dutch and Flemish works came to outnumber those of any other school' in Anna's collection, Wilks suggests that the core devolved from Prince Henry and was then probably supplemented through the activities of the queen's limner, Isaac Oliver, or her Danish connections. Neither possibility is explored, but Wilks further diminishes Anna's achievements by stating that it was the presence of Venetian artworks in Henry's collection that 'truly raised it out of the ordinary'.[81] Such statements are representative of a wider trend in the scholarship of this area, which has focused on identifying classicising Italianate artefacts and interests as the mark of an erudite collector – an identification that is narrow and problematic. Rather than dismissing Anna's collecting activities for not having centred on Italy, her predilection is evidence of her continuing Danish orientation, holding notable parallels with Christian IV's collection of paintings, and, furthermore, with the cultural patronage of Anna and Christian's father, Frederik, and their grandfather, King Christian III (1503–1559).[82] It is reasonable to assume that Anna and Christian developed their appreciation for the artistry of the Low Countries during their years at their father's court, for Frederik – and his advisors Tycho Brahe and Henrik Ranzau – repeatedly looked to the Netherlands for artists and artisans to realise the cultural aims of the king, even if these were inflected with an Italianate aesthetic.[83]

Scholars have long puzzled over the origins of Anna's collection of paintings, which are documented in the inventories of Denmark House and Oatlands Palace. A small number of these paintings – two – have been convincingly traced to Prince Henry's collection, with the logical suggestion that Anna acquired them after her son's death in 1612. However, Wilks's supposition that the *majority* of the queen's collection came from Henry at this time is highly unlikely.[84] The surviving (although incomplete) information on the composition of the two collections is noticeably disparate, and evidence of Anna's artistic agency precedes the prince's collecting activities and continues after his death. Beyond the expected portraits of historical and contemporary European rulers that visualised the queen's genealogical pedigree and international connections – portraits that may have been loosely appropriate for Henry – Anna's collection contained a number of highly personalised paintings of key members of her faction and household, which did not hold relevance for Henry's position at court or his own alliances. Additionally, during her nine years in England prior to Henry's death, and in her seven years after it, Anna not only showed an understanding of the political diplomacy of portraiture but a personal interest in the arts in choosing to patronise her own, comparatively innovative, artists who did not work for the king. This noticeable tendency is discussed in Chapter 5, but the earliest example is Oliver who was attached to the queen's household within a year of her arrival in England.

The small body of Anna's surviving correspondence is almost completely devoid of references to artworks of any sort. The queen's bills and accounts do not include purchase details for artworks, and they contain very few payments to artists. Furthermore, contemporary letters, ambassadorial dispatches, and diaries do not comment on the queen's acquisition or display of any specific pieces of material or visual culture. This paucity of information has contributed to the omission of the queen from scholarship on collecting at the Jacobean court, but the absence of such evidence is not unusual for the period. Even David Howarth writing on Arundel, who he defines as 'the greatest English collector of the Baroque age', concludes that a characteristic of the 'history of collecting in England under the Stuart dynasty' is the 'sheer paucity of evidence', which complicates scholarship on the initiative, connoisseurship, and networks of early modern art patrons.⁸⁵ Looking to the wider European context, similar observations have been made of several celebrated collectors – Queen Christina of Sweden (1626–1689), Duke August of Wolfenbüttel (1579–1666), and Anna's brother, Christian IV – whose correspondence yields few, if any, indications of artistic appreciation or knowledge, and who routinely purchased artworks in large quantities through the efforts of advisors, agents, and/or secretaries having given little specific input.⁸⁶

Firm documentary evidence of agents working to secure artworks for Anna of Denmark are yet to be uncovered, but it is almost certain that such a network was in operation. This could have been occasioned verbally, or in letters now lost, or through any number of intermediaries working between the patron and agent, or between the agent and the painter and/or dealer, that are not yet possible to identify. Since 2010, there has been a flourishing of scholarship on the part and function of the early modern agent in material and visual culture, building on earlier patronage studies that demonstrated the fundamental role of political patron/client relationships to the stability and success of the monarchy.⁸⁷ Research resulting from the project Double Agents, led by Marika Keblusek between 2002 and 2006, has extended our knowledge of the personal, political, and commercial facets of agency and brokerage, stressing the centrality of broad networks, the interrelationship between diplomacy and art, and the commonplace of agents to be involved in 'multiple modes of cultural and political transfer'.⁸⁸

In thinking through reasonable patterns of international movement, mediation, and exchange in relation to the logistics of Anna amassing a sizeable collection of Netherlandish paintings, a compelling solution – and one supported by circumstantial evidence – is that many of them were bought by the Danish secretary, Charisius, while in the United Provinces on diplomatic business for Christian IV in 1607/8. In the narrative that follows, the role of inference is admittedly large, but the notion that paintings were sourced by Charisius in the Netherlands on Anna's behalf, or even on Christian's behalf and then sent to Anna, is extremely plausible. In November 1607, Charisius and Jacob Ulfeldt (1567–1630) were dispatched to The Hague to represent Denmark-Norway in the peace being brokered between the States General and Spain.⁸⁹ Stationed in the United Provinces for the better part of a year, Charisius had an additional task to complete for the Danish King: secure paintings and musical instruments for the royal collection and to encourage Dutch artisans to relocate to Denmark-Norway. Of the former assignment, Charisius was hugely successful and by the close of the embassy in 1608, he had secured 141 paintings and seven musical instruments.⁹⁰

The purchase record of the consignment survives, detailing many of the artists involved and the subject matter of the paintings, although the fate of the contents is uncertain. There is no record of goods arriving in Denmark-Norway, and the Danish palaces were not inventoried until the end of the seventeenth century, giving ample opportunity for the de-acquisition of artworks. In addition, the Danish royal collections were plundered by Sweden during the wars of 1658–1660 and subsequent devastation was wrought by severe fires in 1728, 1794, 1795, and 1884.[91] This leaves the possibility that some of the paintings were originally sent to Anna in England, and definite parallels exist between the consignment and Anna's inventoried collection.[92] Most striking is the heavy weighting towards mythological paintings and scenes from the Old Testament, together with a noticeable interest in landscapes, still lifes, and genre scenes. Furthermore, in one of the few instances where an artist in Anna's collection can be identified – she owned two paintings by one of the Franckens – a further parallel is established with Charisius's consignment, for it too contained work by Franckens.[93] Others are less easy to definitively match, since the inventories of Anna's artworks do not, as was common in the period, include attributions.[94] Nevertheless, clearly defined subjects found in both Charisius's purchases and Anna's collection were numerous: Lucretia, Venus and Adonis, the Raising of Lazarus, the Nativity, the Tower of Babel, a landscape scene of Venice, a still life featuring 'kuchen werk', ten pure landscapes, a banquet scene of the Gods, a night scene of Christ, the Passion of Christ, a painting of an Italian woman, and individual portraits of the first twelve Caesars.[95] It is also conceivable that 'en børen danz [a children's dance]' bought by Charisius was the 'picture of antique boyes dauncinge' at Denmark House.[96]

At the very least, the degree of crossover is strongly suggestive of communication, if not outright exchange and/or gifts. Christian and Anna maintained a high level of contact that, aside from Christian's personal visits to England in 1606 and 1614, was facilitated by the regular exchange of letters, gifts, court personnel, and embassies between Denmark and Scotland, and then England. Charisius himself was frequently chosen by Christian to be the Danish representative. He also maintained correspondence with Anna, and while visiting England in August 1611, Charisius lodged with Anna for several nights at Oatlands.[97] Later, in 1619, Charisius was personally involved in the movement of artworks between the Stuart and Oldenburg courts. From London, on 29 July 1619, Robert Anstruther (1578–c.1644) wrote to Charisius in Copenhagen to confirm that 'Le present porteur vous baisera les Mains de ma part, il a le pourtraitt Du Roy et la Royne pour sa Ma.te' [The present bearer will kiss your hands on my behalf, he has the portrait of the king [James] and the queen [Anna] for his Majesty [Christian]].[98] The Danish king's request had been occasioned by Anna's death in March 1619, and it was Charisius – with his familiarity with the Stuarts, London, and art transportation – who was entrusted to complete the task.

Small spaces: cabinets, closets, and studies

The history of spatial retreat and secrecy in the early modern English interior has traditionally focused on the small room of the closet. Commonly adjoined to the bedchamber, it has been generally conceived as a cloistered reserve for the householder to read, write, or carry out religious devotions or meditations.[99] Recently, Orlin has challenged this interpretation, arguing that the burgeoning demand for closets and studies in sixteenth-century England was an outgrowth of the medieval chest that developed in response to an increase in household goods and the continued desire for their protection.[100] Randle Cotgrave (d.1652) stated as much in his 1611 dictionary, wherein he judged the English cabinet or 'closet, little chamber, or wardrobe' to be the place 'wherein one keeps his best, or most esteemed, substance'.[101] Orlin further emphasises the irregular, shifting nature of this space: variable in location, number, size, contents, function, and even in terminology. There was no 'apparent distinction' between the terms closet and study, and these spaces were suitable for solitude, commune, and select instances of social display; the goods kept therein ranged from 'household stuffs' of linen, fabric, glassware, and furniture, to personal effects such as clothing, to precious belongings including artworks, clocks, books, coins, and pieces of unicorn horn – which were largely determined by rank and wealth.[102] While Orlin focuses on the middling and elite classes of Tudor England, a close reading of the office of the works accounts coupled with the inventories of Denmark House and Oatlands shows that the same was true of royalty in Stuart England. Closets, cupboards, and studies were commonly found in Stuart palaces, and they were not governed by a uniform mode of function or decoration. Importantly, too, the analysis of these rooms furthers our understanding of Anna's directorial role in shaping palace topographies, her understanding and implementation of spatial hierarchies, and how the furnishing of her rooms was highly attuned to function and concomitant audience.

In the first instance, it is significant that Anna's need or desire for these spaces saw their addition and/or refurbishment at all principal Stuart palaces. That they were specifically for Anna's use – and very possibly ordered at her insistence – is made clear by the wording of the entries in the accounts. Thus, a 'litle newe cabinett' (measuring 16 x 14 feet) was built for the queen at Whitehall and was decoratively finished with plastered fretwork featuring 'varieties of woorks and armes' and a wainscot ceiling, while a 'newe cleare storie' window was added to 'the closett Queenes side'; the walls, floor, and ceiling of Anna's study at Greenwich – positioned next to the garden – were newly covered in plaster of Paris; a new 'joyned cupboorde' was made for 'her highnes studdy' at Denmark House; and the floors and ceiling of her study at Hampton Court were lathed and newly plastered while her privy closet there was fitted with a new 'leaning boorde'.[103] The queen's cabinet chamber at Oatlands is only mentioned incidentally in these accounts, but its contents are preserved in the palace inventories, as are the goods Anna kept in her 'studdy' at Denmark House.[104]

In the 1619 inventory of Denmark House, the clerks identified five rooms that could be considered as studies or closets: 'ye roome beyond ye said crosse gallery', 'a little room betweene ye two galleries', 'the little attiring chamber close to the gallery', 'the cabonett', and 'the roome beyond the little beddchamber'.[105] All five rooms housed a variety of paintings and household furnishings (tables, chairs, cabinets, cushions, curtains, mirrors, andirons) but two of them held a considerably greater amount of goods along with items that could be termed collectables or curiosities: those 'beyond' the Little Bedchamber and 'beyond' the Cross Gallery. Judging from Thurley's reconstructive plan of the palace from around 1620, the first of these rooms could be accessed directly from the Great Gallery, the Little Bedchamber, and perhaps also the back stairs, while the latter – in the more removed north-eastern reaches of the palace – was entered through the Cross Gallery and the wardrobes so that both spaces allowed for the queen to be selectively solitary and social (Figure 3.4). This bears interesting parallel with the Danish palaces of Anna's youth, where Frederik's closets – at Copenhagen Castle, Kronborg, and Skanderborg – were similarly marked by a fluidity of privacy and political diplomacy that may well have influenced Anna's later understanding and moulding of court space. Equipped with permanent lathes, Frederik's closets reflected his passion for woodturning and admittance was closely guarded: the king often retired there alone but he also used them for audiences wherein access signalled trust and honour.[106]

Access to Anna's two closets at Denmark House was restricted and they both housed examples of unusual, precious goods, but their location within the wider palace and the volume and type of their contents suggests that they served distinct purposes. The closet next to the Cross Gallery worked in conjunction with it, for both rooms contained objects of visual interest, but the slight remove of the closet allowed Anna to control admittance for favour and prestige. The closet was relatively sparsely furnished thereby giving space for the close inspection of particular items, and it held a number of unusual, finely wrought objects such as candlesticks of yellow amber, a gilt alabaster 'picture' of the Resurrection in a black wooden case, a small tortoiseshell cabinet 'barred wth silver', an elaborate mechanised clock, and curios fashioned from copper, coral, and crystal.[107] It is likely that musicians played here too, providing music – unseen – for the guests walking in the gallery beyond, for the closet contained 'Seaven Lutes two in Cases of old greene Velvett one in a case of orrenge coulor Velvett one other an old Crimsen Velvett Case and the rest in black leather Cases'.[108]

By comparison, the closet next to the Little Bedchamber where Anna slept contained a much greater quantity and array of goods, functioning primarily as a site for 'safe storage'.[109] A large number of boxes, chests, and cabinets were kept here along with pieces of soft furnishings, household items, and clothes, and there was an interesting concentration of scented possessions including rock-crystal boxes of sweet water, a 'Cabonett of pomannder', a wooden box with 'sweet pocketts', and seven sweet bags – two of which were 'very rich' and were presumably employed in the wardrobes. An item probably intended for more immediate use – perhaps in the queen's adjoining bedchamber – was the 'black Ebony Cabonett full of Apothecaries druggs and implemts thereto belonging and a booke inducth describing the perticulers thereof' that was stored in a gilt-green leather case. Many of the cabinets were small and decorative, fashioned from elaborate materials and kept inside individual chests. Thus a 'Cabonett of yellow amber garnished wth silver guilte' was protected within a black ebony box and a 'rich Cabonett of greene Jasper garnished wth silver guilte' lay inside a gilded red-leather case. The presence of a pair of playing tables in 'white and yellow amber garnished with silver', with matching 'Table men and dice', hints at the room having a recreational function although it is more likely, considering the limited amount of space, that they were transported elsewhere for use. Other cabinets were definitely intended for display, such as that upholstered in crimson velvet holding 'Eight peces of purcelane garnished wth silver guilte', or the two white boxes that contained 'fowerteene Images of yellow amber cutt' and 'a Cheyne of Corrall', while other items rewarding close, personal inspection included 'a looking Glass wth some boxes of silver and a globe'.[110] Anna may well have bought select guests here to marvel at some of her objects, but these pieces – like the playing table – could have been easily moved into other rooms of the palace to be displayed to their better advantage.

The queen's closet – her 'cabbinet' – at Oatlands also reads as more of a storage space than a room suited to seclusion or the socio-political. Here was a screen, a small mirror in a gilt-leather case, five folding field tables, a wainscot cupboard, brass andirons, and a suite of furniture (a low chair, two low stools, and three cushions) upholstered in cloth of silver.[111] Certainly, a 'china table of tenne squares', 'a wainscot table wth degrees for books', and a 'square wainescot table' were being held in the closet in 1616, but they were relocated to the book chamber the following year.[112] Aside from the medical text mentioned above, books are not recorded in any of Anna's closet spaces and must have been housed in the book chambers and libraries that were provided for her at Whitehall, Greenwich, Oatlands, Denmark House, and perhaps also Holdenby where 'a presse' was specially ordered for her books.[113] Anna's library at Oatlands contained eighty books, and her household accounts show her to have been an enthusiastic supporter of writers and poets, frequently disbursing money for books and poems that were dedicated to her, and ordering English, French, and Italian titles through her grooms.[114] While in Scotland, Anna, like James, had highly elaborate 'pooks' [bags] made 'for hir maiesteis buikis [books]' in order that they could be easily transported with the queen. Typically fashioned from velvet, they were decoratively finished with strings, 'knoppis and frettis' and passements of silk and precious metal.[115] This additional evidence builds on Knowles's earlier observation of 'the importance of books in Anna's life', showing the queen to have been an avid reader, patron, and linguist, and hinting at Anna's literary activities in Scotland, which it is hoped will become better evidenced.[116]

Music in the queen's household

It is also in the closets at Denmark House that we find evidence of Anna as a music practitioner, adding weight to our knowledge of her as an important, innovative patron of music. The queen's musical interests have been noted by several historians – particularly Andrew Ashbee, John Bergsagel, Lynn Hulse, and those scholars working on John Dowland (1563–1626) and the musical patronage of Christian IV – and some of the warrants and accounts relating to musicians in the Stuart period have been published, but there has been no sustained examination of the breadth or depth of Anna's musical activities.[117] The following discussion brings together the secondary source literature, which is supplemented and extended by new archival material and by a fresh perspective that positions Anna, rather than a male musician, as the focal point.

In addition to the seven lutes kept in the closet next to the Cross Gallery at Denmark House, the scribes recorded an elaborate, probably mechanised, timepiece that commemorated Anna's musical interest: a 'clocke in a Case of Ebony wth trompetts drums and other musicke'.[118] It was possibly an expensive gift from James, who had paid £300 to the Dutchman Hans Nilloe, in August 1609, for 'a clock with music and motions'.[119] Anna's other closet at Denmark House, next to the small bedchamber in which she slept, also housed instruments with 'a p[ai]re of Virginalls in a Case of greene Vuselvett embrodered wth small perles'.[120] Both closets were evidently considered suitable for musical play, but the quantity and location of the instruments reinforces their different uses and audiences as described above. The lutes, as mentioned, anticipate a group of musicians while the pair of virginals were only for one player. Tucked away in Anna's intimate rooms, this may well have been the queen herself, and it is reasonable to suggest that they were the pair Anna earlier commissioned from the instrument maker Robert Henlake, who in February 1607 received £20 for a 'payre of Virginalles by him made for her Ma[jes]t[i]es use'.[121]

The depth of musical culture at Anna's English court stemmed in large part from her Danish upbringing and dynastic connections, the most important of which was her brother Christian. Having both learnt music during their childhood, the pair continued to play as adults, cementing a knowledge and familiarity that enhanced their general appreciation. It is significant that at least four of Frederik and Sofie of Mecklenburg-Güstrow's (1557–1631) children – Elisabeth (1573–1626), Anna, Christian, and Hedevig became noted music patrons.[122] Composers, instrumentalists, singers, and dancers, together with the associated instruments, musical parts, and texts, wound their way between the siblings' courts, adding another layer to the rich fabric of transfer and exchange that operated across the Oldenburg familial network.

At the Danish court of Frederik II, music formed an integral part of the pageantry, plays, dances, and dynastic celebrations that punctured court ceremonial and entertainment, but it had also been a regular feature of court life, for the king maintained three permanent groups of singers, instrumentalists, and trumpeters, comprising forty-seven people.[123] In addition, some, if not all, of his royal children learned musical instruments, with Anna receiving tuition from Thomas Robinson, the English composer and lutenist, in Elsinore (Helsingør).[124] In her adult life in Scotland and England, Anna continued to play music – as did Christian – with both siblings purchasing instruments and music books for their own use. In addition, Anna and Christian, and their two sisters – Elisabeth in Wolfenbüttel and Hedevig in Dresden – were the dedicatees of significant musical tracts, and the siblings exchanged composers and musicians, while Christian chose to purchase instruments and parts in England and engineered further cross-cultural exchange by personally bringing 'his private band' with him to England in 1606, since he was so 'very fond of music'.[125]

In early Stuart England, it was the royal courts together with a few aristocratic households, most notably that of Robert Cecil and Thomas Sackville (1536–1608), that formed the nexus of musical patronage and development.[126] Each of the royal households maintained permanent musicians with a number of 'musical Grooms' of the chamber who, as Ashbee underscores, were important in bridging the divide between the relatively accessible public spaces of performance for banquets, masques, and ceremonial, and the comparatively intimate, personal rooms of the royal family where they played and gave instruction.[127] Music regularly featured in the conveyance of favour and was a suitable background accompaniment for international diplomacy. Anna and Prince Henry both chose music as a medium for showing their esteem for ambassadors (and their representative kingdom). The queen pleased Foscarini with a three-hour audience in which he heard 'her music from a very private gallery', and the Spanish ambassador was 'entertained by some music' before he was treated to stay 'a great while with Her Majesty'.[128] In January 1612, James chose to dine in state while 'a concert of viols and voices and other instruments was heard from a neighbouring chamber, most graceful harmony, but low so as not to interrupt discourse.'[129]

Logically, Anna's musical interest and patronage did not develop suddenly in England, but in comparison to the work on the musical environment of the early Stuart court in England by Ashbee, Bergsagel, and Hulse among others, the musical patronage and activities of the Stuarts in Scotland has been understudied. Music occupied a central role in the everyday life, ceremonial, and entertainments of the Scottish court, and the exchequer rolls indicate that James kept five 'ordinar trumpettouris' – John and William Ramsay, Robert Drummond, Michael Weddell, and Archibald Sim – who each received £23.2s. per term.[130] Four English viol players (Thomas, Robert, James, and William 'Hudsonis') were in attendance at the Scottish court from at least Martinmas 1589, for which they collectively received a fee of £210 per term, and in 1596 they were joined by Robert Leslie.[131] Hudson doubled as a dance instructor, while James's household also hosted two lute players, a fiddler, a minstrel, an organist, and four musicians whose speciality is not recorded.[132]

On the queen's side, trumpeters were likewise in attendance and although unnamed, they were issued the large extraordinary reward of £700 in 1590/91.[133] Of great significance to the consideration of Anna's longstanding value of music, and the musical milieu of the Scottish court more generally, is the English 'musicinar' John Norlie. In November 1601, as music master to the queen, Norlie received the particularly substantial annual salary of £600 Scots at a time when, by comparison, the master of the household received £400 Scots per annum.[134] As many musicians were wont to do in England, Norlie worked for James as well as Anna, receiving patronage from the king between 1601 and 1604.[135] In England, Anna continued to enjoy Scottish music and musicians, employing Malcolm Groate as her 'Musician for Scotch Music' and rewarding 'a Scottish singing woman' in July 1605.[136] Groate remained in Anna's service until her death in March 1619, at which time he was, together three other Scottish musicians, among those granted mourning cloth.[137] Another Scottish musician and composer who benefitted from the queen's patronage in England was Tobias Hume (1579–1645). As Wade and Hulse have outlined, Hume was a notable exponent of the innovative technique of playing the viol in the lyra style, and he dedicated several works to Anna and her siblings Christian and Ulrik.[138] Hulse further elaborates that Anna owned at least one lyra-viol and in November 1608 she bought, presumably for her own use, 'twoe books in folio ruled for the lira and violl'.[139] Yet there has been speculation about the validity of Hume's claim, in 1642, that he had played his hunting song – published in 1607 in *Captain Humes Poeticall Musicke* – 'before two Kings, to the admiring of all braue huntsmen'.[140] New evidence adds weight to Wade's earlier suggestion that Hume was referring to Kings James and Christian and a royal performance in England in 1606: Anna's privy purse accounts for that year include payment to Hume – for 3 April 1606 – at which time Christian was confirmed to visit England.[141] In deference to Anna's patronage, Hume then dedicated *Poeticall Musicke* to the queen and he included, in respect of her close familial ties, honours for her two brothers Christian and Ulrik.[142]

Music across the courts

Mara Wade's research into Hedevig's musical patronage of Heinrich Schütz (1585–1672) and Michael Prætorius (c.1571–1621) has revealed important evidence of cultural exchange and cross-fertilisation operating across the Oldenburg natal network. During Schütz's lengthy term as Kapellmeister at the Dresden court (1615–1672), for example, Hedevig facilitated his periodic attendance at the Danish court where he served as royal Kapellmeister from 1633 to 1635 and again from 1642 to 1644. Prætorius, on the other hand, was the director of music for Heinrich Julius in Wolfenbüttel – the marital court of Hedevig's oldest sister Elisabeth – but he dedicated musical works to Hedevig, Elisabeth, and Christian.[143] Appropriately, for the marriage of Christian IV and Anna Catherine of Brandenburg (1575–1612) in Copenhagen in 1596, Heinrich Julius sent sixteen musicians from Wolfenbüttel to play during the marital festivities.[144] Further transfer between these courts occurred with Heinrich Julius's German organ builder Esaias Compenius (1560–1617). In 1610, probably in collaboration with Prætorius, Compenius built a lavish chamber organ for the duke where the pipes were of a variety of woods including maple, oak, birch, ebony, and satinwood, the veneers were of ivory and the stop knobs of silver.[145] With Heinrich Julius's death in 1613, his widow Elisabeth chose to give the organ to her brother Christian, and Compenius travelled to Frederiksborg Castle in the spring of 1617 to oversee its installation, where it remains in situ.[146]

Musical exchange is also in firm evidence between the courts of Denmark and England, for a number of Danish musicians were in periodic residence at Anna's court in London, some of whom were expressly sent by Christian IV. In 1611, for example, the Danish king sent the composer Mogens Pedersøn (1583–1623), together with three musicians from the Danish royal chapel, to serve Anna in England, where they remained for three years.[147] On their return to Denmark in 1614, the English privy council sanctioned 'A passe for Martin Otto [Martinus Otto], Magneus Peterson [Mogens Pedersøn], Hans Brockrogg [Hans Brachrogge] and Jacob Oven [Jacob Ørn], late servauntes to the Queene's Majestie in place of musitions, to returne to Denmarke, from whence they came, and one man with trunckes of apparel.'[148] The following year, 1615, Otto returned to England and 'by the procurement of our gracious Ladie Queene Anna' was made a gentleman of the chapel royal.[149] Yet the movement of musicians between these nations went both ways, and English musicians who spent time at the Danish court included, perhaps foremost, the lutenist John Dowland and the composer and instrumentalist William Brade (c.1560–1630), as well as Robert Bateman, James Harding, Peter Philips, Anthony Holborne, Edward Johnson, Daniel Norcome, and John Mynors.[150] Dowland's travels are illustrative of the strong musical links that bound the two kingdoms. First entering Christian's service in November 1598, in June 1601 he was entrusted by the Danish king to return to England to buy viols or violins, an Irish harp and some extra strings, and to secure a dancer and a harpist for the Danish court. Later, in August 1603, Dowland again journeyed to England where he met with Anna at Winchester and presented her with his dedication of *Lachrimæ or Seaven Teares*. When, in February 1606, Dowland was dismissed from his post in Denmark, Christian sought another English lutenist to fill his place: Thomas Cutting, then in the service of Arbella Stuart (1575–1615), and who had probably played in front of the Danish king during his visit to England in 1606.[151] It was through the efforts of Anna and Prince Henry that Christian's desire was realised in 1608.[152] When Cutting was to later return to England he, together with Mynors, entered the service of Prince Henry.[153] These channels of exchange further extended through the Oldenburg kinship networks in Germany with Dowland working in both Wolfenbüttel and Kassel, and with Christian IV utilising his familial connections in Wolfenbüttel, Bückeburg, Munich, and Danzig (Gdansk) to secure musicians for the Danish royal chapel.[154]

The queen's musical establishment and patronage

In the same manner as her brother Christian, Anna's musical establishment in England was a truly international grouping of musicians which, as well as the Danes already mentioned, included men from France, Italy, Scotland, and the local English. Providing a summary of the English court in December 1619, the Venetian ambassador was compelled to note that Anna was 'fond of music' and that she kept an international consort with 'excellent French and one Italian performer'.[155] In 1612, Anna engaged a troupe of five French musicians. Highly prized, they not only received large annual pensions – much larger than those of their English counterparts – but got additional money from the queen 'in consideracon of theire Chambr rent'.[156] Around the same time too, Anna received a new Genoese musician, Gioan Marco, who had been in the service of Carlo Emanuele, Duke of Savoy (1562–1630), and may have been the 'Italian performer' later noted by the ambassador. Further, among Anna's householders who received cloth provisions for the attendance of Prince Henry's funeral, in November 1612, were five 'duch' [Danish] musicians, which presumably included the four Danes sent by Christian.[157]

Although the exact composition and use of the queen's consort music is uncertain, her receiver general accounts show a consistent interest in both chamber and theatre music, although many musicians crossed between the two forms. The records are incomplete, but it is clear that Anna's English household supported trumpeters, coronet players, lutenists, violinists, violists, drummers, singers, at least one harpist, and one fifer, and that the queen regularly sanctioned extraordinary gifts and rewards for performances given by male and female musicians, singers, dancers, and even acrobats.[158] With a large, permanent, and international consort of musicians, the queen's household – as has been observed of Cecil's – was ideally suited for apprenticeships and Anna's French musician, Lewes Richart, was charged with the care and 'musical education' of 'two French children, brought up by her [Anna's] command', for which he received £200 per annum.[159]

A number of the instruments and music books required for the queen's consort, and her own personal use, were secured by her musical grooms of the chamber.[160] In March 1604, Daniel Bachelor – a groom and a lutenist – was paid through the privy purse for 'a new violl and a case ... for a booke and for violl & lute stringes', and he was also paid 'for mending of another violl', which, at such an early date in the English reign, may very well have travelled with the queen from Scotland.[161] Lutes and viols also featured in the instruments and music books that another groom of the chamber and musician, the Italian John Maria Lugario, purchased for the queen. Between September 1607 and January 1608, Lugario purchased 'a violle for the consort', 'a litle Lute' for the queen, 'paybookes ruled for song and musick books' as well as 'consort bookes of musick'.[162] Perhaps in respect of the difficulty faced by foreign artisans arriving in London, Anna took responsibility for Lugario's first lodgings – just as she would for her French musicians – paying him sixty shillings in December 1606 'for his Chamber in Kinges Street' for a period of six weeks.[163] The following year, in 1607, Lugario was made a groom of the queen's privy chamber and as well as his retaining fee he was paid a large reward in respect 'of his skill and verie speciall quallity in musick'.[164]

This is a revealing example of the strong financial ties between the royal households, for the reward was ordered by Anna but paid out by the exchequer while Lugario's annual wages for 1608, of £100, were signed off by the king.[165] A significant amount of crossover – more so than in other cultural avenues – occurred with musicians, singers, and composers between the royal courts. The singer Robert Hales, for example, was a groom of Anna's chamber, but he was regularly paid by James for his musical talents and for the year ended Michaelmas 1605, he received payment as one of James's 'musicons for the lutes'.[166] Similarly, Robert Henlake who, as abovementioned, made a pair of virginals for Anna in 1608, had been earlier summoned by the queen to Hampton Court – in the summer of 1607 – to 'repaire a wind Instrumt' and to tend to a second that needed 'prfectinge'.[167] Yet Henlake, together with Andrea Bassano, was in the service of the king, having been appointed for life, on 21 June 1603, to the office of 'keeping, making and repairing of his Majesty's virginals and organs, with other wind instruments', for which he received an annual retainer of £60.[168] Likewise, the famed French violinist, Jacques Cordier (alias Bochan, or Bocan), who doubled as a dancing-master, found overlapping favour with James, Anna, and Arbella Stuart.[169] Such patronage also commonly worked in sequence as musicians moved between patrons, with Alphonso Ferrabosco (c.1575–1628) being one important example. In December 1604, James appointed the English-born composer and viol player to be Prince Henry's music master – in which capacity he is commonly discussed – but what has escaped notice is that Ferrabosco entered royal Stuart patronage in the service of the queen some eleven months earlier.[170] In the queen's privy purse accounts for her first court masque *The Vision of the Twelve Goddesses*, performed at Hampton Court on 8 January 1604, Ferrabosco was paid 100s. for 'making the songes and his imployment'. A further twenty-nine musicians, unfortunately unnamed, were granted £20 for having been 'imploied in the Rock the Temple and for danncinge in the said maske'.[171] Ferrabosco had been in Elizabeth's service and may therefore have been an obvious, or easy, choice for Anna, but the patronage of such an important composer nonetheless reiterates her appreciation and knowledge of music generally, and the central role that it held in her entertainments, which became a highlight of the court calendar over the following decade.

Conclusion

Beyond taste and interest, the surviving inventories of Anna's English residences demonstrate her understanding of the hierarchies and diplomacy of space and material goods. Just as the name of Denmark House came to celebrate the queen's Danish ancestry, so too did much of the interior furnishings and paintings. A large quantity of the portraits depicted the queen's consanguineous relatives, and Anna's identifying badges were seen in various configurations on textiles, pieces of furniture, and even silverware. This was likewise the case at Oatlands, although it is important to recognise that Anna's concern to personalise her residences with visual references to her natal lineage was not unique. An interesting correlative is found with her successor Henrietta Maria at Denmark House, who engaged in a sustained programme of Frenchification as she visually transformed the palace into the domain of a French, Bourbon princess with furniture of the French fashion, and panelling and chimneypieces painted with French designs and the *fleur de lys*. In Henrietta Maria's later decoration of the Queen's House at Greenwich, it was again French iconography that dominated.[172]

For Anna, Denmark-Norway was more than a source of familial pride – it was also the source of much of her knowledge about access and decorum, painting styles, and material furnishings suitable in a royal context. The queen's largest programme of renovation was executed at Denmark House, and while the high level of decorative finishing found precedent in the Tudor palaces of Greenwich and Nonsuch, it was also in firm evidence in Anna's childhood residence of Kronborg. In a similar manner, Anna's painting collection, characterised as it was by a heavy weighting of Dutch and Flemish paintings, did not follow the growing tendency among many English elites to collect Italian – specifically Venetian – artworks, but it importantly connected her to the tastes and preferences that she had witnessed in her father Frederik, and those that continued to be in evidence in the activities of her brother Christian. It was also in Denmark that Anna's understanding of the importance of music to courtly and theatrical settings had been fostered and, together with architecture and painting, music remained one of the central cultural connections between Anna's court and those of her siblings Christian, Elisabeth, and Hedevig in Denmark, Wolfenbüttel, and Dresden respectively. This is not to say that Anna transplanted Danish traditions and modes, completely unmitigated, into Scotland and England. Rather, it was in Denmark-Norway that Anna was first exposed to many of the cultural forms that she espoused in her later life, whereupon they were – to borrow the words of Peter Burke – 'decontextualized and then recontextualized, domesticated or "localized"', which is also true of the queen's wardrobe and even of her householders, as discussed in the next chapter.[173]

Notes

1. K. Acheson (ed.), *The Diary of Anne Clifford, 1616–1619: A Critical Edition* (New York, 1995), 167.
2. The 'privy gallery' most likely refers to the Cross Gallery, which was more private than the Great Gallery and by the time of the mourning period held a much greater quantity of goods as discussed in this chapter. On Clifford's collecting see E. Chew, '"Your Honor's Desyres": Lady Anne Clifford and the World of Goods', in K. Hearn and L. Hulse (eds), *Lady Anne Clifford: Culture, Patronage and Gender in 17th-Century Britain* (Leeds, 2009), 25–42.
3. Acheson (ed.), *Diary*, 63.
4. This reading of Anna has benefited from the earlier work of Griffey and Hibbard on the political value of Henrietta Maria's visual and material agency. See, for example, Griffey, *On Display*; Hibbard, 'Queen's Patronage'; 'Role of a Queen Consort'.
5. See for example, E. Chaney (ed.), *Evolution of English Collecting* (New Haven and London, 2003); P. Croft (ed.), *Patronage, Culture and Power: The Early Cecils* (New Haven and London, 2002); D. Howarth, *Lord Arundel and his Circle* (New Haven, 1985); Smuts, *Court Culture*; Wilks, 'Art Collecting'; T. Wilks (ed.), *Prince Henry Revived*; MacLeod et al., *Lost Prince*.
6. Courtiers generally held responsible for this shift include Robert Cecil, Earl of Salisbury; Henry Howard, Earl of Northampton; George Villiers, Duke of

Buckingham; Robert Carr, Earl of Somerset; Thomas Howard, Earl of Arundel. Female patrons include Aletheia Talbot, Countess of Arundel; Lucy Russell, Countess of Bedford; Jane Meautys, Lady Cornwallis.

7 Dillon, *Language of Space*; M. Fantoni , G. Gorse, and M. Smuts (eds), *The Politics of Space: European Courts c.1500–1700* (Rome, 2009); R. G. Asch, 'The Princely Court and Political Space in Early Modern Europe', in B. Kümin (ed.), *Political Space in Pre-Industrial Europe* (Farnham, 2009), 43–60; T. A. Sowerby, 'Material Culture and the Politics of Space in Diplomacy at the Tudor Court', 47–57, and J. Hennings, 'Diplomacy, Culture and Space: The Muscovite Court', 57–65, both in B. B. Johannsen and K. Ottenheym (eds), *Beyond Scylla and Charybdis* (Odense, 2015).

8 See the consecutive treasury accounts at National Records of Scotland, E21/74, E21/75, and E21/76, and the earlier accounts as published in McNeill (ed.), *Exchequer Rolls*; the works accounts in H. M. Paton (ed.), *Accounts of the Masters of Works*, 2 vols (Edinburgh, 1957); and those of the privy council in D. Masson (ed.), *Register of the Privy Council*, 3 vols (Edinburgh, 1881–1884).

9 Expenditure was accordingly slight, with just over £1,000 disbursed in three years between October 1604 and September 1607: TNA, E351/3240; TNA, E351/3241; TNA, E351/3242. See *CSPV*, vol. 10, no. 207 for the Spanish ambassador being lodged there in April 1604.

10 Colvin, *King's Works*, 255–259; Thurley, *Somerset House*, 33–36.

11 Colvin, *King's Works*, 32.

12 TNA, E351/3244; TNA, E351/3245; TNA, E351/3246; Colvin, *King's Works*, 32–33; C. Gapper, 'Appendix: Fragments', in S. Thurley, *Somerset House* (London, 2009), 77–81.

13 Colvin, *King's Works*, 193–201.

14 Colvin, *King's Works*, 199.

15 Colvin, *King's Works*, 108–109.

16 C. Christensen, *Kronborg: Frederik II's renæssanceslot og dets senere skæbne* (Copenhagen, 1950), 197–198, 208.

17 Christensen, *Kronborg*, 195.

18 U. Reindel, *The King Tapestries: Pomp & Propaganda at Kronborg Castle* (Copenhagen, 2011), 26–27.

19 Christensen, *Kronborg*, 95–96, 98, 195, 206.

20 TNA, E351/3250; TNA, E351/3245; Colvin, *King's Works*, 257; Gapper, 'Appendix', 77–78.

21 TNA, E351/3246.

22 TNA, E351/3245.

23 Quotes from taskwork in TNA, E351/3245; TNA, E351/3246.

24 Colvin, *King's Works*, 255; Thurley, *Somerset House*, 31.

25 Griffey, *On Display*, 73. On the role of Denmark House in the mourning period for Anna of Denmark see J. Field, '"Orderinge Things Accordinge to his Majesties Comaundment": The Funeral of the Stuart Queen Consort Anna of Denmark', *Women's History Review*, forthcoming 2020.

26 TNA, E351/543, fol. 262v.

27 See that cited in n.7 above.

28 Sowerby, 'Material Culture', 49.

29 *CSPV*, vol. 10, nos. 207, 261.

30 L. C. Orlin, *Locating Privacy in Tudor London* (New York and Oxford, 2007), esp. ch. 6.

31 Dillon, *Language of Space*, 6–9; R. M. Smuts and G. Gorse, 'Introduction', in M. Fantoni et al. (eds), *The Politics of Space* (Rome, 2009), 13–35: 13–15.

32 *CSPV*, vol. 10, no. 40.

33 *CSPV*, vol. 10, no. 55.

34 *CSPV*, vol. 10, no. 72: 12 June 1603.
35 Lodge, *Illustrations of British History* 3: 1 (11 June 1590).
36 *CSPV*, vol. 10, no. 384: 15 June 1605.
37 For Ulrik's travels see Wade, 'Duke Ulrik', 244–245.
38 See, for example, Kevin Sharpe's comparison of Kings James and Charles writing that 'where James was informal to the point of familiarity ... Charles was stiff, proud and prudish' in his 'The Image of Virtue: The Court and Household of Charles I, 1625–1642', in D. Starkey (ed.), *The English Court: from the Wars of the Roses to the Civil War* (London and New York, 1987), 226–260: 227.
39 *CSPV*, vol. 19, no. 25: 25 April 1625.
40 *CSPV*, vol. 22, no. 432: 14 June 1630.
41 Examples include: *CSPV*, vol. 10, nos. 102, 104, 166, 191; *CSPV*, vol. 11, nos. 18, 288, 400, 477, 734, 801, 803; *CSPV*, vol. 12, nos. 250, 280, 284, 296, 371, 446, 462, 710, 812; *CSPV*, vol. 14, nos. 112, 139, 206, 741; *CSPV*, vol. 15, nos. 131, 295, 342, 376, 525, 535.
42 *CSPV*, vol. 10, no. 72: 12 June 1603.
43 TNA, E351/543, fol. 262v; TNA, E351/544, fols 8v, 10v, 43v, 60r, 79r, 91v.
44 *CSPV*, vol. 10, no. 166: 8 December 1603; *CSPV*, vol. 12, no. 462: 16 March 1612.
45 *CSP Scotland*, vol. 13, no. 194: 16 August 1598; *CSPV*, vol. 10, no. 515: 27 April 1606.
46 *CSPV*, vol. 12, no. 462: 16 March 1612.
47 For example: Barroll, *Anna of Denmark*, 17, 25–27, and esp. ch. 5, 132–161; Field, 'Anna of Denmark and the Arts', 61–62, 73–76; J. Field, 'Anna of Denmark: A Late Portrait by Paul van Somer', *The British Art Journal* 18 (2017), 50–55: 51; see also Anna's actions in response to the escape of the Laird of Logie and the Gowrie conspiracy as discussed in Chapter 4.
48 Finet, *Finetti Philoxenis*, 12, 13, 19–20, 200; *CSPV*, vol. 10, no. 81: 26 June 1603; Griffey, *On Display*, 21–23.
49 *CPSV*, vol. 15, no. 535: 14 September 1618.
50 *CSPV*, vol. 11, no. 801: 25 February 1610.
51 ESRO, Glynde MS 320, fol. 3r.
52 This was not unusual, and galleries featured in the ceremonial pathways taken by envoys and diplomats under the rule of both Mary I and Elizabeth I, see Sowerby, 'Material Culture', 51.
53 *CSPV*, vol. 14, no. 139; *CSPV*, vol. 10, no. 81; Orlin, *Locating Privacy*, 226–261. Queen Elizabeth similarly used the gallery at Oatlands for audiences, see Sowerby, 'Material Culture', 51.
54 Payne, 'Inventory', 29; Field, 'Funeral of the Stuart Queen', forthcoming; Griffey, *On Display*, 73.
55 Field, 'Funeral of the Stuart Queen', forthcoming.
56 TNA, AO3/1187, fol. 4r.
57 Payne, 'Inventory', 35–36.
58 M. Bencard, 'Ebony and Silver Furniture', in M. Andersen et al. (eds), *Reframing the Danish Renaissance* (Copenhagen, 2011), 325–334: 327, 330–331.
59 Payne, 'Inventory', 35.
60 Payne, 'Inventory', 37–38; Thurley, *Somerset House*, 44; Griffey, *On Display*, 73.
61 Orlin, *Locating Privacy*, 226–261: quotes from 227, 235. Neither gallery is mentioned in the accounts for the dressing of Denmark House for the mourning period; by comparison orders were made for the yard, great hall, chapel, great bedchamber, and the guard, privy, and presence chambers to be hung with black cloth: see Field, 'Funeral of the Stuart Queen', forthcoming; TNA, AO3/1187, fols 11r-v, 17r; 18r
62 Orlin, *Locating Privacy*, 236–238, 241–242; quote from 241.

63 Thurley, *Somerset House*, 36.
64 ESRO Glynde MS 320, fols 1r, 3r, 4r, 5r, 9r, 10r.
65 Payne, 'Inventory', 28–29, 31, 34, 36–37, 40.
66 TNA, E351/3246; Colvin, *King's Works*, 259; Payne, 'Inventory', 37.
67 Payne, 'Inventory', 39, 40.
68 Society of Antiquaries London, MS 137, fols 12v, 37r, 40v. D. King, 'Textile Furnishings', in A. MacGregor (ed.), *The Late King's Goods: Collections, Possessions and Patronage of Charles I in Light of the Commonwealth Sale Inventories* (London and Oxford, 1989), 307–321: 316.
69 S. Murdoch, *Britain, Denmark-Norway, and the House of Stuart* (East Linton, 2000), chs 4 and 5.
70 Peacock, 'Politics of Portraiture', 213, 215–216.
71 The Scottish Jane Drummond entered royal service as a governess to Charles, and she travelled with the queen to England in 1603 where she became first lady and groom of the stool. Mary Middlemore was English and joined the queen's establishment as a maid of honour in 1603. TNA, LR6/154/9; Juhala, 'Household and Court', 91, 329, 334, 335; Payne, 'Aristocratic Women', 280, 283.
72 ESRO Glynde MS 320, fols 7r, 8r. The identity of the 'old Duke of Lenox' as James's grandfather is given in the 1616 inventory of Oatlands: ESRO Glynde MS 315, fol. 2r.
73 Griffey, *On Display*, 71 and ch. 5.
74 Payne, 'Inventory', 36. Royal Collection, London #407377.
75 This finds parallel with Frederik II's practice of using hunting lodges for diplomatic meetings as discussed in Chapter 2, and Sowerby states that Mary I and Elizabeth I likewise used 'areas of royal palaces to which few people were permitted access' as a means of showing 'greater affection and prestige': Sowerby, 'Material Culture', 51.
76 Field, 'Anna of Denmark and the Arts', 58–76; Barroll, *Anna of Denmark*, 131–142.
77 Payne, 'Inventory', 37–39, 44. Anna owned two portraits of Derry by Gheeraerts and Van Somer, and it is reasonable to suggest that portraits of him – and perhaps also of Carew – were concurrently hanging at Denmark House and Oatlands.
78 Rye, *England as Seen by Foreigners*, 163–164. The portrait of Sophia Hedevig remains in the Royal Collection London (406168).
79 Griffey, *On Display*, 69–77; quotes from 71. See also Knowles, 'Images of Royalty', 32.
80 Wilks, 'Art Collecting', 42.
81 Wilks, 'Art Collecting', 44, 35. At Denmark House there were only five artworks whose titles identified Italianate origins: three small paintings (miniatures?) of Venetian women, a landscape of Venice, and 'A Italyan picture of a naked woman': Payne, 'Inventory', 37.
82 K. Neville, 'Christian IV's Italianates. Sculpture at the Danish Court', in M. Andersen et al. (eds), *Reframing the Danish Renaissance* (Copenhagen, 2011), 335–346: 336. Only three paintings in Charisius's consignment can be identified as Italianate: a landscape of Venice and two paintings of 'italianiske signore': E. Nystrøm, 'Jonas Charisius' indkøb af malerier og musikinstrumenterne i Nederlandene 1607–08', *Danske Magazin* 6 (1909): 225–236: 233.
83 Grinder-Hansen, *Danmarks Renæssancekonge*, 234, 237, 239; V. Woldbye, 'Flemish Tapestry Weavers in the Service of Nordic Kings', in G. Delmarcel (ed.), *Flemish Tapestry Weavers Abroad: Emigration and the Founding of Manufactories in Europe* (Leuven, 2002), 91–112: 91, 93, 103. See Chapter 2 for the discussion of the difficulty in determining national styles.
84 Wilks, 'Art Collecting', 42–45.
85 D. Howarth, 'A Question of Attribution: Art Agents and the Shaping of the Arundel

Collection', in H. Cools, M. Keblusek, and B. Noldus (eds), *Your Humble Servant: Agents in Early Modern Europe* (Hilversum, 2006), 17–28: 23.

86 B. Noldus, 'Pieter Isaacsz's Other Life – Legal and Illegal', in B. Noldus and J. Roding (eds), *Pieter Isaacsz (1568–1625): Court Painter, Art Dealer and Spy* (Turnhout, 2007), 151–164: 152; Neville, 'Christian IV's Italianates', 336.

87 On patronage in Stuart England, see the work of David Starkey, Barbara Harris, Linda Levy Peck, and Malcolm Smuts cited in Chapter 1 and the Bibliography.

88 M. Keblusek, 'Introduction', in M. Keblusek and B. Noldus (eds), *Double Agents: Cultural and Political Brokerage in Early Modern Europe* (Leiden, 2011), 1–9: 7. See other chapters in that volume as well as those in Cools et al. (eds), *Your Humble Servant*.

89 B. Noldus, 'Art and Music on Demand', in M. Andersen et al. (eds), *Reframing the Danish Renaissance* (Copenhagen, 2011), 279–301: 281.

90 Noldus, 'Pieter Isaacsz's Other Life', 152.

91 J. Hein, *The Treasure Collection at Rosenborg: The Inventories of 1696 and 1718. Royal Heritage and Collecting in Denmark-Norway 1500–1900*, 3 vols (Copenhagen, 2009), vol. 1, 20–27.

92 Charisius's account is transcribed and published in Nyström, 'Jonas Charisius', 225–236. The original account is: RA, TKUA, Holland C Regnskaber 1607–1627. On Charisius as an agent, with particular focus on his activities in the United Provinces in 1607/8, see Noldus, 'Art and Music on Demand'; Noldus 'Pieter Isaacsz's Other Life', 151–154.

93 It is unclear whether the Franckens purchased by Charisius, or those owned by Anna, were by Frans Francken the Elder (1542–1616) or his son Frans Francken the Younger (1580–1642). For Charisius see Nyström, 'Jonas Charisius', 234; for Anna see J. Steegman, 'Two Unpublished Paintings from the Collection of Charles I', *Burlington Magazine* 99 (1957), 378–380. Note that Steegman suggests that 'their date [is] probably not much earlier than 1615', which, if true, would preclude them from being bought by Charisius.

94 E. Griffey, 'A Brief Description: The Language of Stuart Inventories', *Studi di Memofonte* 12 (2014), online publication. Artists are recorded in Charisius's consignment but, as Noldus cautions, it is not always clear whether they had painted the work or had secured it on behalf of another painter: 'Peter Isaacsz's Other Life', 153.

95 Payne, 'Inventory', 36–40; Nyström, 'Jonas Charisius', 227–229, 232–236; ESRO, Glynde MS 319–320. Of the ten pure landscapes displayed throughout Denmark House, five featured English locations and were therefore unlikely to have been sourced in the Netherlands.

96 Nyström, 'Jonas Charisius', 233; Payne, 'Inventory', 38.

97 TNA, SP75/4, fols 277r–278r; TNA, E351/543, fol. 264r; Riis, *Auld Acquaintance*, 1: 132. For Charisius in England at this time see also TNA, E403/2731, fol. 148v; TNA, E351/543, fols 247v, 250v; *CSPD* (1611–1618), 70–73.

98 RA, TKUA, England, AII.

99 A. Stewart, 'The Early Modern Closet Discovered', *Representations* 50 (1995), 76–100; P. Thornton, *Seventeenth-Century Interior Decoration Decoration in England, France and Holland* (New Haven, 1978), 296–303; M. Girouard, *Life in the English Country House: A Social and Architectural History* (New Haven, 1978), 129–130, 173–174.

100 Orlin, *Locating Privacy*, 301–302, 309, 311.

101 R. Cotgrave, *A Dictionarie* (1611), facsimile edition (Menston, 1968); part quoted in Orlin, *Locating Privacy*, 302, 309, 311.

102 Orlin, *Locating Privacy*, 302–311.

103 TNA, E351/3239; TNA, E351/3241; TNA, E351/3242; TNA, E351/3243; TNA, E351/3244.

104 TNA, E351/3251; ESRO, Glynde MS 320; Payne, 'Inventory'.
105 Payne, 'Inventory', 37, 38, 39, 40–41.
106 Grinder-Hansen, 'Types of Informal Space', 172–173, 178–179.
107 Payne, 'Inventory', 36–37; Griffey, *On Display*, 74.
108 Payne, 'Inventory', 36. As discussed below, James is known to have favoured this arrangement while dining in state.
109 Orlin, *Locating Privacy*, 301.
110 Payne, 'Inventory', 40–42; Thurley, *Somerset House*, 36; Griffey, *On Display*; S. Jervis, '"Shadows, Not Substantial Things". Furniture in the Commonwealth Inventories', in A. MacGregor (ed.) *The Late King's Goods* (London and Oxford, 1989), 277–306: 278, 289.
111 ESRO, Glynde MS 320, fols 5r, 6r, 7r.
112 ESRO, Glynde MS 315, fol. 3r; ESRO, Glynde MS 320, fols 6r, 7r.
113 TNA, E351/3242; TNA, E351/3243; TNA, E351/3245; TNA, E351/3248; ESRO, Glynde MS 314, fol. 4r; ESRO, Glynde MS 320, fols 2r, 4r, 6r-7r, 9r.
114 TNA, SC6/JASI/1646; TNA, SC6/JASI/1648; TNA, SC6/JASI/1650; TNA, SC6/JASI/1655; Knowles, 'Images of Royalty', 27; Field, 'Anna of Denmark and the Arts', 237–240.
115 NRS, E21/76, fols 538–539; NRS, E35/13, vol. 4, p. 10. James also had 'pooks' to carry his books see NRS, E35/13, vol. 1, p. 17.
116 Knowles, 'Images of Royalty', 27.
117 Including A. Ashbee (ed.), *Records of English Court Music*, vol. 4 (Snodland, 1991); J. Bergsagel, 'Danish Musicians in England 1611–14: Newly Discovered Instrumental Music', *Dansk Årbog for Musikforskning* 7 (1973–1976), 9–20; J. Bergsagel, 'Anglo-Scandinavian Musical Relations before 1700', in H. Glahn et al. (eds), *Report of the Eleventh Congress, International Musicological Society*, 2 vols (Copenhagen, 1972), vol. 1, 263–271; L. Hulse, 'Review', *Music & Letters* 73 (1992): 101–103. On Dowland see for example P. Hauge, 'John Dowland's Employment', in M. Keblusek and B. Noldus (eds), *Double Agents* (Leiden, 2011), 193–212; J. Ward, 'A Dowland Miscellany', *Journal of the Lute Society of America* 10 (1977), 5–152; and for printed archival transcripts see Ashbee (ed.), *English Court Music*; H. Cart de Lafontaine (ed.), *The King's Musick: A Transcript of Records Relating to Music and Musicians, 1460–1700* (New York, 1973); and E. F. Rimbault (ed.), *The Old Cheque-Book of Book of Remembrance of the Chapel Royal from 1561 to 1744* (New York, 1966).
118 Payne, 'Inventory', 36.
119 BL Add MS 24705, fol. 5v; F. Devon, *Issues of the Exchequer, Being Payments Made out of His Majesty's Revenues During the Reign of King James I* (London, 1836), 97.
120 Payne, 'Inventory', 41.
121 TNA, SC6/JASI/1648.
122 Heiberg, *Christian IV and Europe*, 136; Hulse, 'Review', 101.
123 Heiberg, *Christian IV and Europe*, 119–142; S. O. Jørgensen, 'Court Culture during the Reign of Christian IV', in B. Noldus and J. Roding (eds), *Pieter Isaacsz* (Turnhout, 2007), 15–31: 23. The work of Helen Watanabe-O'Kelly and Mara R. Wade has been particularly important for informing our knowledge of court festival at the Protestant German courts, see, for instance, H. Watanabe-O'Kelly, *Triumphall shews: Tournaments at German-speaking Courts in the European Context, 1560–1730* (Berlin, 1992); J. R. Mulryne and H. Watanabe-O'Kelly (eds), *Europa Triumphans: Court and Civic Festivals in Early Modern Europe*, 2 vols (Aldershot, 2004); M. R. Wade, *Triumphus Nupitalis Danicus. German Court Culture and Denmark: The Great Wedding of 1634* (Wiesbaden, 1996); M. R. Wade (ed.), *Pomp, Power, and Politics: Essays on German and Scandinavian Court Culture and their Contexts* (Amsterdam, 2003).
124 Hulse, 'Review', 101.

125 *CSPV*, vol. 10, no. 556: 2 August 1606.
126 For Cecil see L. Hulse, 'The Musical Patronage of Robert Cecil, First Earl of Salisbury (1563–1612)', *Journal of the Royal Musical Association* 116 (1991), 24–40; '"Musique which pleaseth myne eare"; Robert Cecil's Musical Patronage', in P. Croft (ed.), *Patronage, Culture and Power* (New Haven and London, 2002), 139–158.
127 Ashbee, *English Court Music*, xi.
128 *CSPV*, vol. 12, no. 284: 28 July 1611; no. 301: 11 August 1611.
129 *CSPV*, vol. 12, no. 415: 13 January 1612.
130 McNeill (ed.), *Exchequer Rolls*, vol. 22, 154, 196–197, 307; McNeill (ed.), *Exchequer Rolls*, vol. 23, 153, 281; NRS, E21/76, fol. 314. Juhala identifies a further ten trumpeters serving in James's household prior to the queen's arrival: Juhala, 'Household and Court', 322.
131 McNeill (ed.), *Exchequer Rolls*, vol. 22, 63. The Hudsons remained in court service at least to 1594, by which time James Hudson was no longer included but the fee was unchanged, see McNeill (ed.), *Exchequer Rolls*, vol. 22, 233, 286.
132 Juhala, 'Household and Court', 315–316.
133 McNeill (ed.), *Exchequer Rolls*, vol. 22, 122.
134 NRS, E23/11/16; NRS, E21/74, fol. 81r; NRS, E24/22. My thanks to Michael Pearce for this reference.
135 Juhala, 'Household and Court', 316.
136 Ashbee, *English Court Music*, ix; TNA, SC6/JASI/1646.
137 TNA, AO3/1187, fol. 38r.
138 Hulse, 'Cecil's Musical Patronage', 143; Wade, 'Duke Ulrik', 253.
139 Hulse, 'Cecil's Musical Patronage', 143.
140 As quoted in Wade, 'Duke Ulrik', 253.
141 TNA, SC6/JASI/1646. In the end Christian did not arrive until 13 July 1606, but he was confirmed before 10 April, see H. N. Davies, 'The Limitations of Festival: Christian IV's State Visit to England in 1606', in J. R. Mulryne and M. Shewring (eds), *Italian Renaissance Festivals and their European Influence* (Lewiston, 1992), 311–335: 320.
142 Hulse, 'Cecil's Musical Patronage', 143; Wade, 'Duke Ulrik', 253.
143 M. R. Wade, 'Widowhood as a Space for Patronage: Hedevig, Princess of Denmark and Electress of Saxony', *Renæssanceforum* 4 (2008), 1–28: 16–22. On the music of the Wolfenbüttel court see A. Spohr, 'Musikalische Widmungen an Herzog Heinrich Julius', in W. Arnold, B. Bei der Wieden, and U. Gleixner (eds), *Herzog Heinrich Julius zu Braunschweig und Lüneburg (1564–1613): Politiker und Gelehrter mit europäischen* (Brunswick, 2016), 283–298.
144 B. Browning, 'Dramatic Activities and the Advent of the English Players at the Court of Heinrich Julius von Braunschweig', in B. Becker-Cantarino and J. Fechner (eds), *Opitz und seine Welt: Festschrift für George Schulz-Behrend* (Amsterdam, 1990), 125–139: 132.
145 H. Vogel, 'The Genesis and Radiance of a Court Organ', in K. J. Snyder (ed.), *The Organ as a Mirror of its Time: North European Reflections, 1610–2000* (Oxford, 2002), 48–59: 49–51.
146 Vogel, 'Genesis and Radiance', 51; Wade, 'Widowhood', 16–17.
147 Bergsagel, 'Danish Musicians in England', 10.
148 H. C. Maxwell Lyte (ed.), *Acts of the Privy Council of England*, vol. 33 (London, 1921), 483; Bergsagel, 'Anglo-Scandinavian Musical Relations', 269.
149 Bergsagel, 'Anglo-Scandinavian Musical Relations', 270.
150 Bergsagel, 'Danish Musicians', 12, 16. For Brade see A. Spohr, 'Networking, Patronage and Professionalism', in D. Smith and R. Taylor (eds), *Networks of Music in the Late Sixteenth and Early Seventeenth Centuries: A Collection of Essays in Celebration of Peter Philip's 450th Anniversary* (Farnham, 2014), 203–214.

151 Hauge, 'John Dowland's Employment', 198–107; Ward, 'Dowland Miscellany', 18–23, 99–107.
152 Ward, 'Dowland Miscellany', 99, 149–151.
153 Bergsagel, 'Danish Musicians', 16.
154 Ward, 'Dowland Miscellany', 18; Moe, 'Italian Music at the Danish Court', 18; Heiberg, *Christian IV and Europe*, 132, 135–136.
155 *CSPV*, vol. 15, no. 658: 19 December 1618 (Relation of England of Foscarini). A 'consort' referring here to a harmonious vocal or instrumental company of musicians: 'consort, n.2'. *OED* Online, Oxford University Press, July 2018, www.oed.com/view/Entry/39728. Accessed 29 October 2018.
156 TNA, SC6/JASI/1648; TNA, SC6/JASI/1650; TNA, SC6/JASI/1655. The French musicians were Lewes Richart, John Chantard, Camille Prevost, Peter de la Mare, and Claud Oliver. With the exception of the latter, who was paid £50 per annum, the other four each received more than £100, which was significantly more than Anna's English fifers, drummers, or trumpeters, who each received an annual stipend of around £20.
157 *CSPV*, vol. 12, no. 551: 10 June 1612; BL, RP 8877.
158 TNA, SC6/JASI/1646; TNA, SC6/JASI/1648; TNA, SC6/JASI/1653; TNA, SC6/JASI/1655; Ashbee, *English Court Music*, 197–206.
159 *CSPD* (1619–1623), 616, no. 38: 22 June 1623; Hulse, 'Musical Patronage of Robert Cecil', 27–28.
160 Musical grooms were not unique to Anna's household and were also part of James's and Elizabeth I's establishments, Ashbee, *English Court Music*, xi; A. Ashbee, 'Groomed for Service. Musicians in the Privy Chamber at the English Court, c.1495–1558', *Early Music* 25 (1997), 185–198.
161 TNA, LR6/154/9. Bachelor had been lutenist to Queen Elizabeth: Ward, 'Dowland Miscellany', 20.
162 TNA, SC6/JASI/1648.
163 TNA, SC6/JASI/1648.
164 Ashbee, *English Court Music*, 16. This was repeated in 1608, see Ashbee, *English Court Music*, 79, 81.
165 TNA, LS13/280, fol. 393.
166 TNA, SC6/JASI/1646; BL Add MS 27404; TNA, E351/543, fols 126v, 147v; Ashbee, *English Court Music*, 21, 26. Hales had served under Queen Elizabeth.
167 Ashbee, *English Court Music*, 200; TNA, SC6/JASI/1650.
168 Ashbee, *English Court Music*, 5; TNA, E351/543, fols 204r, 126v.
169 P. Holman, *Four and Twenty Fiddlers: The Violin at the English Court, 1540–1690* (Oxford, 1993), 175.
170 Ashbee, *English Court Music*, 11; Holman, *Four and Twenty Fiddlers*, 199. Ferrabosco was evidently in the service of the Prince by 28 November 1604 when he was paid for purchasing two viols in cases and one box of strings 'for the use and service of the Prince': TNA, E351/543, fol. 136r.
171 TNA, LR6/154/9.
172 Griffey, *On Display*, 104; Sykes, 'Henrietta Maria's "house of delight"', 332–334: quotation from Griffey.
173 Burke, 'Translating Knowledge', 70.

1 Portrait of Anna of Denmark by Paul van Somer, 1617. Royal Collection Trust / © Her Majesty Queen Elizabeth II 2019.

2 Portrait of Anna of Denmark after Adrian Vanson, c.1595. © Philip Mould & Company.

3 Enamelled gold miniature case set with table diamonds, bearing the monograms of Anna of Denmark, Sofie of Mecklenburg-Güstrow and Christian IV of Denmark, c.1610. © The Fitzwilliam Museum, Cambridge.

4 Portrait of King James VI by Adrian Vanson, c.1595. © Philip Mould & Company.

5 Portrait of James VI and I, attributed to John de Critz the Elder, c.1606. Dulwich Picture Gallery, London.

6 Portrait of Anna of Denmark by John de Critz the Elder, c.1605–1610. © National Portrait Gallery, London.

7 Miniature of Anna of Denmark by Isaac Oliver, c.1604. The Rothschild Collection / © The National Trust, Waddesdon Manor.

8 Miniature of Anna of Denmark by Isaac Oliver, c.1605–1610. © Berkeley Castle, Gloucestershire / Photograph by Peter Yardley.

9 Portrait of King Christian IV of Denmark, after Marcus Gheeraerts the Younger, 1614. Courtesy of the Princeton University Art Museum.

10 Illustrated diagram of the processional order around the royal effigy for the funeral of Anna of Denmark, 1619. Royal College of Arms, London, MS I.4, fol. 13r. Reproduced by permission of the Kings, Heralds and Pursuivants of Arms.

11 Design for the hearse of Anna of Denmark, attributed to Maximilian Colt, 1619. Royal College of Arms, London, MS I.1, p.1. Reproduced by permission of the Kings, Heralds and Pursuivants of Arms.

4

Jewellery and apparel

The early modern body was a socio-political entity constructed through the use of apparel, adornment, and movement. In the courtly community, royal and aristocratic bodies were routinely dressed in costly lengths of fabric – plush velvets, brocades, rich fur, glossy silks – that were covered in lace trimmings, passages of embroidery, precious metal fastenings, and the show of sparkling gems and lustrous pearls. Fashioned from expensive materials that required specialist craftsmanship, these goods literally materialised the wearer's wealth and status, but they often also communicated more personal aspects of identity such as gender, power, piety, and networks of belonging.[1] In his work on the adornment of the noble male body in northern Renaissance Italy, Timothy McCall highlights the interrelationship of visual court culture and socio-political meaning, writing that 'nobility was manifested somatically … by the entire court', for these were 'social arenas in which distinctions of rank were displayed and embodied, in the process simultaneously constituting and illustrating ever-shifting hierarchies enacted by economies of favour, access, and status'.[2] Importantly, the politics of bodily display was available to elite women, who made specific sartorial and accessory choices to legitimise positions, visualise political ambitions, or to show their allegiance, favour, or dynastic membership. Significantly too, this was exercised on a relatively public platform, for not only was the physical body visually appraised by local and visiting dignitaries and elites at court, but it was seen and assessed at distant courts through verbal, written, and pictorial accounts.

In the following chapter, material artefacts are recognised as active repositories of meaning and memory. Drawing on the work of McCall and Leah Clark, pieces of apparel and jewellery are approached as agents that could shape and inscribe the early modern body with signification.[3] Yet this enactment was just one element in a symbiotic dynamic that was in part dependent on the innate lineage of the specific body, and, leading on from this, that *what* was signified was not fixed but changed in accordance with physical setting, socio-political context, and both the individual user and onlooker.[4] The examination of Anna's bodily display centres on her time in both Scotland and England, but particular attention is given to her movement between the Danish, Scottish, and English court spaces. These were key junctures involving Anna's negotiation of established fashions, socio-political formalities, and cultural traditions. The discussion of Anna's self-fashioning extends to her householders – for many were attired through the royal wardrobes and their apparel reflected and enhanced the queen's status and honour. Garments and jewels also flowed between the queen and her servitors in the ritualised world of gift-exchange, which was fundamental to the loyalty and reach of the crown. For Anna, as for many of her royal contemporaries, this courtly convention extended beyond the domestic to the international courtly arena, and it is pertinent to understanding the valuable role the queen played in maintaining dynastic fealty and patronage networks.

Building on the pioneering work of Janet Arnold and Maria Hayward, the recent turn in early modern dress history – headed by cultural historians including Eva Andersson, Sylvène Édouard, Isabelle Paresys, Ulinka Rublack, and Laura Oliván Santaliestra – has focused on uncovering many of the ways in which dress was used and read as a signifier of complex social, economic, political, and religious codes.[5] One of the most emphatic demonstrations of the ability of apparel to showcase national and dynastic identity occurred with movement between courts. For women, this was most commonly occasioned by marriage, for as young princesses they left their natal court – often for the last time – to travel to their new marital kingdom. During this highly politic voyage, they were physical symbols of the families and countries of their birth, but they simultaneously embodied the future of their marital house and kingdom – a duality that turned their bodies into a contentious site for the visualisation of dynastic pride, power, and national belonging. Scholars have, for example, determined that on their marriage to Habsburg royalty, the French princesses Élisabeth of Valois and Élisabeth of Bourbon immediately exchanged their local, French, style of dress for Spanish fashion, in an act that signified the bride's marital subservience and a Habsburg triumph over the houses of Valois and Bourbon.[6] Yet not all early modern royal women shed their native dress after marriage with some, such as Leonor of Castilla (1498–1558), introducing and popularising their natal styles in their new kingdoms.[7]

In England, well-known examples of royal women who retained their homeland fashion on arrival included Catherine of Aragón (1485–1536) and, later, Catherine of Bragança (1638–1705). As Hayward has shown, the arrival of Catherine in 1501 resulted in a flurry of descriptions about her attire, all of which meaningfully stressed that it was 'aftir the manour of her contre'. Later, on her wedding day, a similarly nationalistic interest coloured the eye witness accounts that she wore a 'gown very large, bothe the slevys and also the body' and her attendant 'ladies of Hispayne were arayed' in 'the same fourme ... ther gownes ... aftir their countray maner'.[8] More than 150 years later, Catherine of Bragança travelled to England dressed in Portuguese court fashion whereupon John Evelyn (1620–1706) caustically noted that she 'arrived with her Portuguese ladies in their monstrous fardingales or guard-infantes, their complexions olivader and sufficiently unagreeable. Her Majesty in the same habit, her foretop long and turned aside very strangely.'[9] In both cases, the style of dress inscribed the wearer's body with dynastic and geographic meaning. Thus, elements of the unfamiliar and unfashionable provoked harsh summaries as court onlookers read the foreign styles as evidence that the new consort was loyal to her natal, rather than her martial, house and kingdom. Yet other members of the English body politic warmly embraced Catherine of Bragança's 'monstrous' fashion as a sign of her dynastic value being synonymous with Portuguese wealth and trade opportunities.[10] In between these two queens, England received another foreign consort with the arrival of Anna of Denmark in July 1603. Unlike her predecessor and successor, Anna's entry was not brought about by marriage, but by the succession as King James VI of Scotland added England and Ireland to his dominions. Anna's arrival was further distinguished by it being the second time that she had been the centrepiece of a dynastic cavalcade crossing international borders, having voyaged as a new bride from Denmark-Norway to Scotland in 1590. More interestingly perhaps, and certainly more puzzling, her arrival into Scotland and later into England elicited a markedly different response from her new subjects: silence.

In crossing the North Sea to be crowned the new Queen of Scotland, Anna, together with her extensive retinue and attendant baggage train, required a fleet of sixteen ships, and 'her guard, horses, ships, plate, jewels, apparel' were particularly noted to be 'all so costly it is strange to hear'.[11] The princess was accompanied by 'fourtie personis in goldin chenyeis of guid faschioun' and her 'haill trayne' numbered some 223 people.[12] Then, as mentioned, some fourteen years later James's accession to the English throne necessitated Anna's second, highly charged political journey as she traversed the border dividing the national, linguistic, and cultural identity of Scotland from that of England.[13] Again, reports were eagerly penned. The Venetian ambassador, Scaramelli, stated that Anna reached Windsor in the company of 'two hundred and fifty carriages, and upwards of five thousand horses', while Carleton confidently assured Chamberlain that she was attended by 'a court of ladies and many very fair and goodly ones which were never before seen *in rerum natura*'.[14] In reality, numbers were somewhat less, with a retinue of around 209 people,

215 horses, and seven horse-drawn carriages, but this was a magnificent princely spectacle intended to delight the eye and capture the hearts of the queen's new subjects. A literal embodiment of the Stuart dynasty, the cavalcade was a tool of a political statecraft demanding a high level of material outlay that cost the English crown more than £2,700.[15]

At the very centre of this extraordinary material procession, Anna's royal female body physically signified the wealth, strength, and fashion of dynasty and kingdom. On the occasion of her coming into Scotland, she was pointedly observed to possess a 'rich provision of apparel' that had had 'more than 500 tailors and embroiderers ... at work upon it for three months', and it was reported that her mother Sofie had 'bought many jewels for her, especially pearls'.[16] Indeed, the Danes made specific reference to Anna's jewellery in the marriage treaty, stating that her late father, Frederik II, had determined her dowry at 100,000 guilders but that this was separate to 'the princely gems and other decorations which it is fitting for princesses to wear'.[17] Likewise, when it came to Anna's journey into England in 1603, King James exercised considerable care to outfit the bodies of the queen and her attendants in costly garments and jewels. James's letter to the English privy council makes clear his sartorial needs and expectations, and he explicitly conflates a rich material display with dignity and status, demanding that 'Jewells to be sent for our wyfe [Anna] ... for that we hold needfull for her honor: and ... for horses, lytters, coaches, sadles and other things of that nature'.[18] Later addressing Parliament in 1614, James reiterated his belief that jewels were representative of princely virtue and were thus requisite adornment for the royal body asserting that 'as I shall answere to allmighty god ... my purity [is] like the mettell of golde of my crowne, my firmenes and clearenes like the pr[e]cious stones I weare.'[19] In 1603, James not only required that his consort be equipped with goods from the Tudor wardrobes, but he ordered large amounts of costly textiles – velvet, cloth of gold, cloth of silver, rich taffeta, grosgrain, tabine, tissue, sarcenet, and satin – that was sent into Scotland to be made into new garments for Anna.[20] The queen also received 'one paire of Showes of cloth of gold ... bound aboute wth gold lace' and 'two paire of Spanishe Lether Showes' from the English cobbler Peter Johnson, while six of her Scottish female attendants were provided with fabric for new garments.[21]

There is no doubt that during Anna's bridal journey into Edinburgh, and her later procession into London, the queen cut a magnificent spectacle with her dressed body visually testifying to her dynastic, social, and economic position.[22] But, despite this extraordinary level of riches, Anna's attire – and her appearance more generally – has left surprisingly little trace in the surviving accounts of the two events. Writing of Anna's arrival in Scotland, David Stevenson acknowledges this paucity of information, stating that it 'may not be very remarkable: the trade in princesses was a matter much more of politics than personalities', but suggesting that it resulted from Anna's 'tendency towards melancholy', which prevented her from making 'any impact'.[23] Yet this elides a crucial fact: these entries were expressly intended to make a significant visual impact. They were highly calculated, hugely expensive matters of state, wherein the quantity of the entourage and the quality of the material goods signified the prestige, honour, and power of the associated kingdom. Furthermore, the culturally constructed royal body was not reliant on aspects of character or personality to make statements about socio-political and economic power or dynastic belonging. One plausible explanation for the silence is that those who did witness Anna's entrance – unlike those who watched the arrival of Catherine of Aragón or Catherine of Bragança – did not consider the consort's dress, deportment, jewellery, hair style, or skin colour, to warrant judgement.[24] In other words, Anna of Denmark appeared sufficiently familiar. This supposition is supported by Carleton's opinion that the new queen 'giveth *great contentment to the world in her fashion* and courteous behaviour to the people'.[25] Modelling a 'contentment' of apparel implies that Anna conformed to expectations of *how* an English queen consort should dress – that is, she was attired in sufficiently local fashions. Indeed, Anna may well have been attired in clothing from Elizabeth's wardrobe, for James had given explicit orders that she be sent 'such jewels and other furniture which did appertain to the late Queen [Elizabeth I] as you [the English privy council] think meet for her [Anna's] estate'.[26] Despite James's orders, however, and the oft-quoted belief that 'on leaving Edinburgh' Anna 'generously distributed among the ladies who remained behind, all her jewels, dresses, hangings of her rooms, everything she had, without exception' in readiness for inheriting the riches of Elizabeth's wardrobe, evidence shows that this was only part of the story.[27]

In Scotland, in preparation for Anna's remove, orders were given for her to have new clothes and for existing pieces to be altered. In the weeks before her departure, Anna received new gowns, sets of sleeves, bodies (most commonly of baleen), petticoats, skirts, cloaks, doublets, and footmantles, all of which were presumably made with the fabric that James had ordered for her in England.[28] Several extant gowns needed to be made over into 'ane new vthir [other] fassoun', which required significant amounts of fabric that generally matched the gown.[29] Several entries record enlargements such as the two ells (6.2 feet) of Spanish grey taffeta that were issued 'to eik ane' [to enlarge one] of the queen's gowns 'qlk wes all oppunit out and maid over againe' [which was all opened out and made over again], while 3.5 ells (10.8 feet) of white satin was added to another gown that 'wes alterit lykwayis and maid eftir ye new fassoun' [was altered likewise and made after the new fashion].[30] A third gown of cloth of silver, was fitted with new bodies and sleeves of white Tours taffeta in order that it 'wes all alterit to ane vther fassinn' [was all altered to an other fashion], while a grey velvet gown 'wes lykwayis alterit to ane vthir fassiony' [was likewise altered to an other fashion] with bodies and sleeves of light grey satin lined with red Spanish taffeta.[31] Evidently, considerable amounts of fabric were required and the changes were therefore presumably very noticeable. Leading on from this, it is feasible that the queen's round gowns or Spanish farthingales worn in Scotland were being made over into French, or drum-shaped, farthingales in line with established English court fashion.[32] Irrespective of the exact fashions, it is significant that Anna's move from Scotland to England required her bodily display to be reconfigured to signify her ability and legitimacy to fulfil her new position as consort of the multiple Stuart kingdom.

Despite the efforts made in Scotland, after 'her maties [Anna's] first happie coming' to England, more goods were ordered from milliners, sempters, silkmen, silkwomen, hosiers, embroiderers, linen drapers, woollen drapers, feathermakers, farthingale-makers, and haberdashers. Much of this was for fabrics, lace, and trimmings, but there were also readymade items including 'divers roabes', farthingales, cuffs, ruffs, gloves, fans, garters, gloves, coifs, hats, handkerchiefs, 'ringstrapps',[33] waistcoats, and silk stockings.[34] George Sheeres, apothecary and 'odoriferous servitor', provided sweet bags, sweet waters, and perfumes for Anna's garments, and perhaps also for the royal body, while the cobbler, Thomas Wilson, was paid for 'shooes pantoffles & buskins'.[35] In addition to these new garments, it is almost certain – given the high cost of fabrics in this period – that access to Elizabeth's wardrobe was granted at this point or, if James's orders were followed, some of it had been given to Anna before she left Scotland. This would not have involved the wholesale adoption of existing garments, but a careful process of tailoring and refashioning certain pieces and fabrics in accordance with Anna's size and sensibilities. Whether attired in new apparel, or in altered garments from the Tudor wardrobe, visual evidence confirms that clear efforts were made to configure the new consort in line with current Elizabethan style, thereby adding a visual and physical link between the Tudor and Stuart dynasties. Portraits from Anna's time in Scotland (Plate 2), show her wearing a full, round linen collar, and a wide-set coiffure, while her first English portraits – from around 1603 – register a distinctive shift (Figure 4.1). These portraits conform to the general silhouette seen in contemporary portraits of Elizabeth and elite English gentlewomen, as Anna now wears a square neckline with a standing collar, and a coiffure that is high and narrow. It is uncertain whether this was a reflection of the queen's everyday attire, but it is significant that a specifically Elizabethan mode was chosen for Anna's publicised image, for not only was it seen in oil paintings but in engravings and in Anna's English coronation medal (Figures 4.2 and 4.3). The engraving makes the date of the change explicit, for it occurred in the variant image included in editions of John Jonston's *Inscriptiones* that were printed after 1603.[36]

4.1 Portrait of Anna of Denmark, after John de Critz the Elder, c.1603.

More emphatically than necklines, collars, and hairstyles, it has been the drum-shaped French farthingale that dress historians have heralded as the sartorial link between the Tudor and Stuart queens. Favoured by Anna on coming to England, she continued to wear the style until her death in 1619. In the early days of the English reign, Anna may very well

Jewellery and apparel

4.2 Anonymous engraving of Anna of Denmark, c.1603.

4.3 Medal commemorating the coronation of Anna of Denmark, 1603.

have made use of Elizabeth's extant farthingales, although she was also quick to secure her own, personal farthingale-maker. Rather than patronise Elizabeth's supplier Robert Sibthorpe, Anna employed the services of Robert Hughes, a farthingale specialist based in London.[37] From July 1603, right through until the close of 1618, Hughes fulfilled regular orders for farthingales for the queen and he was among those artificers granted black mourning cloth to walk in Anna's funeral procession in May 1619.[38] In 1617, it was this style of dress that drew the amazement of the Venetian priest Horatio Busino, who famously declared that 'Her Majesty's costume was pink and gold with so expansive a farthingale that I do not exaggerate when I say it was four feet wide in the hips. Her bosom was bare down to the pit of her stomach, forming as it were, an oval.'[39] He clearly did exaggerate, at least in part, but the expansive, drum-shaped farthingale has become synonymous with Anna and dress historians have repeatedly pointed to her insistence that it 'be worn at court long after it ceased to be fashionable', as the result of Anna being 'indebted to images of Queen Elizabeth I'.[40]

Initially, Anna's retention of the drum-shaped farthingale did establish a connection to the deceased Elizabeth, and in the early days of the Stuart's English reign such sartorial consistency contributed to the acceptance and popularity of the new dynasty. However, it must also be recognised that far from being outdated, the drum-shaped farthingale continued to be the height of fashion throughout the 1620s at the courts of Brandenburg, Denmark-Norway, France, Sweden, and Wolfenbüttel.[41] Thus, we find the French queens, Ana María (Anne of Austria), and Maria de Médici, together with many of Anna's female relatives – including Anna Catherine, Maria Eleonora (1599–1655), and Kirsten Munk (1598–1658) – being commemorated in their formal portraits wearing the drum-shaped farthingale throughout the 1610s and 1620s.[42] Indeed, evidence of portrait exchange confirms that Anna knew the style was still in good taste and high usage in her wider familial network. In 1609, the Stuart court received full-length portraits of Anna's older sister Elisabeth, her husband, Heinrich Julius, and individual portraits of their five children: those of Elisabeth, and her three daughters, show them wearing drum-shaped farthingales (Figure 4.4).[43]

Efforts were made to dress Anna's body in Elizabethan fashions for her journey and welcome into England, but her retinue was pointedly shaped to represent both Houses of Stuart and Tudor. On the one hand, Anna's pages of the equerry, the attendants of her coaches and chariots, the lackey appointed to her 'dames of honor', as well as the two pages of honour and the two lackeys assigned to Prince Henry, were all outfitted in garments of the Stuart colours – crimson or scarlet, trimmed and lined with yellow.[44] On the other hand, the heraldic Tudor colours of green and white were noticeable among the apparel of the queen's horses, which included 'horseclothes of white and grene cloth, lined with Canvas & bordered with white and grene cloth', while one of the wagons, together with its attendant horses and the coachman's hammercloth, was embroidered with roses.[45] This Tudor display may well have been the practical result of James's aforementioned request that the privy council send 'horses, lytters, coaches, sadles and other things of that nature' for Anna's journey, but it was also political.[46] As these heraldic colours, monograms, and symbols moved conspicuously through the countryside, James visually underscored his hereditary right to rule the new multiple kingdom as a legitimate descendant of the English House of Tudor.

4.4 Portrait of Princess Dorothea of Braunschweig-Wolfenbüttel, attributed to Jacob van Doort, 1609.

Household livery

As with many early modern noble and royal houses, the Stuarts provided clothing for a quantity of their servitors. These disbursements varied widely in colour and fabric, and household hierarchies were finely enacted through quantity and quality, although specifics were not always recorded in the accounts. For Anna's servitors in Scotland, two ordering systems were enacted through the main cloth supplier, the Scottish merchant and financier Robert Joussie (d.1610). One consisted of orders 'subscryvit with hir majesties [Anna's] awin hand', while the other contained precepts issued to the master of the great wardrobe, Sir George Home of Spott (c.1566–1611), although both streams were covered by the crown, and not by the queen's privy purse.[47] One account, running from 25 May 1592 to February 1596, details Joussie incurring fabric costs of £8,238.18s.5d. Scots for the queen's servants' dress.[48] Contextualised within the court setting where 'nobility was manifested somatically', these records provide insight into the active role of apparel in embodying social hierarchies, dynastic belonging, and honour and reward.[49]

Rather than dynastic livery, the majority of Anna's servitors in Scotland – ushers, pages, tailors, male chamberers, 's[er]uand women', maidens, her Danish cooks, and German minister – were outfitted in black, wherein the quality and quantity of the cloth denoted hierarchical rank and significance.[50] Servants of less importance and who were not readily seen, such as the Danish female cook, Marion, wore cheaper fabrics such as black grosgrain taffeta, London cloth, and frieze. By comparison, those servitors who were more visible and worked in closer physical proximity to the queen were more richly apparelled, but even here careful distinctions were made. For example, two ushers of the queen's chamber – David Morton and James Ogilvie – were both outfitted in black coats, breeches, doublets, and cloaks, but while Morton's outfit cost more than £165 Scots with silk hose, a doublet of 'fine' velvet and a cloak made from ten ells of grosgrain taffeta, Ogilvie was clearly of lesser rank, wearing worsted hose, a doublet of Naples taffeta, and a much shorter cloak made from only three ells of London cloth, the total of which only came to around £80 Scots.[51] More expensive than either outfit was that issued to Anna's Danish secretary, Johannes Calixtus Skien, who received a doublet and breeches of black three-pile velvet, and a cloak of fine grosgrain taffeta lined with fine velvet.[52]

It was not a straightforward case of all servitors wearing black, and many received garments in an array of colours where the determinants remain unclear.[53] Anna's Danish, or perhaps German, gentleman, William Belou (Wilhelm Below) (d.1626), was individualised through orders for garments of bright and varied colours.[54] Between August 1591 and January 1596, for example, he had garments fashioned in violet, red, purple, yellow, green, orange, black, brown, and columbine. Many gentlewomen also received coloured garments, ordered by both James and Anna, the volume of which is suggestive of gift-giving rather than rewards for service and some items were expressly given as extraordinary gifts on the occasion of marriage.[55] More straightforward was the decision to attire the queen's pages and footmen in heraldic livery of the colours of the House of Stuart – red and yellow – equipping them with yellow doublets, scarlet cloaks, coats, stockings, and breeches with cloaks lined with yellow frieze, and the knees of the breeches adorned with yellow trimmings.[56] Stuart dynastic livery was also worn by King James's pages, lackeys, and court trumpeters, and it was issued for representatives travelling abroad and for court ceremonial, such as the baptism of Prince Henry in 1594.[57] For the baptism, six pages were 'cled in reid vellvot' with cloaks lined and faced in yellow, eight lackeys were dressed entirely in red with gold passements and fastenings, and five trumpeters wore yellow velvet hats lined with red, and red doublets, hose, and cloaks wherein the latter was lined and faced with yellow. The significance of the colours worn by other Stuart representatives at the baptism are more difficult to determine, such as the blue and green outfits of the pages of honour – John Murray, Harry Levingston, James Douglas, and Archibald Murray.[58] With the possible exception of the journey into England, where Tudor heraldry also featured, it was the red-and-yellow livery of the House of Stuart that continued in use in England, and it was seen across the households of James, Anna, and Prince Henry. On 25 November 1605, warrants called for eleven of James's pages to be apparelled in crimson velvet and yellow taffeta with buttons and lace of gold.[59] Later, in April 1609, a much larger warrant ordered the embroidery of 330 red livery coats – some of these were to feature James's letters in Venice gold, but the majority were to have red and white roses with a closed (imperial) crown, which pointedly referenced the king's rule over his empire of England, Ireland, and Scotland, and his descent from the Houses of Lancaster and York.[60]

In Scotland, records show apparel pointedly visualising national origins when provisions of English cloth, bombasie, and buroun lining cloth were sanctioned for several of Anna's household servitors in order that they each have 'ane commoun garment for a persoun according to the custome of Denmark'.[61] Paid for by the treasury, the colour or style is not specified, but the shorthand entry suggests that it was distinctive and known to the wardrobe staff. Many of the recipients of these 'commoun garmentis' (liveries) are, perhaps expectedly, identifiable as Danes and included the cupper George Epping (or van Epinghen), and the carver Christopher Carioth (or Carriot), who each had two servants; the secretary Johannes Calixtus Skein; the tailor Paul Rey (Pål Rei); the lackey Hans Feier (or Fyer), and the queen's master cook.[62] Crossing several social hierarchies, the 'custome' may have referred to an expected number of garments, the use of a particular colour, or perhaps a particular cut. It is also possible that this order was given for a specific occasion, for Skein and Feier appear elsewhere in the accounts receiving monochrome apparel, along with Scottish servitors – there being no mention of national custom.[63] Additionally, it is worth noting that Anna had servitors from diverse European kingdoms who were not apparelled according to their origin, such as her two 'laquayis [lackeys] the ane being a Dense [Danish or German] and the uther a Frensche man', both of whom were attired in red and yellow Stuart dynastic livery.[64] On the other hand, the royal Scottish wardrobe did periodically issue clothing that conclusively testified to Anna's dynastic networks as when heraldic liveries were provided for visiting 'dutche [German] larkay[s]'.

In May 1591, the Scottish court received a delegate from the House of Guelf – the marital dynasty of Anna's older sister Elisabeth – and orders were accordingly made to attire the lackey of 'the Duke of Bruniswikis' [Brunswick/Braunschweig] all in green with doublet and breeches of green damask trimmed with green passement and green silk buttons.[65] In 1596, a precept was issued for 'Jacob the Duik of Middleburt his lackay' – a representative from Anna's maternal grandfather Ulric – to be dressed in blue velvet and orange taffeta with gold passements.[66] In September 1593, the Stuarts had hosted a third German footman, from an unspecified court, at which time he was outfitted in a combination of colours with a doublet of orange satin, hose of yellow worsted, and a garment of blue velvet.[67] Through the wear of specific, symbolic colours the lackeys were fashioned into visual signs of their representative ruler. In turn, this reflected directly on the queen consort, for these garments, together with those of the 'Danish custome' worn by her own servitors, meant that an Oldenburg presence was visually manifest at the heart of the Scottish court.

Anna's Danish entourage remained an intrinsic part of the Scottish court throughout her time there. Unlike many early modern royal women, Anna never suffered the expulsion of her bridal entourage in order to force integration.[68] This was despite the fact that some Scots believed she preferred the Danes, with one court attendee observing, in June 1590, that 'our Quein carys a marvelus gravity, quhilk [which], with her partiall solitarines, contrar to the humor of our pepell [the Scots], hath banis[h]ed *all our ladys* clein from her.'[69] Throughout the 1590s, many individual Danes who had journeyed to Scotland in the bridal retinue sought return passage to Denmark, and both James and Anna wrote letters of recommendation and endorsement to Christian IV; many were outfitted with livery for their return journey and/or given extraordinary cash payment.[70] In August 1591, for example, James disbursed £240 Scots to John Gibb 'one of the wallettis [valets] of his heines chalmer to be debursit for certaine deinsmenis [Danish men's] liverayis that past to Denmark'.[71] James's acceptance and generosity was, in part, political. Throughout his regency, and that of his mother Queen Mary (1542–1587), contact between Scotland and Denmark-Norway was slight, but this changed around 1585. From this point onwards, in addition to James and Anna's marriage in 1589, a series of mercantile, military, and political alliances were brokered between the kingdoms, and the maintenance of good relations with the House of Oldenburg developed into a cornerstone of James's international policy.[72] Both Anna and James kept close personal relationships with Christian IV, and there was a high level of exchange between the two kingdoms as diplomats, messengers, gifts, letters – and even royal figures – crossed over the North Sea. Christian himself visited England in 1606 and 1614, and Anna's younger brother Duke Ulrik of Holstein was at the Stuart court in Scotland in 1598 and in England from November 1604 to the end of May 1605.[73] James subsequently granted him a substantial annuity of £1,000, which was still being honoured in May 1614.[74] Repairing Anglo-Danish relations – which had deteriorated during the last years of Elizabeth's reign – was a pressing concern for James on his accession to the English throne. As early as 6 May 1603, James wrote to Christian expressing his hope and belief that 'the quarrels which arose between English and Danish royal subjects ... (whatever they might have been) can easily be put to rest and thoroughly removed owing to our mutual friendship'.[75]

When the Stuarts relocated to London in 1603, several Danish householders chose to remain in the company and service of the queen. Some, such as the Danish maid Katherina Block, journeyed with Anna to England but then, in 1605, chose to return to Denmark, receiving a parting gift of £100 sterling from the queen.[76] Others, such as the German Lutheran chaplain Johan Sering, and another Danish maid Anna Kroas, stayed with the queen until her death, while the sisters Dorothy and Jyngell Silken, also Danish, who served as gentlewomen of the bedchamber, chose to be naturalised in England in 1610.[77] In the list of Anna's householders who walked in her funeral procession, two grooms, John Peterson and Peter Brand, were specifically designated as 'Dutch', a term generally used to refer to a German person but sometimes also used to indicate a Dane.[78] Yet Anna's English household shows that she did not give preferment to her Danish and/or German servitors, for a number of Scots were given important positions: Jane (Jean) Drummond was appointed first lady (groom of the stool); Margaret Stewart, later Countess of Nottingham (c.1591–1639), was made lady of the drawing chamber; Anne Hay and Anna Livingstone (d.1632) became ladies of the bedchamber; Elizabeth Shaw was made a gentlewoman of the bedchamber; Elizabeth and Jane Murray became chamberers, and the chief maid was Barbara Abercrombie.[79] For Anna, those Danish and Scottish servitors – most particularly the women – were an intimate part of her daily life, and on more than one occasion she defended them vociferously. Famously, in August 1592, Anna's Danish serving woman Margaret Vinstarr orchestrated the escape of Sir John

Wemyss, young Laird of Logie, who had been imprisoned on suspicion of treason. Once discovered, James 'charged the Queen [Anna] something sharply with the evil parts of her servant, and so far that they were both in tears' and ordered Margaret's discharge.[80] Refusing to obey, Anna retorted that she would 'rather go to Denmark than part with Mistress Margaret or any others her domestic servants', and by the end of November James had pardoned Logie.[81] This is how the tale has been told and retold over the centuries, but new archival evidence suggests that James was most probably complicit in Logie's escape, the Laird having not only been the king's valet but a firm favourite. In June 1591, James determined that Logie would accompany him to the wedding of Sir John Murray of Tilliebardine's daughter wearing identical apparel and orders were given for each man to have a 'stand of maskerie clayths' made from incarnadine taffeta and gold tock, and trimmed with Florentine ribbons in blue and incarnadine, as well as headpieces made from hard buckram and complete with Venetian masks.[82] From the Duke of Lennox's actions we further learn that Logie was granted access to James's bedchamber, for Lennox was 'in displeasure' with Logie over 'his disobedience shewed in the King's chamber', and in January 1591 he jealously started a quarrel with the Laird in the street which resulted in his being 'commanded from the court for some tyme'.[83] Margaret did remain in Anna's service and favour, receiving large quantities of apparel from the queen and, on 26 October 1593, she was presented with a bed as a wedding present with an expensive set of velvet, damask, and taffeta hangings in orange and white, and trimmed with silver passementerie and a silk fringe. Rather touchingly, the queen shortly afterwards gave Margaret blue velvet 'nicht geir'.[84] When, on the occasion of Margaret's 'depture out of Scotland' (possibly for a trip abroad) in June 1594, Anna ordered her a parting gift of '17 ells of black Napellis [Naples] taffeta … to be hir ane goun'.[85]

A shared sense of national belonging likely furthered Anna's defence of Margaret on this occasion, but her most famous display of loyalty was to the Scottish Ruthven sisters in the aftermath of the Gowrie conspiracy. With the king having narrowly survived an alleged assassination attempt at Gowrie House by John Ruthven, Earl of Gowrie (c.1577–1600) and Alexander Ruthven (1580–1600), on 5 August 1600, an act was passed giving 48 hours to 'all and sundrie personis, man and woman, of the name of Ruthven' to leave court and 'they nor na utheris of the said name of Ruthven' were to come within 10 miles of either James or Anna 'undir the pane of deid'.[86] Resultantly, 'Gowrie's 2 sisters in chiefest credit with the Queen' were 'thrust out of the house from the Queen' and a 'very evil menage' formed between the royal couple.[87] While Anna, reluctantly and begrudgingly, acquiesced to James's orders, she continued to hold Beatrice Ruthven in high regard, and some two years later had her brought into her palace for a clandestine meeting.[88]

Court ceremonial

Although fortunate to only experience subtle changes in apparel, and gradual changes in her household, Anna's move to Scotland was cause for an immediate adaptation to new structures and forms of etiquette, and a host of foreign customs and values. The courts of Anna's childhood and that of her marriage were fundamentally, typologically, different: broadly speaking, the former was ceremonial, while the latter was patriarchal. Thus, the court of Frederik II, during Anna's lifetime, became increasingly formalised with strong hierarchies, complex rules of etiquette, restricted access, high cultural expenditure, and a general focus on the construction and projection of princely magnificence.[89] But at a base level, it was a military institution and it was also itinerant, with half of the chancellery stationed in Copenhagen and the other half travelling through the kingdom with Frederik. In respect of the royal children, some of them spent their early years in Mecklenburg under the care of their maternal grandparents and were then educated by learned nobles but, as Frederik's diary attests, they were frequently present at court where they spent time with their parents.[90] By comparison, the structure, wealth, and resources of James VI's court were little different to that of major Scots landowners. Access to the royal person was considerably freer than that observed at ceremonial courts, and the king was regularly forced to request provisions and/or hospitality from the nobility – not least of all in the preparation for Anna's arrival.[91] These formative differences permeated the culture and customs of the respective courts, and they confronted the newly married pair at their first meeting in 1589. On greeting her husband in Oslo, Anna was alarmed by James's attempt to give her 'a kisse efter the Scotis faschioun at meiting, quhilk scho refusit [which she refused] as not being in the forme of her countrie' and was further horrified that he was still attired in his travelling 'buites and all'.[92] Anna's reaction was not one of personal distaste but of cultural disparity. In fact, the Scottish and English use of kissing as a form of greeting shocked an array of European visitors. It drew comment as early as 1466, when Leo von Rozmital (c.1425–1486), a Bohemian nobleman, observed that 'when guests arrive … the hostess with all her family go out to meet and receive them; and the guests are required to kiss them all, and this among the English was the same as shaking hands among other nations.'[93] Desiderius Erasmus (1466–1536), in 1499, was likewise bemused by the custom, writing to Publio Fausto Andrelini (1462–1518) that 'wherever you come, you are received with a kiss by all; when you take your leave, you are dismissed with kisses; you return, kisses are repeated … wherever you move, there is nothing but kisses.'[94] It was still being remarked upon in 1604 when Juan Fernández de Velasco, Constable of Castile (c.1550–1613), had to greet twenty of Anna's ladies 'according to the custom of the country', which was, of course, with a kiss.[95] By this time, Anna was well accustomed to the tradition, having had it explained to her by James with 'a few wordis prively spoken' back in 1589, after which time the couple were observed sharing 'familiaretie and kisses'.[96]

Cultural influence flowed both ways, and for his part James was struck by the formality, distance, and splendour that characterised the Oldenburg court, and he consequently sought changes to his own style of majesty. As early as March 1590, when the king was still at Kronborg Castle, Robert Bowes, English ambassador in Scotland, recounted that James 'hath reformed th'order of his chamber, allowing ordinarily but iiij [four] gentlemen; th'others be now extraodinarie'.[97] Significantly, Bowes later confirmed, in May 1590, that James had brought these changes back with him to Scotland, where his chamber was now 'kept more private than before … the doors to be kept close, suffering none to have access to his chamber without his pleasure'.[98] The new restrictions on royal access were not universally welcomed and even before James's return, the nobility were incensed by 'the Kinges resolucion to reforme th'estate of his governement' and to establish 'a gard to shoulder and mayntayne this innovacion … [with] promis of th'assistance of th'estate of Denmark'.[99] Indeed, Denmark not only supported the changes, but was readily identified as the cause, as the Scottish court was 'drawen nere to th'order used in Denmark', which would see 'the wholl nobilitie … prejudiced in their auncient priveledges for their free accesse to the king's person, and vote in counsell and matters of estate'.[100] James also commissioned a new royal guard under the leadership of Sir John Carmichael (1542–1600), and the influence of the Danish model on the Scottish court was still palpable in June 1590 when James looked to 'wondrous solitary' after the manner 'of the court of Denmark'.[101] Nevertheless, the Scottish court remained firmly patriarchal, a type that, at least by the turn of the seventeenth century, if not much earlier, was deemed to be 'a symptom of poverty'.[102] The financial difficulties faced by the Scottish crown in the late sixteenth century have been well documented by historians but, significantly, the political premium placed on sartorial display protected the queen's wardrobe from shortfalls in central finance. This is unequivocally demonstrated by Joussie's accounts – one of the main suppliers of fabric to the court – which, rather than being paid through the exchequer, were settled by James with money drawn from his English annuity and borrowed from Maitland.[103] Such circumvention arose from James's knowledge that the high levels of expenditure would incur censure: on 1 February 1596, for example, Joussie recorded that in just under six years he had 'spendit and debursit' £71,513.14*d*. Scots for 'the queins majestie for hir abulziaments [apparel]'.[104] This was only one of several accounts and it excluded both the relatively inexpensive construction costs as well as almost all costly embellishments – spangles, aglets, buttons, pearls, lace, and/or embroidery – that would have been later added by specialists during construction.[105]

Politicking jewels and apparel

As noted at the beginning of this chapter, the early modern body was a social construction formed through clothing and jewellery that both reflected and articulated statements of social and economic status, and political aims and allegiances. Anna's intentional use of such material agency was demonstrable in her first English court masque, *The Vision of the Twelve Goddesses*, performed at Hampton Court on 8 January 1604. Anna's guest of honour for the event was the Spanish ambassador, Don Juan de Tassis, Count of Villamediana (1581–1622), who was accordingly privileged with a canopied seat to King James's right.[106] Taking advantage of Tassis's presence in a relatively public space, Anna made a conscious vestimentary decision to visualise her ongoing verbal politicking for her eldest son to marry the eldest Spanish Infanta. By the time of the masque, a Spanish delegation, led by the Constable of Castile, had been in England for several months in the hope of brokering a peace agreement, and Anna had used this opportunity to inform Velasco of her wish for an Anglo-Spanish marital alliance.[107] In fact, she had 'secretly brought forward a scheme for the marriage of her son' so 'many times and the engagements entered upon on the part of that King [James] went so far', that Velasco had, on his return to Spain, left 'a secret instruction for Don Juan de Tassis … if this negotiation were proceeded with, he might understand what were the conditions upon which it could be admitted.'[108] It was also during this time that Anna performed in *Vision*, where she was observed showing visible favour to Spain with the French ambassador, Christophe de Harlay, Comte de Beaumont (c.1570–1615), reporting that she wore 'a scarf and a red streamer', as an express honour to the Spanish ambassador, Tassis, who was likewise attired in red.[109] For Tassis, this act was likely understood in the context of Anna's marital aims, but it may also have been read by the ambassadors and/or wider audience in the context of the proposed Anglo-Spanish peace, which was also under current discussion. Read in this way, Anna's bodily display could have been taken as evidence of harmonious relations between the two nations, adding weight to the belief that the English were ready to enter formal negotiations. These two readings are not mutually exclusive, but aptly demonstrate how visual signs could convey a multiplicity of meaning dependant on context and recipient.

Bodily adornment again gave presence to Anna's political position in 1610, although this time it was in the context of domestic court faction and the object was a white petticoat. Anna's fondness for petticoats, usually white and covered with elaborate embroidery, was well known with many elites choosing such items as gifts. For New Year 1609/10, Anna received three white petticoats, one of which was lined with plush and covered with an embroidered seascape together with birds, wild beasts, and a variety of fruits. Yet despite Anna's partiality for such garments, and the elegance of this particular example, it was never to touch the queen's body, tainted as it was by having been a gift from James's Chamberlain, Thomas Howard, Earl of Suffolk (1561–1626), against whom (and the Howard faction generally) Anna was staunchly opposed. The figurative design sealed the fate of the garment, for worn by the queen at court it would have been instantly recognisable as a sign of the queen's favour towards the Howards. Too costly to be discarded, but too polarising to be worn, on 17 June 1610 Anna judiciously sent it to her sister Elisabeth in Wolfenbüttel.[110] The only petticoat carrying such a potent political charge that was contrary to Anna's own position, it was, accordingly, the only one out of some twenty-one white petticoats, featuring various types of figurative embroidered designs, that the queen chose to gift beyond the physical borders of the Stuart kingdom.[111] At the Wolfenbüttel court, stripped of its contextual significance, the petticoat was no longer in danger of making a visual statement of allegiance between the Howards and the Stuart queen, and could thus be safely worn and seen as it configured the body of the new wearer – Elisabeth – into a vessel of social privilege and international connection.

Even more illustrative of the ability of clothing to give visual form to favour and allegiance were Anna's actions in Scotland when she ordered pieces of apparel for particular gentlewomen that were identical to her own. In July 1590, Elizabeth Gibb (d.1593) was tasked with making up three matching hats for the queen and her two Danish gentlewomen: Sofie Koss and Katrine Skinkel. Made of red crimson velvet, lined with red Spanish taffeta, and completed with strings of red Florentine ribbon, Anna took special, personal care of the plumage which was fashioned out of five feathers 'quhilks hir majestie resavit for to serve hir majesties hattis'.[112] Anna repeated this coordination in December 1590, when she and her Danish servitors were fitted with matching hats of fine black velvet, as well as 'taffetyes' of black taffeta from Naples with black ribbons from Florence.[113] At this early point of Anna's time in Scotland, such fashioning would have been read as an unmistakeable statement of partiality along lines of personal intimacy and geographic, dynastic allegiance. A second occasion of sartorial sameness occurred in summer 1592, when Anna ordered orange damask gowns with green satin sleeves for herself, for the Danish Margaret Vinstarr, and for the Scottish Mary Stewart, later Countess of Mar (d.1644).[114] Coordinated garments were also issued for Anna's Danish male servitor Belou, who received a coat and a pair of breeches in green stemming and a doublet of orange damask that was faced with orange Spanish taffeta.[115] Crossing over differences in nationality, rank, and gender, these matching garments may well have been intended for wear at a specific court event such as a wedding, where they would have been interpreted by attendees as evidence of the queen's favour and affection.

The elite audience that gathered for a court wedding created an effective platform for Anna's display of royal favour which, beyond corresponding outfits, included the use of space and the giving of gifts. When one of her gentlewomen married, Anna generally gave them articles of clothing, soft furnishings, or pieces of jewellery. These were often ordered specifically such as the 'jewel of gold, set with diamonds' that Anna bought from Heriot for £60 and gave to Jane Mewtes (1581–1659) on her wedding to Sir William Cornwallis of Brome (c.1549–1611) in April 1610.[116] Yet, on the other hand, gifts were also drawn from the queen's personal possessions and when, on 22 June 1612, for example, the Scottish chamberer Anna Livingstone married Alexander Montgomery, Earl of Eglinton (1588–1661), the queen chose to give her three jewels from her own collection.[117] Possessed of royal provenance, these jewels were far more valuable than if the queen had specially purchased them and they intimately bound these two Annas together in a new history of ownership.[118] Space was another political tool that the queen used during weddings to communicate concepts of support, favour, and belonging. In February 1614, and again in March 1617, Anna hosted weddings for her gentlewomen – Jane Drummond and Anne Roper (d.1658) respectively – at Denmark House.[119] Beyond any economic benefit that such generosity might bring, it was an unequivocal statement of the royal privilege and proximity enjoyed by the marital pairs who were marked as members of the queen's network of influence and patronage.

Early modern bodily adornment was an active ingredient in coding social, economic, and political position, and favour, which naturally extended beyond apparel to fastenings, accessories, and pieces of jewellery. Yet the examples discussed remind us that these messages were fluid; it was the *interrelationship* of adornment with the body and context/audience that produced meaning, where a shift in the latter two elements could dramatically alter signification. This is further borne out by Anna's actions in January 1608 when she selected a specific piece of hereditary jewellery invested with memory, history, and meaning to transform her body into a political statement of her wish for Prince Henry to marry the Infanta Ana María.[120] Carefully considering how meaning was produced from the confluence of object, body, political context, and audience, it was during the courtly performance of the *Masque of Beauty* that Anna wore the magnificent gold and diamond collar that had been gifted by Philip II of Spain (1527–1598) to Mary Tudor (1516–1558) on the occasion of their marriage.[121] Plainly bearing their ciphers – P and M – the elite gathering were unmistakeably reminded of the previous Anglo-Spanish marriage and given to understand that the queen consort (and therefore the Stuart monarchy) was desirous to repeat the union. The timing was important, for the marriage of the Stuarts' eldest son, and heir to the throne, Henry, was a central topic of discussion and speculation for there were several suitors: France, Savoy, Spain, and Tuscany. As is now well known, James and Anna preferred Spain, but while the queen's support has been seen as the result of covert Catholic convictions, there was more at stake in a royal marriage than religion: politics and finances.[122] In the first instance, all of Henry's possible brides were drawn from Catholic kingdoms, for James intended to achieve European peace by alternately marrying his children to Catholic and Protestant partners, and the latter was to be achieved through his daughter Elizabeth.[123] Of the Catholic choices, the Habsburgs were of pre-eminent pedigree, political might, and land mass, and their unparalleled wealth meant the Stuarts could hope to gain a larger dowry than that offered by Savoy, Tuscany, or even France.[124] For Anna too, this was a matter of ancestral pride for the Austrian and Spanish Houses of Habsburg were among her consanguineal and affinal kin. On her father's side, this included Isabella of Austria (1501–1526), sister of the all-powerful Holy Roman Emperor, Charles V, who had married Christian II of Denmark-Norway (1481–1559) – Anna's first cousin twice removed, and through her mother's bloodline, Elizabeth of Austria, Queen of Poland (1454–1492) was her great-great-great grandmother. Anna repeatedly reminded foreign emissaries of her Habsburg connections, and when the Venetian ambassador Foscarini came to provide a summary of England in 1618, he was at pains to mention that Anna 'is descended on the female side from the House of Austria in which she takes great pride. She has an intimate friendship with the infanta archduchess [Isabel Clara Eugenia] and calls her sister.'[125] In wearing Mary Tudor's Habsburg gift, Anna visualised the verbal claims that she had been making within the confines of ambassadorial audiences. On a more regular basis, the queen's body likewise gave voice to this genealogy by wearing a miniature of Isabel Clara Eugenia. Requesting the miniature on 24 September 1603, Anna had received it by 28 May 1604, when Charles de Ligne, Prince of Arenburg (1550–1616) was able to write to Archduke Albert (1559–1621) that Anna had promised to wear the portrait as a token of friendship until her death.[126] True to her word, Anna's repeated wear of the miniature resulted in the queen's jeweller, Heriot, being called upon for twice 'mendinge of the tablet' that contained 'the infantors picture'.[127] The high value of the miniature to Anna is well illustrated by her actions in August 1615 when, during a hunt, she lost it and much to James's chagrin called a halt to the chase until it was recovered.[128] By this time, Anna was highly sensitive to the ability of jewelled adornment to shape her body into a statement of dynastic belonging and kinship, having used it as such since her early years in Scotland.

Personalised jewels: miniatures and ciphers

Anna's very first account with Heriot, of May 1593, includes two entries for 'hir majesties Sipher', one of which was set with twenty-eight diamonds and sixteen rubies, and cost more than a third of the entire bill.[129] With this, Anna set the precedent for what was to become a marked pattern of her jewellery patronage: familial ciphers in the form of rings, earrings, pendants, and on miniature cases. Throughout the span of Heriot's bills, Anna purchased no fewer than seventeen jewels bearing her own letters, many of which were given as gifts, and a further eleven jewels featuring an S for her mother Sofie, or a C or C4 for her brother, Christian.[130] One of the most expensive pieces Anna ever bought from Heriot – at a tremendous cost of £300 sterling – combined Christian's letters with her own: a jewel 'wth an A and two CC Sett wth diamonds'.[131] Anna also owned a miniature where the case was decorated with this configuration of letters in diamonds, at a cost of £130 sterling, which probably held a portrait of Christian.[132] An important, comparable example is seen in a miniature of Anna, by Nicholas Hilliard (1547–1619) and his workshop, which retains its original case (Plate 3). Anna owned at least four miniatures of her brother, which, as she informed Christian, she proudly wore 'with the devoted memory of a sister'.[133] In addition to the one just mentioned, a further two of these miniatures allowed for the subject (Christian) to be easily identifiable by onlookers, for one was set under rock crystal, and the other was encased in a tablet decorated with his initial.[134] Anna's fondness for wearing these familial pieces exposed them to damage, and, like the miniature of Isabel Clara Eugenia already mentioned, Heriot was repeatedly charged with repairing Christian's miniatures and jewelled letters.[135] Their ready visibility moved the personal and familial significance into the public and political where the body of the queen consort was assessed by court attendees as a representative of the Stuart and Oldenburg dynasties. This form of jewellery was a common element of Anna's bodily display and, indelibly associated with her, was translated into her visual persona with familial devices appearing in almost all of her portraits – in paint, print, and metal – from around 1610 onwards, which is discussed in Chapter 5.

Personalised ciphers in Scotland and England were, of course, not restricted to Anna of Denmark. Their use as a decorative design dates back to King Edward III (1312–1377), while later examples include Henry VIII, who owned two pendants bearing his letter H; a surviving portrait of Anne Boleyn in the National Portrait Gallery, London, where she wears a necklace with her hanging cipher B; and an extant locket ring set with Elizabeth I's royal letters ER, which was a gift from Edward Seymour, Earl of Hertford (1537–1621).[136] There are numerous other examples, but none of these precedents match the consistency with which Anna pursued this line of personalised adornment, or the extent to which she became identified with them in her portraits. Furthermore, when Anna began purchasing ciphers in Scotland in 1593, it is extremely unlikely that she would have had knowledge that these people owned and/or wore their ciphers as jewels. Rather, it is a very likely possibility that Anna had been exposed to this tradition in Denmark-Norway.

By the mid-sixteenth century, the unparalleled skill of goldsmiths and jewellers operating in Nuremburg and Augsburg had led to the development of a Baltic fashion for intricate ciphers and monograms, a fashion that probably arose from the pronounced use of symbolic insignia among the Armagnacs and Burgundians.[137] Thus, a large number of royal and elite women (many of whom were related to Anna) possessed their own jewelled ciphers, choosing to wear them in their formal portraits. Pertinent examples include Anna's paternal aunt, Anna of Denmark, Electress of Saxony (1532–1585), who commissioned numerous personalised pieces of jewellery and owned at least one of her own ciphers (A), which is extant. When her husband, Augustus (1526–1586), became Elector of Saxony in 1553 he chose to commemorate the event with a jewel that referenced them both: a crowned double A.[138] As Yvonne Hackenbroch has determined, both of these pieces were made in Southern Germany (most probably Nuremburg), where stylistically similar ciphers were produced for Anna of Bavaria (1528–1590) and Caterina Jagellonica, Queen of Sweden (1526–1583). Caterina wore her cipher in her portrait by Lucas Cranach the Younger (1515–1586) from around 1553, and later chose to be buried with it, while Anna of Bavaria's illustrated inventory shows that she likewise owned a pendant bearing her letter A in diamonds and rubies.[139]

The fashion for jewelled letters is also evident among members of Anna of Denmark's immediate family. For example, her younger sister Augusta, Duchess of Holstein-Gottorp (1580–1639), chose to wear identifying letters in formal portraits after her marriage, sitting for Jacob van Doordt (1590–1629) in 1601 in a heavy gold chain with a prominent 'A' pendant. Anna's sister-in-law, Christian's first wife Anna Catherine, owned a bracelet decorated with the enamelled letters AC, which could have referred to her singularly, or to the couple. Certainly, Christian's second wife, Kirsten Munk, sat for portraits wearing elaborate pendants that signified the married pair with the intertwined letters K and C, and in earlier portraits she is seen wearing Christian's jewelled monogram C4.[140] These may have been gifts from Christian, who was partial to giving family members his jewelled badges, having made his mother the present of a bracelet with his crowned monogram on the interior links (Figure 4.5), and giving his eldest sister, Elisabeth, 'Ett smycke medt idell demanter oc ett C' [A piece of jewellery with diamonds all over and a C] in 1595.[141] Later, in June 1611, Christian sent Anna his jewelled monogram 'of splendid diamonds forming a C. and a 4, C. for the first letter of his name, and a 4 because he is the fourth of that name'. Sent on the eve of his invasion of Sweden, Christian's accompanying letter informed Anna that he wanted her to treasure the jewel as a memento.[142] Such sentiments give voice to the surrogate, transposal power of cipher jewellery: they were immortal objects vested with the associated individual's presence and memory. Worn about the person, or held in the hand, these small bejewelled keepsakes strengthened bonds of attachment and identification by stretching beyond the limits of the body's physical existence.

4.5 Danish made (possibly by Dirich Frying in Odense) gold bracelet with niello, rubies, and diamonds, 1593–1600.

Conclusion

The pieces of early modern apparel and accessories discussed in this chapter demonstrate how the wearing of such items constructed the early modern, elite female body into a sign of social, political, economic, and dynastic significance. While these objects were active signifiers, it was really at the point of confluence between the specifics of body, object, audience, and socio-political context that meaning was generated: if and when any of these elements changed, then meaning changed accordingly. To reflect on just two of the many examples examined in this chapter, we have seen how in 1603, with her relocation to London, Anna journeyed south readily equipped with the general silhouette, and even some specific garments, that were in current use among her English subjects. This was a calculated attempt by the Stuarts to construct the new, foreign body of the Stuart consort into a familiar, legitimate symbol of English sovereignty in order to promote the assimilation and popularity of the Scottish dynasty. Then, during Anna's time in England, it was noted that she frequently wore cipher jewels and miniatures referencing contemporary members of the Oldenburg and Habsburg dynasty – a mode of bodily display to be interpreted as statements of allegiance and belonging that visualised Anna's opinion on the marriage alliances of her sons and made manifest the powerful European connections of the House of Stuart. These two instances, together with other cases covered in this chapter, adroitly highlight the role of the body as a site for the materialisation of elite ideologies, which were keenly viewed and appraised by court attendees.

In addition to Anna's own bodily display, those of her servitors and courtiers were a conventional reflection and constituent of her position and privilege. Colours, fabric types, and styles of apparel were strategically disseminated throughout Anna's Scottish household to visualise hierarchies, specific ruling houses, and royal favour. Thus, many of the queen's householders were attired completely in black, but the quality and quantity of these garments enacted a hierarchical scale of social and financial value. By contrast, some members were outfitted in Stuart heraldic livery of red and yellow, while others wore expressly Danish livery – both orders of which could be occasioned by the requirements of ceremonial – while delegates drawn from Anna's wider natal network were hosted by the Scottish court at which time the royal wardrobes equipped them in the full dynastic livery of their representative kingdom. As all of these examples remind us, large amounts of time, money, and consideration were given to dressing the early modern body, which was a powerful vessel for the construction of a multiplicity of meanings that were not only enacted in the physical, fleeting moment but often preserved through portraits, the medium of which is the subject of the following chapter.

Notes

1 T. McCall, 'Brilliant Bodies: Material Culture and the Adornment of Men in North Italy's Quattrocento Courts', *I Tatti Studies in the Italian Renaissance* 16 (2013), 445–490: 447; E. Grosz, *Volatile Bodies: Toward a Corporeal Feminism* (Bloomington, 1994), 23; B. Mirabella, 'Introduction', in B. Mirabella (ed.), *Ornamentalism: The Art of Renaissance Accessories* (Ann Arbor, 2011), 1–10: 2–4; E. Griffey (ed.), *Sartorial Politics: Fashioning Women at the Early Modern Court (1450–1700)* (Amsterdam, 2019).
2 McCall, 'Brilliant Bodies', 451.
3 McCall, 'Brilliant Bodies', 447, 449.
4 This multiplicity of meaning is a sentiment likewise expressed by Mirabella in her study of the ways in which Renaissance handkerchiefs were worn and understood, writing that 'how a handkerchief is read then depends on how it is being used, who is holding it, and in what context.' B. Mirabella, 'Embellishing Herself with a Cloth', in B. Mirabella (ed.), *Ornamentalism* (Ann Arbor, 2011), 59–82: 61–62.
5 S. Édouard, 'The Hispanicization of Elisabeth de Valois at the Court of Philip II', in José Luis Colomer and Amalia Descalzo (eds), *Spanish Fashion at the Courts of Early Modern Europe*, vol. 2 (Madrid, 2014), 237–266: 240–241; Santaliestra, 'Isabel of Borbón's Sartorial Politics', 227–230. Details of several foundational studies by Arnold and Hayward are cited in the Bibliography.
6 Santaliestra, 'Isabel of Borbón's Sartorial Politics', 227–228; Édouard, 'Hispanicization of Elisabeth de Valois', 240–241.
7 Paresys, 'Dressed Body', 250.
8 As quoted in M. Hayward, 'Spanish Princess or Queen of England? The Image, Identity and Influence of Catherine of Aragon at the Courts of Henry VII and Henry VIII', in J. L. Colomer and A. Descalzo (eds), *Spanish Fashion at the Courts* (Madrid, 2014), vol. 2, 11–37: 19. On Spanish fashion see also J. Arnold, *Queen Elizabeth's Wardrobe Unlock'd* (Leeds, 1988), 123–128.
9 W. Bray (ed.), *The Diary of John Evelyn*, 2 vols (London and New York, 1901), 1: 358.

10 M. Hayward, '"The best of Queens, the most obedient wife": Fashioning a Place for Catherine of Braganza as Consort to Charles II', in E. Griffey (ed.), *Sartorial Politics* (Amsterdam, 2019), 227–252: 237–238.
11 *CSP Scotland*, vol. 10, no. 141: 6 July 1589 (Fowler to Walsingham); 124–125, no. 160: 28 July 1589 (Fowler to Asheby).
12 D. Moysie, *Memoirs of the Affairs of Scotland, 1577–1603 from Early Manuscripts* (Edinburgh, 1830), 83.
13 M. Brayshay, 'Long-distance Royal Journeys: Anne of Denmark's Journey from Stirling to Windsor in 1603', *The Journal of Transport History* 25 (2004), 1–21: 2.
14 *CSPV*, vol. 10, no. 91: 10 July 1603; M. Lee Jr. (ed.), *Dudley Carleton to John Chamberlain 1603–1624: Jacobean Letters* (New Brunswick, 1972), 34.
15 Brayshay, 'Long-distance Royal Journeys', 15–16; TNA, AO1/2022/1.
16 *CSP Scotland*, vol. 10, no. 141: 6 July 1589 (Fowler to Walsingham).
17 Graves, 'Danish Account', 80.
18 Ellis (ed.), *Original Letters*, vol. 3, 70–71, no. CCXLI.
19 BL Cotton MS Titus C VII, fol. 121r; C. Murray, '"Great Britaine, all in Blacke": The Commemoration of Henry, Prince of Wales, in a Portrait of his Father, King James I', *The British Art Journal* 12 (2011), 20–25: 22.
20 TNA, LC5/37, fols 309–310.
21 TNA, LC5/37, fols 310, 311, 313. The warrant was given under signet at Winchester, 28 September 1603. The six women were Anna Livingstone, later Countess of Eglinton; Margaret Stewart, later Countess of Nottingham; Jean/Jane Drummond; Anne Campbell, later Marchioness of Huntly (1594–1638); Margaret Hartside (Anna's chamberer in Scotland and England); and either Heleanor Hay, Countess of Livingstone (d.1627) or Margaret Hay, Countess of Dunfermline (c.1592–1659).
22 Griffey makes a similar observation of Henrietta Maria on her entry into England: *On Display*, 40–42.
23 Stevenson, *Scotland's Last Royal Wedding*, 63.
24 The plague must have partly contributed to the silence – it was pronounced in London at the time of Anna's arrival resulting in the ceremonial welcome being cancelled and the number of onlookers would have been significantly reduced.
25 J. Nichols, *The Progresses, Processions and Magnificent Festivities of King James the First*, 4 vols (London, 1828), vol. 1, 190: 28 July 1603 (to Thomas Parry), emphasis mine.
26 Quoted in D. Scarisbrick, 'Anne of Denmark's Jewellery: The Old and the New', *Apollo* 122 (1986), 228–236: 228.
27 *CSPV*, vol. 10, no. 91: 10 July 1603.
28 NRS, E21/76, fols 528–535, 539.
29 NRS, E21/76, fol. 528.
30 NRS, E21/76, fols 529, 530.
31 NRS, E21/76, fols 529, 531.
32 Anna was definitely still wearing round gowns in Scotland at this time with entries for a 'new roungd broun gowne' recorded in May 1603: NRS, E21/76, fol. 532.
33 This refers to the black threads or strings seen tied around rings and women's wrists, and also in their ears, in numerous English portraits of the period. This was probably a fashion Anna brought with her from Denmark for portraits of her sisters wearing black threads are extant: see the Woburn portrait of Anna (Figure 5.1), and that of Hedevig (Staatliche Kunstsammlungen Dresden #2148). For a consideration of this fashion in a specifically English context, see E. Welch and J. Claxton, 'Easy Innovation in Early Modern Europe', in E. Welch (ed.), *Fashioning the Early Modern: Dress, Textiles, and Innovation in Europe, 1500–1800* (Oxford, 2017), 87–109: 90–96.
34 TNA, LR6/154/9: bills dated 26, 27, 28 June 1603.
35 TNA, LR6/154/9. Some of these may have been produced from the orchards and

gardens at Greenwich, which, by 1611, were producing seven gallons of sweet water per annum: BL Add MS 24705, fol. 22v.
36 A. M. Hind, *Engraving in England in the Sixteenth and Seventeenth Centuries: The Reign of James I* (Cambridge, 1955), 49–51, plate 21 (STC 14786; STC 14787).
37 For Sibthorpe see Arnold, *Wardrobe Unlock'd*, 177, 189, 196–197.
38 TNA, LR6/154/9; TNA, SC6/JASI/1646; TNA, SC6/JASI/1653; TNA, SC6/JASI/1655; TNA, AO3/1187, fol. 38v.
39 *CSPV*, vol. 15, 80, no. 131: 22 December 1617.
40 A. Reynolds, *In Fine Style: The Art of Tudor and Stuart Fashion* (London, 2013), 42; E. E. S. Gordenker, 'Isabel Clara Eugenia at the Court of Brussels', in J. L. Colomer and A. Descalzo (eds), *Spanish Fashion at the Courts of Early Modern Europe* (Madrid, 2014), vol. 2, 117–135: 126. This is also posited by S. Vincent, *Dressing the Elite: Clothes in Early Modern England* (Oxford and New York, 2003), 35–36. None of these authors provide any references.
41 According to Arnold, the style began a 'slow decline' in England in 1617: *Patterns of Fashion 4: Cut and Construction of Linen Shirts, Smocks, Neckwear, Headwear, and Accessories for Men and Women c.1540–1660* (London, 2008), 12. See Anne Clifford's comment that while attending court in November 1617, she 'wore my green Damask gown imbroidered, without a farthingale' in Acheson (ed.), *Diary*, 93. Compare with two engravings completed in celebration of the marriage of Charles and Henrietta Maria in 1625 showing the French princess very clearly wearing the drum-shaped farthingale: illustrated Griffey, *On Display*, 56.
42 See that after Pieter Fransz Isaacsz, *Anna Catherine*, 1610–1612, and Michel van Mierevelt, *Maria Eleonora of Brandenburg*, 1619, both in Gripsholm Castle, Stockholm; Jacob van Doordt, *Kirsten Munk*, 1623, Frederiksborg Castle, Hillerød. In the course of writing this book, this perspective was published by C. MacLeod in her chapter: 'Facing Europe: The Portraiture of Anne of Denmark (1574–1619)', in J. Bepler and S. Norrheim (eds), *Telling Objects: Contextualizing the Role of the Consort in Early Modern Europe* (Wiesbaden, 2018), 63–85: 77–78.
43 The portraits remain in the Royal Collection London, RCIN# 405815; 406783; 407222; 404963. Anna's sisters Elisabeth and Augusta were likewise fashioned in French farthingales in their portraits of the early 1600s. See Heiberg, cat nos. 66, 97; Wade, 'The Queen's Courts', figs 3.2, 3.4.
44 NRS, E21/76, fols 554–562.
45 TNA, LC5/37, fol. 296. On the Tudor heraldic colours and livery see M. Hayward, *Dress at the Court of King Henry VIII* (Leeds, 2007), 244–248.
46 Ellis, *Original Letters*, 70–71, no. 241.
47 NRS, E35/14; NRS, E35/13. For the relationship between these two accounts and the system of supply and payment see Field, 'Dressing a Queen', 154–155.
48 NRS, E35/13, vol. 7, p. 9; NRS, E35/14, fols 16r–34v.
49 McCall, 'Brilliant Bodies', 451.
50 NRS, E35/14, fols 24r–27r, 28r–32r.
51 NRS, E35/14, fols 24r, 25r.
52 NRS, E35/14, fols 30r, 24r–v, 26v.
53 Hayward observes as much of Henry VIII's household in her *Dress at the Court*, 248–249.
54 NRS, E35/14, fols 20r–23v. Belou entered Anna's service around 1591 and travelled with the Stuarts to England in 1603, appearing in Anna's household accounts of 1605 as 'William Bellon a Dutch gent and her Mats servant'. He was sent to Denmark in July 1605 and carried letters from James to Christian IV. Belou was still receiving £50 per annum for his position in Anna's household in 1610/11 and was later noted as a 'Danish agent' in England between 1606 and 1626: TNA, SC6/JASI/1646; TNA, LR7/137, fol. 17r; Riis, *Auld Acquaintance*, 2: 281; Meldrum (ed.), *Royal Correspondence*, 51–52.

55 NRS, E35/13; NRS, E35/14; see too J. Field, 'The Wardrobe Goods of Anna of Denmark, Queen Consort of Scotland and England (1574–1619)', *Costume* 51 (2017), 3–27; Field 'Dressing a Queen', 164; M. Pearce, 'Anna of Denmark: Fashioning a Danish Court in Scotland', *The Court Historian* 24 (2019), 138–151: 148.
56 NRS, E21/68, fols 159–162, 234; NRS, E35/14, fol. 24v; NRS, E21/76, fols 244, 424–426, 511–514, 554–555. Note that the shade of red is often clarified, where scarlet and crimson are the most common, but incarnadine is also listed.
57 NRS, E21/68, fols 152–163; NRS, E21/71, fols 102–104; NRS, E21/74, fols 153–154, 156–158; NRS, E21/76, fols 153–162, 245–247, 307, 403–405, 424–428, 479–482, 510. From January 1603, orders are recorded for Prince Henry's pages and lackeys to likewise be attired in red and yellow livery: NRS, E21/76, fols 424–426, 428–429.
58 NRS, E35/13, vol. 7, pp. 1–6.
59 BL Add MS 12498, fols 228v, 230r–v. See also TNA, LC5/37, fols 307–308.
60 BL Add MS 24705, fols 1v, 2r. Livery in red and green, or in a tripartite colour scheme of red, green, and white was also common in Scotland and England, and I have been unable to determine the symbolic significance. See, for example NRS, E35/13, vol. 1, pp. 28–30; BL Add MS 12498, fol. 226r.
61 NLS, Adv. MS. 34.2.17, fols 143r–v. My thanks to Michael Pearce for this reference.
62 Anna had three Danish master cooks between 1590 and 1597: Hans Drier, Hans Popillman, and Joannes Forgius: Juhala, 'Household and Court', 332. More unusually, Anna also had a Danish female cook, Marion: NRS, E35/14, fol. 30r.
63 For Feier see NRS, E35/14, fol. 32r; for Skein see below.
64 NRS, E21/68, fols 161–162.
65 NRS, E35/14, fol. 23r.
66 NRS, E35/14, fol. 34v.
67 NRS, E35/14, fols 26r–v.
68 Examples include Élisabeth of Valois in Spain, and Catherine of Aragón and Henrietta Maria in England: Édouard, 'Hispanicization of Elisabeth de Valois', 239, 241–243; Hayward, 'Spanish Princess or Queen of England?', 17–18; Hibbard, 'Queen's Patronage', 118; Griffey, *On Display*, 50–51.
69 M. Noble, *Historical Genealogy* (London, 1795), 285: 11 June 1590 (William Dundas to Archibald Douglas), emphasis mine.
70 NRS, E35/13, vol. 1, p. 37; NRS, E21/68, fols 158, 164, 170, 178; W. D. Macray, 'Second Report on the Royal Archives of Denmark, and Report on the Royal Library at Copenhagen', in *The Forty-Sixth Annual Report of the Deputy Keeper of the Public Records* (London, 1885), Appendix II, no. 1: 4–5, 7–9, 12–13, 18–19, 34–36, 39; W. D. Macray, 'Third Report on the Royal Archives of Denmark, and Report on the Royal Library at Copenhagen', in *The Forty-Seventh Annual Report of the Deputy Keeper of the Public Records* (London, 1886), Appendix II, no. 5: 26, 28–30, 38–42; J. T. G. Craig (ed.), *Papers Relative to the Marriage of King James the Sixth of Scotland, with the Princess Anna of Denmark* (Edinburgh, 1828), Appendix III, 27; Riis, *Auld Acquaintance*, 2: 288, 294–295; McNeill (ed.), *Exchequer Rolls*, vol. 22, 121; McNeill (ed.), *Exchequer Rolls*, vol. 23, 62.
71 NRS, E21/68, fol. 170. James also outfitted Danish servitors who remained at the Scottish court but continued to be identified by country of origin: NRS, E21/70, fols 233, 234.
72 Murdoch, *House of Stuart*; Murdoch, *Network North*; Riis, *Auld Acquaintance*.
73 See Chapter 1; Riis, *Auld Acquaintance*, vol. 2, 296; Wade, 'Duke Ulrik', 248, 252–254.
74 BL Lansdowne MS 164, fols 78r, 324r. Ulrik's pension was known outside of England and Wade cites it being mentioned in his funeral sermon: 'Duke Ulrik', 252.

75 Meldrum (ed.), *Royal Correspondence*, 4–5.
76 TNA, SC6/JASI/1646.
77 Juhala, 'Household and Court', 330–331; Payne, 'Aristocratic Women', 247; W. A. Shaw (ed.), *Letters of Denization and Acts of Naturalization for Aliens in England and Ireland, 1603–1700* (Lymington, 1911–1932), 13, 16; Murdoch, *House of Stuart*, 3.
78 TNA, AO3/1187, fol. 42v.
79 Payne, 'Aristocratic Women', 280–287; Murdoch, *House of Stuart*, 3–4. In Anna's funeral account, Barbara Abercrombie is listed as a laundry maid: TNA, AO3/1187, fol. 36r.
80 *CSP Scotland*, vol. 10, no. 735: 12 August 1592.
81 *CSP Scotland*, vol. 10, nos. 736, 778: August 1592; 30 November 1592.
82 NRS, E35/13, vol. 1, pp. 33–34. Tullibardine was James's Master Householder and the bride was probably Lilias Murray who married John Grant of Freuchie. My thanks to Michael Pearce for this suggestion.
83 *CSP Scotland*, vol. 10, no. 517: 13 January 1591 (Bowes to Burghley).
84 NRS, E35/14, fol. 19r.
85 NRS, E35/14, fol. 19v.
86 Masson (ed.), *Register of the Privy Council*, vol. 6, 145–146.
87 *CSP Scotland*, vol. 13, part II, no. 535: 6 August 1600 (George Nicholson to Cecil); no. 572: 31 October 1600 (Master of Grey to Cecil).
88 *CSP Scotland*, vol. 13, part II, no. 891: 1 January 1603. The intended purpose of her visit has never been determined.
89 S. Olden-Jørgensen, 'State Ceremonial, Court Culture and Political Power in Early Modern Denmark, 1536–1746', *Scandinavian Journal of History* 27 (2002), 65–76: 67–72; Christianson, 'Terrestrial and Celestial Spaces', 134–136; P. Ahrenfelt, 'Frederik II's Hof: Husholdning og centraladministration', in F. Lundgreen-Nielsen and H. Ruus (eds), *Svøbt i mår: Dansk Folkevisekultur* (Copenhagen, 1999), vol. 1, 327–390: 364–367, 379–383.
90 Grinder-Hansen, *Frederik 2*, 85, 87; Ahrenfelt, 'Frederik II's Hof', 346–348, 352–353.
91 Goodare, 'James VI's English Subsidy', 110–126; Goodare and Lynch, 'James VI: Universal King?' 10, 15–16, 22–23; Riis, *Auld Acquaintance*, 1: 265–266. See also various entries in *CSP Scotland*, vol. 10, especially: nos. 141, 156, 157, 175, 199, 327, 499 (6, 22, 26 July 1589; 11, 29 August 1589; 20 December 1589; 20 November 1590). While in Denmark James had to borrow money from Chancellor Maitland, whose audited accounts survive in BL Add MS 22958.
92 Moysie, *Memoirs of Scotland*, 80–81.
93 Rye, *England as Seen by Foreigners*, 260.
94 Rye, *England as Seen by Foreigners*, 260.
95 Rye, *England as Seen by Foreigners*, 261.
96 Moysie, *Memoirs of Scotland*, 81.
97 *CSP Scotland*, vol. 10, 257, no. 365: 20 March 1590 (to Burghley and Walsingham). See also J. Melville, *Memoirs of His Own Life, 1549–1603* (Edinburgh, 1827), 373, who writes that while James was in Denmark 'ane proclamation, quhilk was send hame [home] to be proclaimed before his Majesties retournyng, that nane [none] of the nobilitie suld com to court on being sent for, and then to bring with them sex persones and na ma [no more]; lykwais every barron to bring bot four.'
98 *CSP Scotland*, vol. 10, no. 404: 23 May 1590 (to Burghley).
99 *CSP Scotland*, vol. 10, no. 391: 24 April 1590 (Bowes to Burghley).
100 *CSP Scotland*, vol. 10, no. 393: 29 April 1590 (Bowes to Burghley); Stevenson, *Scotland's Last Royal Wedding*, 55–56.
101 Quoted in Stevenson, *Scotland's Last Royal Wedding*, 71.
102 Olden-Jørgensen, 'State Ceremonial', 68; Cole, 'State Apartment', 78–79; Stevenson, *Scotland's Last Royal Wedding*, 71–72.

103 NRS, E35/13, vol. 1, p. 1; vol. 3, pp. 2, 3. On these accounts, and Anna's Scottish wardrobe more generally see Field, 'Dressing a Queen'.
104 NRS, E35/13, vol. 7, p. 9. This included a charge of £8,238.18s.5d. Scots for the queen's servitors. Anna was also concurrently spending large sum of money with her jeweller. The accounts vary considerably in terms of the money spent (given in either French crowns or Scottish pounds, or both) and the period of time covered, but none were below 300 French crowns, and they were generally much more, NRS, GD421/1/3. Anna's jewellery is discussed below, and also in J. Field, 'A "Cipher of A and C set on the one Syde with diamonds"', in E. Griffey (ed.), *Sartorial Politics* (Amsterdam, 2019), 139–159.
105 For a comparison to the material goods supplied by Joussie, see those finished garments delivered by Heriot to the queen: NRS, GD421/1/3/14; NRS, GD421/1/3/21.
106 M. A. Sullivan, *Court Masques of James I: Their Influence on Shakespeare and the Public Theatres* (New York, 1973), 14. On the political importance of seating and proximity in regards to ambassadors, see Dillon, *Language of Space*, 76–83.
107 A. J. Loomie, 'Toleration and Diplomacy: The Religious Issue in Anglo-Spanish Relations, 1603–1605', *Transactions of the American Philosophical Society* 53, New Series (1963), 1–60: 24–27.
108 S. R. Gardiner (ed.), *Narrative of the Spanish Marriage Treaty* (London, 1869), 103.
109 Sullivan, *Court Masques of James I*, 14–16; 194, appendix 6.
110 CUL, MS Dd.I.26, fol. 21r. Anna's opposition to the Howards is covered in Chapter 5. For a transcription of this inventory and a discussion of the contents, see Field, 'Wardrobe Goods of Anna of Denmark', and supplementary material.
111 CUL, MS Dd.I.26, fols 9r–v, 10r, 18r–v, 21r, 24r, 25v.
112 NRS, E35/13, vol. 2, pp. 3, 10.
113 NRS, E35/13, vol. 2, p. 13. On taffetas see Field, 'Dressing a Queen', 160–162.
114 NRS, E35/13, vol. 2, p. 55; NRS, E35/14, fols 16r, 17r. This is the same Margaret Vinstarr who, in August 1593, much to James's chagrin, orchestrated the escape of the Laird of Logie as discussed above.
115 NRS, E35/14, fol. 21r; Riis, *Auld Acquaintance*, vol. 2, 281. Belou travelled with the Stuarts to England where he received an annuity of £50: TNA, LR7/137, fol. 17r.
116 Devon, *Issues of the Exchequer*, 104–105.
117 Scarisbrick, 'Anne of Denmark's Jewellery', 200, 212, 213, 226. nos. 64, 196, 200, 321. This was separate to the personal jewel Anna previously gave Lady Livingstone in 1607 when she journeyed to Scotland.
118 L. R. Clark, 'Transient Possessions: Circulation, Replication, and Transmission of Gems and Jewels in Quattrocento Italy', *Journal of Early Modern History* 15 (2011): 185–221: 190–191.
119 McClure (ed.), *Chamberlain*, vol. 2, 62, no. 261. On the festivities surrounding Drummond's wedding see Barroll, *Anna of Denmark*, 140–142; McManus, *Renaissance Stage*, 166–167; Knowles, 'Images of Royalty', 33; Field, 'Anna of Denmark and the Arts', 221–225. On the politics of space in a diplomatic context see Sowerby, 'Material Culture'.
120 On the role of jewellery and gems as both active agent and repository for histories and meanings, Clark, 'Transient Possessions'; Clark, *Collecting Art*, esp. ch. 2.
121 F. Palgrave, *Antient Kalendars and Inventories of the Treasury of the Exchequer*, 2 vols (London, 1836), vol. 2, 301. no. 9; Ungerer, 'Circulation of Gifts', 156–157; D. Scarisbrick, *Tudor and Jacobean Jewellery* (London, 1995), 14, 53, 75–76.
122 A. J. Loomie, 'King James I's Catholic Consort', *Huntington Library Quarterly* 34 (1971), 303–316: 309.
123 G. Redworth, *The Prince and the Infanta: The Cultural Politics of the Spanish Match* (New Haven and London, 2003), 10–14; Murdoch, *House of Stuart*, 45.
124 When Sir John Digby (1580–1654) was attempting to finalise the Anglo-Spanish match in December 1617, James was expecting to receive a staggering two mil-

lion crowns (£600,000 sterling). By comparison, Tuscany offered 600,000 ducats (£150,000 sterling) during negotiations in October 1611; Savoy offered 800,000 ducats (£200,000 sterling) in September 1613; as did France the following year. See J. D. Mackie, *Negotiations between James VI and I and Ferdinand, Duke of Tuscany* (Oxford, 1927), 72; Gardiner (ed.), *Narrative of the Spanish Marriage*, 109–112, 137, 139, 155.

125 *CSPV*, vol. 15, 392, no. 658.
126 Vienna, Haus-, Hof- und Staatsarchiv, *Belgien*, Repertorium P, Abteilung C, Faszikel 44; 45: Arenberg to Archduke Albert, 24 September 1603; 28 May 1604. My thanks to Luc Duerloo for this reference.
127 TNA LR2/121, fols 37r, 42r: May 1611; November 1613.
128 Vienna, Haus-, Hof- und Staatsarchiv, *Belgien*, Repertorium P, Abteilung C, Faszikel 51: Ferdinand van Boisschot to Archduke Albert, 12 August 1615. My thanks to Luc Duerloo for this reference.
129 NRS, GD421/1/3/5.
130 NRS, GD421/1/3/6; NRS, GD421/1/3/10; NRS, GD421/1/3/12; NRS, GD421/1/3/14; NRS, GD421/1/3/16; NRS, GD421/1/3/20; NRS, GD421/1/3/28; NRS, GD421/1/3/43; NRS, GD421/1/3/45; TNA, LR2/122, fols 24r, 25r, 32r, 41v, 43r–v, 44r, 46r–v.
131 TNA, LR2/122, fol. 24r.
132 TNA, LR2/122, fol. 43v.
133 Scarisbrick, 'Anne of Denmark's Jewellery', 234.
134 TNA, LR2/122, fols 34r, 41r; Scarisbrick, 'Anne of Denmark's Jewellery', 220, no. 278; 233, no. 369.
135 TNA, LR2/122, fols 20v, 34r, 41r, 43r.
136 M. P. Siddons, *Heraldic Badges in England and Wales*, 2 vols (London, 2009), vol. 2, part 1, 153–155; D. Scarisbrick, 'Queen Elizabeth's Locket Ring, c.1575', in S. Doran (ed.), *Elizabeth: The Exhibition at the National Maritime Museum* (London, 2003), 12–13. Two other examples in England, but bought in from Europe, include a portrait of Catherine of Aragón, from around 1500, where she wears a necklace with several interlocking links of the initial K, and the cipher necklace that Philip II gave Mary Tudor, which Anna later owned and wore, as noted above. See Y. Hackenbroch, *Enseignes* (Florence, 1996), 271, 272, fig. 257; for Henry VIII see J. Arnold, 'Sweet England's Jewels', in A. S. Cocks (ed.), *Princely Magnificence: Court Jewels of the Renaissance, 1500–1630* (London, 1981), 31–40: 39.
137 Y. Hackenbroch, *Renaissance Jewellery* (London, 1979), 135; Rublack, *Dressing Up*, 8.
138 The pendants belonging to Anna and Augustus of Saxony are illustrated in Hackenbroch, *Renaissance Jewellery*, 135, no. 344; 164, no. 441A and colour plates XI; XIV.
139 Hackenbroch, *Renaissance Jewellery*, 129–136, 150. Anna of Bavaria's remarkable illustrated jewellery inventory is in the Bavarian State Library (Munich) Cod. icon. 429. On the jewels of Anna of Saxony, see E. von Watzdorf, 'Fürstlicher Schmuck in der Renaissance', *Münchner Jahrbuch der bildenden Kunst* 11 (1934); 'Mielich und die Bayerischen Goldschmiedewerke der Renaissance', *Münchner Jahrbuch der bildenden Kunst* 12 (1937). Cranach's portrait of Caterina Jagellonica is in Kraków, Czartoryski Museum.
140 The portrait of Augusta is illustrated in Wade, 'The Queen's Courts', 72, fig. 3.4; the bracelet is illustrated in Heiberg, *Christian IV and Europe*, 176, no. 631. Several versions of the portrait of Kirsten wearing her cipher survive at Rosenborg, Frederiksborg, and in private Danish collections; see those illustrated in Heiberg, nos. 66, 113.
141 RA, *Diverse akter vedr- afregning og kvittance 1588–1660*, B223B. Danske Kancelli, Rentekammeerafdelingen, 1595. My thanks to Camilla Luise Dahl for this reference.
142 *CSPV*, vol. 12, no. 250: 9 June 1611.

5

Representation and self-fashioning

In 1614, Marcus Gheeraerts the Younger was commissioned to paint a full-length portrait of Anna of Denmark. The choice of artist was logical – Gheeraerts was a painter to the court and had painted Anna's portrait from as early as 1609 – but the portrait he painted in 1614 was little short of radical.[1] Now in the collection of the Duke of Bedford and hanging at Woburn Abbey, the portrait is larger than life (212 x 127 cm) and the canvas is dominated by the figure of the queen in formal court dress (Figure 5.1). The scale ensures that Anna is a commanding presence, but it is complemented by careful choices in composition and iconography that produce a dynamic, independent portrait. Positioned in the right of the canvas and turned to the left, Anna occupies the side of greater power which prevents the portrait from being read as a pendant to a portrait of James. By standing in a shadowed architectural alcove that opens onto a manicured cut-turf garden, the painting pointedly commemorates Anna's interest in, and patronage of, garden design and architecture, while her royal identity by birth – rather than marriage – and her specific belonging to the House of Oldenburg is proudly showcased through her personal motto and pieces of jewellery that reference her brother, Christian IV, and her mother, Sofie of Mecklenburg-Güstrow. Unprecedented within the corpus of Anna's painted portraits, these features raise questions around the queen's motivations, her aims, the intricacies of faction and diplomacy that shaped the court at the time of commission, and the intended audience of such an image – questions that lie at the centre of this chapter.

The politics of portraiture

In his seminal article on the politics of portraiture, published in 1994, Harry Berger argued for a re-evaluation of the central role of the sitter

Representation and self-fashioning 153

5.1 Portrait of Anna of Denmark by Marcus Gheeraerts the Younger, c.1614.

as agent, stating that 'a portrait presupposes a desire and decision to be portrayed ... the act of posing ... must always be an intentional act.'[2] In line with Berger's theorisations of the performative fictionality of early modern portraiture, this chapter approaches Anna – as sitter – as the directorial agent of her painted portraits. The queen's distinctive portrait types are therefore examined within the context of their production to ascertain Anna's intention as sitter and director, confirming Joanna Woodall's statement that portraiture was 'responsive' to the changing 'social and political circumstances of the sitter'.[3] Isolating a distinctive shift in the mode of Anna's representation with the Woburn portrait, this chapter is primarily interested in portraits painted of the queen from 1614 onwards, but it discusses the meanings and value tied up in her earlier portraits, and the currency and usage of her image to underscore the political role of the portrait as a proxy for the represented and as a means of information transfer. Media is limited to painted portraits, in easel and in miniature, and to distinct types (rather than variants and reproductions) to centre the argument on Anna's agency in having had physical, or at least verbal, influence on the final image.

The examination of Anna's portraits in this chapter provides, to borrow from Berger, 'insight not into the psychology of the sitter [Anna of Denmark] but into the psychology of self-representation', for the early modern portrait was a social and ideological construct.[4] It shared this basic fact with the elite physical body as discussed in Chapter 4, but it had a distinct difference: while the body was subject to constant, expensive fashioning and refashioning, the portrait arts were comparatively fixed and stable and they were considerably cheaper than fabrics and jewels. As Richard Brilliant has pointed out, 'only physical appearance is naturally visible, and even that is unstable. The rest [of a person's identity] is conceptual and must be expressed symbolically' in a portrait.[5] Writing of sixteenth-century portraiture, Woodall makes a comparable observation, noting that the period saw 'the consolidation of visual motifs and signifying principles' as the physiognomic likeness was repeatedly conceived within a 'visual repertoire' of the full-length format, 'the courtly console table, wooden chairs, curtains, columns, helmets and handkerchiefs' to articulate the 'socio-spiritual authority' and 'elevated status' of the sitter.[6] By uniquely combining an identifiable individual likeness with established visual codes and devices, the portrait arts offered the elite a medium for confirming, or even imagining, themselves in a mode, typological character, or disposition that could be preserved and disseminated. Portraits were a central, political means of communication that transferred information about a person's physicality, and current styles and fashions, but they also circulated knowledge about individual and collective identities such as socio-political belonging, gender, dynastic membership, and religious affiliation. As portraits circulated this information, they reconfirmed the very meaning and relevance of those social structures in which the sitter participated.

In the European courtly community of Anna's lifetime, portraits were often commissioned and/or gifted on occasions of state significance including the attainment of new titles, the birth of an heir, a military victory, or a prospective marriage. The central role of the portrait at these politically charged junctures stemmed from the reflexive relationship it had with the person represented. Alberti famously made this connection clear when, writing in 1435, he asserted that 'painting certainly has in itself a truly divine power, not only because, as they say of friendship, a painting lets the absent be present, but also because it shows [to] the living, after long centuries, the dead … therefore, the faces of the dead, thanks to painting, have in a certain way a very long life.'[7] As Woodall reminds us, the sentiment was not a novel invention of Renaissance thought but had classical origins in the work of Aristotle and it continued well beyond both men into the early modern period.[8] In 1597, Christian IV requested that James VI send full-length portraits of himself 'and the Queen, your wife, Our sister', framing his intention in very similar terms: 'when we have a fairly frequent sight of those who are not with us, we can remember them so much more often and, because of recollection, feel something which gives us delight.'[9]

As a powerful proxy, the portrait occupied a unique, central place in the political arena of early modern dynastic marriage.[10] Easel or miniature portraits of the prospective bride or bridegroom were sent between courts, often accompanied by portraits of the parents, to aid an assessment of the candidate's merits – physically and symbolically.[11] In the case of miniatures, the small, jewel-like format encouraged close inspection as the recipient fostered an attachment to the new spouse prior to their physical arrival. The royal union of James VI and Anna of Denmark was no exception and, when in 1588, James was faced with a choice between Anna and Catherine of Navarre (1559–1604) for his wife, he turned to the physiognomic authority of portraiture to ensure that he made the right decision. Scottish ambassadors were dispatched to both courts and returned with 'pictures of the yong princesses' over which the king deliberated. James spent fifteen days scrutinising the portraits and praying to God 'to moue his hart' to choose the bride who 'wald be metest, and the weall of him slef and his contre', before he was able to announce to the council that he was 'resoluit to mary in Denmark'.[12] The decision was predicated foremost on political and financial considerations, but this remarkable episode evocatively captures the widespread belief in the ability of a painted likeness to capture and convey the typological character and interior virtue of the absent sitter.[13] The use of painted proxies in this manner was common in the period, and just as a physiognomic likeness secured Anna of Denmark's wedded destiny, so too was it the case for other royal queens of England, both regnant and consort, including Catherine of Aragón, Mary Tudor, and

Henrietta Maria.[14] Yet the slippage between portrait and reality was occasionally exposed to disastrous effect as infamously demonstrated by the fate of Anna of Kleve (1515–1540), who was unable to match the standard that Han Holbein's (c.1497–1543) portrait of 1539 had promised Henry VIII.[15]

Dispersing a physical likeness of a particular person in lieu of their physical presence was one of the central uses of the state portrait. Beyond marriage, portraits were gifted as symbolic signs of the approval and support of the person represented. With the signing of the Anglo-Spanish peace in London in 1604 and ratified in Valladolid in 1605, for example, the new amity was sealed with the exchange of miniatures of the Habsburg and Stuart monarchs as well as state portraits of the royal couples and their marriageable children – Prince Henry and the Infanta Ana María.[16] The intermediary abilities of portraiture are even more pointedly demonstrated by the actions of Christian IV who, when not accompanying the Danish embassy to Madrid in 1640, sent his portrait in his stead.[17] Within the Stuart–Oldenburg network, portraits reinforced ties of loyalty and esteem and provided updates on the sitter's appearance and achievements. As outlined in Chapter 4, Anna and Christian gifted each other their portrait miniature on several occasions, but this exchange of painted likeness extended to easel portraits and to other members of the familial network. Writing in 1988, Steffan Heiberg points out that 'close family interrelations' between Denmark-Norway and the multiple Stuart kingdom 'led to an extensive exchange of portraits, which explains the comparatively large number of Danish portraits of that period in England' and that 'there are also a good many English portraits of the English [Stuart] royal house in Denmark.'[18]

Most recently, Catharine MacLeod has considered the place of Anna's visual image within the context of international court portraiture, stating that the artists she patronised and the mode of portrayal that she sought in England were 'part of a European visual court currency'.[19] Building on the work of James Knowles and Lucy Wood, among others, MacLeod confirms the directorial role that Anna exercised over her later visual persona, but she cautions against the tradition of reading it in the shadow of Queen Elizabeth's visual legacy. Rather, MacLeod maps important connections – of artist, iconography, and the physical movement of portraits – between the Stuart and Oldenburg courts to conclude that Anna used 'her own image as a means of forging political, social and visual links between Britain and continental European courts'.[20] MacLeod's chapter is a thoughtful and inspiring contribution to our growing understanding of how the style, iconographies, and variants of Anna's portraiture operated across geographical borders, but it is not, as she acknowledges, 'an exhaustive analysis' – a point that is foremost demonstrated by the omission of Van Somer's notable 1617 portrait of Anna in hunting dress on the grounds that being 'intended for the Queen herself, or her close family, it tells us little about international exchange at this time.'[21] This chapter confirms that Anna pioneered a stylistic break from the isolationist, iconic mode of portraiture shepherded by Elizabeth, but it argues for the Stuarts' careful negotiation of the Tudor legacy, wherein particular links were strategically retained. It also sets Anna's changing visual image firmly within its socio-political framework – domestic and international – thereby giving relevance to her decisions of format, iconography, and audience and increasing our understanding of portraits as objects that engaged with wider cultural, dynastic, and diplomatic concerns.

Portraiture in Scotland under James VI

The textual and visual record of portraiture in sixteenth-century Scotland has fared poorly. There is very little surviving information as to the commissions or payments of the artists who serviced the court, and the number of extant portraits is surprisingly low. The absence of an established painting industry in Scotland was lamented at the time when, in July 1603, Lennox wholly blamed the 'lack of artists' for his inability 'to keep my promise [to send] portraits of yourself [the king], the Queen, and the Princes', but that now he was in England, he would 'not fail' in this task.[22] There were, of course, artists working in Scotland and, as in England, much royal patronage went to artists from Flanders. In September 1581, James appointed the Fleming Arnold van Bronckorst (*fl.*1565–1583) to be his principal painter 'for all the days of his lyvetime', in which capacity he was responsible for 'all the small and great pictures for his Majesty' and was granted an annual pension of £100 Scots. At the very least, Bronckorst completed two portraits of King James, one in full-length format and the other 'fra the belt upward' (three-quarter length), before he returned to London in 1582 and was replaced by another Fleming, Adrian Vanson (d.1610).[23] Vanson worked for the court until the Stuarts left for England and he may have travelled with them, for he was certainly in London by 1604 when he is recorded working on the Dutch triumphal arch that was erected in honour of James's ceremonial entry.[24]

In Scotland, as late as December 1601, Vanson received payment of £20 Scots, 'for ye penting of his maiesties [James's] portratt'.[25] Miniature portraits of the king, either engraved or painted, were concurrently in use as diplomatic gifts, and that same month, as mentioned in Chapter 1, James paid the jeweller Heriot £611.18*s*.4*d*. Scots for 'ane greit cheniyie of gold wt his hienes portrait hingand yairat glk [hanging thereat which] wes gevin to ane gentilmen that came fra ye duik of magilburgh [Mecklenburg]'.[26] While neither of these portraits has been identified, examples of Vanson's work for the crown is extant including an important set of pendants of James and Anna from around 1595 (Plates 2 and 4).[27]

Intended to be hung side-by-side and read together, the figures slightly turn towards each other and follow traditional gendering, with James on the side of greater power (the hierarchic right) and Anna to his left. Elite status is communicated through costly garments and opulent jewels, and James's ermine-lined cloak and sword hilt indicates at (but does not insist on) royal status.[28] There is no trace of the conventions of royal court portraiture which, codified by Tiziano Vecellio (Titian) (1485–1576) and Anthonis Mor (1517–1576) at the Habsburg court, was well known by the late sixteenth century: a full-length format populated with elements such as tables, chairs, curtains, columns, and royal and/or military insignia.[29] Rather, the use of scale, format, and composition produces comparatively intimate portraits of the royal Stuart pair. The paintings are executed on small canvases, in bust length, and the use of cropping forces the figures close to the picture plane. Further, iconographical elements locate their sitters in a particular time and perform a specific, commemorative purpose: the Stuarts as a functioning royal family and the security of the Scottish – and plausibly the English – succession.

The adherence to gendered positioning places Anna as a figure of lesser power, but this is slightly mitigated by the pendants' celebration of the queen for James is configured as *paterfamilias*. Paying visual tribute to his wife, James wears a magnificent hat band fronted with Anna's crowned cipher (A) richly picked out in table diamonds. The quantity of this portrait type of James – with at least four surviving variants – underscores the currency of the royal couple at this juncture and can be plausibly linked to the birth of Prince Henry. As the Stuarts' firstborn child, a son, and a legitimate heir, Henry's arrival was a momentous dynastic event. Although born in February 1594, the prince was not baptised until August, as lengthy preparations were made in Stirling for the rites and celebrations, and international guests were delayed.[30] The timing of the portrait sitting, and James's decision to visually reference his wife, strongly suggests Henry's birth and baptism to have been the motivating event. Indeed, the baptism also gave cause for the prince to have his own first official portrait painted, which was completed a few months later.[31] With the next reign secure and the English succession ever more likely, portraits of the Stuarts were in demand among the Scottish elite and the wider courtly community who sought to demonstrate fealty and support.

In the king's portrait, the queen's cipher is a conspicuous feature through which James honours Anna as a woman, and a queen, who had successfully fulfilled her primary duty with the birth of a male heir the previous year. As seen in Chapter 4, ciphers were an unmistakeable form of identification and personalisation, which led to their common inclusion in pieces of jewellery, clothing, furniture, and soft furnishings.[32] For this reason too, they made good gifts and could be worn as signs of loyalty and/ or deference. On Anna's entry into Edinburgh, 'a faire jewell, of a great price, called the A, was givin to the queene' by the burgh, and it may have been this jewel that James proudly wears in his portrait around 1595.[33] The translation in media – from the object of the jewel being physically worn on the king's body to a painted representation of that moment – did, of course, significantly impact meaning, ownership, and audience.[34] By inclusion in the portrait, the fleeting, temporality of James's wearing and possession of the jewel became fixed and permanent, while access to and knowledge of the king's bodily display expanded beyond the original audience. Further, while James's relationship to the jewel would have been based on its small scale, personal significance, and high economic value, the portrait owners engaged with the jewel from a remove, where it coalesced into a sign of their connection and loyalty to the Stuarts – both king and queen.

Early Stuart portraiture in England

It was another momentous dynastic event that spurred the next surviving painted portrait type of the Stuarts – the succession to the English throne following the death of James's childless cousin, the Tudor Queen Elizabeth in March 1603. As argued in Chapter 4, the painted portraits completed of Anna immediately following her arrival in London reveal a concerted effort to configure her in line with established, Elizabethan fashions. Anna's coiffure was altered from being flat at the crown and wide at the sides, to being raised high on the head with narrow sides, while the full circular ruff gave way to a standing lace collar with a low, square neckline (Figure 4.1). As MacLeod observes, several versions of this portrait exist in several different hands, including one in Vienna, which evidences the widespread demand for images of royalty being spurred by state events.[35] Further, as outlined in Chapter 4, this mode of representation extended beyond paintings to engravings and cast medals that ensured the wide reach of this image type among a broad segment of the Stuart populace and at foreign courts (Figures 4.2 and 4.3). Such self-fashioning was decidedly political. Visual continuity between the Tudor and Stuart queens heightened the initial success and popularity of the Stuarts by helping to quell fears around the arrival of a new and foreign dynasty. It was this mode that continued in John de Critz's portraits of Anna throughout the first decade of the seventeenth century, who James reconfirmed in his office as serjeant-painter on 17 September 1603.[36]

In this portrait type, as it was in the Scottish portraits, Anna occupies the traditionally subordinate side of the sinister (Plates 5 and 6). A subsidiary extension of her husband, she is positioned in the left of the canvas and orientated to the right in order to face the paired portrait of James. De Critz and his studio produced numerous versions of this portrait type, in a variety of formats – full length, half length, and bust length – and with subtle variations in dress, jewellery, and setting – indicating that this was the standard pattern for the new ruling couple of England.[37] Surviving accounts for the first five years of the Stuart reign of England confirm that De Critz was responsible for the portraits that the Stuarts sent to Florence, Lorraine, Ireland, and Vienna, for example, while De Critz also completed versions for local patrons including Salisbury and the Merchant Taylors' Company, the former of whom was a major supporter of the painter.[38] In addition, Anna herself directly engaged De Critz, with her privy purse payments recording £40 'for worke donne for her Ma[jes]t[i]es owne use' in July 1607, although this may have been for decorative work that De Critz regularly completed for the crown, rather than for portraits.[39] Despite considerable royal and aristocratic esteem, De Critz's work as a portraitist abruptly ended with the year 1608. This has been commonly interpreted as a fall from favour as the Stuarts looked to more cosmopolitan artists such as Gheeraerts, but Edward Town has recently determined that it was occasioned by a major loss of eyesight which restricted De Critz to decorative work.[40] It was in this capacity that he continued in crown patronage and, as covered Chapter 6, he was still in high favour in 1619 when he was tasked with the majority of the large heraldic programme for Anna's state funeral.

One extant full-length autograph portrait of Anna, painted by De Critz between 1605 and 1610, is a good example of his artistic proficiency but even as it provides more visual information than Vanson's earlier bust-length portrait, it remains similarly devoid of any signs, symbols, or inscriptions to confirm the identity, lineage, or qualities of the sitter (Plate 6). The interior space is generic, and the portrait is without the familial jewels, mottoes, and references to cultural interests that Anna chose to have included in her later portraits. Rather, in a similar manner to Vanson's portraits, this type by De Critz is concerned with broadcasting material wealth, propriety, abundance, and, through the use of the pendant format, marital union. Coming after the reign of the childless Elizabeth, and the anxiety that had surrounded the heirless succession, the advertisement of such qualities provided a welcome, advantageous contrast. The portrait type highlights difference and distance from the Tudor predecessor, but as mentioned, at this point in time parallels between the two reigns were being concurrently stressed through aspects of Anna's fashion.

The articulation of Tudor-Stuart continuity sought to confirm the legitimacy of the new dynasty, and visual and verbal efforts extended beyond painting to poetry, theatre, and prints. Renold Elstrack (1570–1625), working to a design from John Speed (1552–1629), engraved an elaborate family tree – visualised through portraits – that traced the Tudor-Stuart descent back to the Norman Conquest. Competition among the London print-makers was marked, and at least three contemporaneous versions were published, as well as double portraits of James and Anna flanking an illustrated family tree.[41] As the new queen consort of England, Anna was noticeably conceptualised within the bounds of Elizabeth's iconographic legacy and even the Tudor queen's epithets were recycled. Poets subtly refashioned the Elizabethan appellation 'Oriana' into 'Anna Oriens', and deities who had been commonly associated with the Tudor queen, such as Diana and Cynthia, were reused.[42] Anna herself visibly engaged with Elizabethanism in her first court masque, *The Vision of the Twelve Goddesses*, which was written by Samuel Daniel (1562–1619) and staged at Hampton Court on 8 January 1604. For the performance, the masquers were granted access to Elizabeth's wardrobe goods stored in the Tower of London and while this was not an uncommon practice, the act was noteworthy since spectators recognised the origin of the clothing.[43] Dudley Carleton, in his oft-quoted précis of the masque, alleged that the female performers 'were beholden to Queen Elizabeth's wardrobe' and that the garments had been altered for Anna's gown was 'not so much below the knee but that we might see a woman had both feet and legs, which I never knew before'.[44] The connection was made all the more potent by Anna's decision to appear in the guise of Pallas Athena, the goddess of warfare and wisdom and a potent Elizabethan conceit. Anna thus fashioned herself as the successor of Elizabeth's legacy of female courtly power, an alignment that audience members did not fail to notice.[45]

Miniature portraits of the queen

Echoes of Queen Elizabeth's pictorial legacy crossed over into Anna's portrait in miniature, where the general silhouette and the specifics of dress and hairstyle followed the consort's portrait in large. Anna did not, however, retain Elizabeth's limner, Nicholas Hilliard, but sought a new direction in the patronage of Hilliard's former pupil, Isaac Oliver.[46] Oliver was not new to English court circles, but it was only with the arrival of the Stuarts that he visibly gained favour. Aware of the styles and trends appreciated on the Continent, art historians have suggested that Oliver offered a more naturalistic approach, or a 'continental style', through the use of perspective and shadowing in contrast to the distinctive, hard-edged approach modelled by Hilliard.[47] For his part, James was content to keep Hilliard in his service, a decision that may have been motivated by convenience or by a desire to maintain a level of visual consistency with his predecessor. Either way, James's purported disinterest in the arts has been exaggerated by scholars and if his refusal to give portrait sittings hampered the updating of his image, then he remained well aware of the ability of a portrait to make statements of power, prerogative, allegiance, and honour.[48] In Scotland, in 1601, the court officer Archibald Cornwall was tried, convicted, and executed for trying to sell portraits of James and Anna (belonging to an unnamed debtor) by displaying them on the gallows at the Edinburgh

Cross. In light of this offensive action, James issued a statute against the future misuse of portraits of himself, Anna, and their children, proclaiming that 'for the honour and reverence thai aucht to our soveran Lord [James], his darrest spous [Anna] and childrein, statutes ... that nane [none] of thair maiesteis and graces pictures or portraicts be poyndet [pawned], rowppet [rouped] or compryset [compromised], for ony maner of caus publictlie or privatlie heirafter.'[49] Adding to this, one of the earliest surviving examples of the Stuarts' engagement with the portrait arts following their remove to England comes from James, and it was expressly undertaken with the intention of reaffirming cordial relations with Denmark-Norway following the accession. On 28 December 1603, Hilliard received £19.20s. Sterling 'for his paynes and travell being appoynted by direction to make certayne pictures of his ma[jes]t[i]e which were by his highnes gyven to the Duke of Denmarke embassador'.[50] With similarly political concerns, Anna ordered Oliver to accompany her on her first English progresses so that her portrait in miniature could be given away as reward, as a sign of favour among her new subjects, or in gratitude for lodgings and/or hospitality. Oliver must have been kept extremely busy, for his two acquittances – of 22 March 1605 and 17 June 1605 – were considerable, with £200 sterling declared for 'his great charges in attending her highnes service and for certaine pourtraictures made for her Ma[jes]tie in divers places aswell heere at London as in progresse'.[51] On this occasion, Anna's travels were varied and took her to Rycote in Oxfordshire; Bisham, Hurst, and Newbury in Berkshire; Collingbourne in Wiltshire; and Cobham and Higham in Kent, and necessitated a number of gentry properties being readied for lodging and/or dining.[52] Satisfied with Oliver's talents, on 22 June 1605 Anna appointed him 'her Ma[jes]t[ie]s painter in the art of lymning'.[53]

Two of Oliver's miniatures of Anna survive from the opening years of the Stuarts' time in England which, given the uniqueness of approach and the fresh, sensitive handling, must have followed a personal sitting or, at the very least, were completed with visual knowledge of the queen (Plates 7 and 8). These set the tone for Oliver's subsequent portraits of Anna, as well as those that issued from the workshops of both Oliver and Hilliard, all of which are markedly consistent with only slight variations in jewellery and dress. Anna's mode of portrayal in miniature is therefore relatively consistent, and the surviving quantity suggests the high demand was satisfied by gifts from the queen and independent, elite commissions. Many miniatures of Anna were owned, and indeed worn, as single pieces, but examples do survive in combination with paired portraits of James, and Hilliard (and his studio) produced numerous limned portraits after the type developed by Oliver, which evidences the currency of Anna's image both locally and abroad (Figures 5.2 and 5.3).[54] In all extant miniatures of Anna, unlike her corpus of easel portraits, the queen faces to the right, thereby literally and metaphorically reserving the hierarchic position for James.

Representation and self-fashioning 163

5.2 Miniature of Anna of Denmark from the studio of Nicholas Hilliard, c.1604–1605.

As discussed in Chapter 1, gift-exchange was a central means of preserving the patron–client bonds that anchored the Stuart monarchy. The value of a gift was determined by such criteria as material worth, expert craftsmanship, rarity, and provenance, and one particular object that could fulfil many of these facets was the portrait miniature. Just as the ambassador of Mecklenburg received a jewelled miniature of James as mentioned above, so too did international dignitaries, many of them related to Anna,

5.3 Miniature of King James VI and I by Nicholas Hilliard, c.1610.

receive miniatures of the Stuart queen. This was similarly true of Anna and Christian, who repeatedly gifted each other their miniatures and, on at least one occasion, Anna sent a diamond-encrusted miniature to her mother Sofie.[55] It is reasonable to suggest that the limned portrait of Anna, by Isaac Oliver, remaining in the Danish Royal Collection at Frederiksborg Castle is a result of this familial gift-giving.[56]

Visual and documentary sources show that Anna continued such magnanimity within her own court circle, choosing to give a number of her female chamberers pieces of personalised jewelled adornment. These were highly treasured by the recipient and, as late as 1644, Jane Drummond, who had been Anna's principal lady-in-waiting until 1617, was still in possession of 'a picture case set full of diamonds the midle stone like a heart bigger then the rest, in it Queen Anns picture'.[57] A number of other women close to Anna in England – Anna Montgomerie (née Livingstone), Countess of Eglinton (d.1632), Margaret Seton (née Hay), Countess of Dunfermline (c.1592–1659), and Elizabeth Grey (née Talbot), Countess of Kent (1582–1651) – all chose to commemorate their ownership by sitting for formal portraits wearing jewelled tablets adorned with either A or with AR.[58] Beyond economic and material worth, these miniatures held high cultural, personal, and political value. Worn prominently at court, the jewelled portrait stood proxy for the absent queen consort and shaped the aristocratic female body into a site of social privilege and royal intimacy. Further, the representational interior and denotative exterior of the miniature accrued identity and memory beyond the initial act of gifting and wear; by choosing to wear the jewelled tablet in a formal court portrait, the female sitter preserved their reputation and royal proximity for posterity. Thus, although meanings shift with changes in materiality and with time, even now, after the death of both giver and receiver, and the loss of the original miniature, the extant painting of figure and jewel provides insight into female friendships and allegiances at the early Stuart court.[59]

The Woburn portrait

With the Woburn portrait of 1614 (Figure 5.1), the relationship between the visual personas of Anna and Elizabeth was reformulated. On the one hand, it is important to recognise, as Knowles points out, that the portrait recalls images of Elizabeth to Anna's advantage. Then again, it must also be acknowledged that the connection is superseded by Anna's self-fashioning as a descendent of a royal bloodline, as a member House of Oldenburg, and as a cultural patron.[60] Interestingly, much of what has been argued about Anna in the preceding chapters visually coheres in this portrait: her leading support of innovative building and gardening works is referenced through the classical archway and the symmetrical, ornamental garden; her pride in her royal bloodline and Oldenburg prestige is shown through representational jewellery, her personal motto (discussed below), and a dress embroidered with the peacock feathers of the regal deity Juno. Anna's motivation for reconfiguring her image so dramatically, as is so often the case, is found in the larger socio-political context.

On 22 July 1614, the Stuart court welcomed Anna's brother, Christian IV, to England for a second time. Curiously unannounced, Christian and his entourage travelled incognito into the capital and reportedly made it all the way to the queen's presence chamber at Denmark House before they were recognised.⁶¹ Over the next fifteen days, Christian lodged at Denmark House and Whitehall Palace where he was attended by twenty-three of James's servants.⁶² Time was spent on 'items of business', but Christian also found time to enjoy a regal level of entertainment as banquets, games of tennis, running at the ring, fencing, hawking, hunting, wrestling matches, musical performances, fireworks, and a 'drinking feast' were organised for his enjoyment.⁶³ Significantly, Christian also found time to have his portrait painted by Gheeraerts. The resulting portrait, a version of which is in the Princeton University Art Museum, commemorates Christian's membership in the Order of the Garter; he is shown wearing the insignia of the Order with a magnificently bejewelled Lesser George, and the Garter on his left leg (Plate 9). Painted in the same year and by the same artist as the Woburn portrait of his sister Anna, the two bear marked similarities. Format, pose, and scale are almost identical, and the siblings wear conspicuously large, red ribbons tied around their left arms to visualise Spanish favour. Placed within the unfolding rivalry over *Dominium maris baltici* [Dominion on the Baltic Sea] and the possible Stuart-Habsburg marriage alliance, this was just one of many decisions that Christian made to demonstrate his partiality for Spain while he was in England. Red bands, ribbons, or sashes had long been worn in a variety of forms by Spanish kings, high-ranking military officials, and soldiers as a symbol of the Spanish Empire, for the red band was derived from the red St Andrew's cross of Burgundy, which had been chosen as the emblem of the Spanish Habsburgs by the Burgundian Duke and first Habsburg King in Spain, Philip the Handsome (1478–1506).⁶⁴ Notable examples of the red band being worn around the arm as a visual marker of Habsburg power and allegiance include portraits of Philip II, Philip III, the minister Don Rodrigo Calderón, Count of Oliva (1580–1621), and the military commander Ambrogio Spinola Doria, Marquess of Balbases (1569–1630).⁶⁵

In the first instance, the purpose of Christian's visit to England in 1614 was never made explicit. It confounded contemporaries who speculated widely over 'the reasons for this unexpected visit' with 'each person expressing his own beliefs so that opinions are various and conflicting', and it has continued to draw a variety of interpretations from historians.⁶⁶ Most logically, as Calvin Senning argues, growing opposition in the Baltic had forced Christian to seek personal reassurance from the Stuarts. As Senning recounts, two 'patently anti-Danish' treaties had been signed in spring 1613 between Lübeck and Holland and then in March 1614 between Sweden and the States General. Christian responded to the first treaty by sending Andrew Sinclair (1555–1625) to London to meet with King James and discuss Danish grievances against the Dutch, but the alarm of the second treaty – raising the likelihood of an isolated Denmark-Norway facing aggressive action from Sweden, the Netherlands, and some of the major Hanseatic towns – had Christian personally travel to his brother-in-law to seek support for a 'defensive league'.⁶⁷ To this image of Stuart–Oldenburg relations must be added the Kalmar War of 1611–1613 between Denmark-Norway and Sweden. As Alexia Grosjean and Steve Murdoch have shown, King James followed a particularly daring line of foreign policy that saw him arm both sides. Officially, those British troops sent to Denmark were able to be used by Christian wherever he saw fit, whereas those levied for Sweden were banned from fighting against Denmark and James further obfuscated the movements of the latter by drawing them from Scots regiments stationed in the Dutch Republic. Yet it was these supplementary forces that allowed Sweden to match the Danish war effort, for they were being severely hampered by their ongoing war with Poland-Lithuania.⁶⁸ In fact, as Grosjean determines, 'more Scots serve[d] Sweden than Denmark-Norway throughout the war', and James was also central to the Danish–Swedish peace since he pushed Christian to the negotiation table under threat of withdrawing armed support.⁶⁹ James had levelled the balance of power in Scandinavia, coerced Christian into a mediation, and then had Britain arbitrate the resultant peace of Knäred through the Stuart ambassadors James Spens of Wormiston (d.1632) (for Sweden) and Robert Anstruther (for Denmark-Norway).⁷⁰

In the summer of 1614, Christian was facing the reality of two anti-Danish treaties in Scandinavia and given James's diplomatic weight in the area – and his lukewarm support of Denmark-Norway during the Kalmar War – Christian logically sought personal reassurance of amity from his brother-in-law. While in England, Christian showed 'himself most evilly affected towards the States', requested that James would 'not to help them [the Dutch] if they take the offensive in Flanders', and spoke against 'their excessive aggrandizement', and commercial fishing activities in Greenland.⁷¹ As noted in Chapter 2, Anna's fierce familial loyalty saw her share Christian's opinions, and reports of her antipathy to the Dutch issued out of London.⁷² Beyond entreating his immediate family to share in his hostility, Christian actively cultivated relations with the United Province's traditional enemy: Spain.

In the spring of 1613, a Danish extraordinary embassy was sent to Madrid and proposed an embargo on Dutch shipping in the Øresund if Spain would provide compensation for the annual custom dues. On 17 July 1613, Peiro Priuli, Venetian ambassador in Spain, reported that 'the ambassadors of Denmark took leave of the king [Philip III] yesterday. He made them a present of horses, and has displayed the greatest esteem for them, as he wishes to keep their king well disposed towards him, that monarch [Christian] being at loggerheads with the Dutch.'⁷³ Danish–Spanish cordiality was further advanced in London that year through the activities of the representatives Sinclair and Gondomar. The following year, 1614, after the Danish king arrived in the Stuart capital, it was Gondomar who was honoured with the first of Christian IV's ceremonial audiences.⁷⁴

Gondomar was also treated to the last of Christian's audiences, given on board the king's ship at Gravesend after he had taken leave of King James, which lasted for 'two hours' during which time 'they drank various toasts and at parting the ambassador was honoured with a salute of cannon.'[75] Such partiality was evident throughout Christian's visit, and the ambassadors of Spain and the archduke were noted to 'have been several times with the ministers of that king [Christian], and it is clear that the king of Spain as much as the king of Denmark desires to abuse the States'.[76]

Christian's support of a Stuart–Habsburg marriage through his nephew Charles at this time was another politic strategy in his quest for state security and territorial gains in the Baltic. Through the match, Christian would cement ties to the Habsburgs and bolster Denmark's position against the growing enmity posed by the United Provinces, Sweden, and the Hanseatic League. Christian's interest in the marriage alliance was perceived during his time in England and it was even rumoured that the purpose of his visit was 'to treat with his majesty about a match which is now in parley between his son and the younger daughter of Spain'.[77] It was not the primary motivation for Christian's journey, but it was germane to his wider international strategising at this point. While in London, Christian did speak 'about marrying the prince here [Charles] to a daughter of Spain', and this was notably endorsed by Anna who was described as being 'in favour of it'.[78] The Danish siblings then translated their joint comity for Spain, and concomitant animosity for the United Provinces, into large, full-length portraits by Gheeraerts wherein they mirrored each other in pose, scale, and format, and the show of prominent red favours (Figure 5.1 and Plate 9). It is highly plausible that the siblings wore red bands at court and, by including them in their portraits, sought to stabilise the transience, and extend the reach, of their politicised bodily display. A defensive league with Britain did not result from Christian's visit but, as Senning rightly points out, Christian's presence in London showed 'the closeness of his relations' with the Stuarts and the associated 'threat of Anglo-Danish cooperation in political matters', which were preserved in the new portraits of Oldenburg King and Stuart Queen.[79]

Later portraits by Paul van Somer

In 1617, Anna's visual persona fell to the Flemish artist Paul van Somer (c.1577–1621), who arrived in England from the Low Countries in December 1616.[80] The surviving account of Anna's patronage of Van Somer is posthumous, recording payment of £170 to the artist 'for diverse pictures by him made for the late Queenes Majestie'.[81] Dated to 4 February 1620, the large amount feasibly covers the entire body of work that Van Somer completed for Anna before her death in March 1619. Among these works are the full-length hunting portrait of the queen, signed and dated

1617 (Plate 1), a portrait of her longstanding ally, the Earl of Pembroke, and three full-length portraits of Anna that position the queen in front of architectural features and fantasies painted by other artists (Figure 5.4). One of these shares a historic pairing with a full-length portrait of James by Van Somer, but they are unlikely to have been commissioned as such since both figures turn to the left and lack any background unity.[82] All three portraits use the figure pattern of the Woburn portrait and Anna is again positioned in the right of the canvas, facing to the left, which obviates the paintings from being read as a counterwork to a portrait of James. By comparison, Van Somer's hunting portrait represents a distinct and unique departure, presenting an updated version of the queen that must have resulted from a fresh sitting (Plate 1). Although repeating the orientation of the queen, it is more animated and naturalistic than Gheeraerts's earlier work and Van Somer's portraits that use Gheeraerts's figure type. The link to Anna's cultural endeavours is now made explicit, as the background opens onto a recognisable section of the queen's palace of Oatlands, complete with the new vineyard that she had planted on the south side of the privy gardens and the classical stone gate that she commissioned from Jones the previous year.[83] That said, it is still a composite, carefully fabricated image wherein symbolic referents convey aspects of the queen's virtue, but 'social and artistic limits' of the genre are followed so that pose, expression, and subsidiary elements build an appropriately formal and dignified figure of gravitas.[84]

Evidently pleased with the new painting, Anna chose to hang it at Oatlands, and it is described in the 1617 inventory of the palace as 'Her maiesties owne picture with her horse by her done at large' and was recorded hanging 'in ye gallery next to ye vineyard'.[85] This considered placement, as Knowles writes, produced a *'trompe l'oeil* effect, accentuating the symbolism of the choice of Oatlands in the background, especially the vineyard, its wall, and Inigo Jones's gateway', and unequivocally pictorialising the queen's ownership over the palace and lands in which the viewer was located as they admired the portrait.[86] Here, the viewer was greeted by an image of the queen dressed for the hunt in riding clothes, accompanied by a richly caparisoned horse, a servant of African birth or descent attired in livery, and five greyhounds, with running deer in the middle distance.[87] Acknowledging the racial naming traditions that governed ethnic minorities in early modern England, attempts to identify this individual in the archival record still prove inclusive.[88] He may be the servant problematically described as 'the Moir' in the royal Scottish wardrobe and household accounts of 1590.[89] Unfortunately, the servant's name and position are not recorded in either document, but he was listed together with four pages and three lackeys who, as Michael Pearce has determined, were later noted to be 'pages of the equerry', which suggests that he likewise worked in this capacity.[90] Absent from the 1592 household

5.4 Portrait of Anna of Denmark by Paul van Somer, c.1617–1618.

list, Pearce suggests that he may have died in 1591, but it is also possible that he was given an anglicised name, rendering him indistinguishable in the archival record and that he later travelled with the Stuarts to England in 1603. Granted a subsidiary position in the portrait, his inclusion may have been intended to dramatise the queen's white complexion – a device that became increasingly common in court portraiture as the century progressed.[91]

The portrait commemorates the honourable, princely pastime of the hunt which, as discussed in Chapter 2, was a passion that Anna had had since childhood and one that she continued to enjoy in Scotland and England – with and without James.[92] Of the queen's English residences, Oatlands was primed for hunting and it was Anna's increasingly frequent choice, along with Greenwich, for the summer months. The decision to include a recognisable section of the palace and grounds of Oatlands, and to then hang the portrait in that same palace, underscored Anna's personal, regal entitlement to hunt in the royal forests but, more than this, such self-fashioning symbolically cast Anna in the legacy of Diana, virginal goddess of the hunt, a powerful guardian of women and lunar deity.[93] The use of Diana iconography to stress princely, female virtue held royal precedent, and had been notably employed by Diane de Poitiers (1499–1566) and, more pertinently, Queen Elizabeth.[94] The hanging of the hunting portrait strategically reiterated the connection to Elizabeth, for a portrait of the deceased Tudor queen was placed nearby.[95] The recycling of Elizabethan conceits to stress Anna's princely virtues continues through the invocation of the goddess Pallas Athena, whose common attribute of the owl is seen perching in the oak tree to Anna's right. Pallas Athena was, as McManus writes, 'a singularly Elizabethan icon' and, as noted earlier, Anna had visually linked herself to the goddess of warfare and wisdom, and Elizabeth's courtly body by extension, in the 1604 performance of *Vision*.[96]

A close reading of the iconographic choices in Van Somer's portrait shows the Stuart consort conceptualised as a paradigm of female virtue: chaste, wise, constant. Through the inclusion of the motto and the connection to Elizabeth, the portrait also presents Anna as a powerful, royal woman in her own right, which is reinforced by her masculine pose with right arm akimbo. In his 1644 treatise, *Chironomia, or the Art of Manual Rhetoric*, John Bulwer (1606–1656) unequivocally declared that 'to set the arms agambo [akimbo] or aprank [up rank], and to rest the turned-in back of the hand upon the side is an action of pride and ostentation'.[97] Such traits were appropriate to royalty and the aristocracy and the pose was often used in portraiture where, as Joaneath Spicer asserts, it was 'indicative of boldness or control'.[98] This tradition is complicated by Anna, though, for the gesture was inherently gendered male and it was almost exclusively reserved for male sitters. In fact, Zirka Filipczak argues that it even functioned as an indicator of gender, and when occasionally seen in female portraits, it was tempered by suitably feminine elements such as accessories of fan, gloves, handkerchief, or prayer book, an affable expression, and by having the other hand delicately positioned.[99] This is not true of the queen's hunting portrait, for rather than temper the manliness of Anna's akimbo elbow, the queen's accessories and pose serve as reinforcement. Anna's left hand controls five Italian greyhounds, which links her portrait to a tradition of showing noble males with obedient dogs. This was a pictorial device that, in the words of Woodall, 'enhance[d] the position of the prince as the source of authority' by imaging a 'relationship of command and loyal obedience' which extended beyond the represented dog to the sitter's subjects.[100] Anna's ownership is reinforced denotatively, for each dog wears a collar bearing the queen's diamond-encrusted cipher, AR.

As with the painting of Anna now at Woburn, Van Somer's later portrait vividly articulates the queen's royal status. Importantly, it insists that this was not achieved through the rite of marriage to King James but through Anna's birthright as determined by God. A ribbon boldly flutters above the queen bearing her personal Italian motto *La mia grandezza dal eccelso*, which the Venetian ambassador, Foscarini, contemporaneously translated to 'My Power is from the Most High'. Crucially, Foscarini connected Anna's motto to her unique position as the 'daughter, sister and wife of a king', as well as the mother of the future king of England, Scotland, and Ireland, and declared that the queen claims 'her greatness comes not from the king [James] but from God alone.'[101] In short, the motto articulated Anna's knowledge of, and pride in, her exalted, regal status. Yet this was not an outright challenge to James's superiority but an astute amalgamation of the earthly and celestial that gave Anna scope to reformulate the 'Most High' as being James himself.[102]

In 1598, James famously articulated his opinion on the theory of divine-right monarchy in his treatise, *The Trew Law of Free Monarchies*. As Jenny Wormald has argued, James did not espouse autocracy or absolutism, but sought to reject contractual kingship on the grounds that kings preceded parliaments and therefore should be seen as the original and true makers of law. The Stuart king wholly believed, however, that his position as the legitimate reigning monarch was expressly ordained by God, and so he was answerable only to God.[103] In line with James's advocacy of monarchical divinity, therefore, Anna's motto could be seen to celebrate James as God's appointed ruler and the 'Most High' on earth, but it also allowed her to make a claim for her position having resulted from her sacred birth, rather than the sole derivation of her marriage. Lying at the crux of Anna's identity was her membership in the royal House of Oldenburg – a sentiment that was, as we have seen, repeatedly articulated by the queen in verbal and visual means. The centrality of the motto, and its meaning, is reiterated by its unusual trait of being Anna's only motto, whereas James was associated with at least four personal mottoes, and those connected with Elizabeth I extended to eight.[104] Moreover, unlike James and Elizabeth, whose mottoes were in Latin or French, Anna is unique for insisting on an Italian motto – an interest that continues in the portrait through Jones's classicising gateway, with its Palladian and Serlian elements, and the Italian greyhounds.

The Italianate element

The numerous Italian elements highlight a consistent thread in Anna's cultural agency, which Knowles defines as 'an element of self-conscious internationalism … [being] an interest in Italian culture'.[105] Aside from Knowles, this facet has not been investigated or sufficiently recognised by scholars, but a preference for the Italianate motivated Anna to support certain poets, playwrights, designers, and artists, it encouraged her to add Italian to her repertoire of languages, and it informed her court circle. In Scotland, from 1592 to 1594, Anna learnt Italian from the Reformed writer Giacomo Castelvetro (1546–1616), who subsequently travelled to Denmark, presumably with Anna's introduction. In England, Castelvetro's post was filled by the Italian linguist John Florio (1553–1625), who was also made a groom of the queen's privy chamber.[106] At this point, Anna's dedicated learning drew comment from the court and the Florentine diplomat Ottaviano Lotti (d.1634), described Florio being 'with the Queen all day long teaching her the Italian language and hearing her conversation on all subjects', and that he was entrusted to write 'all her most confidential letters'.[107] Florio bought Italian volumes for Anna and an extant epistle written in the queen's hand in Italian, to the Danish diplomat Jonas Charisius, proves that she could write as well as read the language.[108] Italian culture also permeated Anna's patronage of poetry and theatre in the constant favour shown to Samuel Daniel, whose interest in neoclassical Italian literature was well known, and the theatre of Thomas Campion (1567–1620) who, in contrast to Jonson (supported by James), was heavily influenced by the Florentine *intermedi* with an emphasis on music and dance over poetry.[109] Curiously, this penchant is not in evidence among the paintings Anna owned. The little available evidence that we have, as discussed in Chapter 3, shows that that the queen's collection was marked by Dutch and Flemish works. This was likewise true of Christian IV, who favoured musicians and sculptors with Italian training, or those who were knowledgeable about Italian styles, but whose collection of paintings was Netherlandish. This may have been due to 'financial and geographical realities', as Kristoffer Neville suggests, and borne out by the bulk acquisition made by Charisius in 1607 and 1608.[110] Then again, just as it was argued for architectural forms in Chapter 2, caution must be exercised in assigning a 'national' style to early modern paintings based on country of origin (of the artisan or the place of purchase), and it cannot be discounted that many of the artworks owned by Anna and Christian were inflected with Italianate style and/or tradition with artists having trained in Italy or adhering to Italian trends.

Anna's multilingualism and varied cultural pursuits are notable, but they are not unique in the Danish court. The Stuart queen, King Christian, and their other Oldenburg siblings, were introduced to aspects of Italian culture during childhood, for the Danish court was frequently home to humanist drama, itinerant troupes, and elaborate celebrations featuring international dancers, musicians, and theatrical performers that included the renowned Italian dance master Matthias Zoega (c.1545–c.1605).[111] It was also, as demonstrated in Chapter 2, the site for extensive building and statuary that borrowed heavily from Italianate modes and precepts. Theirs was a childhood that instilled an enduring love for music, dance, theatre, and architecture. Later, Anna sought companions who shared her European outlook and a particular interest in Italian culture. Lucy Harington, Countess of Bedford, one of Anna's closest confidants in England, introduced Daniel to the queen's patronage and Bedford followed Anna's lead with Italian lessons from Florio. The linguist later praised Bedford's aptitude, attesting that 'in Italian as in French, in French as in Spanish, in all as in English [you] understand what you reade, write as you reade, and speake as you write', and in 1614, Castelvetro, Anna's earlier tutor, deemed Bedford to be the suitable dedicatee for the presentation copy of his tract, *Brieve racconto di tutte le radici di tutte l'herbe e di tutte frutti, che crudi o cotti in Italia si mangiano*.[112] Further, at Moor Park in Hertfordshire, one of Anna's companions – either Bedford or Pembroke – commissioned an Italianate garden with suggestive similarities to Anna's earlier work at Denmark House and Greenwich as covered in Chapter 2. When recalling this 'most beautiful and perfect' garden at Moor Park, as it was around 1655, William Temple celebrated its 'very large parterre ... divided into quarters by gravel walks, and adorned with two fountains and eight statues', as well as its orangery, and the grotto that was 'embellished with figures of shell-rock-work, fountains, and water-works'.[113] To this grouping of Italophiles, must be added Southampton whose patronage of Florio, beginning in 1594, predates both Anna and Bedford. It is significant, too, that in 1598 Southampton and Bedford were singled out by Florio as two of the three dedicatees of his Italian–English dictionary, *A worlde of wordes*, which he later expanded, added 'rules for the Italian tongue', and published in 1611 under the new title *Queen Annas new world of words* with a dedication to the queen.[114] Returning to Anna's Italian motto, in the 1617 hunting portrait it gains a conspicuous presence – being considerably more prominent than in any other preceding portrait of the queen in any media (easel, miniature, engraving, or medal) and where it unmistakeably announces the queen's interest in the Italianate and her regal birthright as a member of the House of Oldenburg.

Conclusion

In 1614, with the arrival of Christian IV to England, Anna of Denmark sat for an innovative portrait from the Flemish painter Marcus Gheeraerts. Up until this point, Anna's body of portraits had been produced for the service of the monarchy, highlighting the political strength and security that the Stuarts offered as a healthy, functioning family unit with a secure succession. In 1603, these factors became crucial to the success and popularity of the new Stuart rule of England, for they contrasted positively with the previous reign, although efforts were carefully made – visually and textually – to link the Stuarts to the Tudor dynasty in order to legitimate their claim. Prints of the Stuart couple were thus accompanied by family trees and James's illustrated ancestry was published. Looking to portraits of Anna, noticeable efforts were made to refashion the consort in an Elizabethan mould of fashion and iconography, which extended beyond paintings, prints, and medals to appellations, poetry, and theatre. These changes vividly demonstrate the close relationship between portraiture and politics as Anna's visual persona was melded in response to the changing climate of commission.

With the Woburn portrait of 1614, this fundamentally changed as Anna took the self-determining step to populate her image with information about her pedigree, virtues, cultural activities, and political aims. Yet even as Anna's iconography was increasingly personalised, she retained visual referents to Elizabeth. In Van Somer's portrait from 1617, we still find Anna's virtues being announced by way of Elizabeth through goddesses who were indelibly linked to the Tudor queen – a connection then physically reinforced by hanging the hunting portrait of Anna next to one of Elizabeth. Throughout her time in England, Anna's visual iconography developed to stress her royal bloodline and regal stature – facets that continued to define her posthumous prints and medals. At the time of Anna's death in March 1619, a commemorative medal was issued, depicting the queen in timeless, classicising side-profile pose (associated with Roman emperors) while the obverse features a crowned, full-bearing pine tree, an evergreen symbolic of immortality, and a large swirling ribbon bearing Anna's regal motto.[115] Even more emphatically, posthumous engraved portraits combined the recognisable figure type of the Woburn with verse that paid tribute to Anna's origins and pedigree: 'Great Empresse of the North admiret queene / Like Anne in Ingland, hath not yet bin seene / The daughter, wife, and syster, to a Kinge / Greatnes, and goodnes, from thy grace doth springe.'[116] These were fitting words for a woman so proudly confident of her royal birthright, and the next chapter shows how important Anna's dynastic pedigree was to

James, who staged a monumental state funeral for his late wife fêting her familial glory.

Notes

1. The 1609 portrait, signed and dated, was sent to the Danish court, but was destroyed in the 1859 fire at Frederiksborg: Heiberg, *Christian IV and Europe*, 17, 44–45.
2. H. Berger Jr., 'Fictions of the Pose: Facing the Gaze of Early Modern Portraiture', *Representations* 46 (1994), 87–120: 98.
3. J. Woodall, 'Introduction', in J. Woodall (ed.), *Portraiture: Facing the Subject* (Manchester, 1997), 1–25: 3.
4. Berger, 'Fictions of the Pose', 93.
5. R. Brilliant, *Portraiture* (London, 1991), 9.
6. Woodall, 'Introduction', 2, 3.
7. L. B. Alberti, *On Painting* (Cambridge, 2011), 44, 45.
8. Woodall, 'Introduction', 8.
9. NRS, SP13/128: 10 October 1597.
10. For example, M. Pointon, *Hanging the Head: Portraiture and Social Formation in Eighteenth-Century England* (New Haven and London, 1993), 1; J. Woodall, 'An Exemplary Consort: Antonis Mor's Portrait of Mary Tudor', *Art History* 14 (1991), 192–224.
11. See Gheeraerts being paid in July 1611 for portraits of James, Anna, and Princess Elizabeth that were sent to Brandenburg as part of early marriage negotiations: TNA, E351/543, fol. 268v. Earlier, in February 1610, the Venetian ambassadors, Francesco Contarini and Marcantonio Correr, reported 'there has been some talk of a marriage between this Princess [Elizabeth Stuart] and the son of the Palatine of the Rhine [Friedrich V], and all the royal family are being painted in order to send their portraits to him': *CSPV*, vol. 11, no. 785.
12. Melville, *Memoirs*, 365.
13. Field, 'Anna of Denmark and the Arts', 44–46.
14. Ungerer, 'Circulation of Gifts', 156; Griffey, *On Display*, 83.
15. S. Buck, 'Hans Holbein the Younger: Portraitist of the Renaissance', in S. Buck (ed.), *Hans Holbein the Younger: Portraitist of the Renaissance* (Zwolle, 2003), 11–37: 31.
16. Devon, *Issues of the Exchequer*, 16; Ungerer, 'Circulation of Gifts', 145, 152–156, 159–161.
17. L. O. Larsson, 'Rhetoric and Authenticity in the Portraits of King Christian IV of Denmark', in M. R. Wade (ed.), *Pomp, Power and Politics* (*Daphnis* vol. 32, 2003) (Amsterdam, 2004), 13–40: 13–15.
18. Heiberg, *Christian IV and Europe*, 16–17.
19. MacLeod, 'Facing Europe', 63.
20. MacLeod, 'Facing Europe', 84; L. Wood, 'The Portraits of Anne of Denmark', MA report (Courtauld Institute of Art, University of London, 1981), 40–57; Knowles, 'Images of Royalty', 24, 28, 30–32; Field, 'Anna of Denmark and the Arts', 37, 77–86, 95–98, 120–124.
21. MacLeod, 'Facing Europe', 64, 82.
22. *CSPV*, vol. 10, no. 102.
23. Town, 'A Biographical Dictionary', 179; Juhala, 'Household and Court', 192.
24. Town, 'A Biographical Dictionary', 183.
25. NRS, E21/76, fol. 168.
26. NRS, E21/76, fol. 165.
27. Juhala, 'Household and Court', 192.

28 Vanson's pendants are thought to have been originally three-quarter length – showing James resting his left hand on his sword hilt: K. Hearn (ed.), *Dynasties: Painting in Tudor and Jacobean England 1530–1630* (London, 1995), 173, cat. no. 117; D. Thomson, *Painting in Scotland 1570–1650* (Edinburgh, 1975), 28, cat. no. 14; K. Sharpe, *Image Wars: Promoting Kings and Commonwealths in England, 1603–1660* (New Haven, 2010), 59.
29 On the visual conventions of state portraiture see Woodall, 'Introduction', 2–3.
30 Henry's birth and baptism are discussed in Chapter 6.
31 The portrait is in a private collection and is most recently illustrated in MacLeod et al., *Lost Prince*, 46–47.
32 In England this tendency dates to the reign of Edward III, and for a short overview of the use of letters as decorative designs in medieval and Renaissance England see Siddons, *Heraldic Badges*, vol. 2, part 1, 153–155.
33 D. Calderwood, *The History of the Kirk of Scotland* (Edinburgh, 1842), vol. 5, 97.
34 Clark, 'Transient Possessions', 188.
35 MacLeod, 'Facing Europe', 70.
36 Town, 'A Biographical Dictionary', 67. See also R. Tittler, 'Three Portraits by John de Critz for the Merchant Taylors' Company', *Burlington Magazine* 147 (2005), 491–493.
37 See, for example, those held in public collections at the National Portrait Gallery, London; Scottish National Galleries, Edinburgh; National Trust for Scotland, Aberdeenshire; Government Art Collection, London; Dulwich Picture Gallery, London; National Trust at Loseley Park and Montacute House; Prado Museum, Madrid; Royal Museums Greenwich; Royal Collection, London; St John's College, Cambridge.
38 Town, 'A Biographical Dictionary', 67.
39 TNA, SC6/JASI/1646.
40 E. Town, '"Whilst he had his perfect sight" – New Information on John de Critz the Elder', *Burlington Magazine* 154 (2012), 482–486: 482, 485–486; Town, 'A Biographical Dictionary', 67–68.
41 Knowles, 'Images of Royalty', 21; A. Griffiths, *The Print in Stuart Britain, 1603–1689* (London, 1998), 45–46; Hind, *Engraving in England*, 30–31, plates 4, 5.
42 Lewalski, *Writing Women*, 18; Knowles, 'Images of Royalty', 21, 33–42.
43 E. K. Chambers, *The Elizabethan Stage*, 4 vols (Oxford, 1923), vol. 1, 210; S. J. Steen (ed.), *The Letters of Lady Arbella Stuart* (New York, 1994), 197; McManus, *Renaissance Stage*, 107; Lewalski, *Writing Women*, 30. It should be noted that new garments were also ordered for the masque with nearly £1,000 being paid through the queen's privy purse in December 1603 and January 1604 to mercers and silkmen 'for stuffes and wares ... for her Ma[jes]t[ie]s Maske', see TNA, SC6/JASI/1646. This disproves earlier suppositions that it was wholly reliant on extant Elizabethan garments.
44 Lee (ed.), *Jacobean Letters*, 55, no. 21.
45 McManus, *Renaissance Stage*, 107–109; Lewalski, *Writing Women*, 30.
46 N. Blakiston, 'Nicholas Hilliard: Some Unpublished Documents', *Burlington Magazine for Connoiseurs* 89 (1947), 187–189: 189.
47 Quote from Ungerer, 'Circulation of Gifts', 153. See also J. Finsten, *Isaac Oliver: Art at the Courts of Elizabeth I and James I*, 2 vols (New York, 1981), vol. 1, 117–118; K. Coombs, *The Portrait Miniature in England* (London, 1998), 44.
48 James's art patronage has never been the subject of a major study and statements of his 'disinterest' can be found in, for example, Wilks, 'Introduction', 15; Wilks, 'Art Collecting', 32.
49 M. Wood and R. K. Hannay (eds), *Extracts from the Records of the Burgh of Edinburgh, 1589–1603* (Edinburgh, 1927), 284; Edinburgh City Archives, SL234/1: Register of the Decreets, 1598–1602.

50 TNA, E351/543, fol. 115r.
51 TNA, SC6/JASI/1646; See also Finsten, *Isaac Oliver*, 121.
52 TNA, E351/543, fols 110r, 110v, 111v, 112r, 113v.
53 TNA, SC6/JASI/1646; Finsten, *Isaac Oliver*, 27, 121; M. Edmond, *Hilliard and Oliver: The Lives and Works of Two Great Miniaturists* (London, 1983), 150–151; Wood, 'Portraits of Anne of Denmark', 42; M. Edmond, 'New Light on Jacobean Painters', *Burlington Magazine* 118 (1976), 74–81+83: 74.
54 For example, those by Hilliard in Vienna: Kunsthistorisches Museum, Gemaldegalerie (GG_5477).
55 TNA, LR2/122, fol. 24r.
56 Museum no. 1640-2.
57 Payne, 'Aristocratic Women', 140.
58 Private Collection, Scotland; Dunedin Public Gallery, New Zealand (1–1974); Tate, London (T00398). Anna Livingstone was a Scottish woman of the Bedchamber; Margaret Seton was not a member of Anna's household, but was well connected to the queen through her husband, Alexander, Earl of Dunfermline (1555–1622) who was Lord Chancellor of Scotland from 1604 until his death, one of the councillors appointed manage Anna's finances in Scotland, and Anna's choice of governor for Prince Charles. Elizabeth Grey performed in Anna's 1610 masque, *Tethys Festival*, and was made First Lady of the Bedchamber in 1617 when Jane Drummond was expelled from court.
59 Clark, 'Transient Possessions', 188, 196–197.
60 Knowles, 'Images of Royalty', 24; MacLeod, 'Facing Europe', 77.
61 Nichols, *Progresses*, vol. 3, 13–18; C. F. Senning, 'The Visit of Christian IV to England in 1614', *Historian* 31 (1969), 555–572: 557.
62 TNA, E351/544, fols 26r–27r.
63 TNA, E351/544, fol. 26v; McClure (ed.) *Chamberlain*, vol. 1, 553, no. 211: 4 August 1614 (to Carleton); Senning, 'Visit of Christian IV', 559–560, 567: quote from Chamberlain.
64 G. Parker, *The Army of Flanders and the Spanish Road, 1567–1659: The Logistics of Spanish Victory and Defeat in the Low Countries' Wars*, 2nd ed. (Cambridge, 2004), 139, citing BRB MS. 12622-31, fols 177–200v, Edict of 27 May 1596, clause 41.
65 The portrait of Philip II is in the El Escorial, Monasterio de San Lorenzo; for Philip III see Christie's London, Sale 3699 (July 2011), Lot 519; Calderón's portrait is in the Royal Collection London (404393); versions of Doria's portrait are in the Herzog Anton Ulrich Museum, Braunschweig (GG85) and the Saint Louis Art Museum, Missouri (33: 1934).
66 *CSPV*, vol. 13, no. 346: 1 August 1614; no. 355: 8 August 1614.
67 Senning, 'Visit of Christian IV', 567. See also *CSPV*, vol. 13, no. 703; Heiberg, *Christian IV and Europe*, 59.
68 Murdoch, 'James VI', 15–18; Grosjean, *Unofficial Alliance*, 31–38.
69 Grosjean, *Unofficial Alliance*, 36–37: quote from 36; S. Murdoch, 'Diplomacy in Transition: Stuart-British Diplomacy in Northern Europe, 1603–1618', in A. I. Macinnes, T. Riis, and F. Pedersen (eds), *Ships, Guns and Bibles in the North Sea and Baltic States, c.1350–c.1700* (East Linton, 2000), 93–114: 103, 104.
70 Murdoch, 'Diplomacy in Transition', 103, 104.
71 *CSPV*, vol. 13, nos. 452, 356: 24 October 1614; 8 August 1614. See also Senning, 'Visit of Christian IV', 567; Murdoch, *House of Stuart*, 24–26. Note that this antipathy did not extend to the cultural realm, and Christian continued to seek artistic and architectural expertise from the Northern Netherlands, see Chapters 2 and 3.
72 *CSPV*, vol. 14, nos. 170, 665: 5 February 1616; 2 March 1617.
73 *CSPV*, vol. 13, no. 22: 17 July 1613.
74 Senning, 'Visit of Christian IV', 559, 567–570.
75 *CSPV*, vol. 13, no. 375: 22 August 1614.

76 *CSPV*, vol. 13, no. 375: 22 August 1614.
77 Birch, *Court and Times*, vol. 1, 342: 6 August 1614 (Thomas Lorkin to Thomas Puckering).
78 *CSPV*, vol. 13, no. 356: 8 August 1614.
79 Senning, 'Visit of Christian IV', 571. It was partly hampered by James's wish for Christian to enter an anti-Spanish league with the German states of the Reformed faith, Sweden, the United Provinces, and Venice, see Murdoch, 'Diplomacy in Transition', 97.
80 Town, 'A Biographical Dictionary', 183.
81 TNA, E351/544, f.117v.
82 Field, 'Late Portrait by Paul van Somer', 51; O. Millar, *Tudor, Stuart and Early Georgian Pictures in the Collection of Her Majesty the Queen*, 2 vols (London, 1963), vol. 1, 81–83, cat. nos. 106, 111; Wood, 'Portraits of Anne of Denmark', 48; MacLeod, 'Facing Europe', 82. The portrait of Pembroke is in the Royal Collection (405870) as are two of the three portraits of Anna that Van Somer completed after the Woburn type (405813; 401177) the former illustrated here as Figure 5.4. The third Van Somer portrait, historically paired with a portrait of James, is in the collection of the Duke of Buccleuch at Drumlanrig Castle where the portrait of Anna is reproduced in Knowles, 'Images of Royalty', 29.
83 Colvin, *King's Works*, 212. The vineyard and Jones's work at Oatlands are discussed in Chapter 2.
84 Brilliant, *Portraiture*, 9–11: quotation from 10.
85 ESRO Glynde MS 317. It hung in the gallery for less than a year before being sent to Prince Charles. A marginal notation in ESRO Glynde MS 320, fol. 7r, reads 'Sent to the prinz in St: Jaymes 8 Mar 1618.'
86 Knowles, 'Images of Royalty', 31.
87 For Anna's riding clothes see Field, 'Dressing a Queen', 160–163.
88 H. Imtiaz, *Black Lives in the English Archives, 1500–1677: Imprints of the Invisible* (Burlington, 2008), 12–13.
89 NRS, E35/13, vol. 1, 17–18; Craig, *Papers Relative to the Marriage*, 21, 28, 36, 38.
90 Pearce, 'Anna of Denmark', 143–144.
91 D. Bindman, 'The Black Presence in British Art: Sixteenth and Seventeenth Centuries', in D. Bindman and H. L. Gates (eds), *The Image of the Black in Western Art*, 5 vols (Cambridge, MA, 2010–2014), vol. 3, part 1, ch. 4.
92 The pair were still hunting together in August 1615: Vienna, Haus-, Hof- und Staatsarchiv, Belgien, Repertorium P, Abteilung C, Faszikel 51: Ferdinand van Boisschot to Archduke Albert, 12 August 1615.
93 Knowles states that the association was emphasised by hanging directly opposite Rubens's painting of Diana that remains in the Royal Collection, London (405553), but this cannot be correct for the paintings hung in different galleries. In the 1616 inventory, Rubens's painting was in the South or 'Garden Stone' Gallery, but the inventory of the following year shows that it had been moved to the North Gallery while Anna's portrait was in the South Gallery. See Knowles, 'Images of Royalty', 31; ESRO Glynde MS 315; ESRO Glynde MS 319, fols 7r, 8r.
94 E. Chew, 'The Countess of Arundel', in E. Chaney (ed.), *The Evolution of English Collecting: Receptions of Italian Art in the Tudor and Stuart Periods* (New Haven and London, 2003), 285–315: 301, 313, note 74; R. Strong, *Gloriana: The Portraits of Queen Elizabeth I* (New York, 1987), 125–128; L. Barkan, 'Diana and Actaeon: The Myth as Synthesis', *English Literary Renaissance* 10 (1980): 332–335. For Diane de Poitiers's equivocation with Diana, and a consideration of the flexibility of such ideologies that could be used for different positions, see S. ffolliott, 'Casting a Rival into the Shade: Catherine De' Medici and Diane De Poitiers', *Art Journal* 48 (1989), 138–143.
95 ESRO Glynde MS 320, fol. 7r. On the political significance of portrait arrangements

see Peacock, 'Politics of Portraiture', 215–217. The identification with Diana was continued in the next Stuart reign through Henrietta Maria and the Countess of Arundel, see Chew, 'Countess of Arundel', 301–303; Sykes, 'Henrietta Maria's "house of delight"', 335.

96 McManus, *Renaissance Stage*, 109.
97 J. Bulwer, *Chirologia: or the Natural Language of the Hand and Chironomia: or the Art of Manual Rhetoric* (1644), edited by J. Cleary (Carbondale, 1974), 219.
98 J. Spicer, 'The Renaissance Elbow', in J. Bremmer and H. Roodenburg (eds), *A Cultural History of Gesture* (London, 1991), 84–128: 85.
99 Z. Z. Filipczak, 'Portraits of Women Who "Do Not Keep Strictly to the Masculine and Feminine Genders, as They Call Them"', in K. Van der Stighelen, H. Magnus, and B. Watteeuw (eds), *Pokerfaced: Flemish and Dutch Baroque Faces Unveiled* (Turnhout, 2010), 229–249: 231, 233.
100 J. Woodall, *Anthonis Mor: Art and Authority* (Zwolle, 2007), 143.
101 *CSPV*, vol. 15, no. 658: 19 December 1618 (Relation of England).
102 Field, 'Anna of Denmark and the Arts', 95–100. For an alternative reading of the motto, see Wood, 'Portraits of Anne of Denmark', 51.
103 J. Wormald, 'James VI and I (1566–1625)', *ODNB*; J. Rickard, *Authorship and Authority: The Writings of James VI and I* (Manchester, 2007), 90–91.
104 Field, 'Anna of Denmark and the Arts', 96–97.
105 Knowles, 'Images of Royalty', 27.
106 J. Martin, 'Castelvetro, Giacomo (*bap.* 1546, *d*.1616)', *ODNB*. Notably, Castelvetro also tutored James in Italian. From 1604, Florio received an annual pension of £100, which was significantly higher than most of the grooms, who received £60 per annum. See TNA, LR6/154/9; TNA, SC6/JASI/1646; TNA, SC6/JASI/1648; TNA, SC6/JASI/1650; TNA, SC6/JASI/1653. On Florio's position as Anna's Italian tutor see also Knowles, 'Images of Royalty', 27; Wade, 'The Queen's Courts', 56.
107 Quoted in Knowles, 'Images of Royalty', 27.
108 Rigsarkivet, TKUA England A II, 40.
109 Knowles, 'Images of Royalty', 35; S. Daniel, *Hymen's Triumph*, edited by J. Pitcher (Oxford, 1994), x.
110 Neville, 'Christian IV's Italianates', 338–343; M. Müller and O. Kongsted, 'Christian IV and Music', in S. Heiberg (ed.), *Christian IV and Europe: The 19th Art Exhibition of the Council of Europe: Denmark* (Herning, 1988), 119–141. For Charisius's purchase of artworks in the Netherlands, see Chapter 3.
111 Wade, *Triumphus Nupitalis Danicus*, 22–24, 34–35.
112 Martin, 'Castelvetro'; Hearn, 'Question of Judgement', 222, 224: quote from 222. Not incidentally, both women were celebrated for patronising, authoring, and directing masques, see Hearn, 'Question of Judgement', and the Introduction above. Castelvetro's text has been translated and edited: G. Riley, *The Fruit, Herbs and Vegetables of Italy* (Totnes, 2012).
113 W. Temple, *The Works of Sir William Temple, Bart*, 4 vols (London, 1814), vol. 3, 202–245: 235–237.
114 A. W. Pollard and G. R. Redgrave, *A Short-Title Catalogue of Books printed in England, Scotland & Ireland, and of English Books Printed Abroad, 1475–1640* (London, 1926), 243; F. B. Williams Jr, *Index of Dedications and Commendatory Verses in English Books before 1641* (London, 1962), 5, 161, 204. The 1598 edition is STC 11098; that of 1611 is STC 11099.
115 E. Hawkins, A. W. Franks, and H. A. Grueber (eds), *Medallic Illustrations of the History of Great Britain and Ireland*, 4 vols (London, 1885), vol. 1, 221, cat. no. 75.
116 Quoted in Hind, *Engraving in England*, 59; illustrated plate 29.

6
Ritual and ceremonial

Anna of Denmark died of dropsy on 2 March 1619, and news quickly spread throughout Europe. From France, the Venetian ambassador, Anzolo Contarini, sent dispatch that the Bourbons had 'appointed the Marquis of Trinel [François Juvenal des Ursins, Marquis of Tresnel] as ambassador extraordinary to England to offer condolences upon the queen's death. The mission should do much to further the reconciliation between the two crowns.'[1] Conflating Anna's obsequies with international court politics, Contarini's comment encapsulates the two main threads of this chapter: the queen consort as a figure of reconciliation and negotiation and the use of royal ritual and modes of formalised behaviour to affirm Anna's place, in what historian Linda Levy Peck has termed 'the performance of royal and aristocratic power'.[2] This performance, as Anna Keay asserts, permeated everyday life for 'almost everything a king did in the early-modern period spoke to some extent of his status.'[3] This is similarly true of queens consort and, as the preceding chapters have shown, Anna's activities – from the buildings and gardens she commissioned, to the portraits that she sat for, to the clothes and jewels she chose to wear – all served as a confirmation of status. Rather than the everyday or calendrical, the current chapter focuses on events in the life cycle that fundamentally articulated and confirmed Anna's position as a woman, as queen consort, and as a figurehead of the national religion: the births and baptisms of her children, her churching ceremonies, the betrothal and wedding of her daughter Elizabeth, her position in England during James's progress to Scotland, and her own funeral.[4]

In conception and execution, early modern ceremonial encompassed a complex multiplicity of meaning for both participant and audience. The following discussions show how ritualised conventions, codes of honour and behaviour, and social rankings supported and advanced particular institutions or ideologies, while they concurrently challenged and/or contradicted them. This axiom aligns with Knowles's work on civic ritual in early modern London, wherein he cogently observes that the ceremonial could be appropriated for a variety of divergent positions – often concurrently – writing that even as it 'encouraged obedience and propagandised the state' it could 'simultaneously ... criticise other states, contest a political position, or counsel an alternative political agenda'.[5]

Births

For the queen consort of a hereditary monarchy, no performance was as hotly discussed, as eagerly anticipated, or as crucial to her own position and power, as the rite of motherhood.[6] It was through the production of legitimate, royal children that the continuation of the dynasty and the social and political stability of the kingdom rested. It was an event eagerly anticipated and richly celebrated by both the monarchy and the people, and the responsibility was placed squarely with the queen. Anna amply fulfilled her expected duty with the birth of seven children – five in Scotland and two in England – although only three were to survive infancy. The first three years of the Stuart marriage passed with no visible signs of pregnancy, and the Scottish people grew a 'great disliking of their Queen'.[7] Subsequently, when Anna safely delivered her first child – a healthy son and legitimate heir – at Sterling Castle, on 19 February 1594, joyous celebrations erupted throughout the kingdom, for the news 'wes a great comfort and maiter of joy to the haill pepill, and movit thame to great triumphe, wantonnes, and play, for beanefyres [bonfires] wer set out, and dancing and playing vsit [used] in all pairtes, as gif the pepill had bein daft for mirthe'.[8] The gravity of a prospective Stuart heir had excited the court in the late months of 1593, when a group of courtiers made an elated suggestion to James that the birth should change the very fabric of theological doctrine: 'after the birth of a Prince the common prayer of the people will be "God save the religion and Prince." The king is much occupied with this matter and "conceipte" [concept].'[9] In the end, the prayer remained the same, but the arrival of Prince Henry did bring momentous change: it united the royal bloodlines of Stuart and Oldenburg, it secured the future rule of Scotland, and it increased James's chance of succeeding to the English throne for he was now furnished with a stable, Protestant line.

The political stakes surrounding Henry's birth were extraordinarily high and, not surprisingly, much less fanfare greeted the subsequent Stuart children: Elizabeth, Margaret (1598–1600), Charles, Robert (January–May 1602), Mary (1605–1607), and Sophia (22–23 June 1606). Yet the safe arrival of each legitimate child was still a political triumph for the strength and longevity of the dynasty. Additional sons provided substitute male heirs in the case of accident or death, and marriageable daughters extended and reinforced the dynastic network. Each royal birth also gave cause for the requisite demonstration of Stuart wealth and authority that reaffirmed the socio-political order. James himself articulated as much when he wrote to congratulate his brother-in-law, Christian, on the birth of a son in April 1603 and stated that 'we are moved both for your sake and the sake of the kingdom itself, over which you are ruling; because as children are a source of solace to parents, thus are they a source of support for kings; for the more children there are, the deeper are the roots and the more numerous are the supports, upon which the stability of a kingdom rests.'[10]

Rather than Henry's birth, it is with Anna's second child, and first daughter, Princess Elizabeth – born 19 August 1596 at Dunfermline – that the extant textual record provides insight into the provisions made for the confinement of the Stuart queen. That month, in readiness for the demands of the birth, lengths of fine Holland cloth and the 'fynest small lane [lawn] and camerage [cambric]', new bed hangings in crimson and scarlet, bed coverings, and blankets, 'wer had over to Dumfermelyng to hir majestie', and were promptly followed by more bed coverings and coats for the princess which were carried to the palace in 'ane mekill [large] trunk coffer'.[11] The queen's birthing chamber at Dunfermline was physically redressed in a move that was both practical and symbolic. The material transformation was an anticipated response to the practical needs of the queen and baby, but, as Adrian Wilson recognises, such refashioning concurrently worked to 'confer upon the room a different character, signifying its special function' as the chosen space for the performance of childbirth.[12] This event, Wilson observes, encompassed not only the birth but the process of the lying-in, during which time the mother recuperated.[13] For royal women, this period preceded the birth by several days if not weeks. Physical activity and visitors were restricted, and Anna passed some of this time with needle- or finger-work with 'ane unce of silk for hir majestie to weyffe [weave] with' being ordered during her confinement.[14]

Given the importance of precedent and tradition to the meaning and performance of royal ceremony, the preparations and processes surrounding Elizabeth's birth were repeated for Anna's subsequent confinements. For the births of the fourth and fifth Stuart children – Charles, Duke of Albany, born on 19 November 1600 and Robert, Duke of Kintyre, born on 18 January 1602 – both at Dunfermline – the material provisions for use 'before the time [of the birth] … also sen syne [immediately after]' again included sheets, cradle blankets, pillow cases, lengths of small Holland cloth, as well as clothing for the new baby such as 'sarkis' [shifts], aprons, 'mutchis' [hoods/bonnets], and 'overlayeris' [falling collars].[15] These deliveries also register the place of medicine in childbirth, for specialists were lodged at Dunfermline throughout Anna's confinement and labour. In readiness for Charles's arrival, for example, the royal doctor Martin Schoner and his 'man' – a male servant or assistant – and two midwives were hosted at the birthing palace for four weeks.[16] After the delivery, it was the role of the royal apothecary, Alexander Barclay, to tend to both mother and baby being paid £122.10s. Scots for 'certane drogis medicamentis and uther geir furnissit for hir ma[jes]teis use and hir sone ye duik of Albanie'.[17] This may signal Charles's oft-stated poor health, and/or a difficult birth but, then again, the medical costs associated with Robert's birth were much greater, with Doctor Schoner and the chirurgeon John Nasmith declaring a bill for the significantly larger amount of £666.13s.4d. Scots.[18] In each case, the decision to lodge experts in the residence, coupled with the high costs of treatments, is telling of the significance of the event and the primacy that was placed on the health and care of the queen, who was central to the provision of more royal offspring.[19]

In England, the queen's confinements continued to be dictated by precedence and etiquette. The queen's first English pregnancy began in mid-1604, and by the opening of the new year, preparations had begun at Greenwich to ensure that the palace was suitable for the birth and attendant celebrations. Bills and reports from the period underscore the strict guarding of the ritualised birthing chamber, the large and costly requirements of the childbed, and the physical and spiritual needs of mother and baby. In January 1605, James disbursed £1,498.16d. to cover 'a list' of 'shop keepers artificers and others … for stuff taken of them and for workmanship of divers things made for the childbed of the Queene', and £908.16s for valuable lengths of crimson velvet and damask to make Anna a new bed, while the closed space of the chamber required 'the hire of sundry workmen to trim and wash the plate used in the Queen's privy chamber in the time of her lying in childbed'.[20] By March, the hive of activity at Greenwich Palace led Carleton to report that there was 'much adoe about the Queen's lying down, and great suit made for offices of carrying the white staff, holding the back of the chair, door keeping, cradle rocking, and such like gossips tricks'.[21]

Finally, on 8 April 1605, Anna was safely delivered of her third daughter, and sixth child, who was named after James's mother – Mary. With three children having survived infancy, the succession was already secure, but James's personal response to the occasion and the material and ceremonial display surrounding the birth underscores the significance of the event. As the firstborn Stuart in England, the new princess dramatically increased the popularity and legitimacy of what was still considered by many to be a new and foreign ruling house and, for her father, James, she represented a milestone in the unification of his Scottish and English kingdoms. The day after Mary's birth, James reported to Christian IV that 'our dearest wife had born a most delightful offspring for us … this child which has been so happily conceived and born', crucially adding that 'although this is not our first child, it may nevertheless seem to be the first since it is the first to have occurred for us after the most happy union of our kingdoms.'²² This was further underscored by the choice of name, for Mary's older sisters – Elizabeth and Margaret – had been born in Scotland and named along English, Tudor lines at a time when James was angling for the succession. By 1605, James ruled both kingdoms and Princess Mary was subject to a reversal of tradition being born in England and named along Scottish, Stuart lines. With Mary's birth conceived of as an act of legitimation for the Stuarts, the choice of Greenwich for the ritualised ceremonial was particularly political, for the palace had been used in this capacity for Henry VIII, Mary I, and Elizabeth I, thereby adding a spatial dimension to the Stuarts' function as the inheritors and preservers of the royal Tudor legacy. The celebrations surrounding Mary's birth also give testimony to the importance of the event to the civic fabric of the kingdoms. Prayers were published for Anna's safe delivery of a 'happy issue',²³ and a 'publicke thanksgivinge to God for the same' was held in the Chapel Royal.²⁴

The following year, 1606, Greenwich Palace was again the site of the queen's confinement, and Anna's seventh and last child, Princess Sophia, was born there on Sunday 22 June. A miniature portrait of Anna's treasured brother Christian perhaps provided comfort for the queen during her confinement, for she had paid Heriot to mend a 'tablet of the kinge of denmarkes picture', in May 1606. Then again, given the international stature of the Danish King, Anna may have planned to proudly wear the jewel in the court space of her churching – although the possibilities are not mutually exclusive.²⁵ The monarchy and its subjects were invested in the arrival of another royal Stuart, as the prayer 'for the Queenes safe deliuerance' was reissued and large bills were presented to the exchequer. The precise details of the childbed are missing, but the requirements of a royal Stuart birth were well known by now, following the pattern set by Anna's previous six deliveries, and a continuity of care was established through the midwife Alice Dennis, who had attended at the birth of Princess Mary. A writ for £600 was issued 'for provision of certain linen and other necessaries, as well for the use of the said Queen in her childbed as for the child's body', and the exchequer of the receipt disbursed a further £3,132.9s.10d. on 22 January 1606 towards the extremely large outstanding sum of £18,193.14s. for the queen's confinement.²⁶ It is possible that this total combined charges from the childbeds of both Mary and Sophia, for the specifics of date and/or child are not given, and the two princesses were born close together. Indeed, the size of the bill meant that it was still being paid off nearly three years later.²⁷

Baptisms

The early modern baptismal ceremony was both religious and sociopolitical.²⁸ In the first instance, the ecclesiastical rite prepared the infant's soul for heaven, but the performance of ritual and the associated festivities provided a platform for the creation and upkeep of social and kinship bonds and, in the case of royalty, the reinforcement of court order and subject loyalty. This was affected through the allocation of specific roles, the observance of spatial codes of honour and respect, the creation of knights and elevation of members of the peerage, a liberal use of costly objects, fabrics, and jewels, and a rigorous adherence to traditional orders and regulations.[29] After her births, in keeping with custom, Anna remained in confinement for a period of several weeks before being churched, with the result that she was excluded from the baptismal proceedings held for her children.[30] Despite her physical absence, she was not forgotten. The entire political stage of the baptismal rites and celebrations had been brought to fruition by the achievements of the queen's body, and her central role in the longevity and legitimacy of the monarchy was permanently embodied in the royal child, who now stood proxy for her efforts and success.

Of the Stuart children, it is the baptismal ceremonial for Henry in 1594 that has drawn the interest of historians who have contextualised the event within the wider discourse of European courtly festival and James's dynastic ambitions.[31] This attention is unsurprising given that the most complete textual record survives for Henry's baptism, and that the political significance of the birth resulted in a resplendence of pageantry and formalised ritual. But it was not just Henry who was fêted with an opulent christening, for the birth of Mary was another politically auspicious occasion that gave rise to a public baptism on a magnificent scale. Mary may have been the Stuart's sixth child, and a girl, but she was the first child to be born in England to the rulers of a newly unified Stuart kingdom. By comparison, the scale of expenditure and the international reach of the baptismal celebrations staged for the other Stuart children – Elizabeth, Margaret, Charles, and Robert – were greatly reduced. Nevertheless, the adherence to temporal, spatial, and material traditions of childbirth, confinement, and public baptism bears out James's gratitude for a plurality of royal children whereby each one of them increased the solace, support, and stability of the dynasty. Elizabeth's baptism, at Holyroodhouse on 28 November 1596, was reported to be an occasion of 'little or no triumphe', which was largely due to the financial censure of the Octavians – a commission of eight men entrusted to design and implement strictures to save the royal treasury.[32] Yet efforts were made to stage Stuart identity and liberality: there was a large celebratory banquet, music was provided by violists and taborers, and James and Anna's 'pages lackayis and trumpetours' were outfitted in new clothing, much of which was the conspicuous red-and-yellow dynastic livery of the House of Stuart.[33] This similarly marked the baptisms of Charles and Robert, when clothes were again issued for pages, lackeys, trumpeters, favoured householders, and for each child's nurse and rockers; banquets and festivities were staged and royal liberality extended beyond the confines of court with James disbursing money 'in name of Larges [largesse]'.[34] All three children, like Henry before them, wore white embroidered with gold, although there was no mention of the regal purple velvet robe, encrusted with pearls, that Henry had worn on his ceremonial journey to the chapel.[35]

In the lead-up to the baptism of Princess Mary, reports were eagerly penned of the 'great preparation for the christening chamber, and costly furniture provided for performance of other ceremonies'.[36] The event resulted in one of the highest annual spends at Greenwich during James's reign, with the office of works disbursing more than £2,600.[37] Building focused on the practical needs incurred by the lavish baptismal celebrations as well as effecting a display of Stuart princely magnificence: wealth, prestige, authority, and generosity. The great chapel was fitted with railings 'to keepe out the presse of people', repairs were made to 'very many lodginge and offices aboute the house' in preparation for accommodating guests, large cupboards were built to house plate, the banqueting house was repaired, and a new confectionery, a new wine cellar, and a new cockpit near the friary were constructed. The cock-pit, the tiltyard, and the bear-baiting pit all underwent refurbishment, and new stands for wine and beer were installed in the buttery and the cellar.[38] Boats were hired 'to convey ritche christall cuppes' from the wharf at the Tower of London to Greenwich where they were placed in 'a cuboard of estate sett vpp in the Quenes privye chamber'.[39] Robert Cramner, an officer of the jewel house, was paid to hire two boats and transport 'twoe founts and other riche plate' to Greenwich from the Tower of London for the baptism, and he received further remuneration (along with two other officers) for having hired the seven carts needed to transport additional plate between the two royal properties 'for the furnishing of twoe greate cuboordes of plate for the feasting of the Duke of Holte [Holstein] and ye Archdukes Ambassador'.[40] The three courts at Greenwich were 'hung about with broad cloth', and in the chapel royal 'was erected a most stately canopy of cloth of gold, 12 foot square ... a very rich and stately font of silver and gilt, most curiously wrought with figures of beastes, serpents, and other antycke workes'.[41] As the birth of Princess Mary visually transformed the court, so too did it reshape the social hierarchy for in keeping with tradition, an honours list was drawn up and the ceremony performed the day before the baptism. Significantly, as Barroll has recognised, on this occasion it pointedly emphasised the pivotal role of the consort in the proceedings as it was given over to Anna to choose the nobles to be elevated.[42]

On the day of the christening, 5 May 1605, Elizabeth de Vere, Countess of Derby (1575–1627), a lady of Anna's withdrawing chamber and a niece of Robert Cecil, Earl of Salisbury, carried the infant 'under a cannapee of [cloth of] goold' along a formal processional route, which stretched 'from the Queenes lodgings through both the great Chambers, and through the presence, and downe the winding stayres into the Conduit Court'.⁴³ The queen's chamber, richly hung and furnished for the birth, included a costly ceremonial bed of crimson velvet and damask that would have played a ritual role on the day of the baptism as the starting point of the royal infant's journey to the chapel.⁴⁴ This was likewise observed for Henry, Charles, and Robert, with accounts recording new hangings for the childbed of Charles in taffeta of various colours, those for Robert in the Stuart dynastic colours of red and yellow, and Henry's suite of bedroom furniture – with a bed, stools, chairs, and a tablecloth – all upholstered in orange and violet velvet and taffeta.⁴⁵ For Mary's baptism, music and silence played important symbolic and temporal roles. For the princess's journey from the private chambers to the chapel, an absence of sound – 'a generall scilence' where 'neither voice nor instrument was heard' – reinforced the gravity of the religious and social ceremonial rites that were yet to commence.⁴⁶ This contrasted sharply with the loud organ music that signalled the arrival of the infant into the chapel, the dedicatory anthems that punctuated the service, and the joyous trumpeting that signalled the conclusion of the rites when garter king of arms proclaimed the princess's styles.⁴⁷ The final anthem of the ceremony significantly focused attention squarely on King James as the successful progenitor of the Stuart dynasty. As Richard Turbet argues, this was William Byrd's 'most famous anthem', which had been composed to gain favour with the new monarch by lauding James through the Latin form of his name, *Jacobus*, with a passage from Psalm 81: 'Sing joyfully to God our strength; give loud unto the God of Jacob!'⁴⁸ By concluding with this anthem, as Catriona Murray observes, the joyous baptismal service was given 'a self-congratulating flourish',⁴⁹ which highlighted James's triumph in having fathered 'the first [child] since ... the most happy union of our kingdoms'.⁵⁰

The form of the royal baptismal festivities discussed thus far underscores the socio-political and sacramental primacy of the event but, as edicts make clear, there was also a central civic component. On 24 August 1594, ahead of Henry's baptism, a royal proclamation was issued to manage relations between the Stuart populace and the international ambassadors. It was determined and then announced from the Mercat Cross in Stirling that 'all his Majesteis loving and gude subjects' were to be 'freindlie and courteouslie ... and all disordour foriborne and eshewit quhilk [which] micht be unseamlie or offensive to thame [ambassadors]'. To act on the contrary would not only incur the 'wraith and indignatioun' of the king but would be carried out 'undir the pane of death'.⁵¹ The importance of such proclamations is easily overlooked within the wider panoply of religious and symbolic pageantry that accompanied the baptismal event, but they provide clear evidence of the ways in which royal ceremonial extended beyond the crown and into the kingdom. The general populace was thereby incorporated into the wider fabric of monarchy and a unified front was presented to international guests as Stuart continuity and longevity were fêted. For the baptisms of Charles and Robert, James likewise reinforced ties between crown and subject through his order for money, as mentioned, to be cast 'amongis ye pepill … in name of Larges [largesse]'.[52]

Stuart subjects were included in the overall consideration of the royal baptism, but hierarchical processions, ceremonial roles and rites, and general material splendour reinforced the social order to firmly restate the supreme power and position of the monarchy that now extended into the next generation. In addition to the dignity of the formal rites, the richness of the church interior, and the ranked structure of the court, monarchical supremacy and reverence were enacted through the physical bodies of the king, queen, and infant prince.[53] Traditionally regal colours and expensive fabrics were in use for Prince Henry, whose white satin baptismal gown was striped with gold and lined with plush, over which he wore a purple velvet robe 'very richelie set with pearl'. Further, his ceremonial journey from chamber to chapel was completed under a crimson velvet 'paill' [canopy], trimmed with four 'pandis' [valences] and covered in gold passementerie.[54] In the previous month, July 1594, the great wardrobe had received orders against 'the tyme of the baptysme', for fourteen new outfits for James and Anna – many of which were exceptionally expensive (the majority exceeding £1,000 Scots each) and were made from costly imported fabrics such as Genoese plush and satin, Lucchese velvet, and cloths of gold and silver.[55] Throughout the three-day baptismal honours, such sartorial privilege actively transformed the royal bodies into signs of Stuart wealth, power, and prerogative.

In addition to the clothing choices for himself and his wife, James approached the matter of godparents as an opportunity for strengthening the international position of the Stuarts. For Prince Henry, James furthered his dynastic ambition for the throne of England by appointing his own godmother, Queen Elizabeth, as godmother to Henry, which increased the ecclesiastical and socio-cultural ties and obligations between the houses of Tudor and Stuart. Queen Elizabeth wrote separately to James and Anna to express her 'extreme pleasure' at the news 'of the birth of the young Prince', to give thanks for 'the honourable invitation to assist at the baptism', and to inform them that she had made 'a note of my happy destiny, in beholding my luck so fortunate as to be the baptiser of both father and son, so dear unto me'.[56] It is likely that Henry also had at least one godfather, if not two, but the record of the other appointees does not appear to be extant.[57] Any of the three blood relations of the queen who were representatively present at the baptism – Christian IV, Heinrich Julius of Braunschweig-Lüneburg, and Ulric of Mecklenburg-Güstrow – would have made a fitting choice of godfather, and familial bonds certainly predicated the choice of godparents for Princess Mary.[58] The other plausible contender is the Duke of Lennox, for he was James's cousin, held high rank and favour at court, and played a prominent role in Henry's baptismal ceremony – receiving the infant from the Countess of Mar and passing him to Queen Elizabeth's proxy, Robert Radcliffe, Earl of Sussex (1573–1629).[59] With Mary's baptism in 1605, James suitably chose Lennox to be one of the godparents, a role he shared with familial members and those of sufficient status: James's other consanguineal cousin, Lady Arbella Stuart, Anna's brother, Duke Ulrik of Holstein, and the high-ranking Dorothy Percy, Countess of Northumberland (c.1564–1619).[60] Ulrik had arrived at the English court on 12 November 1604, the cost and honour of which was no small matter. James disbursed welcoming companies and princely hospitality as a sign of respect, while drawing the Danes into his debt. An entourage headed by Henry Onlie was dispatched to Dover to greet Ulrik on arrival to England and provide him with post-horses and carriages, while Sir Lewes Lewknor, master of ceremonies, together with seven servants, was appointed to 'give his attendaunce on him [Ulrik] to be employed by him in such nec[essar]ie occasions as he shoald have need and use'.[61] Several gentlemen ushers and sewers from James's household then took over from Lewknor 'to attende on the Duke of Houlstsen from the firste daie of Marche 1604 [1605] untille the laste daie of Maie nexte ensewinge [ensuing]'.[62] At least £2,000 was separately issued to offset the 'dietts' and 'intertainment' of the duke, his retinue, and the Danish ambassador, Henry Ramelius, and silver vessels were specially sent to Denmark House for the ambassador's service.[63]

In keeping with religious and civic practice, Anna's confinement lasted for several weeks and, as mentioned, removed her from Mary's baptismal celebrations. Despite the queen's physical absence, however, Anna was keenly felt throughout the service in the figure of the princess, whose very existence was testimony to the queen's satisfaction of her role and responsibility as consort. A second proxy for the queen was provided by her brother Ulrik, who played a central, ritualised part in the proceedings and, as one of the godparents, symbolised the investment of the Oldenburg dynasty in the life of the Stuart child. Furthermore, Anna's physical body functioned as a sign of her pivotal role in the event long after the day of the baptism, for James's gratitude and joy had been made manifest in £2,530 worth of diamonds, pearls, and buttons that were 'bestowed by his Majesty upon the Queen'.[64] Importantly, such gifts held more than economic value; they were richly endowed with historic and symbolic meaning. When Anna later wore these jewelled pieces, they actively inscribed her body with the memorialised politics of reproduction and dynasty.[65]

Churching: Catholic and Reformed

The ecclesiastical ritual of churching was a central part of the medieval Catholic church, and it was retained by the Reformed Church of England, although retitled from 'purification' to 'the thanksgiving of women after childbirth ... commonly called the churching of women'.[66] Typically occurring within four weeks of the birth, it was a public celebration of the woman's survival of childbirth and marked her formal return to society, although its Catholic origins and ritualistic elements gave some Puritans cause for complaint. Nevertheless, it remained a widespread practice and more than ninety per cent of mothers belonging to Puritan parishes in early seventeenth-century London chose to undergo the rite.[67] In the context of confessional debate and Puritan opposition, Clare McManus raises the possibility that Anna's absence from the textual record of Prince Henry's baptism points to her physical non-attendance since 'she had wished to be churched and, in the light of the Catholic resonances of such an act had been prohibited from doing so' by the Kirk. This may well have been the case, but it is unlikely to have been due to 'Anna's later conversion to Catholicism' as she suggests.[68] The rite was part of Anna's knowledge and expectation of Lutheran theological practice: it remained widespread in Reformed Scandinavia and, most pointedly, Anna's own mother had been churched.[69] Looking to early modern England, David Cressy notes that the baptismal rite traditionally saw little involvement from the parents where 'mothers had no part to play ... and fathers were permitted no more than a shadowy role.'[70] Instead, this was an event that gave centre stage to other figures in the child's religious, domestic, and social life – notably the godparents and kinsfolk, although a royal context also included the appointed nurse and honourable, favoured members of court.[71]

Anna's return to court after Mary's birth was eagerly anticipated. On 13 May 1605, the Florentine agent, Ottaviano Lotti, happily reported that 'from next week [19 May] her Majesty will let herself be seen in public, and beautiful tilts will be held in those days as is the custom, along with other festivities of mirth.'[72] Not only an occasion for feasting and revelry, the queen's churching involved the visualisation of the social order and a confirmation of her royal position as consort, which centred on the materialisation of her successful body following the long period of its absence. With the nobility regathered in the chapel royal at Greenwich, it was the Dukes of Holstein and Lennox who, having just stood as godfathers to Mary, now served as the queen's supporters – together with James's cousin, Arbella Stuart – and escorted Anna into the chapel up the aisle to her traverse. Following the 'ordinary service of churchinge of women, appointed by the booke [of Common Prayer]',[73] the elaborate ritual turned into a semi-public stage for the display of royal familial strength, unity, and affection: James and Anna met at the altar before 'imbracing each other with great kindnesse, went hand in hand together, untill they came to the Kings presence Chamber doore, where they parted, dooing great reverence each to other'.[74]

Anna's second churching service in England followed after six weeks of confinement at Greenwich. The Stuart's seventh, and last child, Sophia was born 'between the howers of three and fower of the clocke in the morninge' of Sunday 22 June 1606, but she unfortunately grew 'verye weake', was privately baptised the next day, and passed away that same evening.[75] On the following Thursday, Sophia was 'solemnly, conveyed by Bardge covered with Blacke velvet ... unto the Chappell Royall, in Westminster, and was there enterred'.[76] Having not yet been churched, Anna was absent from Sophia's baptism and burial, just as she had been absent for her other children's christening ceremonies.[77] Given the grief of Sophia's death, it was decided that rather than the elaborate ceremonies that had marked Anna's churching after the birth of Mary, Anna would be 'churched pryvatlye in her privie chamber at Greenwich, by Doctor Mountagew, Deane of his Majesties Chappell', who had been responsible for baptising Sophia.[78] The lengthy period of Anna's confinement is indicative of mental as well as physical exhaustion from the birth and almost immediate loss of Sophia. While Ulrik had maintained the Oldenburg presence in the capital after Mary's birth, this time the mantle fell to Anna's other brother Christian, who had coincidentally arrived on 17 July 1606. He took care to visit Anna – together with James, Charles, Elizabeth, and Mary – at Greenwich that month, and he lodged at the palace for several days. Gifting Anna a new miniature portrait of himself 'richly set with jewels', Christian ensured that his sister had an intimate familial image that she could draw comfort from during her time of recuperation, just as Anna had probably taken solace in Christian's portrait during her confinement for the birth of Mary the previous year.[79]

Betrothal and wedding

During her tenure as Stuart queen consort, there was only one royal marriage in which Anna was intimately involved – that of her daughter Elizabeth to Friedrich, Elector Palatine on 14 February 1613. The wedding, an elaborate, costly, and international affair, has drawn much scholarly attention; notably, however, Anna's role – beyond reproaching Elizabeth as 'goodwife palsgrave' – has not been investigated.[80] The textual record of Anna's involvement with Elizabeth's marriage is relatively quiet, especially in comparison to her opinions and actions concerning the marriages of her sons, but it is clear that she was an influential and meaningful figure in the dynastic, political, and cultural schema that surrounded the Stuart–Wittelsbach union. Beyond visualising the prestige and value of the Stuart dynasty through her presence and elaborate adornment, Anna also guided Elizabeth through her first public presentations as a married woman, reaffirmed Elizabeth's belief in her own prestige and entitlement with lasting effect, and equipped her daughter with trusted members of her own household for the marital journey, which contributed to a new generation of cultural exchange and translation.

As with all early modern royal marriages, the match between Elizabeth and Friedrich was predicated on political grounds as James sought to alternately marry his children to Protestant and Catholic partners. It is now well known that the king believed this strategy would establish 'an equilibrium in the power structure of Europe', thereby safeguarding peace and securing James a pivotal, mediatory role.[81] This much was familiar at court, with Chamberlain surmising that 'this match is to the contentment of all well affected people … as beeing a firme foundation for the stablishing of religion', as the Stuarts strategically built affinity and raised their international stature, which facilitated the formation of the Protestant Union with James at its head.[82] Some court attendees believed that extending the Stuarts' affinal network throughout the German lands was redundant given Anna's connections, and just prior to Prince Henry's death, the Venetian ambassador opined that 'a German match would not gain him anything, as all the German Princes are allied to him or to the Queen by blood.'[83] Having selected Anna as his wife on the basis of her natal networks, this fact was well known to James who flattered Christian IV, as quoted in Chapter 1, that 'among all of the princes in Germany … there is almost no one of great name and reputation who does not come in contact with you through kinship or marriage', although Friedrich was one of the highest ranked princes in the empire.[84]

A Wittelsbach and the Elector Palatine, Friedrich was a member of one of the oldest and most venerated German dynasties. He was one of the electors responsible for selecting the Holy Roman Emperor and was the only elector with the power to judge the emperor. Together with the Elector of Saxony, Friedrich held the imperial vicariate allowing the pair to stand proxy for the emperor during his absence or during the interim period between imperial reigns.[85] Anna was well aware of the rights and privilege of the electors palatine, and the wider hierarchical rankings of the empire, for we should remember that her natal house of Oldenburg was linked to many ruling houses throughout the German Empire including prestigious Electoral Saxony, where Anna's brother-in-law was currently in power. Yet she must have wanted her only daughter to mirror her own dynastic success as a princess by birth who became a queen through marriage and she warned Elizabeth that in accepting the match she would irrevocably sink from royal princess to 'goodwife palsgrave'.[86] Such sentiments likewise circled at court and Chamberlain described 'scandalous speaches of him [Friedrich] and the match … [for] some wold embase his meanes, and meannes of estate and title to match with such a lady'.[87]

Efforts were accordingly made to heighten Friedrich's status, with James making him a Knight of the Order of the Garter, on 31 December 1612, and thereby transforming him into 'Prince Palatin (for so he is now stiled)'.[88]

If James and Anna had reservations about Friedrich's merits, these quickly abated following his arrival in London in 1612. Glowing reports of the prince's conduct and appearance issued forth with announcements that 'the Palatine has surpassed expectation, which, on the King's part, was not great', and it was observed of Anna that while she 'seemed not to taste yt [the marriage] so well at first', she has 'since so come about that she doth all she can to grace yt, and takes speciall comfort in him [Friedrich]'.[89] Although disagreements were to later erupt over superiority of rank and bloodline, no cost was spared to celebrate the matrimonial union in a manner appropriate to its political and dynastic significance. Elaborate visual spectacles and entertainments abounded, and one court attendee pronounced 'the whole preparations', which included banquets, masques, dances, fireworks, musical performances, and tournaments, to 'have turned out successful beyond expectation. The expenses have been so great that, in spite of their being very rich, they will feel it for some time.'[90] Indeed, the wedding was the costliest extraordinary ritual of James's entire reign, with expenditure of just over £93,000.[91] In addition to the festivities, bodily adornment was a matter of high importance and significant financial outlay, with luxurious fabrics and jewels being used to send visual messages about social position, wealth, authority, and resources. Rising friction over status thus coalesced into competitive somatic display:

> He [Friedrich] changes his dress every day, and one is richer than another. All the gentlemen he has with him are covered with gold, chains and jewels. He has fifty pages and grooms in crimson velvet liveries embroidered with gold, silver-brocade doublets, and each gentleman of his suite has his own livery. The English gentlemen vie with these, and so the whole city is full of animation.[92]

For the marriage service, the Stuarts engaged in lavish display that conveyed the political and dynastic value of the bride, while their royal presence testified to her legitimacy and networks of belonging:

> The King and Queen took their seats on two great thrones covered with cloth of gold ... The rest of the space was occupied by a great number of ladies and gentlemen of title, so gorgeously dressed that the imagination could hardly grasp the spectacle. The King's cloak, breeches and jacket were all sewn with diamonds, a rope and jewel of diamonds also in his hat, of inestimable value. The Queen had in her hair a great number of pear-shaped pearls, the largest and most beautiful there are in the world; and there were diamonds all over her person, so that she was ablaze. The Princess was in gold and silver. Her hair was down; she wore a crown on her head, studied with jewels and pearls; she had a necklace of diamonds round her neck.[93]

Anna may well have played a role in finalising Elizabeth's elaborate attire, marking her daughter's body with a statement of natal prestige, belonging, and wealth – a statement that could be transported and re-enacted in her new marital home – for she sent Piero Hugon, one of her pages of the bedchamber, to the princess with 'a jewell from her Ma[jes]ty against her highness maryage'.[94]

The queen also exerted influence over Elizabeth's formal activities – undertaken while still in England – and the constituents of her entourage. The wedding party that journeyed from London to Heidelberg between April and June was a magnificent spectacle that stretched to some thirty-four ships, 150 horses, and at least 650 people.[95] For the initial segment, from London to Kent, Elizabeth was accompanied by members of her immediate family and for the first series of public receptions and engagements that she undertook in her new role as a wife and electress, she was advised and attended by her mother, while James and Friedrich went hunting.[96] While Anna did not escort Elizabeth further than Rochester, she retained a degree of authority and connection to her daughter by selecting several of her own musicians, artisans, and householders to make the journey to Heidelberg, which, in addition, assisted in the translation of cultural traditions and fashions from the Stuart to the Palatine court.[97] Perhaps most significant, as mentioned in Chapter 2, was the presence of Salomon de Caus who was to design and outlay magnificent gardens for Friedrich and Elizabeth that contained notable echoes of Anna's earlier gardening achievements at Denmark House. Ties between the courts continued to be strengthened through the passage of additional goods and personnel, with the English Crown spending £106.12s. on the transport costs required to send Elizabeth beer, and Anna ordering one of her maids of honour, Mary Gargrave, to send fans to her daughter.[98] In 1613 and 1614, the Stuarts dispatched midwives to assist Elizabeth with her births, and throughout 1614 a new secretary, a groom of the bedchamber, and three gentlemen servitors followed. This was a pattern still in practice in 1616 when Dowager Lady Harington received a 'passe' to journey to Heidelberg 'with convenient shipping and posthorses for herselfe and her servantes, with transportacion of her provicions' and in 1617 when Elizabeth received horses, servants, and 'diverse necessaries' from England.[99]

The Stuart influence in Heidelberg was not all positive. James and Anna's belief in their superior rank had adverse effects on the Stuart–Wittelsbach marriage long after the celebratory season in London. Elizabeth's sense of her dynastic prestige and place was that as a princess of the multiple Stuart kingdom of England, Ireland, and Scotland, she outranked her husband – as a German count – and she insisted on taking precedence at public ceremonies.[100] As Rebecca Calcagno relates, Friedrich promised James that precedency would be given to Elizabeth, but when he later sought to revoke this pledge – citing superiority as her husband – Elizabeth 'expressed her offense at the idea that they "would set me in a lower rank than them that have gone before me"', and blatantly refused.[101] Elizabeth's determination became highly problematic and by 23 April 1616, Sir Henry Wotton (1568–1639) was compelled to write to James from Heidelberg to outline Friedrich's position 'that it was against the custom of the whole country; that all the Electors and Princes found it strange ... that Kings' daughters had been matched before in his race ... that in the German ground he did compete with the Kings of Denmark and Sweden'.[102] Yet not only did James and Anna make no effort to resolve the situation, but James actively encouraged Elizabeth to keep insisting upon the superior 'quality and honour of her birth' and thanked her for not giving 'way in the matter'.[103] Following the example set by her mother, Elizabeth accomplished her wifely expectations in providing multiple heirs, supplying a channel to her natal family and kinship network, and aggrandising her husband with her 'dynastic and cultural capital', but Friedrich was only able to settle her unbridled sense of genealogical superiority by avoiding all joint appearances in public.[104]

Regency

In 1617, Anna played a supportive, publicly visible role in the governance of England as James embarked on his long-awaited Scottish progress. In January 1617, two months before James's departure, rumours circulated that a regent or a regency council was to rule England in James's absence. Chamberlain was of the belief that Anna 'dreames and aimes at a Regencie during the Kings absence in Scotland', while the Venetian secretary, Giovanni Battista Lionello, confidently named a six-person ruling council to consist of 'the queen [Anna], the prince [Charles], the archbishop of Canterbury [George Abbot], the lord Chancellor [Francis Bacon], the lord Treasurer [Thomas Howard, Earl of Suffolk] and the earl of Worcester [Edward Somerset]'.[105] Based on Chamberlain and Lionello's statements, scholars have interpreted Anna's position to consist of a failed regency and to be proof of her waning influence with James, or, conversely, to be evidence of her appropriation of supreme rule and authority.[106] Bolstered by new documentary evidence, the following discussion discredits Chamberlain and Lionello's claims and contextualises Anna's actions within the rhetoric of Stuart policy and royal gender relations.

The first hint of an English council ruling in James's absence comes from Sir John Throgmorton who, in writing to Carleton on 12 February 1617, recounted that 'the King goes to the Star Chamber, to settle the government during his absence in Scotland.'[107] It is uncertain if it was settled that day, but a draft of remembrances for the king was drawn up by Sir Francis Bacon and Sir Thomas Meautys (1592–1649) on 21 February 1617 and formed the basis of the letters patent that were subsequently issued on 17 March.[108] That same day, 17 March, Carleton received an update from Edward Sherburn that 'the King [has] gone to Theobalds; the Queen and Prince have taken their leave of him; but *the Council who are to remain in England* attend his Majesty, till his visiting is over.'[109] The 'council' to which Sherburn refers was a commission authorised by letters patent with 'full power and authority to graunte and cause to be made for us and in our name under our greate seale of England such comyssions' for the office of Provost Marshal; for 'any busines matter' in Ireland; for the Ecclesiastical Commission; for passing securities for loans to the king from citizens and cities, and for issuing proclamations. It was, the document outlined, James's 'wish and pleasure ... that this our comyssion shall continewe untill our returne from our said journey' to 'our realme of Scotland'.[110] Although directly naming fourteen specific councillors, the letters patent did include 'all and every other the lordes and others of our privie Councell which shalbe here resident [in England]', although a minimum of six members needed to be attendance to make the commission lawful and Abbott, Bacon, Suffolk, or Worcester had to be one of them.[111] Clearly then, contrary to court rumours, neither Anna, Charles, nor a six-person council were granted formal governance of the realm during James's Scottish progress.

On one hand, James's creation of a commission (as opposed to a regency) is another instance of his propensity to use pacification strategies in foreign and domestic – and within that, factional – politics and is not a reflection of patriarchal proclivities or Anna's inabilities.[112] On the other, the Scottish journey provides a significant example of Anna, as she had done throughout the reign, embodying monarchy and authorising royal, court space. With the king's remove to Scotland, Anna promptly relocated the cultural and political heart of the Stuart court from Whitehall to Greenwich. Resident at the riverside palace throughout April and May, Anna drew the commissioners around her, remained a prime subject for the council as they sought to fix her income in case of widowhood, was honoured as the chief spectator in Robert White's (*fl.*1617) masque, *Cupid's Banishment*, and appointed Jones as designer and accountant to begin building her innovative hunting lodge that she funded from her privy purse.[113]

The confluence of queen and council at Greenwich was topical in the court correspondence throughout these months, with Secretary Winwood informing Secretary Lake (who was in Scotland attending the king) that he expected 'the Lords will attend Her Majesty this Easter at Greenwich.'[114] Towards the end of April it was observed that 'the Council meets frequently at Greenwich, where the queen generally lives. The prince is going there to-morrow to stay some weeks,' and public appearances of solidarity and religious conformity between Anna, Charles, and the council were keenly noted as they collectively 'never missed one Lent sermon'.[115] Such unity was repeated by Chamberlain later still when, on 24 May, he penned a full report to Carleton that 'most of the counsaile kepe there [Greenwich] about her [Anna], saving such as have necessarie attendance at the terme, and those come still on Saterday night and tary Sonday. The rest are only absent on Star-chamber dayes, which have ben few or none this terme.'[116] The use of Greenwich for council meetings was not an unusual choice, but, tellingly, when Anna was in residence throughout April and May, the palace was specifically retitled in the privy council register from 'Greenewich' to 'her Majestie's Court at Greenewich'.[117] Anna's galvanising role for the council during the early part of James's Scottish progress suggests she was continuing in the supporting capacity that she had held for the king since at least 1605. It was at this early date, as discussed in the opening chapters of this book, that James decreed the privy council would assemble at Anna's residence during his travels out of from London for 'open air and exercise', and that it would be from the queen that they would receive his written communications.[118]

Beyond the power of Anna's physical presence at Greenwich, the queen's authority was insisted in her decision to take, in the words of McManus, 'the coveted centre-point of power at the head of the hierarchy of the masquing hall' for the performance of *Cupid's Banishment*.[119] Crucially, this was the only time in James's reign that someone other than the king occupied this privileged role during a royal masque.[120] Anna was therefore the physical focal point for the performance and for the elite gathered audience, and her presence – and very identity – was then reiterated through the celebration of her name in needlework and in the physical bodies of the masquers. The queen was presented with embroidered gifts featuring an acorn and a rosemary sprig to symbolise AR for Anna Regina, before the masquers performed a dance choreographed to spell out the royal names: 'Anna Regina in letters; [in] their second masquing dance [forming] Jacobus Rex; [in] their departing dance is [the formation of] Carolus P.'[121] It is highly probable that two of the three Stuarts were in attendance, for Charles was at Greenwich with his mother at this time and evidence of their concord was recently discernible. In December 1616 – in a report reminiscent of the joint politicking earlier observed of Anna and Henry – Sherburn noted that Coke was in line for a barony thanks to 'the Queen and Prince' who 'do much for him'.[122] That same month Anna, as she had likewise done with Henry, wielded power and territorial anger over Charles's household appointments with disastrous consequences for her long-serving first lady and favourite, Jane Drummond. As Chamberlain explained to Carleton, Drummond's husband, Robert Ker (1569/70–1650), 'is not so well pleased with beeing made earle of Roxborough as discontented to be put by the place of Lord Chamberlain to the Prince … His Lady is likewise parting the Quene, beeing become nothing so gracious as heretofore.'[123] The two incidents were intimately connected, for Anna was infuriated by Roxburghe's presumption to secure the Chamberlainship without her blessing and she not only thwarted his aspirations but promptly banished both Roxburghes from court.[124] Anna may well have kept control of Charles's household since Henry's death, for at that time it was noticed that 'the post of Governor to the Prince is being eagerly sought by all the great nobles; but as the Queen has begged the King to leave that duty to her it is likely that he will not refuse to allow the mother to have the charge of her only son.'[125]

With the king in the Scottish realm, political power and monarchical legitimacy resided in England in the figures of consort and heir, who came together at Greenwich in the early months of 1617. The pair's presence located the court at Greenwich and the council, seeking royal sanction for their undertakings, consequently relocated there. Such political unity was, however, short-lived and it had drawn to a close by the end of June when the council recessed for summer. The customary London dispersal drew mention from the Venetian secretary who announced that 'the queen has gone to Oatlands to remain there for the whole summer, and the prince to Richmond. In ten days the Secretary Winwood is to go to Scotland, and the archbishop also is leaving; all the other nobles and gentlemen are leaving London, *as is usual at this time of the year.*'[126] Yet consort and heir had played a key role in smoothing the king's departure from England, for they unified the remaining councillors and upheld the authority, privilege, and dynastic continuity of the monarchy. It was these key tenets which the pair likewise personified in Anna's final extraordinary ritual as consort: her funeral.

Death

On 2 March 1619, the queen passed away at Hampton Court which prompted, some nine weeks later, her state funeral and final interment at Westminster Abbey. Anna's death must have been expected for some time, for she had been suffering from dropsy since at least May 1615.[127] Anna had spent the months of May, October, and November of 1615 in confinement at Greenwich, and while James did not personally visit, his care and concern was seen in his weekly dispatch of letters and in his gifts of dotterels and partridges for Anna's aviary.[128] A large number of doctors, surgeons, and apothecaries were called in for advice and treatment, and James spared no expense on his wife's health: in the last fifteen months of Anna's life, the 'phisicall drugs and medicaments' provided by the French apothecary, Lewes Le Mire, cost more than £700 alone.[129]

In December 1618, with her health continuing to decline, Anna moved to Hampton Court. As one of James's most frequented palaces, it was furnished, staffed, and equipped to a high, comfortable standard, and it increased the ease with which the king could visit. In the final week of

December and throughout January, James made frequent trips to visit Anna (as did Charles and Buckingham), and he ordered that the court spend the Christmas and New Year period at Hampton Court, rather than the customary Whitehall, so that he could be near his wife.[130] Despite continued reports of her 'recovering' condition, Anna began readying herself for death and sent for specific religious paintings to be brought over from Oatlands: 'A picture of our Saviour at his passeon & Maudy'; a 'picture of our Saviour's birth, & ye shepheards coming to him with Gloria in excelsis'; a 'picture of our Saviour, our Lady, Joseph & Mary'; a 'picture of night worke, when ye souldiers put scornefully a reede into our Saviours hand'; and 'An other of our Saviour with ye woman of Samaria'.[131] These images, as Griffey points out, would have 'functioned as part of personal devotion and, for a dying woman, offered faith in the redemption of sins and an exemplar for a noble, Christian death'.[132] Such visual artefacts – mostly prints and paintings – that showed suffering and dying were highly valued for their ability to 'teach the living how to die'.[133] Indeed, the queen made a concerted effort to dutifully look upon the paintings, with one of her attendants reporting that she went 'to hir gallerie everie day allmost, yit still wayk [weak] of hir leggs that scho [she] could not stand wpone them'.[134]

When the day of Anna's death finally arrived, James lost no time in writing to her favourite brother Christian IV, reassuring him that

> Many tokens of both her love and her virtue remain after her life, whence a great desire for her remains in us. But in death itself her sanctity and piety were manifest, which brought us some comfort in her death, certainly in so long an illness as this one, which completely destroyed her strength divine goodness did so much to prepare her spirit for the better life, and before she said farewell to these troubles, she sufficiently persuaded those who were standing by that she had obtained a taste of it. She was blessed by God with keen judgement and sharp senses up to her final condition, so that she eagerly commenced that heavenly journey, which breathes out everything, with the virtues of her spirit joined together.[135]

Having framed Anna's death in personal, familial terms, however, James's 'legitimate grief' swiftly turned political; he tellingly added that 'although this heroine, your sister by whose marriage our affinity was established, has suffered, the intimacy of our future affairs might continue as long as it seems to good to the one who despenses [sic] lifetimes to kingdoms.'[136] Earlier, the queen's declining health had sparked concern among the Danish representatives stationed in England and Anstruther wrote to Danish Chancellor, Christian Friis, to advise that

> since many doubt about my gracious queen's health, and I cannot keep from you they doubt whether her majesty can remain alive much longer, I ask you therefore quite earnestly to consider with his majesty in Denmark [Christian IV] what is most advisable for his majesty for if her majesty is taken through

death before his majesty has seen and spoken with her majesty it is to be feared that it will be outwith his majesty's means ... send someone who he trusts the most to visit her majesty ... and what his majesty further has to deal with could therefore be arranged.[137]

Anstruther continued, making mention of Christian's future visit to England in the spring when 'it would be possible for his majesty to renew his relationship with his majesty here [James] and the prince [Charles] could have great benefit from his majesty's arrival.'[138] The matter – evidently an important one – that Christian had to 'deal with' may refer to Anna's estate, lending credence to Chamberlain's belief that Anna 'meant to have made the king of Denmarke [Christian IV] her executor yf she had had time and leysure'. Chamberlain may well have been in contact with Anstruther, for he likewise expected Christian to return to England, recalling that 'he had greatly insinuated himself of late, and yt is thought yf she [Anna] had lived but three months longer we shold have seene him here once more.'[139] The concern shared by James and Anstruther to restate the Stuart–Oldenburg alliance, recognises Anna's central place in connecting the kingdoms. Her role in this regard was still being keenly noted the following year when the Swedish agent, Johannes Rutgers (1589–1625), wrote to Axel Oxenstierna, Lord High Chancellor of Sweden (1583–1654), of the decline in Stuart–Oldenburg relations, stating that 'The friendship between the Dane [Christian IV] and the Briton [James VI and I] is aging very fast ... Now that the Queen has been snatched away, there is no one in the whole Court of Britain who influences the King in favour of the Dane.'[140] For observers of the Stuart court in the aftermath of Anna's death, it was clear that she had left a diplomatic vacuum in British–Danish relations. Since the arrival of the Stuarts in England, Anna had served as an intercessor between her consanguineal and affinal kin providing the Stuart and Oldenburg dynasties with an informal, familial connection that obviated the need for official agreements. With Anna's death, however, this relationship rapidly shifted. No longer able to work through the conciliatory figure of their wife and sister, the Stuart and Oldenburg Kings were forced to broker a formal alliance. Eventually signed on 29 April 1621, this was the first treaty between the powers in almost two decades, for no official concord had followed in the wake of James's expanded rule over a multiple kingdom in 1603 and the basis of diplomacy rested on personal, familial lines.[141]

Funeral

In respect of Anna's regal rank as the daughter, wife, sister, and mother of kings, the queen's corpse was disembowelled and embalmed.[142] Spatial decisions restated the legitimacy of the Stuart dynasty for Anna's leaded and coffined organs and body were interred in the apsidal chapel of the Henry VII Lady Chapel at Westminster. Here, they joined a legacy of embalmed members from the Houses of York, Tudor, and Stuart including those of Elizabeth I, Mary Queen of Scots, and the Stuarts' own English-born daughters, the Princesses Mary and Sophia.[143] Between the death and interment, more than two months elapsed and the court became a site of frenetic activity. A heraldic state funeral was a carefully orchestrated, costly spectacle that used rank, heraldry, apparel, and formalised ritual to unite the monarchy with its subjects while concurrently enacting the social hierarchy, and confirming the authority, divinity, and legitimacy of the ruling dynasty.

As with so much royal ceremonial, Anna's funeral demanded a vigilant observance of tradition and precedence, but the last funeral held for a queen consort who predeceased the king in England was that of Jane Seymour (b.1508), which had taken place almost a century earlier in 1537. For King James, a more fitting, recent example was found in the 1603 funeral for the regnant Queen Elizabeth I, and he accordingly ordered that Anna's obsequies were to be 'most honourably solemnized and in such manner in all thinges as was Queen Elizabethes Late Queen of Englande'. This edict presented a puzzle to the heralds, who debated 'the difference betwene a quene a kings wife & an absolute sovereigne', and finally concluded that instead of standards and the coat-of-arms with 'crest sword & target' that would accompany a sovereign ruler, there would be nine leading banners showcasing the consort's natal bloodlines, but that Anna would still be honoured with twelve bannerols of descent.[144] In the end, expenditure was vast, even by royal standards, far exceeding the costs of the state funeral held for Prince Henry in 1612 and more than doubling that of Queen Elizabeth.[145]

James's decision to exalt his wife's death in such a magnificent fashion was a diplomatic strategy intended to secure a Stuart–Habsburg marriage that would, in turn, secure European peace.[146] Throughout the first decade of James's English rule, his self-styled persona of *Rex Pacificus* had met with success and praise both locally and abroad as the war with Spain was brought to an end, turbulent relations with Denmark-Norway were peaceably managed, and Stuart diplomats played leading roles in brokering peace between warring European countries.[147] As discussed above, the marriage of his children to Protestant and Catholic partners was a central part of James's strategy to secure peace on the Continent.[148] The former had been successfully achieved in 1613 with the marriage of Elizabeth and Friedrich, which was welcomed by Stuart subjects and celebrated by European Protestant powers. Conversely, however, the Catholic match – sought with Savoy, Tuscany, France, and Spain – was hampered by confessional clauses and oppositional parliamentary subjects in England, which stretched it out over two Stuart bridegrooms and more than two decades. From 1614, this policy centred on Prince Charles and either the French Princess Christine Marie (1606–1663) or the Spanish Infanta María Ana, although James found both matches to have disagreeable conditions.¹⁴⁹ Over the winter of 1617/18, the match with Spain seemed destined for failure as the confessional conditions were finally laid clear in a draft of the marriage treaty: Philip III required religious toleration for all English Catholics, while James only conceded the public exercise of Catholicism by the Infanta and her servitors. Despite this seemingly insurmountable stalemate, when the Bohemian revolt erupted in the spring of 1618 and Ferdinand II (1578–1637) was deposed as king, James's diplomatic response included a refocus on the Spanish marriage.¹⁵⁰ If brokered, James believed he would gain leverage with Philip III who would, in turn, hold sway over his Austrian cousin, Ferdinand, who was at the very centre of the cross-confessional tensions in Bohemia. This, however, was criticised by many of James's subjects, for an alliance with Spain had never been widely popular and it became increasingly unpopular as many perceived it to be a barrier to Britain's ability to intercede on behalf of the Protestant cause in Europe.¹⁵¹ Indeed, pressure for armed Stuart intervention grew domestically and overseas, and in January 1619 the ambassador of the Palatine, Achatius, Baron von Dohna, arrived to seek financial and armed support from both crown and subjects.¹⁵²

It was in this tense, febrile, and delicate cross-confessional climate of European diplomacy that Anna's state funeral was executed. Indeed, in the very period between the queen's death in March and her funeral in May, James pledged 20,000 crowns for the Bohemian cause, and rumours about Stuart military aid began to gain momentum.¹⁵³ Many in England believed that the European situation should have been the top priority for the king's attention and, more importantly, for any state funds, but for James the burial provided an opportunity for a grandiose state occasion that combined religious ritual with civic duty and socio-cultural display to boldly restate the Stuart dynastic and diplomatic position. Thus, the king's decision to pour vast resources into the occasion when the treasury was already over-stretched was a shrewd and strategic political move. The high level of pomp and ceremony that surrounded Anna's funeral made an emphatic statement: the Stuart monarchy had large financial resources, a loyal aristocracy, and powerful alliances throughout the Baltic and German states. This was a monarchy that could be an advantageous ally or a formidable foe and, crucially, it was one furnished with a legitimate and highly marriageable heir in Prince Charles, who was strategically highlighted throughout the event.

Materials of mourning

The main sign of mourning in early modern England was black cloth, and it was often the item of greatest expense in a heraldic funeral.¹⁵⁴ Much more than a sign of wealth, it can be instructively understood, in line with

Knowles's work on early modern civic ritual, as a textile marker of honour and respect, of monarchical allegiance, and of belonging and difference. The foundational axes of civic ritual in London, as Knowles has contended, were 'integration and differentiation', which were signified and enacted through a range of modes including rhetoric, hierarchical order, processional routes, pageants, oaths, and heraldry.[155] At the time of Anna's passing, mourning cloth was used throughout the kingdom and beyond its geographical borders to demonstrate civic, material mourning. Under privy seal, Stuart ambassadors stationed abroad were allocated sums of money for their mourning and Dudley Carleton, resident in the United Provinces, for example, was issued £150 sterling 'for hanginges and scutchions for his house blacke for himself and his family'. Edward Herbert (1582–1648), ambassador in France, likewise received £150 'for the provision of blacks for himself & his retynewe', while Francis Cottington (c.1579–1652), the Stuart agent in Spain, and William Trumbull (1575/80–1635) in Brussels were given £100 for apparelling themselves and their servants.[156] In each case, the cloth firmly identified the ambassadors as civic members of the multiple Stuart kingdom and loyal servants of the Stuart monarchy but, articulated as it was within the physical context of the international, foreign court that the ambassador served, it concurrently defined the ambassadorial body as distinctly other.

The same was true in England, for on the one hand all people allocated cloth to mourn the queen were thereby united in their loyalty to the crown and the very institution of monarchy. But, on the other, the different types of fabric and the various forms of apparel were used to reinforce the social order. Looking to women, the top of the hierarchy (excluding royalty) was occupied by eighteen countesses, each of whom was supplied with tippets and 'Parris heads' or headdresses of fine lawn, the latter of which were elaborately veiled, peaked, pleated, and embroidered.[157] Veiled white headdresses were also issued to one viscountess, seven wives of the sons of earls, eleven earls' daughters, twenty-three baronesses, and thirty-seven knights' wives and gentlewomen, becoming significantly less ornate as rank decreased.[158] At the very end of the social scale were 280 poor women, who were provided with gowns and kerchiefs of Holland cloth for the occasion. There were at least 1,358 people in the funeral procession, which required the great wardrobe to source 12,253 yards of fabric for their apparel.[159] The extensive range of social rank and the associated volume and value of cloth signified the reach and the charity of the crown. This had a twofold significance: it enacted ties between the monarchy and the elite on which the former heavily relied for order and control, and it also tied the court to the city of London for it was the city's poor residents who benefitted from monarchical generosity.[160] This latter connection was spatially reinforced, for it was through London's very streets that the procession moved as it wound its way to Westminster Abbey. The processional route was carefully chosen and carefully prepared. Henry Weekes, paymaster of the office of works, recorded expenditure for readying the streets by filling all holes, and then spreading and levelling the surfaces with gravel. The civic, public element of the ceremonial procession was anticipated in the payment to carpenters 'for framing and setting up vij^c xxxiiij [734] roddes of poste and railes from denmarkehouse in the Strand to the west gate of Westminster Abbey being railed on both sides of the way for Queene Annes funerall'.[161] Welcoming London citizens to participate in the ritualised process of death, the fence also fixed the distance and difference between the royal pageant and the general press of people.

The procession

If rank was enacted through the mourner's apparel, it was also enacted through the physical structure of the procession. According to the heralds, it was to begin with members of the poor and, ascending in rank, move through elite and royal servants, and low-ranking grooms, porters, and other householders. These figures were to be followed by the servants of knights, barons, bishops, viscounts, lords and ladies, and earls and countesses before those office-holders who worked in close proximity to the queen – her male chamberers, ushers, chaplains, musicians, and doctors. This entire section of people was regularly interspersed by ceremonial officials: conductors, trumpeters, and several officers of arms. Next, at the very centre of the procession, came the queen's coffined remains and wooden effigy closely surrounded by prominent mourners: those of significantly high rank and title (countesses and earls), and those who were attached or related to the deceased queen through blood, marriage, or close service, including Prince Charles and the chief mourner, the Countess of Arundel. From this section – which embodied the pinnacle of the social order – the procession then descended through the queen's gentlewomen servants, the female servants of elite women, select householders of James and Charles, and the rear was securely closed by the royal guard.[162] Status further dictated the personnel involved in the funeral service, which was officiated by George Abbott, Archbishop of Canterbury.[163] As the ecclesiastical head of the Church of England, Abbott had overseen the two most significant ceremonial events of the Jacobean period: Henry's funeral in December 1612 and Princess Elizabeth's wedding in February 1613 and, fittingly, as discussed above, he was a privy councillor, a member of the 1617 commission, and a firm ally of Anna, having united with her against the Howard-Carr faction.[164] The funeral service was brought to a close by the senior heraldic authority, Sir William Segar, garter king of arms (c.1554–1633), who proclaimed Anna's styles and parentage, before the trumpets sounded and the dean of Westminster, Dr Robert Tounson (1575–1621), 'dismissed the company wth the peace of God'.[165]

Notable for enacting the hierarchical order of the court, the composition of the queen's funeral procession also testified to the broad nature of her contribution to the cultural climate of the Stuart courts for it included sixty-eight of her specialist servants, 'tradsmen & artificers'. The importance of the queen's sartorial magnificence throughout her life was embodied by the extensive number of clothiers including her farthingale-maker, embroiderer, skinner, silkman, hosier, pinner, haberdasher, and 'shoomaker', many of whom had been in her service throughout her sixteen years in England. Beyond apparel, it was music, jewellery, theatre, and painting that took centre stage as the queen's twelve musicians (including her five French musicians) and sixteen players were joined by her jewellers, easel painters, goldsmiths, and her limner. The queen's long-serving Scottish jeweller, Heriot, walked alongside three other jewellers – Sir William Herrick, Sir John Spillman, and Abraham Harderet – who likewise enjoyed royal patronage but were only used by Anna infrequently.[166] Anna's miniaturist, Isaac Oliver, had died a year earlier and it was his son, the limner Peter Oliver (1594–1648), who took his place walking in mourning for the queen alongside her two favoured easel portraitists, Marcus Gheeraerts and Paul van Somer.[167] The quantity and diversity of the artificers physically embodied the queen's wide cultural interests and activities, reiterating the impact that her patronage had made over the years. Alongside the cultural, the queen's ecclesiastical patronage was realised through her twenty-one chaplains and her almoner, which testified to her support of Protestant preaching while concurrently reinforcing the socio-political tenor of her contribution to Stuart court culture through her affinity to the Pembroke-Southampton faction.[168] As we have seen, Anna's cultural endeavours and political aspirations found repeated alliance with key members of this group, especially the Countess of Bedford, the Earl of Pembroke, and the Earl of Southampton. Importantly, this also included Robert Sidney, Earl of Leicester (hand-picked by the queen to accompany Elizabeth in 1613), who as Anna's long-serving lord chamberlain governed the queen's household above-stairs and, as Peter McCullough determines, therefore oversaw a rotating system for her royal chaplaincy.[169] Thus, not unsurprisingly, the queen's preachers reflected the religious position of the group, upholding her public Protestant position as men 'with solid conformist credentials. Two were even pillars of a notable evangelical revival in the West Country: Edward Chetwynd ... and Samuel Crooke.'[170] Crooke is particularly notable for being the queen's only ordinary chaplain to have published the text of a sermon – 'Death Subdued', which he had delivered to Anna's court at Denmark House on 6 May 1619, between the death and burial of the queen.[171] A conventional piece on the equality of death, Crooke chose, rather fittingly, to dedicate the work to Leicester with a note underscoring the queen's judicious use of amity to bind faction: 'Robert Earle of Leicester ... and to my much honoured and worthy *friends*, the rest that were of the *family* of our late Gracious Mistresse Queen Anne'.[172] Crooke, together with Anna's college of chaplains more generally, strengthened her image of 'confessional acceptability', although the queen's decision to support conformist preaching should also be seen as evidence of her acumen in subordinating religion to politics: as queen consort, she was aware of her role as a 'model of charity and piety', a model that was constantly scrutinised both within and outwith the borders of the multiple Stuart kingdom.[173]

Visualising ancestry and descent

In death, as in life, Anna's body was surrounded by a proud, highly symbolic visualisation of her ancestral pedigree. An astonishing number of flags, pennants, and banners were ordered to adorn Denmark House, Westminster Abbey, and Whitehall Palace, and to be carried in the procession.[174] The majority of the heraldry was executed by the sergeant-painter John de Critz, who was allocated 175 yards of taffeta (in addition to other supports) and must have worked with a team of assistants to paint and/or gild more than 1,000 individual banners, bannerols, pendants, pencells, escutcheons, canopies, pasteboards, and 'Scrowles with words'.[175] Set against the monuments, architectural spaces, and mourners, which were all cloaked in black, the vast quantities of arms and badges would have been resplendent, painted or embroidered as they were in their requisite colours.[176] Of these, two sets of heraldic achievements are worthy of specific mention for giving unequivocal testimony of the centrality of Anna's dynastic identity to her value as queen and for integrating her international ancestry into the history of the multiple Stuart kingdom and its people: the nine great banners that opened the procession and the twelve bannerols that were ordered around the sides of the coffin.[177] These flags are beautifully illustrated in the heralds' manuscript, wherein the various arms are carefully detailed, as is their location in the procession – or their proximity to the coffin – and the identity of the bearer (Plate 10). Affixed to thirteen-foot staves, they were given pre-eminent visibility, towering above the procession. The nine leading banners, in order of appearance, were the Union of Scotland and England; the dynastic house of Oldenburg and Delmenhorst; the Danish territories of Schleswig, Holstein, Stormarn, and Dithmarschen; the historic Danish ancestral tribes of the Vandals and Goths; the kingdoms of Sweden, Norway, and Denmark.[178] The last banner processed immediately in front of the coffin, and as the heraldic centrepiece of the funeral it bore the principal natal and marital quartered arms of the queen: 'the kingdoms of England Denmark Oldenburge Slenswicke Holsten the Vandalls the Gothes'.[179] Behind this showcase, held around the coffin, were twelve bannerols testifying to Anna's wider armigerous alliances.[180] Beyond repeating the territories represented in the nine banners, they extended to the duchies of Saxony, Mecklenburg, and Pomerania, the margraviate of Brandenburg, the fiefdom of Stormarn, the counties of Schauenburg, Delmenhorst, and Sponheim, and the town of Dithmarschen, as well as the personal armorial achievement of Anna's father, Frederik II.

It is difficult to reconcile such an emphatic showcase of dynastic power, subject loyalty, and economic investment with earlier scholarship that has interpreted the funeral as being 'marred by factional interests and a desire to cut costs', and as evidence of Anna's marginalisation and 'loss of power' whereby James prioritised the completion of the Whitehall Banqueting House over her funeral.[181] International context is central to understanding court machinations at this time, and we must remember that, more than court buildings, James was occupied, financially and politically, with the burgeoning of cross-confessional tensions on the Continent that stemmed from the Bohemian revolt in spring 1618. With hundreds of banners and bannerols spelling out Anna's Protestant kinship network, James issued a potent visual reminder to the Catholic leaders of the extensive network to which the House of Stuart belonged.

The funeral hearse customarily bore the heraldic achievements and motto of the deceased. The latter would have been particularly appropriate for Anna of Denmark, for her personal Italian motto – *La mia grandezza dal eccelso* (My power is from the Most High) – had formed a cornerstone of her visual iconography throughout her later life and been liberally applied throughout her main English palaces on pieces of furniture, silverwork, and soft furnishings.[182] However, in the case of Anna's great hearse at Westminster Abbey, it was not her personal motto that took centre stage, but that of King James. Utilising four personal mottoes throughout his life, as well as the traditional French motto of the English monarchy – *Dieu et mon droit* (God and my right) – James made a significant and strategic choice of motto for the hearse. Responding to the current political climate, the king had his biblical motto *Beati pacifici* (Blessed are the peacemakers), repeated at least five times and across two tiers of his wife's catafalque (Plate 11).[183] The maxim reminded onlookers that the multiple Stuart kingdom was currently pursuing a policy of peace, wherein a marriage alliance was favoured over warfare. This was reinforced by the unusual decision to have Prince Charles in the funeral procession (Plate 10). Traditionally, the presence of the heir at a royal funeral stressed the continuity and inviolability of the institution of monarchy, but in this case with the king still alive and well the more specific purpose was to maximise Charles's visibility.[184]

The marriageable suitor in James's wider manoeuvrings with Spain, Charles was to be shown off to his advantage in Anna's funeral as the dutiful son mourning the loss of his mother; as the promising prince commanding his own household of loyal servants; and as the legitimate and rightful inheritor of the dynastic and material wealth of the multiple

Stuart kingdom.[185] As such, mourning apparel was allocated to sixty-one of Charles's householders in the procession, the prince occupied a privileged place of honour walking directly in front of the coffin, and special provisions were made for him in the Abbey where he was allocated an entire pew upholstered in black velvet. Although Anna's death did not signal Charles's attainment of her titles, he still played the principal role in the heraldic offering whereby the deceased's personal rank and entitlements were proclaimed and their armorials were sequentially given over to the officiant and then invested on the heir. Thus, garter king of arms walked Charles to the communion table where he offered a piece of gold on his mother's behalf and then remained there to ceremoniously receive her banners in the reverse order to that seen in the procession.[186] Even after death, Anna continued to fulfil two of the key roles of the consort – negotiation and legitimation.[187] In 1619, during the early stages of the Thirty Years' War, the queen consort was unable to take an active role in counselling James, sheltering opinions at court, or providing access to her wide natal network, but it is fitting that her physical remains, dynastic pedigree, and memory were employed by the king for reconciliatory diplomatic purposes to the benefit of their son and heir Charles.

Conclusion

Anna's involvement in formalised royal ritual and court ceremonial evidences the political role of the queen consort as a figure of dynastic strength, intercession, and legitimisation. These qualities were expressly showcased in Anna's ritualised activities that included childbirth, the baptismal rites and attendant celebrations for her children, her churching, and her funeral. Of these, none was as significant to her strength and value as a royal figurehead as the passage of motherhood. Of crucial importance to the survival of the dynasty, the provision of a legitimate heir was also a matter of state security that ensured ongoing social and political stability. The magnitude of the birth of the Stuart heir, Henry, was seen in the splendid baptismal celebrations that the Stuarts mounted in front of an international audience and it was evocatively captured by their subjects' proposal to change the doctrinal fabric of worship. Each of the seven pregnancies that Anna carried to term were greeted with thanksgiving prayers and joyous celebrations, and while the six that followed Henry, with the exception of Princess Mary, heralded less fanfare, they were still political milestones of joy and celebration as the dynasty safeguarded the succession and enriched its future networks. During the rites and attendant celebrations of the baptisms and the subsequent churching ceremony, it was the body of the queen consort – by proxy or in person – that took centre stage. Having fulfilled her princely obligation to preserve the Stuart dynasty, she was appropriately acclaimed for her virtue and success.

In examining Anna's performance of royal ritual and formalised behaviour at the Stuart courts, this chapter strongly reiterates the dynastic importance of queens consort who, whether as active brokers or passive conduits, provided crucial access to multiple, prestigious international networks. In the case of the Stuarts, Anna of Denmark's Protestant networks were a central component of King James's foreign policy and self-styled persona. They raised his international rank and position and, by extension, facilitated his ability to play the role of the peacemaker, and to be elected head of the Protestant Union in 1613. At the time of Anna's death in 1619, James's letters to her brother, Christian IV, and that of Anstruther to the Danish Chancellor, highlight the queen's valuable position and abilities, as they worried over the future of Stuart–Oldenburg relations in the absence of the connecting force of Anna of Denmark. It was reiterated through the first signing of a formal Stuart–Oldenburg agreement in almost twenty years, and it was clear throughout the funeral proceedings in James's insistence on extremely large quantities of heraldry to visualise Anna's genealogy and networks, and in his decision to accord Charles prominence as the enduring, legitimate embodiment of the unified Stuart and Oldenburg bloodlines.

Notes

1. *CSPV*, vol. 15, no. 830: 10 April 1619.
2. L. L. Peck, 'Building, Buying, and Collecting', in L. Cowen Orlin (ed.), *Material London c.1600* (Philadelphia, 2000), 268–289: 284.
3. A. Keay, *The Magnificent Monarch: Charles II and the Ceremonies of Power* (London and New York, 2008), 2.
4. Anna's wedding and coronations are not included here, for their performative and symbolic, and religious and civic, significance is discussed in McManus, *Renaissance Stage*, 60–96, 118–119, 205–208; Meikle, 'Anna of Denmark's Coronation'.
5. J. Knowles, 'The Spectacle of the Realm: Civic Consciousness, Rhetoric and Ritual in Early Modern London', in J. R. Mulryne and M. Shewring (eds), *Theatre and Government under the Early Stuarts* (Cambridge, 1993), 157–189: 157.
6. Watanabe-O'Kelly, 'Afterword', 231, 234–237; Campbell-Orr, 'Introduction: Court Studies', 17–19.
7. *CSP Scotland*, vol. 10, 574, no. 612: 30 September 1591 (Advertisements from an Englishman in Berwick).
8. Moysie, *Memoirs of Scotland*, 113.
9. TNA, SP 52/51, fol. 60 (12 November 1593: Bowes to Burghley).
10. Meldrum (ed.), *Royal Correspondence*, 11. This was Christian's second child, although his firstborn had survived for less than a month.
11. NRS, E35/13, vol. 8, pp. 59–61; 'Mekil(l adj.'. *Dictionary of the Scots Language*, 2004. Scottish Language Dictionaries Ltd. www.dsl.ac.uk/entry/dost/mekill. Accessed 5 March 2019.
12. A. Wilson, 'The Ceremony of Childbirth and its Interpretation', in V. Fildes (ed.), *Women as Mothers in Pre-Industrial England: Essays in Memory of Dorothy McLaren* (London and New York, 1990), 68–107: 73. See also D. Cressy, *Birth, Marriage,*

& Death: Ritual, Religion, and the Life-Cycle in Tudor and Stuart England (Oxford, 1997), 53–54; C. Murray, Imaging Stuart Family Politics: Dynastic Crisis and Continuity (London and New York, 2017), 18.
13 Wilson, 'Ceremony of Childbirth', 75–78.
14 NRS, E35/13, vol. 8, p. 59. Anna enjoyed weaving and for other orders of silk thread for her 'hir majestie to weif with' see NRS, E35/13, vol. 2, p. 7; NRS, E35/14, fol. 8v; NRS, E21/76, fol. 534.
15 NRS, E21/74, fol. 130.
16 NRS E21/74, fol. 134. This does not seem to have followed in England, where at least one of the midwives in attendance for the birth of Princess Mary at Greenwich Palace was lodged with Thomas Sheffield: TNA, E351/543, fol. 138v.
17 NRS E21/74, fol. 222.
18 NRS, E21/76, fol. 205; Juhala, 'Household and Court', 90.
19 This is explicitly evidenced by King Charles I who, faced with the decision to save either his wife or his firstborn child and son, chose his wife for the reason that she would be able to provide him with more children: Keay, Magnificent Monarch, 10.
20 TNA, E403/2725, fol. 169r; Devon, Issues of the Exchequer, 28; CSPD Addenda, vol. 37, 456, no.11.
21 Sawyer, Memorials of Affairs of State, vol. 2, 52: 10 March 1605.
22 Meldrum (ed.), Royal Correspondence, 44. See also Murray, Imaging Stuart Family Politics, 23–24.
23 Prayers appointed to be vsed in the church at morning and euening prayer by every minister, for the Queenes safe deliuerance set foorth and injoyned by authoritie (London, 1605; STC 16534 and reissued 1606; STC 16537).
24 Rimbault, Old Cheque-Book, 177 (STC 16535).
25 TNA, LR2/122, fol. 20v.
26 TNA, E405/451, fol. 22r; TNA, E403/2726, fols 61r, 125r; Barroll, Anna of Denmark, 104, 201 n. 59.
27 TNA, E403/2727, fol. 147v.
28 Cressy, Birth, Marriage, & Death, 97–194; esp. 98–99, 106–113.
29 Keay, Magnificent Monarch, 12–18.
30 Cressy, Birth, Marriage, & Death, 149–50, 197, 200.
31 M. Bath, '"Rare Shewes and Singular Inventions": The Stirling Baptism of Prince Henry', Journal of the Northern Renaissance 4 (2012), 1–16; M. Lynch, 'Court Ceremony and Ritual', in J. Goodare and M. Lynch (eds), The Reign of James VI (East Linton, 2000), 71–92: 88–91; M. Lynch, 'The Reassertion of Princely Power', in M. Gosman et al. (eds), Princes and Princely Culture 1450–1650 (Leiden, 2003), 199–238; McManus, Renaissance Stage, 79–96; Murray, Imaging Stuart Family Politics, 19–23.
32 Quoted in Lynch, 'Court Ceremony and Ritual during the Personal Reign of James VI', 91. See also Juhala, 'Household and Court', 68, 216.
33 NRS, E35/13, vol. 8, pp. 20, 74; NRS, E35/13, vol. 8, p. 85; Juhala, 'Household and Court', 216–217.
34 NRS, E21/76, fol. 266; NRS, E21/74, fol. 159; Juhala, 'Household and Court', 218–220.
35 NRS, E35/13, vol. 5, pp. 3, 4; W. Fowler, 'A Trve Reportarie' (Edinburgh, 1594) as reprinted in H. W. Meikle (ed.), The Works of William Fowler, vol. 2 (Edinburgh and London, 1936), 181.
36 Sawyer, Memorials of Affairs of State, vol. 2, 57: 6 April 1605.
37 TNA, E351/3240.
38 TNA, E351/3240.
39 TNA, E351/543, fols 129v, 130r.
40 TNA, E351/543, fol. 129v.
41 Stow et al., Annales, 863.

42 Barroll, *Anna of Denmark*, 105.
43 Rimbault (ed.), *Old Cheque-Book*, 167; Stow et al., *Annales*, 863.
44 *CSPD Addenda*, vol. 37, 456, no.11; Murray, *Imaging Stuart Family Politics*, 18.
45 NRS, E21/74, fols 131, 132; NRS, E21/76, fols 182, 231; NRS, E35/13, vol. 5, p. 1. A second 'bed of Estate' was noted by Fowler as being 'richly decored, and wrought with brodered work, containing the story of Hercules and his trauels', see his 'Trve Reportarie', 180.
46 Rimbault (ed.), *Old Cheque-Book*, 167.
47 Rimbault (ed.), *Old Cheque-Book*, 167–169; Murray, *Imaging Stuart Family Politics*, 24. The importance of following tradition is seen in the baptism of Charles Stuart in June 1630, almost thirty years later, where loud organ music was likewise used to announce the arrival of the infant to the chapel: Keay, *Magnificent Monarch*, 15–16.
48 R. Turbet, 'Joyful Singing: Byrd's Music at a Royal Christening', *The Musical Times* 145 (2004), 85–86; Murray, *Imaging Stuart Family Politics*, 24.
49 Murray, *Imaging Stuart Family Politics*, 24.
50 Meldrum (ed.), *Royal Correspondence*, 44.
51 Masson (ed.), *Register of the Privy Council*, vol. 5, 164–165; Murray, *Imaging Stuart Family Politics*, 20.
52 NRS, E21/76, fol. 266; NRS, E21/74, fol. 159; Juhala, 'Household and Court', 218–220.
53 For the interior refurbishment of the chapel see NRS, E35/13, vol. 5, pp. 1, 2; NRS, E35/13, vol. 3, pp. 22, 22A, 22B [these pages are not originally numbered]; Fowler, 'Trve Reportarie', 178–180; *CSP Scotland*, vol. 11, 411–413, no. 326.
54 NRS, E35/13, vol. 5, pp. 3, 4; Fowler, 'Trve Reportarie', 181.
55 NRS, E35/13, vol. 3, pp. 9–18; NRS, E35/13, vol. 4, pp. 4–9.
56 TNA, SP 52/54, fols 3, 4 (August 1594).
57 Cressy, *Birth, Marriage, & Death*, 150.
58 Masson (ed.), *Register of the Privy Council*, vol. 5, 144, n. 2.
59 Fowler, 'Trve Reportarie', 180–181.
60 Stow et al., *Annales*, 863.
61 TNA, E351/543, fols 132r, 132v–133r, 136v, 137r. See also Wade, 'Duke Ulrik', 252–254.
62 TNA, E351/543, fol. 134v. For other charges related to Ulrik's visit see TNA, E351/543, fols 133v, 135v, 137v, 139r.
63 TNA, E403/2724, fol. 215v; TNA, E403/2725, fol. 173v; TNA, E351/543, fols 130r, 139r. Ramelius arrived at the English court in January 1605: Meldrum (ed.), *Royal Correspondence*, 37.
64 Devon, *Issues of the Exchequer*, 48–49; Barroll, *Anna of Denmark*, 104, 201 n. 59. James had carried out this practice on the occasion of Robert's birth too, giving 'one pointit diamont' to 'his dairest bedfallow ye quenis' at a value of £266,13*s*.4*d*. Scots, NRS, E21/76, fol. 266.
65 Clark, 'Transient Possessions', 196–197; McCall, 'Brilliant Bodies', 447, 449–452.
66 Wilson, 'Ceremony of Childbirth', 78; P. Crawford, 'The Construction and Experience of Maternity in Seventeenth-Century England', in V. Fildes (ed.), *Women as Mothers in Pre-Industrial England: Essays in Memory of Dorothy McLaren* (London and New York, 1990), 3–38: 11.
67 Wilson, 'Ceremony of Childbirth', 88.
68 McManus, *Renaissance Stage*, 80. On Anna's religion see Field, 'Anna of Denmark and the Politics of Religious Identity.'
69 M. M. Ahlefeldt-Laurvig, 'Barselskoner i Reformationstiden', *Dragtjournalen* 11 (2017), 4–13: esp. 4–7; Ø. Ekroll, 'State Church and Church State: Churches and

70 Cressy, *Birth, Marriage, & Death*, 149.
71 Cressy, *Birth, Marriage, & Death*, 149–161.
72 J. Orrell, 'The London Stage in the Florentine Correspondence, 1604–1618', *Theatre Research International* 3 (1978), 157–176: 161.
73 Rimbault (ed.), *Old Cheque-Book*, 170.
74 Quoted in Orrell, 'London Stage', 161. See also Barroll, *Anna of Denmark*, 104–107; Payne, 'Aristocratic Women', 116–117.
75 Rimbault (ed.), *Old Cheque-Book*, 170.
76 Stow et al., *Annales*, 883; Rimbault (ed.), *Old Cheque-Book*, 171.
77 Rimbault (ed.), *Old Cheque-Book*, 170.
78 Stow et al, *Annales*, 886; Barroll, *Anna of Denmark*, 107; Rimbault (ed.), *Old Cheque-Book*, 171. The churching took place on Sunday, 3 August 1606; quotation from Rimbault.
79 Birch, *Court and Times*, vol. 1, 67: 12 August 1606 (Mr Pory to Robert Cotton). On Christian's visits to England see Chapter 5; Senning, 'Visit of Christian IV', 555–572; Davies, 'Limitations of Festival', 311–335.
80 On the Palatine marriage see, for example, K. Curran, *Marriage, Performance, and Politics at the Jacobean Court* (Farnham, 2009), 89–127; K. Curran, 'James I and Fictional Authority at the Palatine Wedding Celebrations', *Renaissance Studies* 20 (2006), 51–67; J. R. Mulryne, 'Marriage Entertainments in the Palatinate for Princess Elizabeth Stuart and the Elector Palatine', in J. R. Mulryne and M. Shewring (eds), *Italian Renaissance Festivals* (Lewiston, 1992), 173–196; M. Brayshay, 'The Choreography of Journeys of Magnificence: Arranging the Post-Nuptial Progress of Frederick, the Elector Palatine, and Princess Elizabeth of England from London to Heidelberg in 1613', *Journal of Early Modern History* 12 (2008), 383–408; G. Gömöri, '"A Memorable Wedding": The Literary Reception of the Wedding of the Princess Elizabeth and Frederick of Pfalz', *Journal of European Studies* 34 (2004), 214–224; S. Smart and M. R. Wade (eds), *The Palatine Wedding of 1613: Protestant Alliance and Court Festival* (Wiesbaden, 2013). Notably, Anna is only mentioned in passing.
81 Murdoch, *House of Stuart*, 45. See also S. Smart and M. R. Wade, 'The Palatine Wedding of 1613: Protestant Alliance and Court Festival', in S. Smart and M. R. Wade (eds), *The Palatine Wedding of 1613: Protestant Alliance and Court Festival* (Wiesbaden, 2013), 13–160: 42–45; Redworth, *Prince and the Infanta*, 7–14.
82 McClure (ed.), *Chamberlain*, vol. 1, 427, no. 167: 23 February 1613 (to Winwood); Murdoch, *House of Stuart*, 44–45.
83 *CSPV*, vol. 12, 431, no. 657: 5 October 1612.
84 Meldrum (ed.), *Royal Correspondence*, 98: 13 May 1609.
85 R. Calcagno, 'A Matter of Precedence', in S. Smart and M. R. Wade (eds), *The Palatine Wedding of 1613: Protestant Alliance and Court Festival* (Wiesbaden, 2013), 243–266: 244; Smart and Wade, 'The Palatine Wedding of 1613', 37–38; Brayshay, 'Choreography', 389–390. Quotation from McClure (ed.), *Chamberlain*, 1: 427 (23 February 1613).
86 As quoted in Calcagno, 'Matter of Precedence', 250. On the use of the term 'good-wife' pertaining to a married woman below the level of the gentry see Erickson, *Women and Property*, 99.
87 McClure (ed.), *Chamberlain*, vol. 1, 381, no. 150: 22 October 1612 (to Carleton).
88 McClure (ed.), *Chamberlain*, vol. 1, 403, no. 159: 9 January 1613 (to Winwood).
89 *CSPV*, vol. 12, no. 678: 9 November 1612; McClure (ed.), *Chamberlain*, vol. 1, 427, no. 167: 10 February 1613 (to Winwood).

90 *CSPV*, vol. 12, no. 775: 1 March 1613.
91 Curran, *Marriage*, 89.
92 *CSPV*, vol. 12, no. 680: 9 November 1612.
93 *CSPV*, vol. 12, no. 775: 1 March 1613. See TNA, SP14/72, fol. 50 for Finet's statement that the jewels worn by James, Anna, and Charles were collectively worth £900,000.
94 TNA, E407/57/2, p. 24.
95 M. Lemberg, 'Hessen-Kassel and the Journey up the Rhine of the Princess Palatine Elizabeth in April and May 1613', in S. Smart and M. R. Wade (eds), *The Palatine Wedding of 1613: Protestant Alliance and Court Festival* (Wiesbaden, 2013), 411–426: 412; Brayshay, 'Choreography', 385, fig. 1; 404–405. Brayshay highlights the fluctuating size of the entourage which he estimates to have been, at any one time, between 650 and 2,000 people and notes that on entering Heidelberg on 7 June, it was closer to 10,000.
96 Brayshay, 'Choreography', 387.
97 Wade, 'Dynasty at Work', 507–509; McClure (ed.), *Chamberlain*, vol. 1, 419: 10 February 1613; Brayshay, 'Choreography', 384.
98 BL Lansdowne MS 164, fols 226r, 270r.
99 BL Lansdowne MS 164, fols 250v, 344r, 348r; *CSPD*, vol. 2 (1611–1618), 250, 383; A. E. Stamp (ed.), *Acts of the Privy Council of England*, vol. 35 (London, 1927), 70, 202, 232, 270–271.
100 Calcagno, 'Matter of Precedence', esp. 244–245, 254–258. Calcagno writes that Elizabeth was 'directed by her father, King James', but provides no reference and it is highly possible, especially given Anna's repeated assertions of her own genealogical cachet and her earlier wish for a royal match, that she was involved in directing her daughter's sense of superiority.
101 As quoted in Calcagno, 'Matter of Precedence', 256.
102 Calcagno, 'Matter of Precedence', 257.
103 Calcagno, 'Matter of Precedence', 258–259.
104 Morton, 'Introduction', 5; Calcagno, 'Matter of Precedence', 259.
105 McClure (ed.), *Chamberlain*, vol. 2, 47: 4 January 1617 (to Carleton); *CSPV*, vol. 14, no. 602: 19 January 1617.
106 McManus, *Renaissance Stage*, 180–182; McManus, 'Memorialising Anna of Denmark's Court', 83–86, 88, 89; J. Hallam, 'Re-presenting Women in Early Stuart England: Gender Ideology, Personal Politics & the Portrait Arts' (unpub. PhD diss., University of Pennsylvannia, 2004), 300–301; Roper, 'Unmasquing the Connections', 51. Roper incorrectly identifies the Lord Chancellor as being Sir Thomas Egerton, Baron Ellesmere (1540–1617). Ellesmere resigned from the post on 6 March 1617, and it was granted to Bacon the following day.
107 *CSPD*, vol. 2, 434.
108 Bacon, *Letters*, vol. 6, 140; TNA, SP14/90, fol. 230; *CSPD*, vol. 2, 448.
109 TNA, SP14/90 fol. 225, emphasis mine. James left London on 15 March, he arrived in Scotland on 13 May, then left Scotland on 4 August and arrived back in London on 15 September: Nichols, *Progresses*, vol. 3, 300, 390, 436; TNA, SP14/90, fols 101, 199.
110 TNA, SP14/90, fol. 230.
111 TNA, SP14/90, fol. 230. Those directly named in the commission were George Abbott, Archbishop of Canterbury; Francis Bacon, Lord Keeper of the Great Seal; Thomas Howard, Earl of Suffolk and Lord Treasurer of England; Edward Somerset, Earl of Worcester and Lord Privy Seal; Charles Howard, Earl of Nottingham and Lord Admiral; Thomas Cecil, Earl of Exeter; William Viscount Wallingford; Edward, Baron Zouch and Warden of the Cinque Ports; Edward, Baron Wotton and Treasurer of the King's Household; John, Baron Stanhope; George Lord Carew, Receiver-General to the Queen; Ralph Winwood, Secretary of State; Sir

Fulke Greville, Under-Treasurer of the Exchequer; Sir Julius Caesar, Master of the Rolls.

112 As stressed previously, it must be remembered that this was a *perception* James personally promoted, and it did not prevent him from concurrently seeking armed resolutions to conflict. On this duality see Murdoch, 'James VI', 3–31; S. Murdoch and A. Grosjean, *Alexander Leslie and the Scottish Generals of the Thirty Years' War, 1618–1648* (London, 2014), 30–33, 39, 40–43.

113 See the Introduction and Chapter 1, with Chamberlain observing Jones beginning to build in June 1617; McManus, 'Memorialising Anna of Denmark's Court', 86–87. It is no coincidence that in that same year, 1617, Anna commissioned the authoritative hunting portrait from Van Somer, see Chapter 5.

114 TNA, SP14/91, fol. 55: 16 April 1617. Secretary Winwood was at Greenwich throughout April and May, from where he penned regularly correspondence to Secretary Lake: TNA, SP14/91, fol. 21; TNA, SP14/92, fols 110, 121, 142. For matters touching the queen's income see Spedding et al. (eds), *Life and Letters*, vol. 6, 164–165, 170, 195, 236.

115 *CSPV*, vol. 14, 495, no. 741: 27 April 1617; TNA, SP14/92, fol. 83: 9 May 1617 (George Gerrard to Carleton).

116 McClure (ed.), *Chamberlain*, vol. 2, 76, no. 266: 24 May 1617.

117 TNA, PC2/29, fols 7, 9, 27, 37; TNA, SP15/41, fol. 15. See, by comparison, the meeting of 1 June 1617 having taken place at 'Greenewich': TNA, PC2/29, fol. 51.

118 TNA, SP14/12, fols 19r–v; Chapter 2 above.

119 McManus, *Renaissance Stage*, 180.

120 McManus, 'Memorialising Anna of Denmark's Court', 84–85.

121 McManus, 'Memorialising Anna of Denmark's Court', 90.

122 TNA, SP14/89, fol. 141 (14 December 1616).

123 McClure (ed.), *Chamberlain*, vol. 2, 45, no. 255: 21 December 1616.

124 Payne, 'Aristocratic Women', 59.

125 *CSPV*, vol. 12, 472, no. 732: 5 January 1613.

126 *CSPV*, vol. 14, no. 814: 29 June 1617. Emphasis mine.

127 NLS, Adv. MS. 31.1.3, fol. 119r (10 May 1615).

128 NLS, Adv. MS. 33.1.14, fol. 3v; NLS, Adv. MS. 31.1.3, 119r; TNA, SC6/JASI/1650; TNA, SC6/JASI/1655. Equally, the birds may have been intended for consumption. On the Greenwich aviary see Chapter 2.

129 As well as Mayerne and La Mire, this included the surgeon Cuthbert Toler, who received £30 for three terms ending at Lady Day 1619 (TNA, SC6/JASI/1655); Dr Sam Turner who was paid £220 on 25 July 1619, for 'his attendance on the late Queen' (*CSPD* (1619–1623), 66); and the French apothecary, Gideon de Lawne, who was later made a 'freeman' in consideration of his service to the queen (TNA, AO3/1187, fol. 38v; *CSPD* (1619–1623), 555). All of these medical men walked in the queen's funeral, together with another French apothecary, Edward Le Pluces – and a German apothecary, Johann Woolfe Rumler – as well as an additional ten physicians, three chirurgeons, and three of the physicians' wives, see TNA, SC6/JASI/1655; TNA, AO3/1187, fols 36r, 38r–v, 48r.

130 TNA, E351/544, fols 100r, 100v; McClure (ed.), *Chamberlain*, vol. 2, 196; *CSPD* (1619–1623), 1. The only person noted to be 'constantly with her [Anna]' was the Countess of Derby – presumably Elizabeth de Vere – who, as mentioned above, was a lady of the withdrawing chamber, niece to Robert Cecil, and accorded a privileged role in Mary's baptism. See also Barroll, *Anna of Denmark*, 51–53; Payne, 'Aristocratic Women', 35.

131 *CSPD* (1619–1623), 1, 7, 9, 17; ESRO, Glynde MS 320.

132 Griffey, *On Display*, 71–72.

133 N. Llewellyn, *The Art of Death: Visual Culture in the English Death Ritual c.1500–c.1800* (London, 1991), 7.

134 J. Maidment (ed.), *Miscellany of the Abbotsford Club: Account of the Last Moments of Anne of Denmark* (Edinburgh, 1837), 5.
135 Meldrum (ed.), *Royal Correspondence*, 196–197.
136 Meldrum (ed.), *Royal Correspondence*, 198.
137 RA, TKUA England AII 7. The letter is undated, but internal evidence indicates that it was written after Christmas 1618 and before Anna's death on 2 March 1618/19.
138 RA, TKUA England AII 7.
139 McClure (ed.), *Chamberlain*, 2: 225 (27 March 1619).
140 Riksarkivet (Stockholm), Oxenstierna Samlingen, E 702: 1 January 1620.
141 Murdoch, *House of Stuart*, 2.
142 Embalming allowed for the lengthy time required to stage a heraldic funeral, but evidence suggests that this was a process of rank rather than practicality, for it was observed even for those elites who were buried on the day of their death: C. Gittings, *Death, Burial and the Individual in Early Modern England* (London, 1988), 166; J. Woodward, *The Theatre of Death: The Ritual Management of Royal Funerals in Renaissance England, 1570–1625* (Woodbridge, 1997), 172–174; R. Houlbrooke, *Death, Religion, and the Family in England, 1480–1750* (Oxford, 1998), 340, 342.
143 Field, 'Funeral of the Stuart Queen', forthcoming.
144 RCA, MS I.4, fols 5r, 7v.
145 Field, 'Funeral of the Stuart Queen', forthcoming.
146 On 'non-verbal communication' as a mode of early modern diplomacy generally, see T. Sowerby, 'Early Modern Diplomatic History', *History Compass* 14 (2016), 441–456: esp. 445–447.
147 J. Doelman, *King James I* (Cambridge, 2000), 73–101; Patterson, *James VI and I*, 294–297; Murdoch, *House of Stuart*, 30–36, 38–42; Grosjean, *Unofficial Alliance*, 37–44.
148 The literature on the Thirty Years' War is vast, and the following summarised account is based on T. Cogswell, *The Blessed Revolution: English Politics and the Coming of War, 1621–1624* (Cambridge, 1989), 12–20, 36–53; Murdoch, *House of Stuart*, 44–47; Redworth, *Prince and the Infanta*, 16–26. See also *CSPV*, vol. 15, nos. 594, 614, 793: 20 and 30 November 1618.
149 Murdoch, *House of Stuart*, 45.
150 James also pursued military intervention and by the time Prince Charles and the Duke of Buckingham left for Spain, he had dispatched 6,000 Britons to fight against the Habsburgs – in addition to the five regiments of English and Scots already stationed in the Anglo and Scots-Dutch brigades against Spain – and further supplementary forces were being considered: Murdoch and Grosjean, *Alexander Leslie*, 30–33, 39, 40–43.
151 Note that Stuart ambassadors in Denmark, Sweden, and The Hague were concurrently negotiating for large expeditionary forces to be sent into Europe: Murdoch, *House of Stuart*, 46–47, 49–53.
152 *CSPV*, vol. 15, no. 691: 10 January 1619. In April 1620, James formally authorised von Dohna to travel throughout the English counties to collect revenue for the Bohemian cause, which proved substantial: T. Cogswell, *Home Divisions: Aristocracy, the State and Provincial Conflict* (Manchester, 1998), 35–38.
153 Murdoch, *House of Stuart*, 46–47.
154 R. Kuin, 'Colours of Continuity: The Heraldic Funeral', in N. Ramsay (ed.), *Heralds and Heraldry in Shakespeare's England* (Donington, 2014), 166–189: 167; Houlbrooke, *Death, Religion, and the Family*, 261–262, 264.
155 Knowles, 'Spectacle of the Realm', 166. My thinking on the significance of the ritualised ceremonies associated with Anna's death has been greatly influenced by this chapter.
156 TNA, E403/2705, nos. 8, 18, 28, 37. Issued at Westminster on 12 June, 10 May, 10 June, and 28 July 1619 respectively.

157 TNA, AO3/1187, fol. 28r. The 'Paris' headdress, usually made from white linen, had been worn by women for mourning since at least 1561. There is a possibility that it was stylistically close to a French hood: 'Paris, n. †d' *OED Online*, Oxford University Press, www.oed.com/view/Entry/137915. Accessed 16 June 2018.
158 TNA, AO3/1187, fols 28r–30r.
159 TNA, AO3/1187, fol. 49r. This only refers to mourning apparel and does not include the fabric required for dressing royal residences, furniture, or funeral monuments.
160 Knowles, 'Spectacle of the Realm', 170.
161 TNA, AO1/2422/49.
162 RCA, MS I.4, fols 8r–14v; TNA, AO3/1187, fols 30r–49r.
163 McClure (ed.), *Chamberlain*, vol. 2, 237, no. 327 (to Carleton).
164 *CSPV*, vol. 12, nos. 727; 732, 775: 29 December 1612; 11 January 1613; 1 March 1613.
165 BL Harley MS 5176, fol. 239v.
166 As discussed in Chapter 4, Anna kept her own accounts with Heriot and used him regularly, but other jewellers who serviced the court – including Herrick, Spilman, Hardaret, Arnold Lulls, and Nicasius Russell, and the goldsmith Nicholas Howker, for example – were patronised by the queen for ambassadorial gifts that were then paid through the exchequer, and were also called upon for refashioning some of the Crown Jewels for the queen. For Anna's patronage of jewellers besides Heriot see Field, 'Anna of Denmark', 132–134, 161–163, 196–197; Devon, *Issues of the Exchequer*, 29, 48–49, 59; J. Hayward, 'The Arnold Lulls Book of Jewels and the Court Jewellers of Anne of Denmark', *Archaeologia* 108 (1986): 227–237.
167 TNA, AO3/1187, fols 39r–40r, 48r. See also, Knowles, 'Images of Royalty', 25.
168 McCullough lists the eighteen chaplains given as 'Chaplaines to the Queene', but additional chaplains are included under the heading of 'His Ma[jes]t[ie]s Chaplaines' with entries for 'Mr fforsith to the K & Q' and 'Dr White to the Queene', as well as a separate entry for Gabriel Price as 'Chaplaine to ye Q[ueen]': TNA, AO3/1187, fols 37v–38r, 47v; McCullough, *Sermons at Court*, 172, n. 13.
169 McCullough, *Sermons at Court*, 4, 173. Sidney had been Anna's Lord Chamberlain since her arrival in England: TNA, SC6/JASI/1646. On the Pembroke-Southampton faction, many of whom have been referred as the 'Essex group' or 'Sidney group' see Chapters 1 and 5; Barroll, 'Court of the First Stuart Queen', 200–205; Barroll, *Anna of Denmark*, 40–44, 51–53, 135–136; Lewalski, *Writing Women*, 23–25; Payne, 'Aristocratic Women', 35, 38–44; M. O'Connor, '"Silvesta was my instrument ordained?": Lucy Harington Russell, Third Countess of Bedford as Family Marriage Broker', *Sidney Journal* 34 (2016), 49–65: 49–51, 55–56.
170 McCullough, *Sermons at Court*, 171–172.
171 McCullough, *Sermons at Court*, 173.
172 S. Crooke, *Death Subdued, or, The Death of Death* (London, 1619): STC (2nd ed.) / 6065 (emphasis mine); V. Larminie, 'Crooke, Samuel (1575–1649)'. *ODNB* (Oxford, 2008).
173 Watanabe-O'Kelly, 'Afterword', 233, 238.
174 RCA, MS. I.4, fol. 5v.
175 TNA, AO3/1187, fols 12v–13v; 18v. For details of the heraldic constituents see Field, 'Funeral of the Stuart Queen', forthcoming.
176 TNA, AO3/1187, fol. 5v.
177 RCA, MS. I.4, fol. 7v, 13r.
178 TNA, AO3/1187, fol. 13v; RCA, MS I.4, fols 8r–11v.
179 RCA, MS. I.4, fol. 12v; TNA, AO3/1187, fols 6r, 10v, 16v, 20r–v; Kuin, 'Colours of Continuity', 168.
180 RCA, MS. I.4, fol. 13r. The remains of Queen Elizabeth were likewise surrounded by twelve bannerols during her funeral procession: TNA, SP14/1, fol. 105v.

181 Woodward, *Theatre of Death*, 166; McManus, *Renaissance Stage*, 202–203.
182 On Anna's use of, and identification with, her personal motto, see Chapters 3 and 5 above; Field, 'Late Portrait by Paul van Somer', 52; Field, 'Anna of Denmark and the Arts', 77–82.
183 For a succinct summation of domestic tensions surrounding the proposed Stuart–Habsburg match in the late 1610s and of the growing concerns over the Palatinate, see Cogswell, *Blessed Revolution*, 6–20.
184 More expectedly, Charles was the chief mourner at the funeral of King James in 1625: Gittings, *Death, Burial and the Individual*, 221.
185 For the wider argument see Field, 'Funeral of the Stuart Queen', forthcoming.
186 BL Harley MS 5176, fol. 238. On the practice of the Offering see Kuin, 'Colours of Continuity', 175–180. Two black cushions 'to offer uppon' and one black carpet 'for the offeringe' were fitted at Westminster Abbey: TNA, AO3/1187, fols 5r, 9v.
187 Watanabe-O'Kelly, 'Afterword', 238–240.

Conclusion

On 12 June 1625, England welcomed a new Stuart queen consort with the arrival of Henrietta Maria, the French Bourbon princess who had married King Charles by proxy at Notre Dame Cathedral a month earlier.[1] In her journey from France to England, Henrietta Maria transitioned from princess to queen consort as she entered a new kingdom and a new marital dynasty. Along with jointure properties, furnishings, and patterns of access and display, Henrietta Maria inherited a set of expectations, responsibilities, and obligations. This was a mantle determined by tradition and recently shaped by Anna of Denmark. Having died six years earlier, Anna remained firm in the collective memory, and her economic position, material possessions, and legal rights were well documented. In fact, even before her marriage to Charles, Henrietta Maria was framed and counselled by way of Anna of Denmark's legacy. Conceptualised as the 'true Mirror of her [Anna's] most gracious qualities', Henrietta Maria was to provide King Charles with 'a kinde of mother in a wife, so like Her, who may serve Him for his mothers picture, at all times to looke on, with a respective, loving, joyfull remembrance, to see his mother living in Her'.[2] Henrietta Maria had to negotiate and adapt Anna's example consortship and one event offers pointed insight into the significance of precedence and the dynamics of the royal relationship for consorts.

As discussed in Chapter 4, Anna never endured the expulsion of her natal retinue, which commonly befell early modern consorts. Moreover, she was allowed to make her own decisions about her household personnel throughout her life, wherein she chose to retain a mix of Danish, Scottish, and English attendants. This was a precedent that Henrietta Maria knew and wanted, but it was one that Charles eventually rejected as the French retinue drew criticism and complaint for their purportedly devious intriguing and unsettling political and religious influence.

On 7 August 1626, Andrea Rosso, the Venetian secretary to England observed that 'the quarrels between their Majesties do not cease, but even become more and more bitter. It seems that the queen herself spoke to the king and told him that she desired no more for the regulation of her household than his mother Queen Anne enjoyed.'[3] Unlike Anna's entourage, however, Henrietta Maria's French, Catholic contingent were considered an obstacle to her assimilation and marital concord, being blamed for several 'misdemeanours' and for 'ill craftie counsells'.[4] As a result, despite Henrietta Maria's wishes – and Stuart precedent – Charles determined 'to be master' and expelled the French entourage.[5] This was a move motivated by personal, political, and religious considerations: it showcased his resolve to control his wife and it dramatically proved to parliament, as Griffey argues, that the king was willing to act against the wishes of 'the French monarchy and Catholic cause'.[6] While precedent was respected as an essential legitimising force for early modern hereditary monarchies, this episode clearly demonstrates the overriding power of the individual marital relationship and the specific socio-political context.

This book has located Anna of Denmark within the unique courtly environs that she inhabited as queen consort of Stuart Scotland and England. Chiefly concerned with Anna's cultural interests and agency, it has conceptualised her activities within the established axioms of consortship, while being sensitive to the relationships, traditions, modes, and etiquettes that she managed, negotiated, appeased, and was often able to shape and exploit. Throughout it all, Anna is repeatedly evidenced as an Oldenburg princess who never lost sight of – or pride in – her genealogical lineage. This was a prime constituent of her desirability as a bride and an ongoing factor in her value as a consort. The lynchpin of Stuart–Oldenburg relations, Anna created and maintained a valuable passageway between the multiple kingdoms ruled by her husband and brother, through which dynastic amity was established and communication, people, customs, and objects were subsequently able to filter.

It was Anna's early experiences in Denmark-Norway, coupled with her enduring relationships with her siblings and with other members of her extensive familial network, that were typically the source of knowledge and motivation for her cultural endeavours. As she built affinity (and faction), strategically used amity, and celebrated her family and lineage, Anna translated fashions, modes, and traditions from the Baltic and Germanic states into the courtly realm of Stuart Scotland and England. She did this by governing patterns of access at her court, nurturing new and existing relationships (locally and internationally) directing building work on her palaces and in her gardens, choosing to dress her body in particular clothes and jewels, and seeking artisans from beyond the borders of the Stuart kingdoms. With her death in 1619, Anna's strong, clear iconographic independence was subsumed by James and bestowed on Charles.

More than an occasion of loss for Anna, it was a triumph of her political power as James was moved to publicly stage a post-death alliance between the Stuart and Oldenburg kingdoms: their dynastic heraldry was seen coalescing in the figure of Prince Charles and an official alliance sealed future unity between the two ruling houses.

Beyond restating the centrality of Anna's dynastic heritage to her consortship, a central aim of this book has been to reassess the character, structure, and complexities of her relationship with James. By utilising recent models of patronage, frameworks of gender, and the conceptualisation of political culture, the analyses herein have complicated the traditional approach to early modern royal relationships as uneven, yet complementary pairings.[7] Rather than hold a fixed position vis-à-vis her husband the king, Anna occupied different positions at different times as she variously modelled separation, collaboration, and submission. Such fluidity was facilitated by a distinct confluence of factors: Anna's ancestral value, her reproductive success that sustained the Stuart dynasty, the polycentric nature of the English court, her relationship with courtiers and faction, and James's style of kingship. These findings raise ongoing questions about the formative and enduring place of natal heritage for early modern women and whether this is specific to those of royal status, to individual consorts, or whether it filtered down to the aristocracy.

A socially delineated variance is certainly admissible in Anna's financial situation and privileged proximity to the king – with significant consequences for her sphere of agency – that was unlikely to have been shared by titled or landed women. Such discoveries suggest that scholars may have to rethink using broad categories of analysis, such as elite or noble, in the study of these two classes in Stuart England. In working through the determinative influence of dynasty, in-depth studies of Anna's three sisters would, for example, be of particular value in establishing whether it was local circumstances at the marital court that led her natal heritage to be of particular value and/or allowed it to gain overt expression or if it remained a cornerstone of agency for them all. Such avenues of research would also further our understanding of the part played by concomitant factors of network, amity, and clientelism, while broadening our grasp of the connections and exchanges that bridged the British, Scandinavian, and Germanic courts in the early Stuart period. By exploring the opportunities and restrictions that Anna negotiated, this book has cast further light on the subtleties and intersections that knitted the personal to the political, and it contributes to a growing engagement with early modern concepts and constructs of kingship and consortship. There is more to be uncovered about Anna – such as relationships with powerful men at court, calendrical rituals, and her engagement with buildings, gardens, and portraiture in Scotland – but it is hoped that this reassessment of her contribution, impact, and marriage dynamics, coupled with the new archival evidence presented herein, will provide impetus for future studies of the nature of consortship broadly and for ongoing contributions to the fundamental reframing of Anna of Denmark specifically.

Notes

1 On Henrietta Maria's marriage, wedding ceremony, and bridal journey see Hibbard, 'Translating Royalty'; Griffey, *On Display*, ch. 2; Britland, *Drama at the Courts*, 15–37, 48–52, 63–64.
2 As quoted in Griffey, *On Display*, 64.
3 *CSPV*, vol. 19, no. 685; Griffey, *On Display*, 64.
4 As quoted in E. Griffey, 'Express Yourself? Henrietta Maria and the Political Value of Emotional Display at the Stuart Court', *The Seventeenth Century* 35 (2019), 1–26: 6.
5 Quoted in Griffey, *On Display*, 64. See also Griffey, 'Express Yourself?', 6–9.
6 Griffey, *On Display*, 64.
7 Most recently outlined by Watanabe-O'Kelly, 'Afterword', 238.

Select bibliography

Archival Sources

Austria

Haus-, Hof- und Staatsarchiv: Vienna
Belgien, Repertorium P, Abteilung C: Faszikel 44–57.

Denmark

Statens Arkiver Rigsarkivet: Copenhagen
TKUA 63-2 to 63-4: Tyske Kancelli, udenrigske afdeling, Speciel del, England (1602–1714).
TKUA 75-1 and 75-2: Tyske Kancelli, udenrigske afdeling, Speciel del, Skotland (1487–1619).
Diverse akter vedr- afregning og kvittance: Danske Kancelli, B223B Rentekammeerafdelingen (1588–1660).

England

British Library: London

Add MS 12498:	Volume of the Collections made by Sir Julius Caesar, Judge of the High Court of Admiralty, and Master of the Rolls, temp. James I: 1603–1625.
Add MS 24705:	Calendar by Charles Devon of Writs of the Great and Privy Seals: 1605–1608, 1609, 1611, 1618.
Add MS 27404:	Accounts of Queen Anna of Denmark's Jointure: 1606; 1612.
Cotton MS Titus C VII:	Miscellaneous papers, temp. Elizabeth I (1558–1603) to James I (1603–1625).
Harley MS 5176:	The Creation of Henry Prince of Wales, 1610, and his Funeral, 1612: mostly in Camden's own hand, as also several things following are ... Funeral of Ann, Queen of J. I.

Lansdowne MS 164: A Volume in Folio, filled with Papers of Exchequer Business: 1558–1625.
RP 9392: Autograph accounts sheet of payment for work on Anna of Denmark's new garden at Greenwich: 1609–1610.

Cambridge University Library: Cambridge
MS Dd.I.26: An Inventory of the Wardrobe of the Queen Consort of James I: 1608–1611.

East Sussex Record Office: Brighton
The Glynde Place Archives (Early Trevor Family): Oatlands: The Standing Wardrobe
GLY MS 314–323: Detailed inventories of hangings, carpets, furniture and pictures at Oatlands Manor: 1608–1619.

Parliamentary Archives: London
Records of the House of Lords: Private Bill Office: Private Acts 1 James I
HL/PO/PB/1/1603/1J1n35: An Act of Confirmation of the Jointure of the most High and Mighty Princess Anne, Queen of England, Scotland, France and Ireland.

Royal College of Arms: London
MS. I.4: Funerals of Kings, Princes, etc.

Society of Antiquaries: London
MS 137: Inventory of Denmark House: November 1627.

The National Archives: London
Auditors of the Imprest and Commissioners of Audit: Declared Accounts
AO1/2022/1: Sir M. Darell, a Controller of the Household. Journey of the Queen, the Prince and the Lady Elizabeth, from Berwick to Windsor: 1603.
AO1/2422/49: Surveyors and Paymasters: H. Wickes: 1618–1619.
AO1/2485/344: Sir J. Trevor. Works and repairs at Oatlands Park: 1616–1618
AO1/2487/356: I. Jones, Surveyor at Greenwich and Oatlands: 1616–1618.

Auditors of the Imprest and Successors: Various Accounts
AO3/1187: Wardrobe: Royal Funerals and Coronations. Funeral of Anna of Denmark: 1619.

Chancery and Supreme Court of Judicature: Patent Rolls
C66/1610: Part 4: 1603–1604.
C66/1626: Part 20: 1603–1604.
C66/1631: Part 4: 1604–1605.
C66/1924: Part 27: 1611–1612.
C66/1990: Part 13: 1613–1614.

Exchequer: Pipe Office: Declared Accounts: Works and Buildings: Surveyors and Paymasters
E351/3239:   A. Kerwyn: 1603–1604.
E351/3240:   A. Kerwyn: 1604–1605.
E351/3241:   A. Kerwyn: 1605–1606.
E351/3242:   A. Kerwyn: 1606–1607.
E351/3243:   A. Kerwyn: 1604–1605.
E351/3244:   A. Kerwyn: 1609–1610.
E351/3245:   A. Kerwyn: 1610–1611.
E351/3246:   A. Kerwyn: 1611–1612.
E351/3247:   A. Kerwyn: 1612–1613.
E351/3248:   A. Kerwyn: 1613–1614.
E351/3249:   A. Kerwyn: 1614–1615.
E351/3250:   A. Kerwyn and H. Wickes: 1615–1616.
E351/3251:   H. Wickes: 1616–1617.
E351/3252:   H. Wickes: 1617–1618.
E351/3253:   H. Wickes: 1619–1620.

Exchequer: Pipe Office: Declared Accounts: Miscellaneous
E351/3389:   I. Jones, Surveyor at Greenwich and Oatlands: 1616–1618.
E351/3391:   H. Wickes, Paymaster. Building a banqueting-house at Whitehall, and a pier in Portland Island for stone: 1619–1622.

Exchequer: Pipe Office: Declared Accounts: Treasurers of the Chamber
E351/543:   Lord John Stanhope: 1596–1612.
E351/544:   Sir W. Uvedale: 1613–1627.

Exchequer of Receipt: Issue Rolls and Registers
E403/2705:   Privy Seal Rolls: 1619–1620.
E403/2724:   Order Books: 1604.
E403/2725:   Order Books: 1605.
E403/2726:   Order Books: 1606–1607.
E403/2727:   Order Books: 1607–1608.
E403/2728:   Order Books: 1608–1609.
E403/2729:   Order Books: 1609–1610.
E403/2730:   Order Books: 1610–1611.
E403/2731:   Order Books: 1611–1612.
E403/2732:   Order Books: 1612–1613.

Exchequer of Receipt: Jornalia Rolls, Tellers' Rolls, Certificate Books, Declaration Books and Accounts of Receipts and Issues
E405/451:   Tellers' Views of Accounts: 1606.

Exchequer of Receipt: Miscellaneous Rolls, Books, and Papers
E407/57/2:   Expenses of Princess Elizabeth: Lord Harrington's Account: 1613.

Records of the Lord Chamberlain and other officers of the Royal Household: Great Wardrobe
LC5/37: Copies of Warrants: 1593–1603.

Office of the Auditors of Land Revenue and Predecessors: Miscellaneous Books
LR2/121: Inventory of wardrobe of Queen Anna taken by Lord George Carew by her commission: April 1611.
LR2/122: Volume of accounts of George Heriot, Jeweller to Queen Anna, taken by Auditor Povey as ordered by warrant of Lord Chief Justice Coke, February 1617: 1605–1615.

Office of the Auditors of Land Revenue and Predecessors: Receivers' Accounts, Series 1
LR6/154/9: Queen Anna's Jointure: Declaration of account of Sir George Carew, Vice-Chamberlain and Receiver General: 1603–1605.

Office of the Auditors of Land Revenue and Predecessors: Receivers' Accounts, Series 2
LR7/137: Queen Anna's Jointure: Ministers' Accounts: 1603–1604; 1604–1605; 1605–1606; 1610–1611.

Lord Steward's Department: Miscellaneous Books
LS13/280: Household: original papers of Sir Julius Caesar: 1603–1625.

Records of the Privy Council: Registers
PC2/29: Records of James I: 1 April 1617–31 October 1618.

Special Collections: Ministers' and Receivers' Accounts: Divers Counties: Possessions of Queen Anna. Declaration of Receiver-General's Account
SC6/JASI/1646: 1604–1605.
SC6/JASI/1648: 1606–1607.
SC6/JASI/1650: 1614–1616.
SC6/JASI/1651: 1615–1616.
SC6/JASI/1653: 1616–1617.
SC6/JASI/1655: 1618–1620.

Secretaries of State: State Papers Domestic, James I
SP14/1: Warrant to Sir John Fortescue, Master of the Wardrobe… for the Service of the Queen in the Closet: 1603.
SP14/12: Copy of the King to the Council: 9 January 1605.
SP14/27: Draft of the Bill for Assurance of the house of Theobalds and divers manors and other lands to the Queen, for life, with reversion to the Crown, and for assurance of other manors and lands: 29 May 1607.
SP14/40: The Lord Treasurer to the Officers of Customs of the Port of London: Undated, 1608?
SP14/67: Letter of Jane Drummond to Earl of Salisbury: November 1611.

SP14/72:	Letter of John Finet to Dudley Carleton: February 1613.
SP14/75:	Statement of Grants of Offices and Lands made to Thomas Sheffield and Lord [Northampton?] in Greenwich: December? 1613.
SP14/75:	Earl of Northampton to Thomas Lake: 9 December 1613.
SP14/75:	Earl of Northampton to Thomas Lake: 11 December 1613.
SP14/86:	Analysis of the Queen's Revenue and Proposed Expenditure: March 1616.
SP14/86:	Account of the Queen's Receiver for the copyholds of Spalding and Gedney, &c.: March 1616.
SP14/86:	Plan devised by Sir Edward Coke for payment of the Queen's Debts: March? 1616.
SP14/90:	Edward Sherburn to Dudley Carleton: 8 February 1617; 17 March 1617.
SP14/90:	Projected Stages of His Majesty's Journey to, and return from, Scotland: March? 1617.
SP14/90:	Copy of Commission, to Continue till His Majesty's return out of Scotland: 21 March 1617.
SP14/91:	Lord Carew and Secretary Winwood to Secretary Lake: 5 April 1617.
SP14/91:	Secretary Winwood to Secretary Lake: 16 April 1617.
SP14/92:	John Chamberlain to Dudley Carleton: 4, 21 June 1617.
SP14/92:	Secretary Winwood to Secretary Lake: 18, 22, 27 May 1617.
SP14/91:	George Gerrard to Dudley Carleton: 9 May 1617.
SP14/141:	Confirmation to Earl of Northampton of the Office of Keeper of Greenwich Park, and the Herbage and Pannage of the Same: December 1613.

Secretaries of State: State Papers Domestic, Edward VI – James I: Addenda
SP15/41:	The Council to Sir Edward Conway and Sir William Bird: 4 May 1617.

Secretaries of State: State Papers Scotland Series I: Elizabeth I
SP52/48:	Robert Bowes to Lord Burghley: 28 January 1592.
SP52/50:	Occurents in Scotland: 7 April 1593.
SP52/67:	George Nicholson to Sir Robert Cecil: 7 April 1601.

Secretaries of State: State Papers Foreign: Denmark
SP75/4:	Account of Robert Anstruther of the Charges of Doctor Jonas Charisius, Ambassador of Denmark in England: August; September 1611.

Kent County Council: Kent
Sackville Family: Cranfield Collection
U269/1/OW15:	Building work at Greenwich Palace: 1617–1618.
U269/1/OW145:	King James to the Commissioners of the Treasury: 13 March 1618; 2 May 1619.

Scotland

National Library of Scotland: Edinburgh

Adv. MS. 31.1.3:	Volume from the collection (Adv.MSS.31.1.1–6) of the Rev. James Scott, minister of the East Church, Perth (1733–1818).
Adv. MS. 33.1.14:	Denmilne State Papers, vol. 32.
Adv. MS. 34.2.17:	Papers Concerning the Exchequer and Royal Rents, 1591.

National Records of Scotland: Edinburgh
Exchequer Accounts and Vouchers

E21/68:	Sir Robert Melville of Murdocairnie, Treasurer depute: 1590–1592.
E21/71:	Walter, Commendator of Blantyre, Treasurer: 1596–1597.
E21/74:	Alexander, Master of Elphinstone, Treasurer: 1600–1601.
E21/76:	Sir George Home of Greenlaw, Treasurer: 1601–1604.
E23/11:	Sir George Home, Treasurer, and Sir John Arnot, Treasurer-depute: 1601–1602.
E23/12:	Sir George Home, Treasurer, and Sir John Arnot, Treasurer-depute: 1604–1605.
E24/22:	Sir David Murray of Gospertie, Comptroller: 1600–1601.
E35/13:	The king's and queen's apparel furnished by Robert Jousie, Merchant, at the direction of Sir George Home, Master of the Wardrobe: 1590–1600.
E35/14:	Apparel furnished to the queen and her gentlewomen and servants: 1591–1596.

Papers of the Erskine Family, Earls of Mar and Kellie

GD124/10/82:	King James VI to Queen Anna: May 1603.

Personal and Executry Papers of George Heriot: Accounts and Receipts for Jewels

GD421/1/3/5:	Itemised account supplied to the Queen: May 1593.
GD421/1/3/6:	Itemised account supplied to the Queen: May 1593.
GD421/1/3/10:	Itemised account supplied to the Queen: 1596–1597.
GD421/1/3/12:	Itemised account supplied to the Queen: April–August 1598.
GD421/1/3/14:	Itemised account supplied to the Queen: April–July 1600.
GD421/1/3/16:	Itemised account supplied to the Queen: September 1600–January 1601.
GD421/1/3/20:	Itemised account supplied to the Queen: Aug. 1601–June 1602.
GD421/1/3/21:	Itemised account supplied to the Queen: November–December 1602.
GD421/1/3/28:	Itemised account supplied to the Queen: August 1604–July 1605.
GD421/1/3/43:	Itemised account supplied to the Queen: March 1612–March 1615.
GD421/1/3/45:	Itemised account supplied to the Queen: February 1612–November 1617.

State Papers Miscellanea
SP13/128: Letter from King Christian IV to King James VI: 10 October 1597.

Edinburgh City Archives: Edinburgh
SL234/1: Register of the Decreets, 1598–1602.

Sweden

Riksarkivet (National Archives): Stockholm
Oxenstiernska samlingen Axel Oxenstierna av Södermöre.
Oxenstierna Samlingen, E 702: 1 January 1620.

Primary Sources

Akrigg, G. P. V., ed. *Letters of King James VI and I*. Berkeley, 1984.
Alberti, Leon Battista. *On Painting*, edited and translated by Rocco Sinisgalli. Cambridge, 2011.
Birch, Thomas. *The Court and Times of James I*. 2 vols. London, 1849, reprint 1973.
Boyd, William, Henry Meikle, Annie Cameron, M. S. Giuseppi and J. D. Mackie, eds. *Calendar of the State Papers Relating to Scotland and Mary, Queen of Scots ... Preserved in the Public Record Office, the British Museum and Elsewhere in England*. 13 vols. Edinburgh, 1915–1969.
Bray, William, ed. *The Diary of John Evelyn*. 2 vols. London and New York, 1901.
Bulwer, John. *Chirologia: or the Natural Language of the Hand and Chironomia: or the Art of Manual Rhetoric* (1644), edited and introduced by James Cleary. Carbondale, 1974.
Calderwood, David. *The History of the Kirk of Scotland*, edited by Thomas Thomson. 7 vols. Edinburgh, 1842.
Castelvetro, Giacomo. *The Fruit, Herbs and Vegetables of Italy*, edited and translated by Gillian Riley. Totnes, 2012.
Cotgrave, Randle. *A Dictionarie of the French and English Tongues* (1611), facsimile edition. Menston, 1968.
Craig, James Thomson Gibson, ed. *Papers Relative to the Marriage of King James the Sixth of Scotland, with the Princess Anna of Denmark*. Edinburgh, 1828.
Crooke, Samuel. *Death Subdued, or, The Death of Death*. London, 1619.
Daniel, Samuel. *Hymen's Triumph* (1615), edited by John Pitcher. Oxford, 1994.
De Caus, Salomon. *Les Raisons des forces Mouvantes*. Frankfurt, 1615.
De Lafontaine, Henry Cart, ed. *The King's Musick: A Transcript of Records Relating to Music and Musicians, 1460–1700*. New York, 1973.
Devon, Frederick. *Issues of the Exchequer, Being Payments Made out of His Majesty's Revenues During the Reign of King James I*. London, 1836.
Edelen, George, ed. *The Description of England: The Classic Contemporary Account of Tudor Social Life*. Washington and New York, 1994.
Ellis, Henry, ed. *Original Letters Illustrative of English History*. 3 vols. London, 1969.
Giuseppi, M. S., ed. *Calendar of the Manuscripts of the Most Hon. the Marquis of Salisbury*, vol. 17. London, 1938.
Finet, John. *Finetti Philoxenis: som choice observations of Sr. John Finett knight, and master of the ceremonies to the two last Kings... etc*. London, 1656.

Gardiner, Samuel Rawson, ed. *Narrative of the Spanish Marriage Treaty*. London, 1869.

Lee, Maurice Jr., ed. *Dudley Carleton to John Chamberlain 1603–1624: Jacobean Letters*. New Brunswick, 1972.

Lodge, Edmund. *Illustrations of British History, Biography and Manners in the reigns of Henry VIII, Edward VI, Mary, Elizabeth, and James I … etc.*, 3 vols. London, 1791.

Lyte, H. C. Maxwell, ed. *Acts of the Privy Council of England*, vol. 33. London, 1921.

McClure, Norman Egbert, ed. *The Letters of John Chamberlain*. 2 vols, Philadelphia, 1939.

McNeill, George Powell, ed. *The Exchequer Rolls of Scotland: Rotuli Scaccarii Regum Scotorum*. 2 vols. Edinburgh, 1903–1908.

Macray, William Dunn. 'Second Report on the Royal Archives of Denmark, and Report on the Royal Library at Copenhagen'. In *The Forty-Sixth Annual Report of the Deputy Keeper of the Public Records*. London, 1885.

—. 'Third Report on the Royal Archives of Denmark, and Report on the Royal Library at Copenhagen'. In *The Forty-Seventh Annual Report of the Deputy Keeper of the Public Records*. London, 1886.

Maidment, James, ed. *Miscellany of the Abbotsford Club: Account of the Last Moments of Anne of Denmark*. Volume First. Edinburgh, 1837.

Masson, David, ed. *The Register of the Privy Council of Scotland*. 8 vols, Edinburgh, 1881–1894.

Meikle, Henry, ed. *The Works of William Fowler, Secretary to Queen Anne, Wife of James VI*. 3 vols. Edinburgh, 1914–1940.

Meldrum, Ronald M., ed. *The Royal Correspondence of King James I of England (and VI of Scotland) to his Royal Brother-in-Law, King Christian IV of Denmark, 1603–1625*. Hassocks, 1977.

Melville, Sir James of Halhill. *Memoirs of His Own Life, 1549–1603*. Edited by T. Thomson. Edinburgh, 1827.

Moysie, David. *Memoirs of the Affairs of Scotland, 1577–1603 from Early Manuscripts*. Edited by James Dennistoun. Edinburgh, 1830.

Nichols, J. *The Progresses, Processions and Magnificent Festivities of King James the First*. 4 vols. London, 1828.

Noble, Mark. *An Historical Genealogy of the Royal House of Stuarts, from the reign of K. Robert II, to that of K. James VI*. London, 1795.

Palgrave, Sir Francis. *Antient Kalendars and Inventories of the Treasury of the Exchequer*. 2 vols. London, 1836.

Paton, Henry M., ed. *Supplementary Report on the Manuscripts of Mar and Kellie preserved at Alloa house, Clackmannanshire*. London, 1930.

—, ed. *Accounts of the Masters of the Works for Building and Repairing Royal Palaces and Castles*. Edinburgh, 1957.

Pollard A. W. and G. R. Redgrave. *A Short-Title Catalogue of Books printed in England, Scotland & Ireland, and of English Books Printed Abroad, 1475–1640*. London, 1926.

Prayers appointed to be vsed in the church at morning and euening prayer by every minister, for the Queenes safe deliuerance set foorth and injoyned by authoritie (London, 1605; STC 16534 and reissued 1606; STC 16537).

Rimbault, Edward F., ed. *The Old Cheque-Book of Book of Remembrance of the Chapel Royal from 1561 to 1744*. New York, 1966.

Rushworth, John. *Historical Collections of Private Passages of State, Weighty Matters in Law, Remarkable Proceedings in Five Parliaments Beginning the Sixteenth Year of King James, Anno 1618 and Ending the Fifth Year of King Charles, Anno 1629*. London, 1659.

Rye, William Brenchley. *England as Seen by Foreigners in the Days of Elizabeth and James the First*. London, 1865.

Sawyer, Edward. *Memorials of Affairs of State in the Reigns of Q. Elizabeth and K. James I Collected (chiefly) from the Original Papers of the Right Honourable Sir Ralph Winwood, Kt. Sometime one of the Principal Secretaries of States*, 3 vols. London, 1725.

Shaw, William A. *Letters of Denization and Acts of Naturalization for Aliens in England and Ireland, 1603–1700*. Lymington, 1911–1932.

Spedding, James, Robert Leslie Ellis, and Douglas Denon Heath, eds. *The Life and Letters of Francis Bacon*. 6 vols. London, 1861–1874; electronic edition: Virginia, 1998.

Stamp, A. E., ed. *Acts of the Privy Council of England*, vol. 35. London, 1927.

Steen, Sara Jayne, ed. *The Letters of Lady Arbella Stuart*. New York, 1994.

Stow, John, George Buck, and Edmund Howes. *Annales, or Generall Chronicle of England, begun first by maister Iohn Stow, and after him continued and augmented with matters forreyne, and domestique, anncient and moderne, vnto the ende of this present yeere 1614*. London, 1615.

Temple, William. *The Works of Sir William Temple, Bart.* 4 vols. London, 1814.

Williams Jr, Franklin. B. *Index of Dedications and Commendatory Verses in English Books before 1641*. London, 1962.

Wood, Marguerite and R. K. Hannay, eds. *Extracts from the Records of the Burgh of Edinburgh, 1589–1603*. Edinburgh, 1927.

Secondary Source Literature

Aasand, Hardin. '"To Blanch an Ethiop and Revive a Corse": Queen Anne and *The Masque of Blackness*'. *Studies in English Literature* 32 (1992): 271–285.

Acheson, Katherine, ed. *The Diary of Anne Clifford, 1616–1619: A Critical Edition*. New York, 1995.

Ahlefeldt-Laurvig, Mette Maria. 'Barselskoner i Reformationstiden'. *Dragtjournalen* 11 (2017): 4–13.

Ahrenfelt, Pernille. 'Frederik II's Hof: Husholdning og centraladministration'. In *Svøbt i mår: Dansk Folkevisekultur 1550–1700*, edited by Flemming Lundgreen-Nielsen and Hanne Ruus, vol. 1, pp. 327–390. Copenhagen, 1999.

Algazi, Gadi, Valentin Groebner, and Bernhard Jussen, eds. *Negotiating the Gift: Pre-Modern Figurations of Exchange*. Göttingen, 2003.

Andersen, Michael, Birgitte Bøggild Johannsen, and Hugo Johannsen, eds. *Reframing the Danish Renaissance: Problems and Prospects in a European Perspective*. Copenhagen, 2011.

Andersson, Eva. 'Foreign Seductions: Sumptuary Laws, Consumption and National Identity in Early Modern Sweden'. In *Fashionable Encounters: Perspectives and Trends in Textile and Dress in the Early Modern Nordic World*, edited by Tove Engelhardt Mathiassen, Marie-Louise Nosch, Maj Ringgaard, Kirsten Toftegaard, and Mikkel Venborg Pedersen, pp. 15–31. Oxford, 2014.

Andrea, Bernadette. 'Black Skin, The Queen's Masques: Africanist Ambivalence and Feminine Author(ity) in the Masques of *Blackness* and *Beauty*'. *English Literary Renaissance* 29 (1999): 246–281.

Arnold, Janet. 'Sweet England's Jewels'. In *Princely Magnificence: Court Jewels of the Renaissance, 1500–1630*, edited by Ann Somers Cocks, pp. 31–40. London, 1981.

—. *Queen Elizabeth's Wardrobe Unlock'd*. Leeds, 1988.

—. *Patterns of Fashion 4: Cut and Construction of Linen Shirts, Smocks, Neckwear, Headwear, and Accessories for Men and Women c.1540–1660*. Conceived and illustrated by Janet Arnold; completed with additional material by Jenny Tiramani and Santina M. Levey. London, 2008.

Asch, Ronald. 'The Princely Court and Political Space in Early Modern Europe'. In *Political Space in Pre-Industrial Europe*, edited by Beat Kümin, pp. 43–60. Farnham, 2009.

Ashbee, Andrew, ed. *Records of English Court Music*. 9 vols. Vols 1–4 published Snodland, 1986–1991; vols 5–9 published Aldershot, 1991–1996.

—. 'Groomed for Service. Musicians in the Privy Chamber at the English Court, c.1495–1558'. *Early Music* 25 (1997): 185–197.

Ashley, Maurice. *House of Stuart: Its Rise and Fall*. London, 1980.

Baillie, Hugh Murray. 'Etiquette and the Planning of the State Apartments in Baroque Palaces'. *Archaeologia* 101 (1967): 169–199.

Barkan, Leonard. 'Diana and Actaeon: The Myth as Synthesis'. *English Literary Renaissance* 10 (1980): 317–359.

Barroll, Leeds. 'The Court of the First Stuart Queen'. In *The Mental World of the Jacobean Court*, edited by Linda Levy Peck, pp. 191–208. Cambridge, 1991.

—. 'Theatre as Text: The Case of Queen Anna and the Jacobean Court Masque'. *Elizabethan Theatre* 14 (1996): 175–193.

—. 'Inventing the Stuart Masque'. In *The Politics of the Stuart Court Masque*, edited by David Bevington and Peter Holbrook, pp. 121–143. Cambridge, 1998.

—. *Anna of Denmark, Queen of England: A Cultural Biography*. Philadelphia, 2001.

Bath, Michael. '"Rare Shewes and Singular Inventions": The Stirling Baptism of Prince Henry'. *Journal of the Northern Renaissance* 4 (2012): 1–16.

Bellany, Alastair. *The Politics of Court Scandal in Early Modern England: News Culture and the Overbury Affair, 1603–1660*. Cambridge, 2002.

Bencard, Mogens. 'Ebony and Silver Furniture at Frederiksborg Castle'. In *Reframing the Danish Renaissance: Problems and Prospects in a European Perspective*, edited by Michael Andersen, Birgitte Bøggild Johannsen, and Hugo Johannsen, pp. 325–334. Copenhagen, 2011.

Berger Jr., Harry. 'Fictions of the Pose: Facing the Gaze of Early Modern Portraiture'. *Representations* 46 (1994): 87–120.

Bergsagel, John. 'Anglo-Scandinavian Musical Relations before 1700'. In *Report of the Eleventh Congress, International Musicological Society*, edited by Henrik Glahn, Søren Sørensen, and Peter Ryom, vol. 1, pp. 263–271. Copenhagen, 1972.

—. 'Danish Musicians in England 1611–14: Newly Discovered Instrumental Music'. *Dansk Årbog for Musikforskning* 7 (1973–1976): 9–20.

Bindman, David. 'The Black Presence in British Art: Sixteenth and Seventeenth Centuries'. In *The Image of the Black in Western Art*, edited by David Bindman and Henry Louis Gates, 5 vols; vol. 3, part 1, pp. 235–270. Cambridge, MA, 2010.

Black, Virginia. 'Beddington – "the best Orangery in England"'. *Journal of Garden History* 3 (1983): 113–120.
Blakiston, Noel. 'Nicholas Hilliard: Some Unpublished Documents'. *Burlington Magazine for Connoiseurs* 89 (1947): 187–189.
Bold, John. *Greenwich: An Architectural History of the Royal Hospital for Seamen and the Queen's House*. London, 2000.
Bracken, Susan and Robert Hill. 'Sir Isaac Wake, Venice and Art Collecting in Early Stuart England: A New Document'. *Journal of the History of Collections* (2012): 183–198.
Braunmuller, A. R. 'Robert Carr, Earl of Somerset, as Collector and Patron'. In *The Mental World of the Jacobean Court*, edited by Linda Levy Peck, pp. 230–250. Cambridge, 1991.
Brayshay, Mark. 'Royal Post-Horse Routes in England and Wales: The Evolution of the Network in the Later-Sixteenth and Early-Seventeenth Century'. *Journal of Historical Geography* 17 (1991): 373–389.
—. 'Long-distance Royal Journeys: Anne of Denmark's Journey from Stirling to Windsor in 1603'. *The Journal of Transport History* 25 (2004): 1–21.
—. 'The Choreography of Journeys of Magnificence: Arranging the Post-Nuptial Progress of Frederick, the Elector Palatine, and Princess Elizabeth of England from London to Heidelberg in 1613'. *Journal of Early Modern History* 12 (2008): 383–408.
—. *Land Travel and Communications in Tudor and Stuart England*. Liverpool, 2014.
Brilliant, Richard. *Portraiture*. London, 1991.
Britland, Karen. *Drama at the Courts of Queen Henrietta Maria*. Cambridge, 2006.
Bromley, James. *Intimacy and Sexuality in the Age of Shakespeare*. Cambridge, 2012.
Browning, Barton. 'Dramatic Activities and the Advent of the English Players at the Court of Heinrich Julius von Braunschweig'. In *Opitz und seine Welt: Festschrift für George Schulz-Behrend*, edited by Barbara Becker-Cantarino and Jörg-Ulrich Fechner, pp. 125–139. Amsterdam, 1990.
Bucholz, R. O. 'Going to Court in 1700: A Visitor's Guide'. *The Court Historian* 5 (2000): 198–211.
Buck, Stephanie. 'Hans Holbein the Younger: Portraitist of the Renaissance'. In *Hans Holbein the Younger: Portraitist of the Renaissance*, edited by Ariane van Suchtelen and Quentin Buvelot, pp. 11–37. Zwolle, 2003.
Burke, Peter. 'State-Making, King-Making and Image-Making from Renaissance to Baroque: Scandinavia in a European Context', *Scandinavian Journal of History* 22 (1997): 1–8.
—. 'Translating Knowledge, Translating Cultures'. In *Kultureller Austausch in der Frühen Neuzeit*, edited by Michael North, pp. 69–77. Cologne, 2009.
Butler, Martin. *The Stuart Court Masque and Political Culture*. Cambridge and New York, 2008.
Calcagno, Rebecca. 'A Matter of Precedence: Britain, Germany, and the Palatine Match'. In *The Palatine Wedding of 1613: Protestant Alliance and Court Festival*, edited by Sara Smart and Mara Wade, pp. 243–266. Wiesbaden, 2013.
Campbell-Orr, Clarissa, ed. *Queenship in Britain, 1660–1837: Royal Patronage, Court Culture and Dynastic Politics*. Manchester, 2002.
—. 'Introduction: Court Studies, Gender and Women's History, 1660–1837'. In

> *Queenship in Britain, 1660–1837: Royal Patronage, Court Culture and Dynastic Politics*, edited by Clarissa Campbell-Orr, pp. 1–53. Manchester, 2002.

—. ed. *Queenship in Europe 1660–1815: The Role of the Consort*. Cambridge, 2004.

—. 'Introduction'. In *Queenship in Europe 1660–1815: The Role of the Consort*, edited by Clarissa Campbell-Orr, pp. 1–15. Cambridge, 2004.

Capp, Bernard. 'Separate Domains? Women and Authority in Early Modern England'. In *The Experience of Authority in Early Modern England*, edited by Paul Griffiths, Adam Fox, and Steve Hindle, pp. 117–145. Basingstoke and London, 1996.

—. *When Gossips Meet: Women, Family, and Neighbourhood in Early Modern England*. Oxford, 2003.

Chambers, Edmund Kerchever. *The Elizabethan Stage*. 4 vols. Oxford, 1923.

Chaney, Edward, ed. *The Evolution of English Collecting: Receptions of Italian Art in the Tudor and Stuart Periods*. New Haven and London, 2003.

—. 'The Italianate Evolution of English Collecting'. In *The Evolution of English Collecting: Receptions of Italian Art in the Tudor and Stuart Periods*, edited by Edward Chaney, pp. 1–124. New Haven and London, 2003.

—. and Peter Mack, eds. *England and the Continental Renaissance*. Woodbridge, 1990.

Chettle, George H. *The Queen's House, Greenwich*. London, 1937.

Chew, Elizabeth. 'The Countess of Arundel and Tart Hall'. In *The Evolution of English Collecting: Receptions of Italian Art in the Tudor and Stuart Periods*, edited by Edward Chaney, pp. 285–315. New Haven and London, 2003.

—. '"Your Honor's Desyres": Lady Anne Clifford and the World of Goods'. In *Lady Anne Clifford: Culture, Patronage and Gender in 17th-Century Britain*, edited by Karen Hearn and Lynn Hulse, pp. 25–42. Leeds, 2009.

Christensen, Charles. *Kronborg: Frederik II's renæssanceslot og dets senere skæbne*. Copenhagen, 1950.

Christianson, John R. 'The Spaces and Rituals of the Royal Hunt: King Frederik II of Denmark (1559–1588)'. In *Beyond Scylla and Charybdis: European Courts and Court Residences outside Habsburg and Valois/Bourbon Territories 1500–1700*, edited by Birgitte Bøggild Johannsen and Konrad Ottenheym, pp. 159–171. Odense, 2015.

—. 'Terrestrial and Celestial Spaces of the Danish Court, 1550–1650'. *The Court Historian* 12 (2007): 129–153.

—. 'The Hunt of King Frederik II of Denmark: Structures and Rituals'. *The Court Historian* 18 (2013): 165–187.

Clark, Leah R. 'Transient Possessions: Circulation, Replication, and Transmission of Gems and Jewels in Quattrocento Italy'. *Journal of Early Modern History* 15 (2011): 185–221.

—. *Collecting Art in the Italian Renaissance Court: Objects and Exchanges*. Cambridge, 2018.

Cogswell, Thomas. *The Blessed Revolution: English Politics and the Coming of War, 1621–1624*. Cambridge, 1989.

—. *Home Divisions: Aristocracy, the State and Provincial Conflict*. Manchester, 1998.

Colvin, Howard M. *The History of the King's Works*. Vol. IV (1485–1660). London, 1982.

Coombs, Katherine. *The Portrait Miniature in England*. London, 1998.
Coster, Will. 'The Churching of Women, 1500–1700'. In *Women in the Church*, edited by W. J. Sheils and Diana Wood, pp. 377–387. Oxford, 1990.
Cramsie, John. *Kingship and Crown Finance under James VI and I, 1603–1625*. London, 2002.
Crawford, Katherine. *European Sexualities, 1400–1800*. Cambridge, 2007.
—. *The Sexual Culture of the French Renaissance*. New York, 2010.
Crawford, Patricia. 'The Construction and Experience of Maternity in Seventeenth-Century England'. In *Women as Mothers in Pre-Industrial England: Essays in Memory of Dorothy McLaren*, edited by Valerie Fildes, pp. 3–38. London, 1990.
—. *Women and Religion in England 1500–1720*. London and New York, 1993.
Cressy, David. *Birth, Marriage, & Death: Ritual, Religion, and the Life-Cycle in Tudor and Stuart England*. Oxford, 1997.
Croft, Pauline. 'Robert Cecil and the Early Jacobean Court'. In *The Mental World of the Jacobean Court*, edited by Linda Levy Peck, pp. 134–148. Cambridge, 1991.
—. 'Can a Bureaucrat Be a Favourite? Robert Cecil and the Strategies of Power'. In *The World of the Favourite*, edited by J. H. Elliott and L. W. B. Brockliss, pp. 81–95. New Haven and London, 1999.
—, ed. *Patronage, Culture and Power: The Early Cecils*. New Haven and London, 2002.
Crum, Roger J. 'Controlling Women or Women Controlled? Suggestions for Gender Roles and Visual Culture in the Italian Renaissance Palace'. In *Beyond Isabella: Secular Women Patrons of Art in Renaissance Italy*, edited by Sheryl E. Reiss and David G. Wilkins, pp. 37–51. Kirksville, 2001.
Cuddy, Neil. 'The Revival of the Entourage: The Bedchamber of James I, 1603–1625'. In *The English Court: From the Wars of the Roses to the Civil War*, edited by David Starkey, pp. 173–225. London, 1987.
—. 'Reinventing a Monarchy: The Changing Structure and Political Function of the Stuart Court, 1603–88'. In *The Stuart Courts*, edited by Eveline Cruickshanks, pp. 59–86. Stroud, 2000.
Curran, Kevin. 'James I and Fictional Authority at the Palatine Wedding Celebrations'. *Renaissance Studies* 20 (2006), pp. 51–67.
—. *Marriage, Performance, and Politics at the Jacobean Court*. Farnham, 2009.
Davies, H. Neville. 'The Limitations of Festival: Christian IV's State Visit to England in 1606'. In *Italian Renaissance Festivals and their European Influence*, edited by J. R. Mulryne and Margaret Shewring, pp. 311–335. Lewiston, 1992.
Davis, Natalie Zemon. *The Gift in Sixteenth-Century France*. Oxford, 2000.
Daybell, James, ed. *Women and Politics in Early Modern England, 1450–1700*. Aldershot, 2004.
—. 'Introduction: Rethinking Women and Politics in Early Modern England'. In *Women and Politics in Early Modern England, 1450–1700*, edited by James Daybell, pp. 1–21. Aldershot, 2004.
Dent, John. *The Quest for Nonsuch*. 2nd edn. Sutton, 1981.
De Jonge, Krista. 'Antiquity Assimilated: Court Architecture 1530–1560'. In *Unity and Discontinuity. Architectural Relations between the Southern and Northern Low Countries 1530–1700*, edited by Krista De Jonge and Konrad Ottenheym, pp. 55–78. Turnhout, 2007.
—. 'A Netherlandish Model? Reframing the Danish Royal Residences in a European Perspective'. In *Reframing the Danish Renaissance: Problems and Prospects*

in a European Perspective, edited by Michael Andersen, Birgitte Bøggild Johannsen, and Hugo Johannsen, pp. 219–233. Copenhagen, 2011.

—and Konrad Ottenheym, eds. *Unity and Discontinuity: Architectural Relations between the Southern and Northern Low Countries 1530–1700*. Turnhout, 2007.

Dillon, Janette. *The Language of Space in Court Performance, 1400–1625*. Cambridge, 2010.

Doelman, James. *King James I and the Religious Culture of England*. Cambridge, 2000.

Dunbar, John. *Scottish Royal Palaces: The Architecture of the Royal Residences during the Late Medieval and Early Renaissance Periods*. East Linton, 1999.

Edmond, Mary. 'New Light on Jacobean Painters'. *Burlington Magazine* 118 (1976): 74–81+83.

—. *Hilliard and Oliver: The Lives and Works of Two Great Miniaturists*. London, 1983.

Édouard, Sylvène. 'The Hispanicization of Elisabeth de Valois at the Court of Philip II'. In *Spanish Fashion at the Courts of Early Modern Europe*, edited by José Luis Colomer and Amalia Descalzo, vol. 2, pp. 237–266. Madrid, 2014.

Ekroll, Øystein. 'State Church and Church State: Churches and their Interiors in Post-Reformation Norway, 1537–1705'. In *Lutheran Churches in Early Modern Europe*, edited Andrew Spicer, pp. 277–309. Farnham, 2012.

Erickson, Amy. *Women and Property in Early Modern England*. London, 1993.

Fantoni, Marcello, George Gorse, and Malcolm Smuts, eds. *The Politics of Space: European Courts c.1500–1700*. Rome, 2009.

ffolliott, Sheila. 'Casting a Rival into the Shade: Catherine De' Medici and Diane De Poitiers'. *Art Journal* 48 (1989): 138–143.

Field, Jemma. 'Anna of Denmark: A Late Portrait by Paul van Somer'. *The British Art Journal* 18 (2017): 50–55.

—. 'The Wardrobe Goods of Anna of Denmark, Queen Consort of Scotland and England (1574–1619)'. *Costume* 51 (2017): 3–27.

—. 'Anna of Denmark and the Politics of Religious Identity in Jacobean Scotland and England, c.1592–1619'. *Northern Studies* 50 (2019): 87–113.

—. 'Dressing a Queen: The Wardrobe of Anna of Denmark at the Scottish Court of King James VI, 1590–1603'. *The Court Historian*, 24 (2019): 152–167.

—. 'A "Cipher of A and C set on the one Syde with diamonds": Anna of Denmark's Jewellery and the Politics of Dynastic Display'. In *Sartorial Politics: Fashioning Women at the Early Modern Court (1450–1700)*, edited by Erin Griffey, pp. 139–159. Amsterdam, 2019.

—. '"Orderinge Things Accordinge to his Majesties Comaundment": The Funeral of the Stuart Queen Consort Anna of Denmark'. *Women's History Review*, forthcoming 2020.

Filipczak, Zirka Zaremba. 'Portraits of Women Who "Do Not Keep Strictly to the Masculine and Feminine Genders, as They Call Them"'. In *Pokerfaced: Flemish and Dutch Baroque Faces Unveiled*, edited by Katlijne Van der Stighelen, Hannelore Magnus, and Bert Watteeuw, pp. 229–249. Turnhout, 2010.

Finsten, Jill. *Isaac Oliver: Art at the Courts of Elizabeth I and James I*, 2 vols. New York, 1981.

Fisher, N. R. R. 'The Queenes Courte in her Councell Chamber at Westminster'. *English Historical Review* 108 (1993): 314–337.

Franke, Birgit. 'Salomon de Caus (1576–1626) and the Grotto Phenomenon in Court

Art', pp. 202–204, in 'Building Policy and Urbanisation during the Reign of the Archdukes: The Court and its Architects', coordinated by Krista de Jonge. In *Albert and Isabella: Essays*, edited by Werner Thomas and Luc Duerloo, pp. 191–219. Turnhout, 1998.

Gapper, Clare. 'Appendix: Fragments of Decorative Plasterwork'. In *Somerset House: The Palace of England's Queens, 1551–1692*, by Simon Thurley, pp. 77–81. London, 2009.

Girouard, Mark. 'The Smythson Collection of the Royal Institute of British Architects'. *Architectural History* 5 (1962): 21–184.

—. *Life in the English Country House: A Social and Architectural History*. New Haven, 1978.

—. *Elizabethan Architecture: Its Rise and Fall, 1540–1640*. New Haven and London, 2009.

Gittings, Clare. *Death, Burial and the Individual in Early Modern England*. London, 1988.

Gömöri, George. '"A Memorable Wedding": The Literary Reception of the wedding of the Princess Elizabeth and Frederick of Pfalz'. *Journal of European Studies* 34 (2004): 214–224.

Goodare, Julian. 'Scottish Politics in the Reign of James VI'. In *The Reign of James VI*, edited by Julian Goodare and Michael Lynch, pp. 32–54. East Linton, 2000.

—. 'James VI's English Subsidy'. In *The Reign of James VI*, edited by Julian Goodare and Michael Lynch, pp. 110–125. East Linton, 2000.

— and Michael Lynch. 'James VI: Universal King?' In *The Reign of James VI*, edited by Julian Goodare and Michael Lynch, pp. 1–31. East Linton, 2000.

Gordenker, Emilie E. S. 'Isabel Clara Eugenia at the Court of Brussels'. In *Spanish Fashion at the Courts of Early Modern Europe*, edited by José Luis Colomer and Amalia Descalzo, vol. 2, pp. 117–135. Madrid, 2014.

Gowing, Laura. *Gender Relations in Early Modern England*. Harlow and New York, 2012.

Graves, Peter. 'The Danish Account'. In *Scotland's Last Royal Wedding: The Marriage of James VI and Anne of Denmark*, by David Stevenson, pp. 79–122. Edinburgh, 1997.

Griffey, Erin. 'A Brief Description: The Language of Stuart Inventories'. *Studi di Memofonte* 12 (2014), online publication.

—, ed. *Henrietta Maria: Piety, Politics and Patronage*. Aldershot, 2008.

—. 'Introduction'. In *Henrietta Maria: Piety, Politics and Patronage*, edited by Erin Griffey, pp. 1–11. Aldershot, 2008.

—. *On Display: Henrietta Maria and the Materials of Magnificence*. New Haven, 2015.

—. 'Express Yourself? Henrietta Maria and the Political Value of Emotional Display at the Stuart Court'. *The Seventeenth Century* 35 (2019): 1–26.

—, ed. *Sartorial Politics: Fashioning Women at the Early Modern Court (1450–1700)*. Amsterdam, 2019.

Griffiths, Antony. *The Print in Stuart Britain, 1603–1689*. London, 1998.

Grinder-Hansen, Poul. *Frederik 2: Danmarks Renæssancekonge*. Copenhagen, 2013.

—. '"Im Grünen": The Types of Informal Space and their use in Private, Political and Diplomatic Activities of Frederik II, King of Denmark'. In *Beyond Scylla and Charybdis: European Courts and Court Residences outside Habsburg and*

Valois/Bourbon Territories 1500–1700, edited by Birgitte Bøggild Johannsen and Konrad Ottenheym, pp. 171–183. Odense, 2015.

Groebner, Valentin. *Liquid Assets, Dangerous Gifts: Presents and Politics at the End of the Middle Ages*, translated by Pamela E. Selwyn. Philadelphia, 2002.

Grosjean, Alexia. *An Unofficial Alliance: Scotland and Sweden, 1569–1654*. Leiden and Boston, 2003.

Grosz, Elizabeth. *Volatile Bodies: Toward a Corporeal Feminism*. Bloomington, 1994.

Gunther, R. T. *Early British Botanists and their Gardens*. Oxford, 1922.

Hackenbroch, Yvonne. *Renaissance Jewellery*. London, 1979.

—. *Enseignes*. Florence, 1996.

Hamling, Tara. *Decorating the 'Godly' Household: Religious Art in Post-Reformation Britain*. New Haven and London, 2010.

Harris, Barbara. 'Women and Politics in Early Tudor England'. *The Historical Journal* 33 (1990): 259–281.

—. 'Aristocratic Women and the State in Early Tudor England'. In *State, Sovereigns, and Society in Early Modern England: Essays in Honour of A. J. Slavin*, edited by Charles Carlton, Robert L. Woods, Mary L. Robertson, and Joseph S. Block, pp. 3–24. Stroud, 1998.

—. 'The View from my Lady's Chamber: New Perspectives on the Early Tudor Monarchy', *Huntington Library Quarterly* 60 (1999): 215–247.

—. *English Aristocratic Women, 1450–1550: Marriage and Family, Property and Careers*. Oxford, 2002.

Harris, John. 'Disneyland in Greenwich: The Restoration of the Queen's House'. *Apollo* 122 (1990): 256–260.

—. 'Inigo Jones and the Courtier Style'. *Architectural Review* 154 (1973): 17–24.

— and Gordon Higgott. *Inigo Jones: Complete Architectural Drawings*. London and New York, 1989.

—, Stephen Orgel, and Roy Strong. *The King's Arcadia: Inigo Jones and the Stuart Court*. London, 1973.

Hauge, Peter. 'John Dowland's Employment at the Royal Danish Court: Musician, Agent – and Spy?'. In *Double Agents: Cultural and Political Brokerage in Early Modern Europe*, edited by Marika Keblusek and Badeloch Noldus, pp. 193–212. Leiden, 2011.

Hawkins, E., A. W. Franks, and H. A. Grueber, eds. *Medallic Illustrations of the History of Great Britain and Ireland*. 4 vols. London, 1885.

Hayward, John. 'The Arnold Lulls Book of Jewels and the Court Jewellers of Anne of Denmark'. *Archaeologia* 108 (1986): 227–237.

Hayward, Maria. *Dress at the Court of King Henry VIII*. Leeds, 2007.

—. 'Spanish Princess or Queen of England? The Image, Identity and Influence of Catherine of Aragon at the Courts of Henry VII and Henry VIII'. In *Spanish Fashion at the Courts of Early Modern Europe*, edited by José Luis Colomer and Amalia Descalzo, 2 vols, vol. 2, pp. 11–37. Madrid, 2014.

—. '"The best of Queens, the most obedient wife": Fashioning a Place for Catherine of Braganza as Consort to Charles II'. In *Sartorial Politics: Fashioning Women at the Early Modern Court (1450–1700)*, edited by Erin Griffey, pp. 227–252. Amsterdam, 2019.

Heal, Felicity. *Hospitality in Early Modern England*. Oxford, 1990.

—. 'Royal Gifts and Gift-Exchange in Sixteenth-Century Anglo-Scottish Politics'. In *Kings, Lords and Men in Scotland and Britain, 1300–1625: Essays in Honour of Jenny Wormald*, edited by Steve Boardman and Julian Goodare, pp. 283–300. Edinburgh, 2014.

—. *The Power of Gifts: Gift-Exchange in Early Modern England*. Oxford, 2014.

Hearn, Karen, ed. *Dynasties: Painting in Tudor and Jacobean England 1530–1630*. London, 1995.

—. 'A Question of Judgement: Lucy Harington, Countess of Bedford, as Art Patron and Collector'. In *The Evolution of English Collecting: Receptions of Italian Art in the Tudor and Stuart Periods*, edited by Edward Chaney, pp. 221–239. New Haven and London, 2003.

Heaton, Gabriel. *Writing and Reading Royal Entertainments: From George Gascoigne to Ben Jonson*. Oxford, 2010.

Heiberg, Steffan, ed. *Christian IV and Europe: The 19th Art Exhibition of the Council of Europe: Denmark*. Herning, 1988.

Hein, Jørgen. *The Treasure Collection at Rosenborg Castle: The Inventories of 1696 and 1718. Royal Heritage and Collecting in Denmark-Norway 1500–1900*, 3 vols. Copenhagen, 2009.

Henderson, Paula. 'The Architecture of the Tudor Garden'. *Garden History* 27 (1999): 54–72.

—. 'A Shared Passion: The Cecils and their Gardens'. In *Patronage, Culture and Power: The Early Cecils*, edited by Pauline Croft, pp. 99–120. New Haven and London, 2002.

—. *The Tudor House and Garden: Architecture and Landscape in the Sixteenth and Early Seventeenth Centuries*. New Haven and London, 2005.

Hennings, Jan. 'Diplomacy, Culture and Space: The Muscovite Court'. In *Beyond Scylla and Charybdis: European Courts and Court Residences outside Habsburg and Valois/Bourbon Territories 1500–1700*, edited by Birgitte Bøggild Johannsen and Konrad Ottenheym, pp. 57–65. Odense, 2015.

Hibbard, Caroline. 'The Role of a Queen Consort: The Household and Court of Henrietta Maria, 1625–1642'. In *Princes, Patronage, and the Nobility*, edited by Ronald Asch and Adolf Birke, pp. 393–414. Oxford, 1991.

—. '"By Our Direction and For Our Use": The Queen's Patronage of Artists and Artisans seen through her Household Accounts'. In *Henrietta Maria: Piety, Politics and Patronage*, edited by Erin Griffey, pp. 115–139. Aldershot, 2008.

Higgott, Gordon. 'The Design and Setting of Inigo Jones's Queen's House 1616–40'. *The Court Historian* 11 (2006): 135–149.

Hind, Arthur Mayger. *Engraving in England in the Sixteenth and Seventeenth Centuries: The Reign of James I*. Cambridge, 1955.

Holman, Peter. *Four and Twenty Fiddlers: The Violin at the English Court, 1540–1690*. Oxford, 1993.

Houlbrooke, Ralph. *Death, Religion, and the Family in England, 1480–1750*. Oxford, 1998.

Howard, Deborah. *Scottish Architecture: Reformation to Restoration, 1560–1660*. Edinburgh, 1995.

Howarth, David. *Lord Arundel and his Circle*. New Haven, 1985.

—. 'A Question of Attribution: Art Agents and the Shaping of the Arundel Collection'. In *Your Humble Servant: Agents in Early Modern Europe*, edited by Hans Cools, Marika Keblusek, and Badeloch Noldus, pp. 17–28. Hilversum, 2006.

Hufton, Olwen. 'Reflections of the Role of Women in the Early Modern Court'. *The Court Historian* 5 (2000): 1–13.

Hulse, Lynn. 'The Musical Patronage of Robert Cecil, First Earl of Salisbury (1563–1612)'. *Journal of the Royal Musical Association* 116 (1991): 24–40.

—. 'Review of "Records of English Court Music, vol. 4, by Andrew Ashbee"'. *Music & Letters* 73 (1992): 101–103.

—. '"Musique which pleaseth myne eare"; Robert Cecil's Musical Patronage'. In *Patronage, Culture and Power: The Early Cecils*, edited by Pauline Croft, pp. 139–158. New Haven and London, 2002.

Hyman, Wendy Beth, ed. *The Automaton in English Renaissance Literature*. Farnham, 2011.

Imtiaz, Habib. *Black Lives in the English Archives, 1500–1677: Imprints of the Invisible*. Burlington, 2008.

Jansson, Maija. 'Measured Reciprocity: English Ambassadorial Gift Exchange in the 17th and 18th Centuries'. *Journal of Early Modern History* 9 (2005): 348–370.

Jervis, Simon. '"Shadows, Not Substantial Things". Furniture in the Commonwealth Inventories'. In *The Late King's Goods: Collections, Possessions and Patronage of Charles I in Light of the Commonwealth Sale Inventories*, edited by Arthur MacGregor, pp. 277–306. London and Oxford, 1989.

Jørgensen, Sebastian Olden. 'Court Culture during the Reign of Christian IV'. In *Pieter Isaacsz: Court Painter, Dealer and Spy*, edited by Badeloch Noldus and Juliette Roding, pp. 15–31. Turnhout, 2007.

Kaufmann, Thomas DaCosta. *Court, Cloister, and City: The Art and Culture of Central Europe 1450–1800*. Chicago, 1995.

Keay, Anna. *The Magnificent Monarch: Charles II and the Ceremonies of Power*. London and New York, 2008.

Keblusek, Marika. 'Introduction: Double Agents in Early Modern Europe'. In *Double Agents: Cultural and Political Brokerage in Early Modern Europe*, edited by Marika Keblusek and Badeloch Noldus, pp. 1–9. Leiden, 2011.

Kettering, Sharon. *Patrons, Brokers and Clients in Seventeenth-Century France*. New York and Oxford, 1986.

—. *Patronage in Sixteenth and Seventeenth Century France*. Aldershot, 2002.

King, Donald. 'Textile Furnishings'. In *The Late King's Goods: Collections, Possessions and Patronage of Charles I in Light of the Commonwealth Sale Inventories*, edited by Arthur MacGregor, pp. 307–321. London and Oxford, 1989.

Knight, Caroline. 'The Cecils at Wimbledon'. In *Patronage, Culture and Power: The Early Cecils*, edited by Pauline Croft, pp. 47–66. New Haven and London, 2002.

Knowles, James. 'The Spectacle of the Realm: Civic Consciousness, Rhetoric and Ritual in Early Modern London'. In *Theatre and Government under the Early Stuarts*, edited by J. R. Mulryne and Margaret Shewring, pp. 157–189. Cambridge, 1993.

—. '"To Enlight the Darksome Night, Pale Cinthia Doth Arise": Anna of Denmark, Elizabeth I and the Images of Royalty'. In *Women and Culture at the Courts of the Stuart Queens*, edited by Clare McManus, pp. 21–48. Basingstoke, 2003.

—. *Politics and Political Culture in the Court Masque*. London, 2015.

Kragelund, Patrick. *A Stage for the King: The Travels of Christian IV and the Building of Frederiksborg Castle*. Copenhagen, 2019.

Kuin, Roger. 'Colours of Continuity: The Heraldic Funeral'. In *Heralds and Heraldry in Shakespeare's England*, edited by Nigel Ramsay, pp. 166–189. Donington, 2014.

Laitinen, Riitta. 'Church Furnishings and Rituals in a Swedish Provincial Cathedral from 1527 to c.1660'. In *Lutheran Churches in Early Modern Europe*, edited by Andrew Spicer, pp. 311–331. Farnham, 2012.

Larminie, Vivienne. 'Crooke, Samuel (1575–1649)'. *Oxford Dictionary of National Biography*. Oxford, 2008.

Larsson, Lars Olof. 'Rhetoric and Authenticity in the Portraits of King Christian IV of Denmark'. In *Pomp, Power and Politics: Essays on German and Scandinavian Court Culture and their Contexts*, edited by Mara Wade (*Daphnis* vol. 32, 2003), pp. 13–40. Amsterdam, 2004.

Lawson, Jane, ed. *The Elizabethan New Year's Gift Exchanges, 1559–1603*. Oxford, 2013.

Lazzaro, Claudia. 'The Villa Lante at Bagnaia: An Allegory of Art and Nature'. *Art Bulletin* 59 (1977): 553–560.

—. *The Italian Renaissance Garden*. New Haven and London, 1990.

Lee, Maurice. *Great Britain's Solomon: James VI and I in His Three Kingdoms*. Urbana and Chicago, 1990.

Lemberg, Margaret. 'Hessen-Kassel and the Journey up the Rhine of the Princess Palatine Elizabeth in April and May 1613'. In *The Palatine Wedding of 1613: Protestant Alliance and Court Festival*, edited by Sara Smart and Mara R. Wade, pp. 411–426. Wiesbaden, 2013.

Lewalski, Barbara Kiefer. *Writing Women in Jacobean England*. Cambridge, MA, 1993.

Lindley, David. 'Embarrassing Ben: The Masques for Frances Howard'. *English Literary Renaissance* 16 (1986): 343–359.

Llewellyn, Nigel. *The Art of Death: Visual Culture in the English Death Ritual c.1500–c.1800*. London, 1991.

Lockhart, Paul Douglas. *Denmark, 1513–1660: The Rise and Decline of a Renaissance Monarchy*. Oxford, 2000.

—. *Sweden in the Seventeenth Century*. New York, 2004.

Lockyer, Roger. *James VI and I*. London and New York, 1998.

Loomie, Albert Joseph. 'Toleration and Diplomacy: The Religious Issue in Anglo-Spanish Relations, 1603–1605'. *Transactions of the American Philosophical Society* 53, New Series (1963): 1–60.

—. 'King James I's Catholic Consort'. *Huntington Library Quarterly* 34 (1971): 303–316.

Lundkvist, Sven. 'The Experience of Empire: Sweden as a Great Power'. In *Sweden's Age of Greatness, 1632–1718*, edited by Michael Roberts, pp. 20–57. London, 1973.

Lynch, Michael. *Scotland: A New History*. London, 1991.

—. 'Court Ceremony and Ritual during the Personal Reign of James VI'. In *The Reign of James VI*, edited by Julian Goodare and Michael Lynch, pp. 71–92. East Linton, 2000.

—. 'The Reassertion of Princely Power in Scotland: The Reigns of Mary Queen of Scots and King James VI'. In *Princes and Princely Culture 1450–1650*, edited by Martin Gosman, Alasdair Macdonald and Arjo Vanderjagt, pp. 199–238. Leiden, 2003.

McCall, Timothy. 'Brilliant Bodies: Material Culture and the Adornment of Men in North Italy's Quattrocento Courts'. *I Tatti Studies in the Italian Renaissance* 16 (2013): 445–490.

McCullough, Peter. *Sermons at Court: Politics and Religion in Elizabethan and Jacobean Preaching*. Cambridge and New York, 1998.

McEvansoneya, Philip. 'Italian Paintings in the Buckingham Collection'. In *The Evolution of English Collecting: Receptions of Italian Art in the Tudor and Stuart Periods*, edited by Edward Chaney, pp. 315–336. New Haven and London, 2003.

MacKechnie, Aonghus. 'James VI's Architects and their Architecture'. In *The Reign of James VI*, edited by Julian Goodare and Michael Lynch, pp. 154–169. East Linton, 2000.

Mackie, John Duncan. *Negotiations between James VI and I and Ferdinand, Duke of Tuscany*. Oxford, 1927.

MacLeod, Catharine, Timothy Wilks, R. M. Smuts, Rab MacGibbon. *The Lost Prince: The Life and Death of Henry Stuart*. London, 2012.

MacLeod, Catharine. 'Facing Europe: The Portraiture of Anne of Denmark (1574–1619)'. In *Telling Objects: Contextualizing the Role of the Consort in Early Modern Europe*, edited by Jill Bepler and Svante Norrheim, pp. 63–85. Wiesbaden, 2018.

McManus, Clare. *Women on the Renaissance Stage: Anna of Denmark and Female Masquing in the Stuart Court (1590–1619)*. Manchester, 2002.

—. 'Introduction: The Queen's Court'. In *Women and Culture at the Courts of the Stuart Queens*, edited by Clare McManus, pp. 1–17. Basingstoke, 2003.

—. 'Memorialising Anna of Denmark's Court: *Cupid's Banishment* at Greenwich Palace'. In *Women and Culture at the Courts of the Stuart Queens*, edited by Clare McManus, pp. 81–99. Basingstoke, 2003.

—. 'When Is a Woman Not a Woman? Or, Jacobean Fantasies of Female Performance (1606–1611)', *Modern Philology* 105 (2008): 437–474.

Martin, John. 'Castelvetro, Giacomo (bap. 1546, d.1616)'. *Oxford Dictionary of National Biography*. Oxford, 2004.

Mauss, Marcel. 'Essai sur le Don. Forme et Raison de l'Échange dans les Sociétés archaïques', *L'Année sociologique*, n.s., 1 (1923–1924), 30–186.

—. *The Gift*, expanded edition selected, annotated, and translated by Jane I. Guyer. Chicago, 2016.

Meikle, Maureen. 'Anna of Denmark's Coronation and Entry into Edinburgh, 1590: Cultural, Religious and Diplomatic Perspectives'. In *Sixteenth-Century Scotland: Essays in Honour of Michael Lynch*, edited by Julian Goodare and A. A. MacDonald, pp. 277–294. Leiden, 2008.

—. 'A Meddlesome Princess: Anna of Denmark and Scottish Court Politics, 1589–1603'. In *The Reign of James VI*, edited by Julian Goodare and Michael Lynch, pp. 126–140. East Linton, 2000.

—. and H. Payne, 'From Lutheranism to Catholicism', *The Journal of Ecclesiastical History* 64 (2013), 45–69.

Metzer, Wolfgang. 'The Perspective of the Prince: The Hortus Palatinus of Friedrich V and Elizabeth Stuart at Heidelberg'. In *The Palatine Wedding of 1613: Protestant Alliance and Court Festival*, edited by Sara Smart and Mara Wade, pp. 567–596. Wiesbaden, 2013.

Millar, Oliver, ed. 'Abraham van der Doort's Catalogue of the Collections of Charles I'.

The Thirty-seventh Volume of the Walpole Society. London, 1958–1960, pp. iii–256.
—. *The Tudor, Stuart and Early Georgian Pictures in the Collection of Her Majesty the Queen*, 2 vols. London, 1963.
Mirabella, Bella. 'Introduction'. In *Ornamentalism: The Art of Renaissance Accessories*, edited by Bella Mirabella, pp. 1–10. Ann Arbor, 2011.
—. 'Embellishing Herself with a Cloth: The Contradictory Life of the Handkerchief'. In *Ornamentalism: The Art of Renaissance Accessories*, edited by Bella Mirabella, pp. 59–82. Ann Arbor, 2011.
Moe, Bjarke. 'Italian Music at the Danish Court during the Reign of Christian IV: Presenting a Picture of Cultural Transformation'. *Danish Yearbook of Musicology* 38 (2010/11): 15–32.
Morgan, Luke. *Nature as Model: Salomon De Caus and Early Seventeenth-Century Landscape Design*. Philadelphia, 2007.
Morton, Adam. 'Introduction: Politics, Culture and Queens Consort'. In *Queens Consort: Cultural Transfer and European Politics, c.1500–1800*, edited by Adam Morton and Helen Watanabe-O'Kelly, pp. 1–14. London, 2017.
—. and Helen Watanabe-O'Kelly, eds. *Queens Consort: Cultural Transfer and European Politics, c.1500–1800*. London, 2017.
Müller, Mette and Ole Kongsted. 'Christian IV and Music'. In *Christian IV and Europe: The 19th Art Exhibition of the Council of Europe: Denmark*, edited by Steffan Heiberg, pp. 119–141. Herning, 1988.
Mulryne, J. R. 'Marriage Entertainments in the Palatinate for Princess Elizabeth Stuart and the Elector Palatine'. In *Italian Renaissance Festivals and their European Influence*, edited by J. R. Mulryne and Margaret Shewring, pp. 311–335. Lewiston, 1992.
—. and Margaret Shewring, eds. *Italian Renaissance Festivals and their European Influence*. Lewiston, 1992.
—, eds. *Theatre and Government under the Early Stuarts*. Cambridge, 1993.
—. and Helen Watanabe-O'Kelly, eds. *Europa Triumphans: Court and Civic Festivals in Early Modern Europe*, 2 vols. Aldershot, 2004.
Murdoch, Steve. *Britain, Denmark-Norway, and the House of Stuart, 1603–1660: A Diplomatic and Military Analysis*. East Linton, 2000.
—. 'Diplomacy in Transition: Stuart-British Diplomacy in Northern Europe, 1603–1618'. In *Ships, Guns and Bibles in the North Sea and Baltic States, c.1350–c.1700*, edited by Allan I. Macinnes, Thomas Riis, and Frederik Pedersen, pp. 93–114. East Linton, 2000.
—. 'James VI and the Formation of a Scottish-British Military Identity'. In *Fighting for Identity: Scottish Military Experience c.1550–1900*, edited by Steve Murdoch and A. MacKillop, pp. 3–31. Leiden, 2002.
—. *Network North: Scottish Kin, Commercial and Covert Associations in Northern Europe, 1603–1746*. Leiden and Boston, 2006.
—. and Alexia Grosjean. *Alexander Leslie and the Scottish Generals of the Thirty Years' War, 1618–1648*. London, 2014.
Murray, Catriona. '"Great Britaine, all in Blacke" The Commemoration of Henry, Prince of Wales, in a Portrait of his Father, King James I'. *The British Art Journal* 12 (2011): 20–25.
—. *Imaging Stuart Family Politics: Dynastic Crisis and Continuity*. London and New York, 2017.

Neville, Kristoffer. 'Christian IV's Italianates. Sculpture at the Danish Court'. In *Reframing the Danish Renaissance: Problems and Prospects in a European Perspective*, edited by Michael Andersen, Birgitte Bøggild Johannsen, and Hugo Johannsen, pp. 335–346. Copenhagen, 2011.

Noldus, Badeloch. *Trade in Good Taste: Relations in Architecture and Culture Between the Dutch Republic and the Baltic World in the Seventeenth Century*. Turnhout, 2004.

—. 'Pieter Isaacsz's Other Life – Legal and Illegal'. In *Pieter Isaacsz (1568–1625): Court Painter, Art Dealer and Spy*, edited by Badeloch Noldus and Juliette Roding, pp. 151–164. Turnhout, 2007.

—. 'Art and Music on Demand – A Portrait of the Danish Diplomat Jonas Charisius and his Mission to the Dutch Republic'. In *Reframing the Danish Renaissance: Problems and Prospects in a European Perspective*, edited by Michael Andersen, Birgitte Bøggild Johannsen, and Hugo Johannsen, pp. 279–301. Copenhagen, 2011.

Nyström, Eiler. 'Jonas Charisius' indkøb af malerier og musikinstrumenterne i Nederlandene 1607–08'. *Danske Magazin* 6 (1909): 225–236.

O'Connor, Marion. 'Godly Patronage: Lucy Harington Russell, Countess of Bedford'. In *The Intellectual Culture of Puritan Women, 1558–1680*, edited by Johanna Harris and Elizabeth Scott-Baumann, pp. 71–83. New York, 2011.

—. '"Silvesta was my instrument ordained?": Lucy Harington Russell, Third Countess of Bedford as Family Marriage Broker'. *Sidney Journal* 34 (2016): 49–65.

Olden-Jørgensen, Sebastian. 'State Ceremonial, Court Culture and Political Power in Early Modern Denmark, 1536–1746'. *Scandinavian Journal of History* 27 (2002): 65–76.

Orlin, Lena Cowen, ed. *Material London, c.1600*. Philadelphia, 2000.

—. *Locating Privacy in Tudor London*. New York and Oxford, 2007.

Orrell, John. 'The London Stage in the Florentine Correspondence, 1604–1618'. *Theatre Research International* 3 (1978): 157–176.

Ørum-Larsen, Asger. 'Uraniborg – The Most Extraordinary Castle and Garden Design in Scandinavia'. *Journal of Garden History* 10 (1990): 97–105.

Ottenheym, Konrad. 'Introduction'. In *Unity and Discontinuity: Architectural Relations between the Southern and Northern Low Countries 1530–1700*, edited by Krista De Jonge and Konrad Ottenheym, pp. 1–15. Turnhout, 2007.

—. and Krista De Jonge. 'The Architecture of the Low Countries and its International Receptions, 1480–1680: A Bird's Eye View'. In *The Low Countries at the Crossroads: Netherlandish Architecture as an Export Product in Early Modern Europe (1480–1680)*, edited by Konrad Ottenheym and Krista De Jonge, pp. 15–30. Turnhout, 2013.

—. and Krista De Jonge, eds. *The Low Countries at the Crossroads: Netherlandish Architecture as an Export Product in Early Modern Europe (1480–1680)*. Turnhout, 2013.

Paresys, Isabelle. 'The Dressed Body: The Moulding of Identities in Sixteenth-Century France'. In *Cultural Exchange in Early Modern Europe: Forging European Identities, 1400–1700*, edited by Herman Roodenburg, vol. 4, pp. 227–258. Cambridge, 2007.

Parker, Geoffrey. *The Army of Flanders and the Spanish Road, 1567–1659: The Logistics of Spanish Victory and Defeat in the Low Countries' Wars*, 2nd ed. Cambridge, 2004.

Parrott, Vivienne. 'Celestial Expression or Worldly Magic? The Invisibly Integrated Design of Uraniborg: A Look at some Philosophical Aspects of the Ground Plan of Tycho Brahe's House and Garden'. *The Garden History Society* 38 (2010): 66–80.

Patterson, William B. *King James VI and I and the Reunion of Christendom*. Cambridge, 1997.

Payne, M. T. W. 'An Inventory of Queen Anne of Denmark's "Ornaments, Furniture, Householde Stuffe, and Other Parcells" at Denmark House, 1619'. *Journal of the History of Collecting* 13 (2001): 23–44.

Peacock, John. 'The Politics of Portraiture'. In *Culture and Politics in Early Stuart England*, edited by Kevin Sharpe and Peter Lake, pp. 199–228. Basingstoke, 1994.

Pearce, Michael. 'Anna of Denmark: Fashioning a Danish Court in Scotland'. *The Court Historian* 24.2 (2019): 138–151.

Peck, Linda Levy. 'Court Patronage and Government Policy: The Jacobean Dilemma'. In *Patronage in The Renaissance*, edited by Guy Fitch Lytle and Stephen Orgel, pp. 27–46. Princeton, 1981.

—. *Northampton: Patronage and Policy at the Court of James I*. London, 1982.

—. 'An Introduction'. In *The Mental World of the Jacobean Court*, edited by Linda Levy Peck, pp. 1–17. Cambridge, 1991.

—. *Court Patronage and Corruption in Early Modern England*. London, 1993.

—. 'Building, Buying, and Collecting'. In *Material London, c.1600*, edited by Lena Cowen Orlin, pp. 268–289. Philadelphia, 2000.

—. *Consuming Splendor: Society and Culture in Seventeenth-Century England*. Cambridge, 2005.

Perry, Curtis. '1603 and the Discourse of Favouritism'. In *The Accession of James I: Historical and Cultural Consequences*, edited by Glenn Burgess, Rowland Wymer, and Jason Lawrence, pp. 155–176. Basingstoke, 2006.

Pilkinton, Mark C., ed. *Records of Early English Drama: Bristol*. Toronto, 1997.

Pointon, Marcia. *Hanging the Head: Portraiture and Social Formation in Eighteenth-Century England*. New Haven and London, 1993.

Pollnitz, Aysha. 'Humanism and the Education of Henry, Prince of Wales'. In *Prince Henry Revived: Image and Exemplarity in Early Modern England*, edited by Timothy Wilks, pp. 22–65. London, 2007.

Ravelhofer, Barbara. *The Early Stuart Masque: Dance, Costume and Music*. New York, 2006.

Redworth, Glyn. *The Prince and the Infanta: The Cultural Politics of the Spanish Match*. New Haven and London, 2003.

Reindel, Ulrik. *The King Tapestries: Pomp & Propaganda at Kronborg Castle*. Copenhagen, 2011.

Reiss, Sheryl E. and David G. Wilkins. 'Prologue'. In *Beyond Isabella: Secular Women Patrons of Art in Renaissance Italy*, edited by Sheryl E. Reiss and David G. Wilkins, pp. xv–xvii. Kirksville, 2001.

Reynolds, Anna. *In Fine Style: The Art of Tudor and Stuart Fashion*. London, 2013.

Rickard, Jane. *Authorship and Authority: The Writings of James VI and I*. Manchester, 2007.

Riis, Thomas. *Should Auld Acquaintance Be Forgot ... Scottish–Danish Relations c.1450–1707*. 2 vols. Odense, 1988.

Roberts, Michael. *Gustavus Adolphus: A History of Sweden, 1611–1632*. 2 vols. London, 1958.

Roeck, Bernd. 'Introduction'. In *Cultural Exchange in Early Modern Europe: Forging European Identities, 1400–1700*, edited by Herman Roodenburg, vol. 4, pp. 1–29. Cambridge, 2007.

Roper, Louis H. 'Unmasquing the Connections between Jacobean Politics and Policy: The Circle of Anna of Denmark and the Beginning of the English Empire, 1614–18'. In *'High and Mighty Queens' of Early Modern England: Realities and Representations*, edited by Carole Levin, Jo Eldridge Carney, and Debra Barrett-Graves, pp. 45–59. New York, 2003.

Rublack, Ulinka. *Dressing Up: Cultural Identity in Renaissance Europe*. Oxford, 2010.

Santaliestra, Laura Oliván. 'Isabel of Borbón's Sartorial Politics: From French Princess to Habsburg Regent'. In *Early Modern Habsburg Women: Transnational Contexts, Cultural Conflicts, Dynastic Continuities*, edited by Anne J. Cruz and Maria Galli Stampino, pp. 225–243. Farnham and Burlington, VT, 2013.

Scarisbrick, Diana. 'Anne of Denmark's Jewellery: The Old and the New'. *Apollo* 122 (1986): 228–236.

—. *Tudor and Jacobean Jewellery*. London, 1995.

—. 'Queen Elizabeth's Locket Ring, c.1575'. In *Elizabeth: The Exhibition at the National Maritime Museum*, edited by Susan Doran, pp. 12–13. London, 2003.

Schwarz, Kathryn. 'Amazon Reflections in the Jacobean Queen's Masque'. *Studies in English Literature* 35 (1995): 293–319.

Scott, Alison. *Selfish Gifts: The Politics of Exchange and English Courtly Literature, 1580–1628*. Madison, NJ, 2006.

Senning, Calvin F. 'The Visit of Christian IV to England in 1614'. *Historian* 31 (1969): 555–572.

Sharpe, Kevin. 'The Image of Virtue: The Court and Household of Charles I, 1625–1642'. In *The English Court: from the Wars of the Roses to the Civil War*, edited by David Starkey, pp. 226–260. London and New York, 1987.

—. *Politics and Ideas in Early Stuart England: Essays and Studies*. London, 1989.

—. *Image Wars: Promoting Kings and Commonwealths in England, 1603–1660*. New Haven, 2010.

Shephard, Robert. 'Sexual Rumours in English Politics: The Cases of Elizabeth I and James I'. In *Desire and Discipline: Sex and Sexuality in the Premodern West*, edited by Jacqueline Murray and Konrad Eisenbichler, pp. 101–122. Toronto, 1996.

Siddons, Michael Powell. *Heraldic Badges in England and Wales*. 2 vols. London, 2009.

Skovgaard, Joakim. *A King's Architecture: Christian IV and his Buildings*. London, 1973.

Smart, Sara, and Mara R. Wade. 'The Palatine Wedding of 1613: Protestant Alliance and Court Festival'. In *The Palatine Wedding of 1613: Protestant Alliance and Court Festival*, edited by Sara Smart and Mara R. Wade, pp. 13–60. Wiesbaden, 2013.

—, eds. *The Palatine Wedding of 1613: Protestant Alliance and Court Festival*. Wiesbaden, 2013.

Smuts, R. Malcolm. *Court Culture and the Origins of a Royalist Tradition*. Philadelphia, 1987.

—. 'Cultural Diversity and Cultural Change at the Court of James I'. In *The Mental World of the Jacobean Court*, edited by Linda Levy Peck, pp. 99–113. Cambridge, 1991.

—. 'Art and the Material Culture of Majesty in Early Stuart England'. In *The Stuart Court and Europe: Essays in Politics and Political Culture*, edited by R. Malcolm Smuts, pp. 86–112. Cambridge, 1996.

—. 'Prince Henry and his World'. In *The Lost Prince: The Life and Death of Henry Stuart*, edited by C. MacLeod et al., pp. 19–31. London, 2012.

—. and George Gorse, 'Introduction'. In *The Politics of Space: European Courts c.1500–1700*, edited by Marcello Fantoni, George Gorse and R. Malcolm Smuts, pp. 13–35. Rome, 2009.

—. and Melinda J. Gough. 'Queens and the International Transmission of Political Culture'. *The Court Historian* 10 (2005): 1–13.

Sowerby, Tracey A. 'Material Culture and the Politics of Space in Diplomacy at the Tudor Court'. In *Beyond Scylla and Charybdis: European Courts and Court Residences outside Habsburg and Valois/Bourbon Territories 1500–1700*, edited by Birgitte Bøggild Johannsen and Konrad Ottenheym, pp. 47–57. Odense, 2015.

—. 'Early Modern Diplomatic History'. *History Compass* 14 (2016): 441–456.

Spicer, Joaneath. 'The Renaissance Elbow'. In *A Cultural History of Gesture: From Antiquity to the Present Day*, edited by Jan Bremmer and Herman Roodenburg, pp. 84–128. London, 1991.

Spohr, Arne. 'Networking, Patronage and Professionalism in the Early History of Violin Playing: The Case of William Brade'. In *Networks of Music in the Late Sixteenth and Early Seventeenth Centuries: A Collection of Essays in Celebration of Peter Philip's 450th Anniversary*, edited by David Smith and Rachelle Taylor, pp. 203–214. Farnham, 2014.

—. 'Musikalische Widmungen an Herzog Heinrich Julius als Dokumente seines musikkulturellen Handelns'. In *Herzog Heinrich Julius zu Braunschweig und Lüneburg (1564–1613): Politiker und Gelehrter mit europäischen*, edited by Werner Arnold, Brage Bei der Wieden, and Ulrike Gleixner, pp. 283–298. Brunswick, 2016.

Starkey, David. 'Introduction'. In *The English Court: from the Wars of the Roses to the Civil War*, edited by David Starkey, pp. 1–25. London, 1987.

—. 'Intimacy and Innovation: The Rise of the Privy Chamber, 1485–1547'. In *The English Court: from the Wars of the Roses to the Civil War*, edited by David Starkey, pp. 71–119. London, 1987.

— ed. *The English Court: from the Wars of the Roses to the Civil War*. London, 1987.

Steegman, J. 'Two Unpublished Paintings from the Collection of Charles I'. *Burlington Magazine* 99 (1957): 378–380.

Stevenson, David. *Scotland's Last Royal Wedding: The Marriage of James VI and Anne of Denmark*. Edinburgh, 1997.

Stewart, Alan. 'The Early Modern Closet Discovered'. *Representations* 50 (1995): 76–100.

Stockton, William and James R. Bromley. 'Introduction: Figuring Early Modern Sex'. In *Sex before Sex: Figuring the Act in Early Modern England*, edited by William Stockton and James R. Bromley, pp. 1–23. Minneapolis, 2013.

Stokes, James, ed. *Records of Early English Drama: Somerset*. 2 vols. Toronto, 1996.

Strong, Roy. *Tudor & Jacobean Portraits*. 2 vols. London, 1969.

—. *The Renaissance Garden in England*. London, 1979.

—. *Henry Prince of Wales and England's Lost Renaissance*. London, 1986.
—. *Gloriana: The Portraits of Queen Elizabeth I*. New York, 1987.
—. 'Sir Francis Carew's Garden at Beddington'. In *England and the Continental Renaissance*, edited by Edward Chaney and Peter Mack, pp. 229–238. Woodbridge, 1990.
—. *The Artist and the Garden*. New Haven, 2000.
Sullivan, Mary Agnes. *Court Masques of James I: Their Influence on Shakespeare and the Public Theatres*. New York, 1973.
Sykes, Susan Alexander. 'Henrietta Maria's "house of delight": French Influence and Iconography in the Queen's House, Greenwich'. *Apollo* 133 (1991): 312–336.
Thomson, Duncan. *Painting in Scotland 1570–1650*. Edinburgh, 1975.
Thornton, Peter. *Seventeenth-Century Interior Decoration in England, France and Holland*. New Haven, 1978.
Thurley, Simon. *The Royal Palaces of Tudor England: Architecture and Court Life*. New Haven, 1993.
—. 'Architecture and Diplomacy: Greenwich Palace under the Stuarts'. *The Court Historian* 11 (2006): 125–135.
—. *Somerset House: The Palace of England's Queens, 1551–1692*. London, 2009.
Tittler, Robert. 'Three Portraits by John de Critz for the Merchant Taylors' Company'. *Burlington Magazine* 147 (2005): 491–493.
Tomlinson, Sophie. *Women on Stage in Stuart Drama*. Cambridge, 2005.
Town, Edward. '"Whilst he had his perfect sight" – New Information on John de Critz the Elder'. *Burlington Magazine* 154 (2012): 482–486.
—. 'A Biographical Dictionary of London Painters, 1547–1625'. *The Seventy-Sixth Volume of the Walpole Society*. London, 2014, pp. 1–237.
Traub, Valerie. *Thinking Sex with the Early Moderns*. Philadelphia, 2016.
Turbet, Richard. 'Joyful Singing: Byrd's Music at a Royal Christening'. *The Musical Times* 145 (2004): 85–86.
Ungerer, Gustav. 'Juan Pantoja De La Cruz and the Circulation of Gifts between the English and Spanish Courts, 1604–5'. *Shakespearean Studies* 26 (1998): 145–186.
Vincent, Susan. *Dressing the Elite: Clothes in Early Modern England*. Oxford and New York, 2003.
Vogel, Harald. 'The Genesis and Radiance of a Court Organ'. In *The Organ as a Mirror of its Time: North European Reflections, 1610–2000*, edited by Kerala J. Snyder, pp. 48–59. Oxford, 2002.
Wade, Mara R. *Triumphus Nupitalis Danicus. German Court Culture and Denmark: The Great Wedding of 1634*. Wiesbaden, 1996.
—. 'The Queen's Courts: Anna of Denmark and Her Royal Sisters – Cultural Agency at Four Northern European Courts in the Sixteenth and Seventeenth Centuries'. In *Women and Culture at the Courts of the Stuart Queens*, edited by Clare McManus, pp. 49–80. New York, 2003.
—, ed. *Pomp, Power, and Politics: Essays on German and Scandinavian Court Culture and their Contexts. Daphnis* vol. 32, Amsterdam, 2003.
—. 'Widowhood as a Space for Patronage: Hedevig, Princess of Denmark and Electress of Saxony'. *Renæssanceforum* 4 (2008): 1–28.
—. 'Duke Ulrik as Agent, Patron, Artist: Reframing Danish Court Culture in an International Perspective c.1600'. In *Reframing the Danish Renaissance: Problems and Prospects in a European Perspective*, edited by Michael Andersen,

Birgitte Bøggild Johannsen, and Hugo Johannsen, pp. 243–263. Copenhagen, 2011.
—. 'Dynasty at Work: Danish Cultural Exchange with England and Germany at the Time of the Palatine Wedding'. In *The Palatine Wedding of 1613: Protestant Alliance and Court Festival*, edited by Sara Smart and Mara R. Wade, pp. 479–514. Wiesbaden, 2013.
Walsham, Alexandra. *Church Papists: Catholicism, Conformity, and Confessional Polemic in Early Modern England*. Woodbridge, 1993.
Ward, John. 'A Dowland Miscellany'. *Journal of the Lute Society of America* 10 (1977): 5–152.
Watanabe-O'Kelly, Helen. *Triumphall shews: Tournaments at German-speaking Courts in the European Context, 1560–1730*. Berlin, 1992.
—. 'Afterword: Queens Consort, Dynasty and Cultural Transfer'. In *Queens Consort: Cultural Transfer and European Politics, c.1500–1800*, edited by Helen Watanabe-O'Kelly and Adam Morton, pp. 231–249. London, 2017.
Watzdorf, E. Von. 'Fürstlicher Schmuck in der Renaissance'. *Münchner Jahrbuch der bildenden Kunst* 11 (1934).
—. 'Mielich und die Bayerischen Goldschmiedewerke der Renaissance'. *Münchner Jahrbuch der bildenden Kunst* 12 (1937).
Welch, Evelyn, ed. *Fashioning the Early Modern: Dress, Textiles, and Innovation in Europe, 1500–1800*. Oxford, 2017.
—. and Juliet Claxton. 'Easy Innovation in Early Modern Europe'. In *Fashioning the Early Modern: Dress, Textiles, and Innovation in Europe, 1500–1800*, edited by Evelyn Welch, pp. 87–109. Oxford, 2017.
Williams, Ethel Carleton. *Anne of Denmark: Wife of King James VI of Scotland, James I of England*. London, 1970.
Wilkins, David G. 'Introduction: Recognising New Patrons, Posing New Questions'. In *Beyond Isabella: Secular Women Patrons of Art in Renaissance Italy*, edited by Sheryl E. Reiss and David G. Wilkins, pp. 1–17. Kirksville, 2001.
Wilks, Timothy. 'Robert Carr, Earl of Somerset (1587–1645), Reconsidered'. *Journal of the History of Collections* 1 (1989): 167–177.
—. 'Art Collecting at the English Court from the Death of Henry, Prince of Wales to the Death of Anne of Denmark (November 1612– March 1619)'. *Journal of the History of Collections* 9 (1997): 31–48.
—. '"Forbear the Heat and Haste of Building": Rivalries among the Designers at Prince Henry's Court, 1610–12'. *The Court Historian* 6 (2001): 49–65.
—. 'Introduction: Image and Exemplarity'. In *Prince Henry Revived: Image and Exemplarity in Early Modern England*, edited by Timothy Wilks, pp. 10–21. London, 2007.
— ed. *Prince Henry Revived: Image and Exemplarity in Early Modern England*. London, 2007.
—. 'Introduction'. In *The Lost Prince: The Life and Death of Henry Stuart*, edited by C. MacLeod et al., pp. 11–17. London, 2012.
Wilson, Adrian. 'The Ceremony of Childbirth and its Interpretation'. In *Women as Mothers in Pre-Industrial England: Essays in Memory of Dorothy McLaren*, edited by Valerie Fildes, pp. 68–107. London, 1990.
Woldbye, Vibeke. 'Flemish Tapestry Weavers in the Service of Nordic Kings'. In *Flemish Tapestry Weavers Abroad: Emigration and the Founding of Manufactories in Europe*, edited by Guy Delmarcel, pp. 91–112. Leuven, 2002.

Woodall, Joanna. 'An Exemplary Consort: Antonis Mor's Portrait of Mary Tudor'. *Art History* 14 (1991): 192–224.

—. 'Introduction: Facing the Subject'. In *Portraiture: Facing the Subject*, edited by Joanna Woodall, pp. 1–25. Manchester, 1997.

— ed. *Portraiture: Facing the Subject*. Manchester, 1997.

—. *Anthonis Mor: Art and Authority*. Zwolle, 2007.

Woodward, Jennifer. *The Theatre of Death: The Ritual Management of Royal Funerals in Renaissance England, 1570–1625*. Woodbridge, 1997.

Wormald, Jenny. 'James VI and I (1566–1625)'. *Oxford Dictionary of National Biography*. Oxford, 2014.

Wunder, Heide. 'Gender Norms and their Enforcement in Early Modern Germany'. In *Gender Relations in Early Modern German History: Power, Agency and Experience from the Sixteenth to the Twentieth Century*, edited by Lynn Abrams and Elizabeth Harvey, pp. 39–57. London, 1996.

—. *He Is the Sun, She Is the Moon: Women in Early Modern Germany*, trans. Thomas Dunlop. Cambridge, MA and London, 1998.

Wynne-Davies, Marion. 'The Queen's Masque: Renaissance Women and the Seventeenth-Century Court Masque'. In *Gloriana's Face: Women, Public and Private in the English Renaissance*, edited by S. P. Cerasano and Marion Wynne-Davies, pp. 79–104. Hemel Hempstead, 1992.

Unpublished Theses

Carney, Sophie. 'The Queen's House at Greenwich: The Material Cultures of the Courts of Queen Anna of Denmark and Queen Henrietta Maria, 1603–69'. PhD Thesis, University of Roehampton, 2013.

Cole, Emily. 'The State Apartment in the Jacobean Country House, 1603–1625'. DPhil Thesis, University of Sussex, 2010.

Field, Jemma. 'Anna of Denmark and the Arts in Jacobean England'. PhD Thesis, University of Auckland, 2015.

Francis, Jill. '"A ffitt place for any Gentleman"? Gardens, Gardeners and Gardening in England and Wales, c.1560–1660'. PhD Thesis, University of Birmingham, 2011.

Fry, Cynthia. 'Diplomacy & Deception: King James VI of Scotland's Foreign Relations with Europe (c.1584–1603)'. PhD Thesis, University of St Andrews, 2014.

Hallam, Jennifer. 'Re-presenting Women in Early Stuart England: Gender Ideology, Personal Politics & the Portrait Arts'. PhD Thesis, University of Pennsylvannia, 2004.

Juhala, Amy. 'The Household and Court of King James VI of Scotland, 1567–1603'. PhD Thesis, The University of Edinburgh, 2000.

Middaugh, Karen Lee. '"The Golden Tree": The Court Masques of Queen Anna of Denmark'. PhD Thesis, Case Western Reserve University, 1994.

Payne, Helen. 'Aristocratic Women and the Jacobean Court, 1603–1625'. PhD Thesis, University of London, 2001.

Wilks, Timothy. 'The Court Culture of Prince Henry and his Circle, 1603–1613'. PhD Thesis, University of Oxford, 1987.

Wood, Lucy. 'The Portraits of Anne of Denmark'. MA report, Courtauld Institute of Art, University of London, 1981.

Index

Figures and plates are given in italics

Abbot, George, Archbishop of
   Canterbury 197, 205, 214 n.111
Alberti, Leon Battista 44–45, 155
ambassadorial audiences 8–9, 22, 37
   n.25, 49, 76 n.37, 91–93, 106, 138,
   167–168
Anna Catherine of Brandenburg 108,
   129, 143
Anstruther, Robert 101, 167, 200, 201
Aristotle 155
Arundel, Thomas, Earl of 10, 19, 98, 99
Augusta, Duchess of Holstein-Gottorp
   143, 147 n.43

baptism 158, 181, 185–190, 191, 192,
   209
birth 158, 181, 182–185, 191, 192,
   195, 196, 209
Brade, William 109
Brahe, Tycho 45, 60, 64, 99
books 9, 102, 104–105, 110

cabinets 9, 86–87, 93, 102–104
Carew, George Earl of Totnes 34, 46,
   63, 74 n.16, 97, 98, 115 n.77, 214
   n.111
Carr, Robert, Duke of Somerset 20,
   25–30, 72
Catherine of Aragón 75 n.21, 121, 124,
   151 n.136, 155, 156
Caus, Salomon de 58–60, 61, *62*, 63,
   68, 73, 81 n.136, 195
Cecil, Robert, Duke of Salisbury 20,
   43, 48–49, 57, 78 n.86, 106, 110,
   187
Charles, Duke of Albany and York, later
   King of England 84, 90–91, 96,
   157, 182, 183–184, 186–187, 188,
   189, 196, 197, 198–199, 200, 201,
   202, 208–209, 219, 220, 221
Charisius, Dr Jonas 18, 100–101,
   173
Christian IV, King of Denmark-Norway
   32, 51, 55, 93, 96, 99, 100, 101,
   105, 106, 107–109, 112, 133,
   134, 142, 143–144, 152, 155, 156,
   164, 165–168, 173–174, *175*, 183,
   184–185, 189, 192, 193, 200, 201,
   210, 220, *plate 9*
churching 181, 185, 191–192, 209,
   213 n.78
ciphers
   as decorative feature 10, 86, *86*, *87*,
     93, 95–96, 132, 198
   in jewellery 140, 142–145, *144*, 151
     n.136, 158, 159, 165, 172
clocks 93, 102, 103, 105
clothing 120–129, *126*, *127*, *128*, *130*,
   138–139, 147 n.41, 187, 189, 194
   livery 129, 131–133, 145, 169,
     186–187, 194
   for mourning 107, 109, 204, 209
   and national fashion 121–122, 124,
     132–133, 139
   and Queen Elizabeth's wardrobe
     123, 124–126, 128–129

clothing (*cont.*)
  for servants 121, 123, 131–133, 135, 139–140, 145
Colt, Maximilian 87, *plate 11*
Commonwealth Sale 96
Compenius, Esaias 108
confessional identity 23, 30–31, 191–192, 206–207
consortship 1–3, 19–23, 181, 207, 209, 210, 220–222
Critz, John de, the Elder 87, 159–160, 207, *plates 5 and 6*

Daniel, Samuel 161, 173, 174
Derry, Tom 97, 98, 115 n.77
devotional objects 103, 200
dining 53, 92, 106–107, 116 n.108, 162, 166, 186
Dowland, John 105, 109
Drummond, Jane (Jean) 27, 43, 77 n.65, 97, 115 n.71, 134, 140, 146 n.21, 165, 178 n.58, 198
Dunfermline 46, 50, 51–52, 53, 71, 72, 183

Elisabeth, Duchess of Braunschweig-Lüneburg 106, 108, 112, 129, 133, 139, 143, 147 n.43
Elizabeth I, Queen of England 85, 97, 111, 124, 125, 129, 134, 142, 156, 159, 160, 161, 165, 171, 173, 175, 185, 189, 190, 202
Elizabeth Stuart, Princess 53, 61, 181, 182, 183, 185, 186, 192–196, 202, 205, 206
embalming 201, 202, 215 n.142
English succession 21, 31, 48, 90, 122, 158, 159, 160, 175, 184, 185, 209
Erskine, John, Earl of Mar 20

Ferrabosco, Alphonso 111, 119 n.170
finance 6, 7, 45–47, 68, 73, 88, 137–138
Florio, John 173, 174, 180 n.106
fountains 58–60, 61, 62, 79 n.115, 174
Frederik II, King of Denmark-Norway 51–52, 60, 64–66, 68, 85–86, 96, 99, 103, 106, 112, 123, 141, 208
Frederiksborg Castle 56, 65, 78 n.76, 93, 103, 108, 136, 164
fretwork 85, 86, 87, 102
Friedrich, Elector Palatine 53, 192–194, 195–196, 202

funeral 109, 160, 176, 181, 199, 201–209, *plates 10 and 11*

gardens 7, 12, 44–45, 53, *54*, 56–61, *62*, 63, 85, 95, 102, 152, 165, 174
garden house 65–68, *66*, 69, 71
Gheeraerts, Marcus, the Younger 152, *153*, 160, 166, 168, 169, 175, 176 n.11, 206, *plate 9*
gift-exchange 3, 7, 11, 12, 19, 22, 29, 32–35, 48, 57, 101, 105, 110, 121, 132, 134, 135, 138–139, 140–141, 142, 143–144, 156, 157, 158–159, 162–165, 190, 192, 195, 198, 199, 212 n.64, 217 n.166
Gondomar, Diego Sarmiento de Acuña, Count 97, 167–168
Gowrie Plot 21, 135
Greenwich Palace 1–2, 8, 22, 26, 30, 44, 46, 47, 48, 49, 50, 52, 58–59, 60–61, 63–67, *64*, 68–69, 71, 72, 85, 93, 102, 111, 112, 174, 184, 185, 187, 191–192, 197–198, 199
  aviary 60–62, *62*, 112 n.6, 199

Hampton Court 18, 30, 41 n.82, 47, 48, 49, 53, 75 n.31, 102, 110, 111, 138, 199, 200
Hedevig, Electress of Saxony 34, 106, 108, 112, 146 n.33
Heinrich Julius, Duke of Braunschweig-Lüneburg 33, 34, 42 n.103, 45, 108, 129, 189
Henrietta Maria, consort of King Charles I 1, 6, 14 n.3, 17 n.44, 62, 75 n.21, 97, 98, 111, 156, 179 n.95, 211 n.19, 219–220
Henry VIII, King of England 46, 60, 75 n.21, 97, 142, 156, 185
Henry, Prince of Wales 8, 12, 17 n.44, 20, 21, 23, 24–26, 32, 53, 61, 84, 98, 99, 106, 109, 111, 129, 132, 140–141, 156, 157, 158, 182, 183, 186, 187, 188–189, 191, 193, 198, 199, 202, 205, 209
heraldry 95–96, 102, 129, 132, 202, 204, 207–208, 209, 210
Herbert, William, Earl of Pembroke 20, 25, 26, 30, 62, 97, 169, 174, 206
Heriot, George 32, 140, 141, 142, 157, 185, 206
Hilliard, Nicholas 142, 161, 162, *163*, *164*, *plate 3*
Home, George, Earl of Dunbar 25, 29

Howard-Carr faction 25, 26, 27, 29, 39 n.50, 98, 139, 205
Howard, Henry, Duke of Northumberland 26, 71–72
Hume, Tobias 107–108
hunting 2, 22, 23, 33, 47, 65, 68, 107, 115 n.75, 166, 171, 179 n.92, 195, 197

Isabel Clara Eugenia, Archduchess of the Netherlands 97, 141, 142

James VI and I, King of Scotland and England 8, 19, 20–23, 27, 28–30, 33, 43, 47–50, 53–56, 68, 69, 73, 97, 98, 101, 105, 106–107, 108, 110, 111, 117 n.115, 123, 124, 125, 132, 133, 134, 141, 155, 157, 158–159, 160–162, 163, *164*, 166, 167, 169, 171, 172, 182, 183, 184–185, 187, 188, 189, 190–196, 197, 198, 199, 200, 201, 202–203, 208, 210, 220–221, *plate 4*
jewellery 9, 91, 123, 124, 140–145, *144*, 194, 195, 212 n.64
jointure 1–2, 6, 11, 19, 21, 43, 45–47, 50, 51, 71, 219
Jones, Inigo 1, 44, 63, *64*, 65, 66, 67, 68, 69, *70*, 70, 73, 82 n.165, 169, 173, 197

Kalmar War 167
Knäred, Treaty of 167
Kronborg Castle 63–67, 86, *86*, *87*, 96, 103, 112

lying-in 183–184, 185, 186, 190, 192

Maitland, Sir John of Thirlestane 20, 21, 71, 72, 82 n.161, 137
Margaret Stuart, Princess 182, 185, 186
marriage 108, 121–122, 123, 132, 134, 136, 140, 143, 152, 155, 156, 166, 168, 172, 176 n.11, 181, 182, 192–195, 200, 202–203, 205
Mary I, Queen of England 140, 141, 151 n.136, 155, 185
Mary Stuart, Princess 31, 182, 184–185, 186, 187–188, 191, 202, 209
masques 5, 7, 27, 30, 38 n.33, 106, 111, 135, 138, 140, 161, 171, 177 n.43, 178 n.58, 194, 197, 198

medicine 104, 183–184
practitioners 125, 184, 199, 215 n.129
Middlemore, Mary 97, 115 n.71
miniatures 8, 12, 32, 141, 142, 154, 155, 156, 157, 161–165, *163*, *164*, 174, 185, 192
mottoes 10, 86, 95, 152, 160, 165, 171, 172–175, 208
Munk, Kirsten 129, 143
music 3, 5, 11, 35, 100, 103, 105–112, 173, 186, 188, 194, 206

Nonsuch Palace 30, 46, 47, 48, 71, 72, 75 n.21, 85, 112

Oatlands Manor 2, 8–9, 30, 46, 47, 48, 50, 52, 68, 69–71, *70*, 72, 95, 98, 103, 104, 169, 171, 200
Oldenburg, House of 3–4, 10, 11, 33, 34, 35, 51, 84, 97, 106, 108, 109, 133, 134, 137, 142, 145, 152, 156, 165, 172, 174, 175, 193, 207, 220
Oliver, Isaac 12, 26, 39 n.52, 98, 99, 161–164, 206, *plates 7 and 8*

paintings 98–101, 103, 112, 173–174, 200
Pedersøn, Mogens 108
Pembroke-Southampton faction 20, 26, 27, 39 n.50, 206–207, 217 n.169
Philip II, King of Spain 140, 166
Philip III, King of Spain 97, 166, 167, 203
portraiture 96–98, 101, 111, 125, 129, 143, 152–166, *163*, *164*, 168–175, *170*, 176 n.11
as proxy 154, 155–156, 165
Prætorius, Michael 108
progresses 22, 30, 32, 47–48, 49–50, 76 n.41, 162, 181, 196–199

regency 196–199
Robert Stuart, Duke of Kintyre 182, 183, 184, 186–187, 188, 189, 212 n.64
Russell (née Harington), Lucy, Countess of Bedford 25, 62, 174, 206

Schaw, William 51
Schütz, Heinrich 108
Sering, Johan 30, 134

Sinclair, Andrew 166, 167
Sofie of Mecklenburg-Güstrow 32, 106, 123, 142, 143, 152, 164
Somer, Paul van 156–157, 168–173, *170*, 175, 206, *plate 1*
Somerset (Denmark) House 2, 8–9, 30, 44, 47, 49, 50, 52–55, *54*, 56–60, 72, 85, 86–89, *88*, 93–98, *94*, 101, 102, 103, 105, 111, 112, 140, 166, 174, 195, 207
  Mount Parnassus 56, 59–60, 61
Sophia Stuart, Princess 31, 182, 185, 192, 202
spatial politics 43, 83, 84, 89–93, *94*, 95, 101, 140, 183, 184, 185, 186, 197–198, 201, 204–205
Sterling Castle 182
Stewart, Ludovic, Duke of Lennox 20, 135, 157, 190
Stolbovo, Treaty of 55–56
Stuart, Arbella 109, 111, 190, 191
Stuart, House of
  and marriage matches 31, 32, 91, 97, 138, 140–141, 145, 156, 166, 168, 176 n.11, 193, 202–203, 208
Stuart–Oldenburg relations 13, 33–34, 56, 101, 133–134, 166–168, 182, 190, 192, 201, 210, 220, 221
sweet bags 104, 125

textiles 9, 84, 89, 93, 95, 96, 101, 103, 104, 105, 111, 123, 135, 140, 184, 187, 188, 189, 192, 209
Thirty Years' War 13, 203, 209

Ulric, Duke of Mecklenburg-Güstrow 33, 98, 133, 157, 189
Ulrik, Duke of Holstein 90, 107–108, 134, 187, 190, 191, 192
Uraniborg 45, 60, 63–65

Vanson, Adrian 157, *plates 2 and 4*
Villiers, George, Duke of Buckingham 10, 19, 22, 27–29, 112 n.6, 200
vineyards 69, 81 n.150, 169
Vinstarr, Margaret 134–135, 139

Wells 50
Whitehall Palace 30, 48, 49, 52, 54, 69, 102, 166, 197, 200, 207, 208
Wriothesley, Henry, Earl of Southampton 20, 26, 30, 98, 174, 206

EU authorised representative for GPSR:
Easy Access System Europe, Mustamäe tee 50,
10621 Tallinn, Estonia
gpsr.requests@easproject.com

www.ingramcontent.com/pod-product-compliance
Lightning Source LLC
Chambersburg PA
CBHW061130010526
44117CB00024B/3000